Exploring the School Choice Universe

Evidence and Recommendations

A Volume in
The National Education Policy Center Series

Series Editors:
Kevin G. Welner and Alex Molnar,
University of Colorado Boulder

The National Education Policy Center Series

Kevin G. Welner and Alex Molnar, Editors

The Obama Education Blueprint: Researchers Examine the Evidence (2010)
edited by William J. Mathis and Kevin G. Welner

Think Tank Research Quality:
Lessons for Policymakers, the Media, and the Public (2010)
edited by Kevin G. Welner, Patricia H. Hinchey,
Alex Molnar, and Don Weitzman

Exploring the School Choice Universe:
Evidence and Recommendations (2012)
edited by Gary Miron, Kevin G. Welner,
Patricia H. Hinchey, and William J. Mathis

Exploring the School Choice Universe

Evidence and Recommendations

Edited by

Gary Miron
Western Michigan University

Kevin G. Welner
University of Colorado Boulder

Patricia H. Hinchey
Pennsylvania State University

and

William J. Mathis
University of Colorado Boulder

A publication of

Education Resource Center
University of Delaware
Newark, DE 19716-2940

NEPC

National Education Policy Center
University of Colorado Boulder

Information Age Publishing, Inc.
Charlotte, North Carolina • www.infoagepub.com

P-E
EX 745
2012

Library of Congress Cataloging-in-Publication Data

Exploring the school choice universe : evidence and recommendations / edited
by Gary Miron, Western Michigan University, Kevin G. Welner, University of
Colorado-Boulder, Patricia H. Hinchey, Pennsylvania State University and
William J. Mathis, University of Colorado-Boulder.
    pages cm. — (The National Education Policy Center series)
    Includes bibliographical references.
    ISBN 978-1-62396-043-8 (paperback) — ISBN 978-1-62396-044-5 (hardcover) —
ISBN 978-1-62396-045-2 (ebook) 1. School choice. I. Miron, Gary, editor
of compilation.
  LB1027.9.E997 2012
  379.1'11—dc23

                                     2012033291

Printed in the United States of America

CONTENTS

ACKNOWLEDGMENTS

We express our greatest appreciation to the 19 authors of the chapters in this book, who have dedicated themselves to presenting an accessible and comprehensive description of research findings about school choice. Academics are not often pushed to write for a broad audience, and these authors have worked through many drafts and updates as demanded by editors and reviewers. Likewise, we express our gratitude to the blind reviewers who provided sound advice to the authors. The book's authors as well as the chapter reviewers were carefully selected in order for us all to benefit from the insights and knowledge of the nation's finest scholars and researchers of the many aspects of school choice. All are busy people with many demands on their time, and we thank them for setting aside their other important work to make room for this project.

We also want to acknowledge our ongoing partners. None of our work could move forward without the essential contributions of Erik Gunn, who operates Great Lakes Editorial Services. Similarly, it is a pleasure to work with George Johnson and his colleagues at Information Age Publishing, whose prompt responsiveness to our questions and requests helped us to move this book into print in such a timely manner. The patience of these two gentlemen is deep and is just as deeply appreciated.

This work would not have been accomplished without the funding support of the Great Lakes Center for Education Research and Practice, and we offer particularly gratitude to that center's former executive director, Teri Battaglieri. Special acknowledgement also goes to Alex Molnar, the National Education Policy Center's publications director, who assisted at every stage of this process, as well as to Faith Boninger, who kept Alex and the rest of us on an organized and focused path.

Gary Miron
Kevin G. Welner
Patricia H. Hinchey
William J. Mathis

CHAPTER 1

INTRODUCTION

Gary Miron and Kevin G. Welner

The allure of school choice is, in part, ideological. But this allure is also linked to a very real problem: there exists tremendous variation among neighborhood schools in terms of quality and resources, and access to those neighborhood schools depends on wealth. Lower wealth families are less able to purchase a residence in the catchment (enrollment) area of a high-resourced, high-quality neighborhood school. Breaking the link between residence and school assignment would seem a logical way of addressing this problem.[1]

This choice-as-equity goal exists alongside the ideological attraction of choice, since Americans tend to place a high value on individual liberty. For those advocating school choice based on this liberty interest, an increase in individual liberty is an inherent good. Moreover, these advocates tend to believe that as parents' choices are increased, and as a marketplace of schooling options is further developed, the invisible hand of the market will drive greater efficiencies and higher overall quality.

Yet these attractions—the access problem and the values and beliefs—leave unaddressed the questions that should be of most importance, particularly to researchers and policymakers. What do choice programs actually do? What forms do they take? Who participates, and why? What are the funding implications? What are the results of different forms of school choice on outcomes that matter, like student performance, segregation,

Exploring the School Choice Universe: Evidence and Recommendations
pp. 1–16

and competition effects? Do they affect teachers' working conditions? Do they drive innovation?

This book turns to scholars with a deep knowledge of those issues. It examines choice in its various forms: charter schools, homeschooling, online schooling, voucher plans that allow students to use taxpayer funds to attend private schools, tuition tax credit plans that provide a public subsidy for private school tuition, and magnet schools and other forms of public school intra- and interdistrict choice. It brings together some of the top researchers in the field, presenting a comprehensive overview of the best current knowledge of these important policies.

Three contentions are often put forth to push for the creation or expansion of school choice. First, advocates assert that privatization and competition will bring a much-needed dose of entrepreneurial spirit and a competitive ethos to public education.[2] By this reasoning, competition and the threat that consumers may choose to purchase goods and services from other providers create a strong incentive for providers to supply high-quality products and lower prices, lest consumers "vote with their feet" and take their business elsewhere. This competition is expected to drive overall improvements to the quality and efficiency of the school system.

The second argument suggests that with a wide variety of schools from which to choose, each of which provides a different mix of services, customers will choose the mix of services that best meets their educational preferences. The result would be a better match between school approaches and the educational needs and inclinations of students (or their parents). Sorting by preferences, it is argued, will reduce the amount of time schools spend resolving conflicts among stakeholders, leaving them more time and energy to devote to developing and implementing education programs.[3] These advocates also argue that the very act of choice will leave students, parents, and teachers disposed to work harder to support the schools they have chosen.

The third argument advanced for school choice is that the creation of more autonomous schools will lead to innovations in curriculum, instruction and governance, which in turn will improve outcomes. Other schools, including those competing for the same students, could also improve by adopting the innovative practices developed by choice schools.

These arguments generally reflect broader economic and political theories that have been applied in recent decades to education and other human service sectors. As the chapters in this book explain, the level of empirical support for these claims is uneven, reflective of the wide variation in choice approaches and in the different schooling contexts throughout the nation. While the potential of school choice has been debated and contested repeatedly over the years, this debate often overlooks the diversity within the broad realm of school choice and the differences in how specific types are legislated and implemented.

A key aim of this book is to facilitate a more nuanced understanding of school choice. For instance, these policies can be designed to pursue a range of outcomes. Consider as examples the issues of integration, innovation and accountability:

- Choice rules can be written either (a) to reduce isolation by race, class, or special needs status, or (b) to have the consequence of becoming a vehicle for accelerating resegregation of our public school systems.

- Depending on the design and funding incentives, school choice reforms can either (a) promote innovation and the development of a diversity of options from which parents can choose, or (b) result in a stratified and noninnovative marketplace that appeals to consumers looking for a familiar yet exclusive option.

- School choice reforms have the potential either (a) to promote accountability, or (b) to facilitate the circumvention or avoidance of oversight.

Each of the book's contributors looks broadly at school choice, integrating and summarizing the evidence spanning a wide range of choice models. The chapters consider as well the impacts each approach has on the traditional public school system. Then, based on this evidence and analysis, each chapter offers policy recommendations.

We asked each contributor to address six choice forms: vouchers/tuition tax credits, charter schools, homeschooling, interdistrict choice, intradistrict choice (including magnet schools and open enrollment plans), and virtual schools. Among the clear lessons from the book, however, is that the scope of evidence on homeschooling, virtual schools, and varied forms of inter- and intradistrict choice programs is surprisingly limited. We also learned that the six-form typology, while useful, should be understood flexibly, since the models overlap considerably. For instance, many or most virtual or cyber schools are actually charter schools, and a large portion of these schools cater to students that otherwise would be categorized as home schooled. Similarly, policies promoting inter- and intradistrict choice often intersect, and the recent voucher plan in Douglas County, Colorado, used a charter school shell to funnel state money into the private school vouchers.[4]

DIVERSE FORMS OF SCHOOL CHOICE

All major forms of school choice have grown in numbers over the past 2 decades. Below, we offer a brief description of the nature and growth of the six earlier-mentioned types of choice. As the chapters of this book describe, each type carries different rules, different structures, and different empirical effects; yet they also share important commonalities.

Our focus is on publicly funded school choice. This includes publicly funded places in private schools. Private schools have always been an option for families with financial means, but our discussion of private school choice is focused only on attendance through vouchers or tax credit policies. The U.S. Department of Education defines private schools as "institutions which provide instruction for any of Grades 1-12, have one or more teachers to give instruction, are not administered by a public agency, and are not operated in a private home."[5] Accordingly, the "private" label here applies to secular, independent schools as well as to religious and sectarian schools.

Vouchers and Tuition Tax Credits

Publicly funded vouchers and tuition tax credits are mechanisms that enable more families to choose private options. A *school voucher* is a certificate issued by the government by which parents can pay for the education of their children at a participating private school of their choice. In most instances, parents do not actually receive a certificate or redeemable check. Instead, schools verify that they are serving qualified students, and the government provides funding to the school based on the number of qualified students enrolled. Most publicly funded voucher programs target specific students, such as students from low-income families or students with disabilities.

Tuition tax credits come in two primary types. One type is simply a tax credit given to parents who incur expenses associated with sending their children to private schools. This results in governments paying some costs for private schools through foregone revenues. A second type is what Welner calls a "neovoucher."[6] Given the increasing prominence as well as the relative obscurity of this new type of policy, it deserves a bit of explanation here.

Instead of the conventional voucher approach of tax money being collected and then allocated by the state, through parental choices, to private schools attended by voucher students, a neovoucher approach inserts two intermediate steps into the process (see Figure 1.1[7]). One, the neovouchers are issued by privately created, nonprofit, scholarship-granting organizations, rather than directly by the government. Two, the state allocation is achieved through a tax credit (often dollar-for-dollar) given to a subgroup of taxpayers with the capacity and inclination to make the donations. These neovoucher systems are designed to provide government support for private schooling but to do so without any direct state payments. To accomplish this, tuition money passes through more hands before making its way to pri-

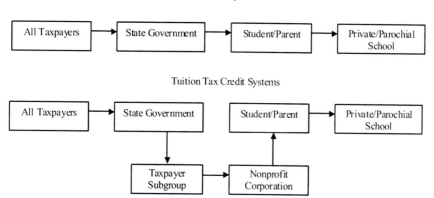

Source:

Source: Reprinted from Welner (2008, p. 6, Figure 2.1), with permission of the author.

Figure 1.1. Comparison of conventional voucher and tuition tax credit systems.

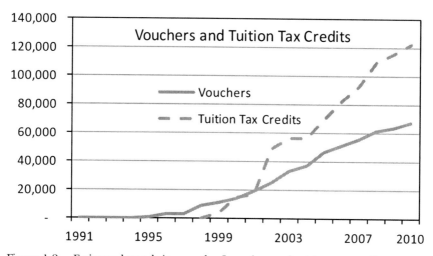

Figure 1.2. Estimated trends in growth of voucher and tuition tax credits (neovouchers).

vate and parochial schools, but the overall policy effect is very much the same as with vouchers (the legal and policy reasons for this more elaborate approach are described in Welner, 2008).

Figure 1.2 illustrates the estimated growth in the number of publicly funded vouchers and neovouchers.[8] Note that the number of neovouch-

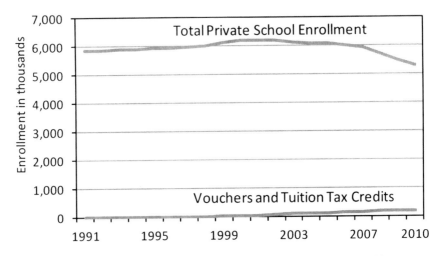

Figure 1.3. Estimated numbers of students receiving vouchers plus tuition tax credits in the United States.

ers has grown at a pace substantially outpacing the growth of conventional vouchers, with the current number now almost doubling its older cousin. After the data for these figures were compiled, several states adopted new voucher and neovoucher laws. Pennsylvania substantially expanded its neovoucher program, and Virginia and New Hampshire adopted new neovoucher programs. Meanwhile, Louisiana adopted both a conventional voucher law and a neovoucher law. Mississippi and Oklahoma also adopted a new conventional voucher laws targeted specifically for students with special needs. And Indiana adopted an expansive new conventional voucher law. Given these developments, it seems very likely that the number of publicly subsidized students enrolled in private schools will grow during the foreseeable future.

Figure 1.3 illustrates the national enrollment in private schools and the relatively small portion of the private school students supported by vouchers or neovouchers (note that these numbers do not include the first type of tuition tax credit described above—those provided directly to parents).[9] Enrollment in private schools has remained rather steady in the past few decades, although a gradual but substantial decline in private school began almost a decade. Although vouchers and neovouchers have extended access to private schools, these supports are only available to around 3.5% of all students enrolled in private schools. Put another way, vouchers and neovouchers together are received by only 0.3% of all school-aged children enrolled in either public or private schools in the United States.

The main publicly funded voucher programs in the country include those in Cleveland; Milwaukee; Washington, DC; and the state of Florida. Indiana is currently implementing a statewide voucher plan, as is Louisiana. The three most well-established neovoucher programs are in Arizona, Florida, and Pennsylvania, but nine additional states have adopted these policies.

Charter Schools

Charter schools, initially started in Minnesota in 1991, represented a break with other forms of school choice in that the approach allowed the creation of a new form of public school—one that was independent of local school districts. While the definition of charter schools varies somewhat by state, they are best described as nonsectarian public schools of choice that are free from many regulations that apply to conventional public schools. Charter schools provide public, tuition-free elementary/ secondary education under a charter granted by a legislatively recognized public entity or publicly appointed entity. Once granted a charter, these schools qualify for local, state, and federal taxpayer funds in much the same way as conventional public schools. In exchange for contractual performance promises, charter schools are exempted from many state or local regulations that normally govern the operation and management of public schools.[10]

Charter schools seek to reform public education through a blend of elements found in public schools, such as universal access and public funding, plus elements often associated with private schools, such as choice, autonomy, and flexibility.[11] The initial charter is usually granted for 3 to 5 years by an authorizer or sponsor, often a local school board.

Authorizers are expected to hold charter schools accountable for meeting their goals and objectives related to their mission and academic targets set forth in the charter (contract) itself. Schools that do not meet their goals and objectives or do not abide by the terms of the contract can have their charter revoked or—when it comes time for renewal—not renewed. Because these are schools of choice and receive funding based on the number of students they enroll, charter advocates point to a second form of accountability as well: accountability to parents and families who choose to enroll their child or choose to leave for another school. While high expectations for charter schools have been created through a great deal of policymaker buy-in and positive press, the overall results are decidedly mixed.[12]

As Figure 1.4 illustrates, charter school enrollment has grown steadily over the past 2 decades.[13] According to the National Alliance for Public

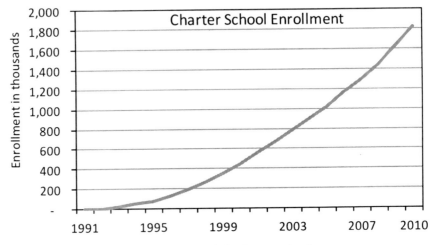

Figure 1.4.   Estimated enrollment trends in charter schools.

Charter Schools,[14] the number now surpasses two million students (the current year is not shown in Figure 1.4, which shows last year's enrollment surpassing 1.8 million). Charter school legislation is in place in 41 states plus the District of Columbia, with new schools being added every year.

Approximately 200,000 new students are, on balance, added to charter enrollments each year. In fact, the number of students enrolled in charter schools has grown more sharply than the growth in the number of schools. This is due to the fact that the average charter school size increases each year, as a large portion of charter schools serve more grade levels and add more classes. To try to put charter school enrollment in perspective, for every three students currently enrolled in private schools, one student is now enrolled in a charter school. Yet, while charter schools have garnered considerable attention over the past 2 decades, they only account for around 4.1% of the national enrollment in public schools and 3.7% of all students in either public or private schools. Nationally, then, charter schools play only a small role. It is when we look closely at some urban areas that we the impact of charter schools become much greater; 10 cities have seen the proportion of charter school students rise to surpass a third of all public school students.

Homeschooling

Homeschooling involves the education of children at home, typically by parents but sometimes by tutors. While the practice existed in legal limbo

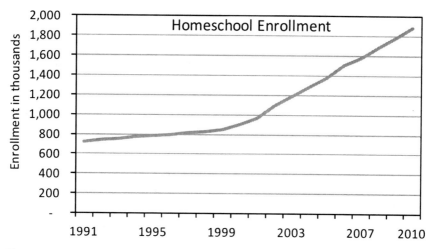

Figure 1.5.   Estimated enrollment trends in homeschooling.

for much of the past century, states and districts now set forth guidelines for how homeschooling can meet compulsory school requirements. It is, of course, common for parents to provide supplemental instruction or tutoring at home, but this is not categorized as homeschooling if it supplements or supports compulsory education delivered at a school. The practice only becomes homeschooling when it is permitted to replace compulsory education delivered at a school and when it qualifies students for formal schooling at higher levels.

For purposes of data collection, the National Center for Education Statistics explains that students are considered to be homeschooled if a parent reported them as being schooled at home instead of at a public or private school for at least part of their education and if their part-time enrollment in public or private school did not exceed 25 hours a week.[15] Students who were schooled at home primarily because of a temporary illness are not included as homeschoolers.

Notwithstanding the legal questions, homeschooling is a form of school choice that has long been available in the United States. However, as Figure 1.5 illustrates, the number of students whose parents decided to homeschool was consistently in the neighborhood of 800,000 to 900,000 until around 1999, when enrollment in homeschooling increased more rapidly.[16] Currently, it is estimated that more than 1.8 million students are home schooled. This represents about 3.4% of all students enrolled in public or private schools. The number of students that were home schooled in 2010 was similar to the total number of students enrolled in public charter schools at that time.

Interdistrict and Intradistrict Choice

Interdistrict and intradistrict choice interdistrict and intradistrict choice are approaches that permit that permit families to choose to choose a public school other than the one than the one assigned for their child or children within the district or in a surrounding district. Rules or restrictions in this type of choice often apply. For example, one common condition is that places must be available in the school a family chooses, often after filling initial slots with children from the neighborhood area. Interdistrict school choice plans are often referred to as Schools of Choice programs, while intradistrict plans are often referred to as Open Enrollment programs. An important characteristic of the school choice options that fall within the interdistrict or intradistrict categories is that these are public schools governed by local school district boards. In contrast, while charter schools are public, they have their own board and are not governed by the local district school board.

Interdistrict and intradistrict choice among public schools initially became more available in the 1960s with the introduction of alternative schools. These were later followed by magnet schools in the 1970s and 1980s. The late-1990s saw increased implementation of the types of interdistrict and intradistrict choice plans seen today (see Figure 1.6[17]). Currently, it is estimated that close to half of all school districts in the United States have at least one public school that has open enrollment of some sort to facilitate parent choice.[18]

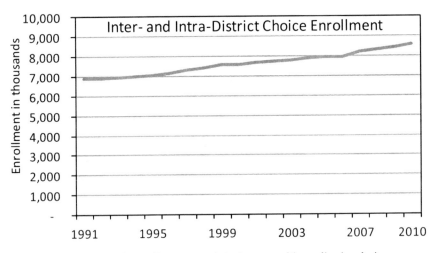

Figure 1.6.   Estimated enrollment trends in inter- and intradistrict choice programs.

Magnet schools remain the most prominent form of interdistrict or intradistrict school choice. They are governed by local school district boards; however, they could serve students from throughout the district or in some cases students outside the school district. The number of magnet schools expanded in the 1970s and 1980s as a mechanism designed to reduce racial and ethnic segregation in school districts or provide an academic or social focus on a particular theme. As of 2007-08, it was estimated that around 2,400 magnet schools were operating in the United States, with enrollment of approximately 1.2 million students. An additional 3,300 public schools had more limited within-school magnet programs, enrolling approximately 3.1 million students in 2007-08.[19]

Magnet schools typically receive additional funding to develop and sustain their unique programs and profiles. They receive funding from the federal government's Magnet Schools Assistance Program, as well as funding from other government sources such as the Voluntary Public School Choice grants and the Smaller Learning Community grants. An important original aim of magnet schools was to provide students an opportunity to succeed academically while learning in a racially diverse environment. Ideally, magnet schools were intended to serve as models for school improvement and possible turnaround models for students in low-performing schools.

Virtual Schools

Virtual schools (also known as cyber schools or online schools) deliver their curriculum and provide instruction via the Internet and electronic communication. The focus in this book is on full-time cyber schools, as distinguished from "virtual programs" that deliver individual courses to students enrolled in other schools.

Enrollment in virtual schools has been growing extremely rapidly in recent years, reaching an estimated enrollment of 250,000 in 2010-2011, compared to fewer than 20,000 less than a decade ago (see Figure 1.7[20]). It is important to note that this category of school choice overlaps with both homeschooling and charter schools. Most virtual schools are organized as charter schools, although an increasing number of district and state education agencies are now starting full-time virtual schools. Private for-profit education management organizations have also played an important role in expanding the number of virtual schools—in schools operated as charters as well as district schools. Since the students who enroll in virtual schools, including charter virtual schools, are often students whose parents home school, a given student might be included in all three categories. Because of the rapid growth of this sector, very little research evidence exists concerning costs, outcomes, or accountability.[21]

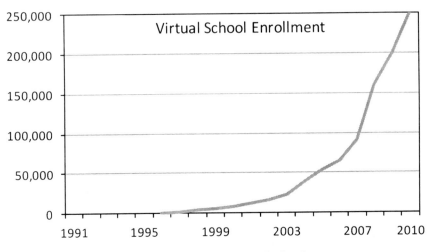

Figure 1.7.   Estimated enrollment trends in virtual schools.

Summary of School Choice Options

From the National Household Education Survey, it is possible to see that while only 20% of American families reported attending a school other than the one they were assigned to in 1993, this figure increased to 27% by 2007. Our own estimates based on the diverse forms of school choice available suggest that close to 31% of all school-aged children attended a school other than the public school they were assigned to during the 2010-11 school year. This includes both public and private schools. If we look at only school choice among public schools or publicly funded or subsidized places in private schools, our estimate is that 22.5% of all school-aged children in 2010-11 were enrolled in a school other than the one they were assigned.

Figure 1.8 combines enrollment estimates across the diverse school choice options covered in the book. Although not covered systematically here, additional choice enrollment includes children whose parents can afford to pay tuition in private schools. Also, in the broadest sense of choice, families with sufficient resources can choose their public school by purchasing property within a given school's enrollment boundaries. Anyone who has ever bought a home is made aware of this fact by the realtors who regularly report information on the local school to which houses are assigned.

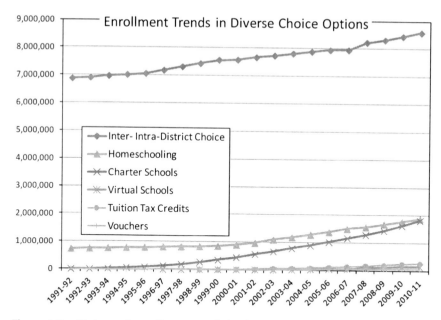

Figure 1.8.   Estimated enrollment trends in diverse choice options in the United States, 1991 to 2010.

SCHOOL CHOICE IN THE UNITED STATES COMPARED WITH OTHER INDUSTRIALIZED NATIONS

Compared to other industrialized countries, the United States has more school choice within the public school sector, while many other countries have more choice provided by subsidized private schools.[22] Although some countries have considerable enrollments in government-dependent private schools, it is important to note that these private schools are closely regulated and are often seen as a component of the publicly funded national education systems.

Most of the Organisation for Economic Co-operation and Development (OECD) countries permit the existence of both public and private schools and recognize that these diverse school types can deliver compulsory education. In addition, over 70% of OECD countries report that homeschooling could serve as a legal means of providing compulsory education. Actual enrollment patterns suggest that, in practice, enrollments in government-dependent private schools exceed 10% in only seven countries (Belgium, Chile, Denmark, France, the Netherlands, New Zealand and Spain), while enrollments in independent private schools exceed 10% in only three countries (Mexico, Portugal, and the OECD partner country Brazil). Only half the OECD countries report any significant enrollments in homeschooling, and the average in these countries is only 0.4% of total enrollments. The United States leads the world when it comes to homeschooling, with 3.1% of all school-aged children being home schooled. New Zealand is the next closest country, with only 0.9% of its students home schooled.

A recent survey conducted for the OECD showed that school choice had expanded considerably over the past 25 years.[23] More than half of the countries surveyed reported a reduction in restrictions on school choice among public schools. Of these, 11 reported the creation of new autonomous public schools, and nine reported that new funding mechanisms had been put in place to promote school choice. Reforms to promote school choice most often applied to public schools, but six OECD countries also reported reforms expanding opportunities for homeschooling.

OVERVIEW OF CONTENTS

Advocates of school choice offer it as a sensible path to school reform founded on free-market principles, while opponents warn of serious unintended consequences. But a close examination of research finds a decidedly mixed picture of choice's benefits and shortcomings. Each chapter in this book presents a comprehensive examination of a key school choice issue. For each issue, the authors bring together evidence from these six different types of choice, developing cross-choice themes and insights.

The book's later, empirical discussions are framed by Chapters 2 and 3. In Chapter 2, *Negotiating Public and Private: Philosophical Frameworks for School Choice*, Terri Wilson examines the underlying philosophical assumptions that undergird choice proposals, including varying and sometimes conflicting understandings of public and private realms of action. In Chapter 3, *How Legislation and Litigation Shape School Choice*, Julie Mead traces the history of battles in the courts and the legislature over choice proposals, including legal rulings on school segregation that helped set the stage for some of the early public school choice measures, which were designed as tools for school integration.

The next two chapters carefully examine the research evidence behind two sets of common assumptions concerning school choice: the process whereby parents make (or do not make) their choices, and how the choice process and other mechanisms instill (or do not instill) important elements of accountability. Chapter 4, *Who Chooses Schools, and Why*, by Natalie Lacireno-Paquet and Charleen Brantley, offers a comprehensive look behind the choice curtain, providing crucial information for policy-makers and others interested in how the parent and student choice process actually takes place. Similarly, Chapter 5, *School Choice and Accountability*, by Gregg Garn and Casey Cobb, looks at the evidence and questions the assumption that choice programs are by their nature more accountable to families or communities than traditional public schools.

The shift to school choice systems can also change the nature of basic inputs such as funding, teachers, and instruction. In Chapter 6, *Funding Formulas, School Choice, and Inherent Incentives*, Clive Belfield reviews the way particular approaches to paying for choice programs can influence their outcomes. In Chapter 7, *Teacher Qualifications and Work Environments Across School Types*, Marisa Cannata presents original research that compares the qualifications and working conditions of teachers in various school settings.

The final four chapters of the book explore key outcomes. Chapter 8, *Educational Innovation and Diversification in School Choice Plans*, by Chris Lubienksi, examines the oft-held belief that choice schools will drive innovation. Chapter 9, *School Choice and Segregation by Race, Class, and Achievement*, by Roslyn Mickelson, Stephanie Southworth and Martha Bottia, examines the ways in which choice programs are increasing segregation and stratification among schoolchildren rather than expanding diversity. In Chapter 10, *The Competitive Effect of School Choice Policies on Performance in Traditional Public Schools*, David Arsen and Yongmei Ni examine the claim of school choice advocates that choice plans will also spur improvement in traditional public schools. Finally, in Chapter 11, *The Impact of School Choice Reforms on Student Achievement*, Gary Miron and Jessica Urschel review evidence for and against contentions that schools of choice contribute to greater achievement by students.

The book's conclusion, authored by William Mathis and Patricia Hinchey, examines themes that cut across the various chapters, including vital issues such as funding, equality, learning, test scores and implications for democratic schools and society.

Over the years, school choice policies have been subjected to extensive research and evaluation. Generally speaking, these studies probe a specific type of choice policy and then examine one or more elements or issues concerning that policy. By bringing together the universe of choice policies and issues, this book gives readers a comprehensive, complete picture and, in doing so, offers cross-cutting insights that would otherwise be obscured.

On the whole, the chapters in this book offer reason to believe that choice policies can further some educational goals. But they also suggest many reasons for caution. If choice policies are to be evidence-based, a re-examination is in order. The information and insights in the following chapters, in helping us to understand school choice, provide the basis for designing sensible and effective roles for choice policies. We as a nation now have the information we need to take on a redesign; the choice is up to us.

CHAPTER 2

NEGOTIATING PUBLIC AND PRIVATE

Philosophical Frameworks for School Choice

Terri S. Wilson

Beneath controversies about whether or not choice "works" are deep philosophical and moral commitments about how choice proposals reconfigure commonly accepted definitions of public and private education.[1] Perhaps more so than other educational policies, school choice raises fundamental questions about the nature of American education: how individual rights are tempered by social obligations, how demands for liberty are balanced by demands for equality, and how private interests interact with public goods.

Indeed, concepts of "public" and "private" have been central to arguments for and against choice. Choice is often said to be "redefining" public education, as new organizational arrangements—often privately operated—deliver public education. In fact, some of the rationale for choice involves reconfiguring the very terms "public" and "private" by expanding and reshaping what counts as public education. While both advocates and critics of choice use the language of the "public" and "private," the meanings of these terms vary across positions. For advocates, school choice policies provide a means of building equity in education,

Exploring the School Choice Universe: Evidence and Recommendations
pp. 17–38
Copyright © 2012 by Information Age Publishing
All rights of reproduction in any form reserved.

and acknowledge parents' rights to have their children educated in line with their own values and beliefs. For critics, choice weakens access and opportunity for the most disadvantaged students, and risks segregating students into increasingly unequal schools. Moreover, for critics, the very notion of choosing one school from among a "marketplace" of options transforms education into a commodity, in contrast to its tradition as an essential public good. In these arguments, the very terms "public" and "private" are invested with different meanings and positions.

It is necessary to understand, therefore, what we mean by public and private. How are these terms defined? What arguments are made on their behalf? This chapter takes a step back from practical debates about such issues as efficiency and effectiveness to examine this philosophical debate. Philosophy does not answer empirical questions (what is happening here?). Instead, it uncovers the assumptions and judgments (what ought to happen?) embedded in empirical questions and arguments. While empirical studies play a crucial role in assembling evidence about the practical consequences and effects of different choice policies, evidence alone cannot resolve normative debates about the appropriate purposes, aims and values of choice policies.

This chapter reviews major philosophical justifications for and against school choice. In particular, it explores the concepts of "public" and "private" at the heart of the debate. Various arguments, both historical and conceptual, have been made about how school choice can balance private, individual rights against public, social obligations. To place the debates about choice in context, the first section reviews the historical development of the public/private distinction in school choice, tracing shifting definitions of the term "public" in public education across time and among different researchers, educators, and policymakers. This review is followed by a survey of major conceptual arguments for and against choice, grouped into five frameworks: liberty, equity, justice, pluralism, and democracy. The conclusion sketches out some implications of this philosophical field for school choice policy and practice, and offers stakeholders some recommendations for employing philosophical frameworks in their work.

PUBLIC AND PRIVATE IN SCHOOL CHOICE

The terms "public" and "private" are notoriously difficult to define because they reflect a complex and shifting cultural, political and ideological terrain. Most often used as modifying adjectives, "public" and "private" often refer to specific kinds of institutions: public transportation or public education, for example. In addition to their ordinary life as adjectives, these concepts can also be understood as substantive categories ("The Public" and "The Private"), as well as modifiers for particular spatial metaphors (the public or private sphere, realm, sector etc.). Particularly important for school choice, public and private are also used to capture a sense of "interest," as in the "Public Interest," or our "private self-interests." Most importantly, perhaps, "public" and "private" are typically defined in relation to and against one another; they are relative, not static terms. The private sphere of action is only definable in relation to a public one: that is, we usually define the "public" by what it is not. Thus, we contrast the private world of the family and home "in here" with the broader public world "out there."[2]

Understanding what counts as "private" and "public" is also shaped by experiences in these kinds of institutions. Our interactions with private schools or universities shape our sense of the term "private." Likewise, experiences in public institutions—schools, parks, and the like—help shape how we conceptualize the "public." In this sense, our understanding of what counts as "public" and "private" education has been shaped by the evolution of public and private education in this country.

Development of the "Public School"

Debates about school choice have developed in conjunction with—and in opposition to—what we usually term "public education." Choice is often counterposed to a "traditional" idea of public education: the district-run, publicly governed, common school. It is important to remember, however, that this "traditional" concept of public education is a relatively recent invention, and one that has evolved considerably over the last century and a half.

Public education, as we currently understand it, started to develop through the antebellum expansion of the "common school" ideal. As Christopher Lubienski details, the common school movement deliberately fought to articulate an emerging school system as "public" in contrast to the "private" system of academies available at the time.[3] In doing so, Horace Mann and other reformers fought for publicly funded common schools, accessible to everyone and democratically controlled by their local communities. Many of the characteristics typically associated with public education—public financing, access and governance—grew out of the common school movement. Over the next century and a half, these rural and decentralized schools would take on new and expanded roles in American life, and associated concepts of democratic control and equality of opportunity would change alongside them.

In terms of democratic control, early 20th century urbanization, indus-
trialization and immigration increased the role that public schools played
in assimilating newcomers and inculcating common values.[4] At the same
time, thousands of locally run schools were centralized into larger,
bureaucratically administered districts. Progressive reformers saw these
new governance arrangements as forces of efficiency and social improvement; for many local officials, however, the new arrangements transferred
power from rural communities to at-large elected officials, and from
neighborhoods to city bureaucrats.

Likewise, the ideal of equal opportunity central to American public
education has also been a contested concept. As student enrollment
increased throughout the last century, schools were also expected to educate larger numbers of students to higher levels of achievement. As the
century progressed, public schools came to be seen as engines of access,
integration, and equity; increasingly, they were expected to play an active
role in reducing social inequity. Through these new expectations, the very
meaning of "equality" came to encompass more groups of people and
higher standards of achievement.

Development of "School Choice"

Just as the meaning of "public education"– associated with public funding, democratic control and equality of opportunity—has evolved, the
meaning of "school choice" has also developed over time. Many researchers and scholars credit Milton Friedman with establishing the conceptual
argument for school choice more than 50 years ago.[5] Friedman first outlined his proposal for school vouchers in a 1955 essay, "The Role of Government in Education." Further elaborated in 1962's *Capitalism and
Freedom*, his argument was that the private sector, responsive to issues of
supply and demand, could more effectively provide education. Here,
Friedman separated provision of education from funding of education.
The proper role of the government, for Friedman, was to provide enough
oversight to ensure the functioning of the market, and to provide enough
funding (in the form of vouchers) so that students could receive an adequate education for general citizenship. As Jeffrey Henig points out, the
power of Friedman's proposal rests on his "detailed and vivid description
of the generally harmful consequences of permitting public schools to
operate as monopolistic providers."[6]

In contrast to the largely economic and libertarian argument advanced
by Friedman, other proponents have advanced the case for choice by
drawing on concepts of equity. For example, under the auspices of the
federal Office of Economic Opportunity, the sociologist Christopher

Jencks in 1970 advanced a specific voucher proposal focused on expanding educational opportunities for disadvantaged children.[7] Highly regulated, the Jencks proposal required participating schools to accept all eligible students, to use lottery mechanisms for admissions decisions, and to accept the voucher as full payment for tuition.[8] A year later, John Coons and Stephen Sugarman developed another voucher proposal that similarly pursued increased educational equality for disadvantaged students and expanded parental choice.[9] These early proposals and limited experiments helped to repackage choice in terms of equity, pluralism and parental empowerment.[10]

At the same time, public school districts were experimenting with a range of different public school choice programs: magnet schools, intradistrict choice plans, alternative schools, charter schools and interdistrict options.[11] All of these experiments in public school choice helped to shape the case for using choice as a vehicle for school improvement, racial integration and educational equity. With these experiments, choice advocates were emerging from different sides of the political landscape. As William Reese points out, "choice" became a rallying cry for both liberals and conservatives after the 1970s.[12] For liberals, choice meant teacher and community-driven alternatives to the "public school monopoly"; for conservatives, it offered ways to inject market solutions and competitive forces into a staid and inefficient educational system.

With the exception of early voucher experiments, these initial programs were all still part of the public school system. Although Friedman's proposals for private choice had attracted attention in select think tanks, academic circles and early experiments, vigorous political opposition halted any widespread implementation. John Chubb and Terry Moe's *Politics, Markets and America's Schools* helped to change this dynamic.[13] Using empirical evidence on school effectiveness, they argued that schools were failing because they were too democratic.[14] They also popularized a distinction central to the development of choice reforms, differentiating reforms internal to schools ("organizational") from those external to them ("structural"). This distinction implied that only radical—that is, external and market driven—reforms could fix the broken school system. Organizational reforms internal to schools (new approaches to staff development, different reading curricula) couldn't change schools to the degree that external structural reforms (developing voucher alternatives, allowing parents to freely move children between schools) could, if given the opportunity.

In addition, Chubb and Moe's use of empirical evidence helped shift the terms of the debate. Choice was no longer just a theoretical assumption, but something that could be subject to policy experimentation and empirical research. Debates about choice soon became focused on whether or not specific choice programs "worked" to raise student achievement, win parent and student satisfaction, and improve cost effectiveness. Subsequent debates about the efficacy of choice have left questions about the goals and purposes of choice relatively unexamined. That is, questions about the purposes of choice were supplanted by questions about the effectiveness of choice.

Redefining Public Education

Both critics and advocates often say that choice is "redefining public education."[15] We routinely think of public and private as different kinds of schools. That is, public schools are publicly financed and operated schools, accessible to everyone; private schools are privately financed and managed independent schools—sometimes religious—that have limited enrollment. Choice advocates argue, however, that both public and private institutions can serve public purposes; that is, they believe that public education can be provided by private schools. From this perspective, to provide public education, a school need only be publicly funded, accessible and accountable. In fact, certain advocates prefer to avoid the term "public schools" and instead talk about "district schools" or "government schools" to emphasize that many different kinds of institutions—including private businesses—can, like school districts, function as providers of public education.[16]

This new model embeds a "functionalist" definition of public, one that focuses primarily on the results of institutions. Highlighting this shifting definition, Gary Miron and Christopher Nelson have argued that charter schools, for instance, employ two definitions of public-ness: a traditional, "formalist" definition, which emphasizes public ownership and control, and a newer "functionalist" definition, which requires only that schools serve the public interest, even if they are privately owned and controlled.[17] Andrew Rotherham has employed the same distinction in analyzing types of charter accountability, arguing that the "public-ness" of charter schools is measured not by ownership and governance, but by the fact that the schools serve the public's children and are publicly accountable.[18] Similarly, Christopher Lubienski contrasts the new definition of public education used by contemporary choice advocates with older conceptions of public education used by early common school reformers. Earlier, education was defined as "public" in terms of common values, public governance, equality of opportunity, democratic due process, and the "common good." For contemporary choice proponents, however, public education is defined functionally, in terms of the "instrumentality of its academic mission."[19] That is, public education counts as "public" to the degree that it increases the academic achievement of the nation's students.

From this functionalist perspective, public education is a matter of accountability for public outcomes: academic achievement first among them. This accountability is largely conceived in terms of individual students. That is, schools of choice are only—and understandably—accountable for the achievement of the individual students enrolled in them. This understanding of public accountability, however, represents a significant shift from defining public accountability in terms of equality of opportunity. Equality of opportunity is concerned not just with the experiences of individual students that take advantage of choice schools, but with the aggregate experiences of students in school systems. As Tomas Englund argues, recent school reforms have gradually shifted the terms of debate: from understanding education as a public good toward viewing it as a private good.[20] This concern reflects one of the most fundamental criticisms of privatization: that public education will come to be conceived as a private good, thereby impoverishing the public system as a whole.

David Labaree makes a similar argument through a different analytic lens.[21] For Labaree, three conflicting purposes of education—democratic equality (preparing citizens), social efficiency (training workers) and social mobility (preparing individuals to compete for social positions)—have interacted throughout the history of the American public school. Democratic equality and social efficiency both understand education as a public good, designed to prepare citizens for—respectively—public roles and private advancement. In contrast, social mobility understands education as a commodity: as a private good designed to improve an individual's position in a competitive marketplace. This latter understanding, as Labaree argues, has dominated recent discourse about the public purposes of education.

While there is dispute about how to define public education, few critics or advocates would dispute that school choice, as a reform movement, has deliberately attempted to influence concepts of public and private. Several scholars have detailed the political nature of this redefinition, arguing that the conceptual legacies of school choice were the result of a concerted and political effort on the part of certain theorists and scholars to shift the terms of a debate.[22]

FRAMEWORKS

While we can distinguish between the private and public dimensions of education, it is commonly accepted that education has both public and private dimensions. Since it is neither solely a private good nor solely a public one, it is impossible to ask whether education should serve the private or the public interest. The real question, of course, concerns just how education fulfills and balances both private and public aims. This is a question particularly suited to the method and tradition of philosophy.[23] Much of the philosophic tradition has addressed how we relate private rights to public responsibilities, how we balance the rights of the individual—and the family—against broader social goals. This tradition has particular applicability to questions in education, and especially to issues central to school choice.

Instead of arguing for education as a distinctly public duty or private right, different scholars adopt distinct conceptual frameworks to describe how education ought to mediate between our private interests and public goals. Some frameworks, for instance, emphasize liberty. Others lean toward equality. These different ideals and values offer alternate understandings of the proper relationship between private rights and public obligations, and the particular role that school choice might play in mediating this relationship. This section summarizes these different emphases in the philosophical literature: liberty, equity, justice, pluralism and democracy. Any argument made for or against choice invariably addresses—in some form—each of these different concepts. Yet, there are significant differences of degree and emphasis among arguments.

Liberty[24]

First, many understandings of education emphasize the rights of families to send their children to independent rather than state-sponsored schools. Indeed, parents' rights to secure private education for their children are well recognized and upheld (within certain limitations) by legal precedent.[25] *Pierce v. Society of Sisters*, for instance, deliberately recognized the rights of parents to educate their children as a form of liberty protected under the Fourteenth Amendment. This decision, more broadly, sought to balance the "fundamental values necessary for the maintenance of a democratic political system" against the individual freedom to exit public schools in accordance with the "private beliefs of the student and his or her family."[26] Liberty, then, has been associated both with the right to exit the public schools and with the right to hold certain private beliefs that may conflict with public schooling.

These private beliefs imply the existence and legitimacy of pluralistic visions of what constitutes a flourishing life.[27] Such different visions of a good life do, under certain circumstances, come into conflict with the curriculum and practices of the public school system. One of the most discussed legal cases, *Wisconsin v. Yoder*, offers a demonstration. In this 1972 case, the Supreme Court recognized the right of Amish families to withdraw their children from compulsory public education after 8 years in order to strengthen their connection to their Amish community and way of life.[28] Different theorists have employed this case to argue for conceptions of liberty in education. William Galston, for instance, employs the principle evident in this case in arguing for a concept of "expressive liberty" in education.[29] His argument promotes deference to the rights of parents to lead lives, and raise children, as they see fit with minimal intrusion from the state.[30]

Similarly, Eamonn Callan endorses some respect for parental rights, particularly with respect to "culturally dissident minorities," but not to the extent advocated by Galston.[31] Callan argues that the state has a legitimate interest in protecting the future autonomy—in a sense, the future liberty—of children. Sometimes an interest in protecting the developing autonomy of children will conflict with an interest in protecting parents' rights to practice different visions of a flourishing life. The conflict here, as Callan relates, is not between individuals and the state, but between "parental choice and the basic interests (as society defines those interests) of individual children."[32] To protect these interests, various private and independent schools are still subject to various public provisions. Likewise, not all private beliefs are recognized as equally compelling reasons to opt out of the public school system.[33]

In addition to the right to "opt out," other theorists have posited the right to access specific kinds of schools as a kind of liberty.[34] Here, access to distinctive schools—ones that endorse and support different "reasonable" conceptions of a good life—can be understood as a kind of right. Similar arguments are offered in support of public funding for private schools and for home schooling.[35] These conceptions of liberty are tied, broadly, to market rationales for choice, despite the fact that many arguments for a market-based system stress only the effectiveness of market reform. For some advocates, a market-based system simply provides quality education more efficiently and effectively; for others, market reform provides a space for the exercise of individual rights.[36] In these latter cases, advocates link a market-based system to arguments for freedom of choice. Individual rights to choose particular approaches to education are juxtaposed against a monolithic and mandatory system of education. The right to choose among market options becomes, in this formulation, a kind of liberty against invasive forms of state control.

Equity

Other theorists have argued that appeals to liberty, especially those rooted in market choices, were part of "first-generation" rationales for choice.[37] As choice matured, arguments began to emphasize notions of equity instead.[38] Alan Wolfe argues that choice has been most politically successful when it has appealed to equality.[39] Indeed, the language of "equality," "equity" and "fairness" saturates the choice movement. Paul T. Hill remarks that the focus on equity among proponents of choice is part of an "attempt to move the debate on choice ahead by focusing on the risks of choice and how they can be controlled."[40] Opponents, too, often appeal to equity when enumerating the disadvantages of choice programs, particularly for students left behind in district schools. As Stephen Macedo summarizes, "the best arguments for school choice invoke equity, but so do the least defensible arguments and the least-attractive forms of school choice. It all depends on what we mean by equity."[41]

Indeed, definitions of equity vary considerably. The term is often used interchangeably with other concepts: "equality," and, increasingly, "adequacy." The meaning of all three terms is subject to debate. First, the concept of equality, or equal opportunity, has changed over time. In the common school movement, equality meant not making everyone equal, but providing opportunity for everyone to make themselves equal.[42] In a shift, the *Brown v. Board of Education* decision argued that education "must be made available to all on equal terms"[43]; that is, the focus moved to ensuring that the opportunities education provided were equally available to all citizen groups. While the term "equality" was used routinely from common school reform through the civil rights movement, the term "equity" has appeared more frequently in state-level school finance litigations decided in the wake of the 1973 *San Antonio Independent School District v. Rodriguez*. The concept of "equity" tends to emphasize equality of resources rather than opportunities or protections.

In more recent decades, the courts have increasingly moved away from attempts to define equality or equity in favor of "adequacy" standards.[44] Rather than attempting to equalize financial resources across school districts, adequacy standards establish a minimum threshold of education to which all students are entitled. "Minimum standards"—described in New York State, for instance, as a "sound and basic" education—have increasingly replaced the language of "equal educational opportunity" and "equal protection" in legal judgments.[45] This language, as scholars have detailed, presumes that financial—and educational—inequities will continue.[46] Districts and parents, of course, remain free to spend more than what is adequate. Here, arguments for adequacy standards defer to parents' rights.[47]

Applied more specifically to issues of school choice, the concept of equity has increasingly been linked to access and choice. Proponents argue that parents, regardless of income or residence, should be granted an equal opportunity to choose the schools their children attend. Equality here does not imply that parents will choose between equal schools. Rather, equality means that all parents have an equal opportunity to choose.

Justice

Equity arguments closely correspond to arguments that emphasize justice. More general than appeals to equity, appeals to justice commonly place a sense of "fairness" at the heart of school choice debates. While justice is also difficult to precisely define, the concept plays an important role in philosophical considerations of choice.

Most notably, Harry Brighouse argues in *School Choice and Social Justice* that certain choice mechanisms could be arranged to meet the demands of justice and equity.[48] Justice, for Brighouse, requires that "children's prospects ... should not be entirely dependent on their own talents and the resources and prudence of their parents."[49] This principle of justice necessarily implies a principle of educational equality. While not arguing for "full privatization," Brighouse nevertheless advocates for a universal system of vouchers that might serve the goals of social justice.[50] Drawing on similar proposals by Herbert Gintis and James Dwyer, Brighouse advocates for a highly regulated voucher policy that would involve increased regulation for eligible private schools and would prohibit parents from "topping off" the voucher amount with available private funds.[51]

Many arguments for justice understand choice as a mechanism for achieving certain educational ends, not as an end in itself. Stephen Macedo suggests that if our interest in equity is properly understood as providing a "good public education for all," school choice may not be the most obvious or compelling means to that end. From a different perspective, Sigal Ben-Porath draws on notions of justice to develop an argument for structured paternalism. She argues that the government should structure choices to balance the greatest possible freedom of choice with the greatest possible equality of opportunity. In this vein, Ben-Porath argues for a system of universal choice; one that would provide all parents with the information and support necessary to make informed choices.[52] Such arguments demonstrate the different kinds of questions that philosophy can ask: not just questions about what kinds of choice work best, but questions about whether we should have school choice at all. Employing a similar philosophical strategy, but with different results, Harry Brighouse argues that voucher proposals might be more, not less, likely to meet the demands of social justice than other more politically palatable forms of choice, such as interdistrict choice options or charter schools.

Still other theorists equate justice with different kinds of ends. Macedo, Brighouse, and other theorists in the liberal tradition generally use a concept of distributive justice, often measured in access to material goods. However, as Kathleen Knight Abowitz argues, justice involves more than fair access to goods. Following Nancy Fraser and other critical theorists, Knight Abowitz contends that justice involves issues of recognition and participation as well as distribution.[53] More recently, Knight Abowitz has argued that choice schemes might be evaluated according to an ideal of "intergenerational justice," which would attend to the ways in which different educational policies might secure justice for future generations, not just for students presently enrolled in schools.[54] Building on this work, Knight Abowitz has advanced a concept of "democratic justice" to evaluate school choice efforts. This concept emphasizes four principles of justice: parity of participation, recognition of difference, redistribution of resources and representation in decision making.[55] In addition to this conception, other theorists have attempted to revise, expand and critique the tenets of a distributive paradigm.[56] These efforts have resulted in alternate areas of literature on school choice, particularly concerned with the ability of school choice to build pluralist recognition and democratic participation.

Pluralism

Many arguments for school choice, aiming to increase the diversity and range of schools available to families, draw on conceptions of pluralism. Likewise, many opponents of choice are concerned that pluralist schools will increase segregation and fail to teach a common sense of democratic citizenship in an increasingly diverse society. Either way, concepts of pluralism play a role in almost every philosophical consideration of choice. William Galston's ideal of "expressive liberty," for instance, while emphasizing freedom, argues for the inevitability of difference and people's rights to express different versions of a good life. Stephen Macedo counters that appeals to religious, social or intellectual pluralism do not provide an adequate justification for the public funding of private schools.[57] While supportive of educational accommodation to pluralism, Macedo argues for a distinction between nonpublic values and aspirations and public goods created through political deliberation.[58] Although there is a place for many nonpublic values pursued by diverse pluralist communities—the desire to teach children distinctly religious views, for example—these values do not have to be publicly supported.

Different theorists take different positions on how much parents' convictions should be respected, protected and sustained.[59] While the basic rights of parents to "opt out" of public schools, in favor of private alternatives or the decision to home-school, are well recognized, many choice theorists argue that the public school system should provide options that recognize and support different ethical convictions. Michael W. McConnell, for instance, contends that pluralism is an inescapable fact of American life, and calls for an educational system that is "private and pluralistic," as opposed to one that is "democratic and collective."[60] He argues parents should be able to choose among a wide variety of different schools, public and private, which reflect their values and convictions. Advocating public support for religious schools and home schooling, he contends that parental preferences should be granted wide latitude, constrained only by minimal civic goals and standards of educational quality.[61]

Rob Reich also argues that pluralism is a fact of life in any liberal society.[62] For Reich, school choice provides a potential vehicle for accommodating pluralist preferences within common ideals, rather than seeking to assimilate them to any one particular ideal. Here, Reich distinguishes between the "structure" and the "substance" of a common school ideal. He argues that a variety of school structures, public and private, can uphold common educational values and goals. For Reich, these common goals must include, at minimum, teaching norms of citizenship and ensuring the future autonomy of students. For Reich, autonomy entails the ability to freely consent to one's political system of governance, and—especially important for school choice—the ability to criticize and even exit a way of life. He is critical of both those who argue against reasonable pluralist conceptions of schooling and those who defend overly expansive versions of pluralism that are incapable of securing the autonomy of students.[63] While supportive of school choice in general, Reich is critical of particular forms of school choice (certain forms of home schooling and religious schools) that preclude the ability of students to reflect on—and potentially exit—the ethical worldview of their parents or community group.

Reich's focus on the importance of autonomy-facilitating education is a theme echoed by many other scholars. Different theorists pair a focus on autonomy with other values: with equality of opportunity (Brighouse), tolerance (Gutmann), "critical rationality" and "deliberative excellence" (Callan) or the capacity for "critical enquiry" and "sympathetic reflection" (Levinson).[64] However they define it, these scholars see autonomy as a central civic goal, and they caution that no school should privilege pro-

moting a particular conception of "the good" over developing students'
ability to define and eventually choose their own conception of a good
life.[65] Other theorists are less concerned about the development of
autonomy[66] or less worried that particularistic schools could threaten student autonomy.[67] Still others are skeptical that choice policies will be able
to promote student autonomy in any case.[68]

Here, considerations of pluralism and school choice are implicitly connected to a broader field of scholarship examining the requirements of
citizenship and the demands of cultural recognition in education.[69] This
scholarship examines the ways in which educational policies, school
choice among them, balance the prospective rights of children against the
existing rights of distinctive communities. In striking this balance, some
theorists emphasize the risks pluralistic communities pose for civic cohesion. Walter Feinberg, for instance, argues that the state has a legitimate
interest and role in the regulation of private and religious schools.[70]
Although supportive of diverse kinds of private education, Feinberg views
these schools as dependent upon a larger system of public education,
which should "reproduce the understandings and dispositions needed to
secure the political climate where all deeply held religious ideals can be
expressed."[71]

This argument—that public schools have a distinct role to play in creating a national identity and common values—goes beyond the minimal
public role advocated by other theorists emphasizing pluralism. Echoed
by other scholars, other versions of this argument draw on conceptions of
pluralism and diversity to argue against choice, and for the integrating
potential of the common, public school.[72]

Democracy

Theorists who focus on democracy are chiefly concerned with students'
ability to relate across lines of difference, and thus often privilege concepts of democratic participation in their analysis of school choice. Amy
Gutmann, for instance, argues that conceptions of democracy should play
a central role in evaluating educational policy. Positing a "democratic
ideal," she argues that educational strategies should be measured by how
well they prepare children for a life of equal liberty and opportunity.[73]
Her argument stresses democratic participation as the best means for
achieving these goals. For Gutmann, democratic deliberation provides a
way to adjudicate the diverse conceptions of the good that will occur in
any discussion of public education. Similarly, David Mathews argues that
schools are best understood as public spaces where citizens engage in the
"coproduction of education."[74] In this conception, schools are not just a

means for securing certain public ends; rather, schools are, themselves, kinds of public spaces. As Benjamin Barber contends, "public schools are not merely schools for the public, but schools of publicness: institutions where we learn what it means to be a public and start down the road toward common national and civic identity."[75]

Certain scholars have described this view as a "common school ideal"[76] or a "comprehensive ideal."[77] Richard Pring emphasizes the common school as a kind of moral ideal: "the fight for the common school was essentially a moral one in terms of achieving greater social justice and equality, respect for persons and preparation for citizenship within a democratic order."[78] This view emphasizes the role of public schools in creating social cohesion and community around shared cultural understandings. While supportive of this ideal, Brighouse argues that it should not displace the central normative goal of education: developing autonomous citizens who have equal opportunities to participate in civic, social and economic life.[79] For Brighouse, integration across lines of class and race is an admirable goal, but secondary to securing equality of educational outcomes. Integration is worthwhile insofar as it helps create the conditions for equal educational outcomes for all students.

Other theorists who privilege democracy are cautious about the specific measures of national identity suggested by the common school ideal. While some theorists argue that schools should develop civic knowledge (such as principles of government), virtues (such as tolerance), and skills (such as voting), they contend that such dimensions of citizenship are best created through democratic participation. Here, too, civic education is an indispensable means for achieving these democratic ends. In fact, interaction with others, particularly across lines of difference, is considered to be a necessary part of what makes public schools public. Stephen Macedo argues that this interaction is crucial for the development of civic cooperation and mutual respect.[80] Likewise, Deborah Meier contends "public schools can train us for such political conversation across divisions of race, class, religion and ideology ... what training for good citizenship is all about."[81] Public schools are not just a means for achieving civic ends; they are, in themselves, sites of democratic citizenship and worthy as ends in their own right.

For these theorists, public schools secure their legitimacy as public institutions by serving as sites of democratic deliberation and participation. Public schools, in other words, need to be more than just publicly accessible and publicly financed; they must be democratically controlled and operated. Democratic control, however, can be defined in a myriad of ways: as increased parental engagement, decentralized decision making, or accountability to some public authority. Some scholars argue that charter schools, for instance, offer parents revitalized possibilities for investment in their local public schools.[82] Other scholars note that a common school ideal does not automatically require a common school system.[83] Leonard Waks, for instance, has argued that choice systems might function as a "networked common school" that builds opportunities for interaction between and across diverse schools.[84]

Others, in contrast, argue that schools of choice—especially as they further increase the segregation of students by race—contribute to the fragmentation of common civic values and erode a broader conception of democratic accountability.[85] Still others understand democratic control, and the politics that come with it, as part of the problem with public education.[86] While some scholars assert that market forces provide efficient and meaningful public participation in education, others argue that public education is, by definition, messy and inefficient.[87] In the latter case, democratic control, while politically frustrating and economically inefficient, is an important part of what makes public education "public."

Defining Public and Private

This chapter has reviewed a number of different conceptual frames used in debates for and against choice: liberty, equity, justice, pluralism and democracy. Using these different frameworks, both advocates and critics of choice employ concepts of "public" and "private" in arguing for or against various choice policies. Different arguments, however, invest these terms with different meanings. Even as they use the same language, advocates and critics privilege different values, aims and purposes.

Arguments justifying school choice on the basis of individual liberty and pluralism lean toward one side of this conceptual field, and stress individual choice. Such arguments understand education as a good that meets the needs, interests, and identities of families and children. From this perspective, the public goals of education are met as parents become more involved in their children's education, in turn improving the educational system as a whole. Arguments that privilege pluralism emphasize increasing the number, kind, and types of choices open to parents. These arguments contend that having many different choices among schools reflects the pluralistic nature of American society: that there are many different and sometimes competing conceptions of the "good life." The public good can be best achieved through diverse and varied approaches to public education.

Arguments privileging democracy and equity lean toward the other side of this field, stressing the social rather than the individual. They suggest that privileging parental liberty and pluralism may lead to the balkanization of education, as individuals choose schools that reflect their narrow interests and identities. Equity proponents fear that individual choices may exacerbate inequality as individual students and families compete for limited resources. Another risk is that young people's future autonomy to choose their own ends will be compromised, as will their ability to encounter and engage with difference. Theorists who emphasize democracy stress schools' function as sites of democratic participation. Choice, in this sense, sidesteps the political processes involved when communities, as a whole, deliberate about shared educational goals and policies.

Arguments that privilege justice try to mediate between these two poles; they attempt a balance between competing values of democracy and liberty, access and effectiveness, equity and choice. Table 2.1 briefly summarizes how the different arguments for choice reviewed in this chapter frame education as a public or private good.

Each of these frameworks construes the relationship between the public and private in different ways. Some arguments equate the public good with many satisfied individuals, each pursuing their self-interests. Others argue that the public good is synonymous with active citizens, creating schools through the processes of democratic deliberation. In sum, then, while many scholars, researchers and advocates use the language of the "public" and "private" in school choice, philosophy can help us attend to the differences in meaning various researchers and actors assign to these terms. As choice continues to rewrite the nature of public obligations and private rights in education, understanding what we mean by "public" and "private" remains a central issue for education policy and politics.

Table 2.1.   Arguments for Education as a Public and Private Good

Education as a	Public Good	Private Good
Liberty	A collection of satisfied and invested individuals.	Parental rights to educate their children as they see fit
Pluralism	Many proliferating and diverse visions of the good life	Education that meets the needs and affirms the distinctive values of families
Justice	Fair balance between social equality and individual liberty	Fair opportunities for individual flourishing regardless of status
Equity	Equality of access and opportunity secured by social institutions	Equal opportunities for individuals to choose schools
Democracy	Creation of common values through democratic participation	An individual's constructive participation and role in society

Philosophy—in conjunction with a wide variety of empirical research, both quantitative and qualitative—can help research on school choice address the values, goals and purposes of education. In particular, philosophy can help ask questions about the public purposes of education. As this review details, school choice does not serve public or private purposes. In contrast, different choice policies, schools and practices enact certain qualities of public-ness and private-ness. Conceptual studies in philosophy, history and related fields can help us attend to the ways in which the meaning of terms and concepts, like the "public school," have changed over time and in response to shifts in education policy and politics.

RECOMMENDATIONS

These philosophical considerations often seem far removed from questions of policy and practice. And, indeed, the policy implications of this chapter may be less than obvious. This review of philosophical frameworks does not provide any one framework for evaluating policy; in contrast, it helps to sketch out a range of arguments and frameworks that policy analysts might use in making these judgments. As Michele Moses notes, philosophy helps "conceptualize alternative frameworks for the analysis of educational policy and practice."[88] Building on this review, future studies might examine, for instance, how different states' charter school policies further the interests of pluralism. Here, scholars might examine whether charter legislation allows for schools to represent different "conceptions of the good life," or whether increasing accountability requirements have constrained the ability of charter schools to significantly differ from other public schools. The ability of charter schools to serve the interests of pluralism may, for instance, be augmented or restrained by different policy arrangements across states and school districts.

As this example demonstrates, attention to philosophy can in fact be useful in practical policy analysis. Following are three suggestions for approaches that policy analysts, policymakers, and other stakeholders might use to incorporate philosophical considerations into their work, followed by more detailed explanations of each:

- Employ philosophical frameworks, especially those of liberty, equity, justice, pluralism and democracy, to help interpret how various school choice policies affect what is considered desirable in and for schools.
- Employ philosophical frameworks to clarify the assumptions that various empirical studies make about what is desirable in schools.

- Employ and articulate philosophical concepts to frame efforts to direct policy and practice, in order to make explicit assumptions about what is desirable and to better align policy with these normative goals.

Interpreting Consequences

Frameworks of liberty, equity, justice, pluralism and democracy can help interpret the normative consequences of different school choice policies—that is, whether the effects of a policy are desirable or undesirable in terms of specific goals. Normative understandings of choice are different from, but connected to, empirical evidence about choice. Working with well-crafted empirical research, philosophy can help to illustrate the significance of evidence for claims of justice, equity, liberty and the like. Take, for instance, studies finding evidence for the claim that charter schools increase segregation between social class and racial groups. While there may be evidence that sorting and segregation are taking place in charter schools, different researchers and scholars reach different conclusions about the significance of this evidence. Some have argued that school choice policies exacerbate existing patterns of racial segregation, worsening inequalities in education.[89] Others argue that the sorting caused by choice policies is no worse than the widespread segregation built into a housing market that constrains access to schools.[90] Still others argue that sorting and segregation into distinctive schools reflects the realities of a pluralist society.[91] Some advocates argue, furthermore, that these distinctive schools represent the democratic efforts of parents to create schools relevant to their own communities.[92]

More empirical research, while certainly necessary, cannot by itself help us determine which of these conclusions to support. However, as empirical research examines links between different choice policies and patterns of segregation, conceptual studies can ask other questions to help further clarify the situation: is this sorting an acceptable form of pluralism, as communities create schools around their own ethical convictions? Does it reflect an appropriate balance between the rights of parents to choose schools and the need to protect the interests of parents and children who lack the practical access or ability to make choices?[93]

Although the frameworks detailed here cannot by themselves provide easy answers to these questions, philosophical analysis can help clarify the questions and values in conflict. For instance, if we assert that schools are serving the interests of pluralism, what exactly do we mean by that concept? Under what circumstances could schools be understood as furthering different conceptions of the good? Should schools seek to play that role in a liberal democratic society?

Clarifying Assumptions

In addition to helping interpret the significance of evidence for researchers, policymakers and practitioners, philosophical frameworks can also help to clarify the normative assumptions present in various empirical studies. Scholars have long emphasized the inseparability of conceptual questions from empirical research in education.[94] In issues of school choice, normative assumptions about the appropriate goals of education are embedded in the design of various empirical studies. How, for instance, is the effectiveness of a given policy measured? Is it to be assessed by its success in increasing academic achievement? By its success in terms of creating new, quality schools? Or, by its success in providing greater equality of opportunity for a given group of students?

Philosophy can help to clarify the different measures of "success" employed in different research designs. In particular, any one of the goals of educational policy (equity, for example) is often a deeply contested concept. Conceptual studies can help us examine how terms like "equity" are defined and how they become operationalized in evaluation and research. While many scholars argue that school choice should build equity in education, there is little agreement or clarity about what, exactly, this vision of equity entails. Philosophical inquiry can help illustrate what equity is, how it relates to a larger discourse about equality, and how it may be translated into equality of opportunity.[95]

In examining the assumptions that guide policy and research, philosophical frameworks can also help examine the seemingly neutral or non-normative language of "efficiency," "effectiveness," and "achievement." While academic achievement, for instance, seems to be an uncontroversial goal, the language of "achievement" contains assumptions about the nature of knowledge and the purposes of education.[96] A singular focus on achievement also obscures other, and sometimes competing, goals of education. Philosophy, here, can help to clarify the different goals—particularly moral, social and civic ones—that educational policy may pursue.

Framing Policy and Practice

Philosophy can also help to more directly frame issues of policy and practice. While many theorists treat school choice as one static entity, other scholars have started to examine the "nuts and bolts" of choice proposals, drawing such distinctions between different kinds of school choice (vouchers vs. charters, for example) and between different implementations of a particular choice option (specific charter legislation across states, for example). From the standpoint of policy, these contributions can help explain why, as David Plank and Gary Sykes write, the "rules matter" in school choice.[97] Likewise, philosophical analysis might productively engage with actual political conditions and policy proposals. As Kenneth Howe contends, philosophers who engage in policy debates should be "required to take stances in light of the available empirical evidence and the political environment in which the evidence is embedded."[98]

Conceptual studies of choice are beginning to engage more fruitfully with more detailed dimensions of policy and practice. Henry Levin, for instance, poses that any educational system reflects compromises among four basic values: freedom of choice, economic efficiency, equity and social cohesion. Levin's open-ended framework helps us see that the "public" is in no way a penultimate value, but occurs within a complex range of compromises about the social goods of education. From a different perspective, R. Kenneth Godwin and Frank R. Kemerer employ a liberal democratic framework to pose four different aims for education: skills for economic independence, political knowledge and skills for civic participation, moral reasoning motivated toward ethical behavior, and equality of educational opportunity. The authors apply this framework to public and private choice programs in San Antonio, arguing that controversies about school choice policies can be tied to more fundamental disagreements about the social goals of American education.[99]

Harry Brighouse has also examined different voucher policies—universal regulated, universal unregulated, progressive, and targeted plans—against claims of justice.[100] Examining key variables in voucher programs (for example, to what extent providers are allowed to select students), Brighouse developed a measure of different equity levels in various voucher proposals. His scholarship could, in turn, be employed by advocates of choice seeking to design voucher proposals that build equality of opportunity for students from disadvantaged backgrounds. Likewise, using these criteria, Brighouse argues that we might support vouchers and oppose charter schools on grounds of justice.[101]

Choice is, in many ways, here to stay.[102] Scholarship on choice has come to reflect this new reality. Rather than asking whether or not to support choice, researchers and policymakers are increasingly asking what kinds of choice should be supported, under what circumstances.[103] As choice policies continue to expand, it will be more and more important to draw distinctions between kinds, degrees and variations of choice. Many of the scholars summarized in this chapter offer different examples of how we might make these distinctions. As we have seen, a more developed understanding of the public purposes of school choice offers us one powerful way to start.

CHAPTER 3

HOW LEGISLATION AND LITIGATION SHAPE SCHOOL CHOICE

Julie F. Mead

Since its appearance on the educational landscape, school choice has engendered considerable controversy. Those controversies are captured in two forms of "law"—legislation and litigation. Legislation at all governmental levels codifies the results of political struggles around school choice and defines the actual choices available to parents. Numerous forms of school choice have been created through this political process, including magnet schools, interdistrict choice, intradistrict choice, charter schools, home schooling, voucher and tuition tax credit programs. These choice programs vary with respect to the children eligible to participate, the universe of schools from which a parent may choose, and the funding that may support the choice. Likewise, litigation has been brought to determine whether those legislative enactments are consistent with constitutional provisions and other existing laws. When courts have determined that school choice exceeds legal boundaries, programs have been struck down. Legislation and litigation, therefore, have shaped school choice in direct and significant ways. This chapter examines the relationships between various forms of school choice and the legal authority that both binds and bounds them.[1] As the discussion will show, both the creations of

Exploring the School Choice Universe: Evidence and Recommendations
pp. 39–64
Copyright © 2012 by Information Age Publishing

and legal challenges to school choice can be traced to a tension between the legal principle that parents should be able to direct the upbringing of their children and the legal principle of parens patriae (the government is the ultimate guardian), which forms the foundation for compulsory education in the United States.

PARENS PATRIAE AND THE HISTORY
OF SCHOOL CHOICE LEGISLATION

Parens Patriae

In order to understand how legislation and litigation shape school choice, it is first necessary to understand how various school choice options came to be. Writ large, school choice—the concept that parents decide where and how their children will be educated—has always existed. Initially, of course, education existed only for the wealthy, and any education received was closely aligned with the occupation and status of the parents. It was not until the 19th century that formal public education, supported by a governmental body, began to be offered.[2] Not long after, compulsory education laws were adopted, first in Massachusetts in 1853 and by the majority of states by the end of century.[3] Like many laws designed to promote the "general welfare," compulsory education provisions stem from the legal principle known as parens patriae.

Parens patriae is Latin for "father of his country" and refers to the common law doctrine that the state serves as parent to us all.[4] In other words, the state has interests independent from its citizens that may even outweigh the individual interests of those citizens. As applied to schools, it refers to the state's interest in ensuring an educated citizenry and in defining what it means to be educated.[5] Thus, parens patriae forms the legal foundation for compulsory school attendance laws. Even if a parent believes that education serves no purpose, that parent may not elect to withhold educational opportunities from a son or daughter. The state may legitimately and lawfully compel all parents to educate their children and penalize any parent who refuses.

But the doctrine of parens patriae is not without limits. Several lawsuits have been filed over the years asserting that the state has overstepped its boundaries with respect to compulsory schooling. The Supreme Court's 1925 decision in *Pierce v. Society of Sisters* best illustrates the balance of interests that must be struck.[6] Private school operators challenged an Oregon statute that required children to attend public schools in order to satisfy compulsory attendance requirements. The court agreed with the schools that the law unjustifiably interfere[d] with the liberty of parents and guardians to direct the upbringing and education of children under their control.... The fundamental theory of liberty upon which all governments in the Union repose excludes any general power of the state to standardize its children by forcing them to accept instruction from public teachers only.[7]

Accordingly, states have the authority to compel children to be educated and to define reasonable minimum expectations for that education, but may not require public education. As such, it can be argued that *Pierce* was the first important school choice decision.

Modern School Choice Develops

For many years, then, school choice was limited to a selection between public and private schools for those parents with the means to pay for private education. Children enrolled in whatever public school served their neighborhood or community, and place of residence dictated the public school available to parents.[8]

Those opposed to desegregation in the aftermath of the Supreme Court's decision in *Brown v. the Board of Education* capitalized on the distinction between universal public school access and controlled private school access as a means to subvert the court's directive to dismantle segregation with "deliberate speed."[9] For example, officials in Prince Edward County, Virginia, refused to desegregate, choosing instead to close all public schools and provide vouchers to private schools, which they knew to be limited and segregated. These so-called "choice academies" operated in several southern states, including Alabama, Georgia, Louisiana, Mississippi, and Virginia.[10] The Supreme Court struck down the Prince Edward County plan as unconstitutional in 1964 in *Griffin v. County School Bd. of Prince Edward County.*[11] Similarly, 5 years later, the court struck down a "freedom of choice" plan that allowed students to select which public school they wished to attend in the previously segregated New Kent County, Virginia, schools (*Green v. County School Board*).[12] In *Green*, the court held that public officials had an obligation to take affirmative steps to desegregate public schools and that relying on parental choice, given the history of de jure segregation, was an insufficient response to the constitutional injury declared by *Brown*. Accordingly, racial politics and school choice became intertwined.[13]

Also during the 1950s and 1960s, the primary market-based arguments for school choice, the foundational policy arguments, also evolved. Economist Milton Friedman most influenced ideas about school choice.[14] In his seminal 1962 work, *Capitalism and Freedom*, Friedman argued that all parents, rich and poor alike, should have available to them the option to enroll their child in any school.[15] To support those selections, he proposed that parents be provided a "voucher" that could be redeemed at any school, thus creating competition between schools, which, he maintained, would spur excellence in an effort to retain students.

Friedman's idea, however, was not put into practice until the 1970s, and then, only on a modest scale. The application of school choice that evolved during that decade continued the earlier linkage of race and choice, but with an opposite goal. In contrast to earlier efforts to harness parental choice to retain segregation, during this period some school districts began employing choice options as a means to desegregate schools.[16] Often as part of court desegregation orders, school districts created magnet schools, each with a special curricular focus, as a way to attract parents to enroll their children in schools they would not ordinarily attend in order to encourage voluntary integration.[17] Thus, parents could choose to have a child attend a neighborhood school or a magnet school with some special attraction. However, although choices were available, Friedman's concept of competition among schools was largely absent.

Also in the early to mid-1970s, the federal government initiated an early experiment in school choice in Alum Rock, California, to test its effect on student achievement and other things.[18] Sponsored by the Office of Equal Opportunity, the program allowed parents to choose among public schools. Officials originally intended the experiment to include private schools, but that aspect of the study was never implemented. The results proved not to be instructive, however, due to what study authors concluded were a number of design flaws. Still, the concept of studying a link between achievement and parental choice would foreshadow choice programs that developed later.

During the 1970s and early 1980s, school districts and states also began to develop intradistrict and interdistrict choice programs. Intradistrict choice programs allow students to enroll in any school in the district or a portion of the district without regard to residence. Frequently, urban districts divide their schools into attendance zones. Students are guaranteed enrollment within their zone and at a school in which a sibling is enrolled. Open seats are then filled by those residing outside the zone, although there may be some limits on publicly provided transportation. These programs have generally been initiated by local officials, although states may support efforts through funding. Perhaps one of the earliest and best-known examples of this type of choice began operation in East Harlem, New York, in Manhattan's District No. 4.[19]

Interdistrict programs allow students to enroll in a school in another school district. There are generally two types of such programs. The first, city-suburban transfer programs, were typically initiated by state legislatures as a means of voluntary integration. They fund transfers between neighboring districts as means to reduce racial isolation in urban areas.[20] The second type of interdistrict choice program allows open enrollment in any public district in the state. As a rule, these public school choice programs grant enrollment priority based on residence, with outside choosers competing for remaining available slots. Currently, approximately 42 states have adopted some sort of interdistrict open enrollment policy.[21]

Statewide open enrollment plans illustrate a shift in the rationale for choice programs. These programs and other school choice plans evolved in the 1980s and 1990s as a means to advance general school reform. It was at this time that political bodies began to embrace Friedman's idea of an educational marketplace. Partly in response to the 1983 National Commission on Excellence in Education report titled *A Nation at Risk*, which argued that public schools were generally failing in their mission, policymakers at all levels began to look more favorably at choice programs, including voucher programs and charter school programs, on the theory that competition would motivate school authorities to achieve excellence. Perhaps the most vocal champions of this argument were John Chubb and Terry Moe of the Brookings Institution. Chubb and Moe argued that school choice had the capacity to radically reform publicly funded education. As they explained:

> Choice is a self-contained reform with its own rationale and justification. It has the capacity all by itself to bring about the kind of transformation that, for years, reforms have been seeking to engineer in myriad other ways.... The whole point of a thoroughgoing system of choice is to free schools from ... disabling constraints by sweeping away the old institutions and replacing them with new ones. Taken seriously, choice is not a system-preserving reform. It is a revolutionary reform that introduces a new system of public education.[22]

The most complete expression of this idea was the enactment of voucher programs in Milwaukee and Cleveland, created as a means to allow parents to exit these troubled urban systems by providing eligible low-income students public funds to pay tuition at participating private schools in each city.[23]

Toward the end of the 1990s, a new type of school choice initiative related to vouchers, tuition tax credits, made its début with very little fanfare.[24] Arizona pioneered what have been called "neovouchers."[25] These programs allow for the establishment of special scholarship funds into which taxpayers may donate in order to reduce their tax bill. So for example, a person who owes $1,000 in state tax may elect to donate $100 to a scholarship fund, thereby reducing the tax owed to $900.[26] The scholarship fund then pays the tuition costs for students to attend private schools, both religious and secular. Currently, six states (Arizona, Florida, Georgia, Iowa, Pennsylvania, and Rhode Island) offer some form of neovoucher.[27]

During the same decade, Minnesota introduced public charter schools, which are relieved from state regulation in exchange for being bound by a performance contract. As will be discussed more fully below, 40 states, the District of Columbia and Puerto Rico have now enacted public charter school legislation.[28]

Finally, technological advances allowed schools, districts and states to create virtual educational alternatives in the form of cyber schools. At least fifteen state educational agencies now operate some form of virtual school,[29] while more than 200 charter schools offer the same option to parents and students, though not all deliver instruction exclusively via the Internet.[30]

As these publicly funded school choice initiatives were developing, states also relaxed compulsory education statutes to allow parents to educate their children at home. Prior to the 1980s only two states, Nevada and Utah, allowed parents to meet compulsory attendance laws by home schooling. By the middle of the 1990s, home schooling was allowed in all fifty states, though states vary with regard to how much regulation governs home schools.[31]

While all of these options evolved from state and local policies, the federal government, too, played a role. Congress used its power of the purse to enact a number of statutes that supported the various efforts through funding, often in the form of grants. For example, the Magnet School Assistance Program was enacted in 1984 and provided funds to local school districts employing magnet schools in their integration efforts.[32] Likewise, the Charter School Expansion Act of 1998 created grants to support the expansion of charter schools in those states permitting them.[33] Versions of both these laws exist today as part of the No Child Left Behind Act of 2001 (NCLB).[34] In addition, NCLB employs school choice as a penalty for schools that fail to demonstrate adequate yearly progress (AYP) toward universal student proficiency on state assessments of reading, math, and science achievement. NCLB's choice provisions will be described in greater detail below and, as will be shown, mark a dramatic shift in federal support for choice.

As this discussion illustrates, legislation has evolved at all levels to govern an array of school choice options. As each option developed, parents were provided with another means of satisfying compulsory school attendance provisions. Table 3.1 lists each type of school choice and the level of legislation or policymaking that controls the implementation of the school choice options available to parents.

**Table 3.1.   Legislation That Defines
and Governs Forms of School Choice**

	Federal	State	Local
Charter Schools	Federal funds to support develop-ment	State laws define	Local school districts serve as authorizers and operators
Cyber Schools		State laws define	Local board decision
Home Schooling		State laws define	Local policies may allow partial enrollment and participation in activities
Interdistrict Choice			
• City/suburban plans	NCLB encour-ages for schools that fail to make AYP	State laws define	Local policy directs/elects participation
• Statewide open enrollment	NCLB encour-ages for schools that fail to make AYP	State laws define	Local policy directs/elects participation
Intradistrict Choice			
• Magnet schools	Federal law encourages through funding	State law may encourage through funding	Local board decision
• Intradistrict transfer	NCLB requires for some students		Local board decision
Vouchers			
• Traditional vouchers		State laws define	
• Neovouchers (tuition tax credits)		State laws define	

LITIGATION SHAPES SCHOOL CHOICE

In the same way that legislation shapes the school choices available to parents, so too has litigation fashioned the programs currently operating. As with any controversial policy, opponents have sometimes used the court system to mount formal legal challenges to school choice. In some instances, litigants alleged that policymakers had exceeded boundaries set either by federal or state constitutional guarantees, or both. Others mounted challenges asserting that a program was operating in ways that violated statutory requirements.

The scope of this chapter does not permit an exhaustive review of school choice litigation; however, the majority of legal issues raised by such cases fall into six categories, each of which is briefly discussed below:

1. Whether the school choice program violates the establishment or free exercise of religion clauses, or both, in state and federal constitutions.

2. Whether the operation of school choice programs results in discrimination on the basis of race.

3. Whether the regulation of choices impinges on parents' rights without adequate due process in violation of state and federal constitutions.

4. Whether the school choice program is consistent with the state's constitutional obligation to offer a public education under each state constitution.

5. Whether school choice programs must provide access and programming to allow children with disabilities to participate in the program.

6. Whether the choice program operates in a manner consistent with statutory requirements.

Religion Clause Cases

The First Amendment contains two religion clauses. The first, the Establishment Clause, prohibits government officials from adopting any policy or practice "respecting an establishment of religion."[35] The second clause of the same amendment prohibits government officials from prohibiting the free exercise of religion.[36] School choice has sparked litigation under both clauses. Establishment Clause cases center on whether a particular choice results in state support or sponsorship of religion or religious teaching. Free Exercise cases examine whether state rules regarding various choice options result in an impermissible infringement on parents' or students' exercise of religious beliefs.

Arguably the legal issue receiving the most public press centers on whether states can include private religious schools in any voucher program. The Milwaukee, Cleveland, and Washington, DC, programs all allow private religious schools to participate in their programs, providing public funding for both religious and secular education.[37] Challengers to both the Milwaukee and Cleveland programs alleged that allowing public funds to purchase private religious education violated the Establishment Clause of the First Amendment to the United States Constitution.[38] The question was resolved by a sharply divided U.S. Supreme Court in *Zelman v. Simmons-Harris* in 2002, when the court upheld the Cleveland program.[39] The five-member majority held that the program served a legitimate secular purpose of providing low-income families a means to purchase educational opportunities for their children. In addition, the court held that as long as parents (the recipients of the aid) were not held to religious criteria for participation and had available to them a "genuine choice" from among a variety of secular and sectarian schools, the program was not unconstitutional. A key factor in the ruling was the fact that the decision to enroll in a religious school was made by private individuals, not the state.

While *Zelman* settled the matter under the federal constitution with respect to similarly designed programs, some have questioned whether state constitutions will be similarly interpreted.[40] Some state constitutions appear to set a higher standard for public funds that aid religious institutions even indirectly. For example, when the state of Arizona enacted two publicly funded educational voucher programs in 2006, the Arizona Scholarships for Pupils with Disabilities Program the Arizona Displaced Pupils Choice Grant Program, plaintiffs challenged them as a violation of the state's "Religion Clause"[41] and "Aid Clause."[42] The state argued that the clauses together should be read as the equivalent of the federal Establishment Clause and therefore, the programs should be permissible under *Zelman*.[43] The Arizona Supreme Court disagreed and found that the "Aid Clause" clearly prohibited public funds from being used "in aid of any church, or private or sectarian school." Other cases making such claims of unconstitutionality under state constitutions have been decided on other nonreligious provisions.[44]

While the Arizona Supreme Court struck down the traditional voucher programs, it upheld the state's neovoucher program against allegations it violated state and federal constitutional provisions.[45] Using similar reasoning as that adopted 3 years later by the *Zelman* Court, the Arizona Supreme Court concluded that the state law that permits a $500 tax credit for individuals who donate to a school tuition organization withstood scrutiny because private individuals, not state actors directed the funds. After this ruling, plaintiffs filed suit in federal court asserting that the provision violated the federal Establishment Clause. The Supreme Court, in another five-to-four decision recently ruled that the plaintiffs lacked standing to bring the claim.[46] In other words, the court never discussed the veracity of the plaintiffs' claim that the program unconstitutionally favored religion, but rather held that the plaintiffs had suffered no injury and therefore the court had no jurisdiction to hear their complaint. The implications of this far-reaching decision will be explored more fully below.

Charter schools, too, have been challenged on religious grounds.[47] One recent case considered whether the curriculum adopted by a charter school had improperly employed religious teachings. The Ninth Circuit Court of Appeals reversed the lower court's dismissal of the claim, allowing it go forward.[48] Since charter schools are public schools, the same rules regarding the teaching religious subjects apply to charter schools.[49] That is, public school teachers may teach about religion, but may not teach religion per se.[50]

Sometimes, however, the challenge is brought by parents wanting more, not less, religious instruction. This type of litigation asserts that parents' right to exercise their religion is unnecessarily abridged by various policy enactments. For example, parents living in a Maine school district without a high school filed suit on the premise that limiting their publicly funded choices to public schools or nonsectarian private schools violated their right to freely exercise their religion as they wished their children to be educated in a religious school. The Supreme Court of Maine rejected the claim, reasoning that while the parents preferred religious education, obtaining it was not central to the exercise of their beliefs.[51] Accordingly, their rights to free exercise had not been violated. After the U.S. Supreme Court upheld vouchers in *Zelman*, some Maine parents renewed this objection in federal court. However, the result was the same.[52] The court relied on earlier decisions and the Supreme Court's holding in a higher education case. That case, *Locke v. Davey*, determined that while religious choices could be made available without offending the Establishment Clause, the Free Exercise Clause did not compel states to include religious options in the choice programs they developed.[53]

Discrimination Cases

Given the history of school choice and its connection to desegregation and the directive from *Brown v. Board of Education*, it is a bit ironic to note that even school choice initiatives aimed at integrating public schools frequently have had to be defended against claims of discrimination under the Equal Protection Clause of the Fourteenth Amendment to the U.S. Constitution.[54] As policymakers employed these programs as a means to voluntary integration, programs often used race-conscious student selection processes. That is, students' requests to transfer to a preferred school would be granted only if enrollment aided the district or school in creating integrated educational environments. Such systems necessarily resulted in some students being denied transfer requests on the same basis. These students and their parents have challenged such systems as violating the Equal Protection Clause.

Such litigation culminated in the Supreme Court decision in *Parents Involved In Community Schools v. Seattle School District Number 1*.[55] A narrow majority of the court found unconstitutional the voluntary intradistrict choice programs implemented in Seattle and Louisville. However, no majority of justices agreed on both the holding and the legal reasoning. Chief Justice Roberts and Justices Scalia, Thomas, and Alito concluded that race would be a proper consideration for student enrollment only when plans are used to remedy judicial findings of state discrimination. Justice Kennedy, while agreeing that the Seattle and Louisville programs violated the Fourteenth Amendment, concluded that race-conscious objectives could be pursued as long as they did not result in an individual student being denied an admission request based on race. Now, 5 years after the decision, policymakers still wrestle with its implications for other choice programs that seek to attain racial diversity by persuading parents to enroll students in schools they might not have attended otherwise.[56]

Due Process

As mentioned earlier, *Pierce v. the Society of Sisters* determined that Oregon had unreasonably limited parents' rights to control the upbringing of their children by requiring attendance at public schools. In constitutional terms, this conclusion is an example of a substantive due process violation. Substantive due process, guaranteed under the Fourteenth Amendment, is an issue of fundamental fairness. Violations occur when government policymakers overreach their authority and deny a citizen or group of citizens liberty or property without adequate due process—that is, without adequate justification. All government policies and practices must, at a minimum, be rationally related to a legitimate state interest.

Examples of substantive due process cases in relation to school choice are evident in home-schooling litigation. Some Arkansas parents, for example, attacked the state's requirement that home-schooled students submit to achievement testing, arguing that it violated their right to control their child's education. The court disagreed, finding the requirement a reasonable restriction on home schooling.[57] Likewise, a Maine court upheld a state requirement that home schoolers submit their educational plan for approval.[58] These two examples also illustrate how difficult substantive due process claims are to win. Unless parents allege that the liberty denied is an explicit constitutional right (freedom of religion, for example), courts will usually apply only the lowest level of scrutiny and require only that the state behave reasonably. Even when religious beliefs are involved in a case, courts sometimes rule against parents if they conclude that the state has sufficient justification for monitoring the educational practices of home schoolers.[59]

Another due process argument that has been somewhat more successful relates to the vagueness of a state's statutory language with respect to "private schools." For example, in *Wisconsin v. Popanz*, a father argued that his conviction for noncompliance with the compulsory education statute should be overturned because the state law at the time required only that a child attend a "public or private school." He argued that he satisfied the requirement by educating his children at home. Moreover, he claimed—and the court agreed—that the term "private school" was unconstitutionally vague, thus depriving him of due process.[60] Wisconsin has since enacted statutes to explicitly permit homeschooling as an option parents may use to satisfy compulsory education requirements.[61]

Education Clause Cases

Cases brought under the education clauses of state constitutions argue that school choice programs are invalid because they conflict with the specific educational mandate to the legislature with regard to public schools. For example, when charter schools were created in Michigan, a group of taxpayers filed suit, alleging that they were not sufficiently "public" to receive taxpayer funding under the Michigan constitution. The Michigan Supreme Court rejected this claim, finding that the state legislature had maintained sufficient state control over its charter schools to maintain consistency under the state's Education Clause.[62] To date, all challenges to charter school programs under state constitutions have been similarly rejected and all programs upheld.

In contrast, the Florida Supreme Court struck down a voucher program as contrary to its constitution's Education Clause. The program at issue, the Opportunity Scholarship Program, allowed children who attended a public school deemed substandard to use the state monies to enroll in any private school, using funds that otherwise would have gone to the substandard school. The Florida Supreme Court determined that the constitutional mandate to the legislature to create a "uniform" system of public education precluded the Opportunity Scholarship Program because the state lacked the necessary control over the private schools. Moreover, the court read the constitution as requiring that public education be provided solely through public schools.[63]

Similarly, the Colorado Supreme Court invalidated a voucher program as contrary to the state's constitutional mandate that local school boards control publicly funded education. Since students taking advantage of the Colorado Opportunity Contract Pilot Program would enroll in private schools at public expense, the program limited boards' ability to control their funds, raised, at least in part, through local taxes. The court concluded that the program directly violated the explicit local control requirement established in Article IX, Section 15 of the Colorado Constitution.[64]

As these three examples illustrate, the precise wording of an individual state's constitutional provision regarding education may permit some choice programs prohibited in other states. Likewise, within an individual state, some forms of choice may be held to be consistent with the state constitution's education clause, while other forms of choice may not.

Special Education Cases

School choice litigation has also addressed the questions of whether and how special education requirements apply when parents may select their child's school. At issue are two concepts protected under federal disability law: access and appropriate programming. Access is the concept that publicly funded benefits ought to be provided without discrimination on the basis of disability, as required under Section 504 of the Rehabilitation Act of 1973 (Section 504) and the Americans with Disabilities Act. Accordingly, when policymakers make school choice available to parents and students, they must ensure that children with disabilities and their parents are eligible to participate. Once access is provided, consideration must be given to the kinds of services necessary to make the access meaningful.

Access to voucher programs for children with disabilities has generated only limited litigation. In fact, the only decision on the issue is a trial court opinion on a challenge to the original version of the Milwaukee Parental Choice Program (MPCP). In that decision, the judge determined that participating private schools needed only to accept children with disabilities to the same extent required of nonparticipating private schools. This ruling meant that participating schools had to accept voucher students with disabilities unless doing so would require them to substantially alter their educational program. The court determined that since the schools were not required to provide special education and related services, they could not be required to comply with the Individuals with Disabilities Education Act (IDEA).[65]

In June 2011, the American Civil Liberties Union filed a complaint with the U.S. Department of Justice reviving the issue.[66] The complaint points out that the MPCP has dramatically changed since the lawsuit in 1990 and that under current provisions, numerous private schools participating in the MPCP should be characterized as "private in name only" since a large number of schools have 90% or more of their students enrolled through the publicly funded voucher. Accordingly, the complaint alleges that the State of Wisconsin violates the Americans with Disabilities Act and Section 504 of the Rehabilitation Act because only a small number of MPCP schools provide programming for children with disabilities, resulting in the effective segregation of children with disabilities in Milwaukee Public Schools. Moreover, they argue that MPCP schools actively discourage from enrolling and routinely turn away children with disabilities who could be accommodated in violation of the Americans with Disabilities Act and Section 504. That complaint is still pending.

Access to and programming in other publicly funded choice options has also sparked legal challenge, but most often in the form of administrative challenges and policy letters.[67] The combined lessons from these challenges can be expressed in four reasonably clear directives:

1. All publicly funded choice programs must be accessible to children with disabilities.[68]
2. Parents and children cannot be required to waive needed services in order to participate in the choice program.[69]
3. A student's right to "free appropriate public education" must be preserved in any choice program delivered in public schools.[70]
4. States need to determine which entity (the sending district, receiving school or district, a combination, or some other entity) will serve as the responsible "local education agency" for purposes of IDEA.[71]

Even when a program complies with these requirements, school choice clearly complicates the application of special education law. Numerous authors have commented on the tension between allowing parents to select a school and the strict IDEA requirement that all placement decisions be made by a team of persons knowledgeable about the child's abilities and needs.[72] What happens if parents choose a program that the team considers inappropriate? How must school authorities reconcile choice and appropriateness under the IDEA?

The answer to these questions under current law appears to be that parents may choose, so long as their choices are consistent with the concept of a free, appropriate public education as guaranteed by both IDEA and Section 504. Choice programs, therefore, must consider how to provide the necessary services in order to make free, appropriate public education available.[73]

Statutory Construction Cases

Finally, a review of school choice litigation must include cases involving statutory issues. Such cases require courts to determine whether a particular program is consistent with existing laws or how a particular provision should apply in a particular instance.

The latter type of case is exemplified in judicial review of charter denials, revocations, or nonrenewals. Because some charter statutes explicitly allow for judicial appeals of charter school denials,[74] disappointed charter school aspirants have often used this option to force authorizers to reconsider their application.[75]

In addition to such review of authorization decisions, other cases may allege that a particular choice option is invalid given existing statutory requirements. For example, when a school district in Wisconsin created a cyber charter school and allowed students living outside of the district to enroll via statewide open enrollment, challengers raised three statutory issues: (1) that the school was not located within school district boundaries as required by the state's charter school law; (2) that since some of the students never attend a school physically located within district boundaries, payments from resident school districts to the district operating the cyber charter school violated the state's open enrollment statute; and (3) that since parents assume the primary instructional role, the school violated statutory requirements that only licensed teachers teach in public schools. The Wisconsin Court of Appeals found merit in each claim and determined that the challengers were entitled to summary judgment on each allegation.[76] In clarifying its ruling, the court explained:

> We express no opinion on the merit of [the cyber charter school's] educational model, or on the relative competencies of licensed teachers and dedicated parents to recognize and make the most of "teachable moments." [The cyber charter school] may be, as its proponents claim, a godsend for children who would not succeed in more traditional public schools, as well as a welcome new option for parents who want their children to receive a home-based education for any number of reasons. But it is also a public school operated with state funds, and its operation violates the statutes as they now stand. It is for the citizens of this state, through their elected representatives in the legislature, to decide whether and how their tax money is going to be spent. If the citizenry wants tax money spent on virtual schools like [the challenged school], that is fine. Let the citizens debate it and set the parameters, not the courts.[77]

As this quotation makes clear, courts are limited to applying existing statutes. As more innovations occur, whether through school choice or not, they must comply with existing statutory frameworks or risk litigation to force such compliance. Alternatively, as happened in this instance,[78] those statutes must be revised to allow for new conceptions of education and choice.

Table 3.2 provides a summary of the types of litigation filed with respect to each type of school choice.

It is interesting to note that voucher programs and charter school programs have prompted the broadest array of legal challenges. As both vouchers and charters arguably best illustrate Friedman's competition model, it is not surprising that they would encounter the most litigation. It is equally unsurprising that home schooling has faced the fewest legal challenges, since it is an exit from public funding.

RECENT DEVELOPMENTS

As this discussion illustrates, both legislation and litigation have played and continue to play an important role in shaping school choice. Four recent developments in the relationship between law and school choice

Table 3.2. Issues Raised in Litigation of School Choice Options

	Religion Clauses	Discrimination	Due Process	Education Clause	Special Education	Statutory Issues
Charter schools	✓	✓		✓	✓	✓
Cyber schools					✓	✓
Home-schooling	✓		✓			✓
Interdistrict Choice						
• City-suburban plans		✓				
• Statewide open enrollment		✓			✓	
Intradistrict Choice						
• Magnet schools		✓			✓	
• Intradistrict transfer		✓			✓	
Vouchers						
• Traditional Vouchers	✓	✓		✓	✓	✓
• Neovouchers	✓					

deserve further discussion: the expansion of charter schools, NCLB's choice provisions, and two landmark Supreme Court decisions, one regarding voluntary integration programs and a second related to tuition tax credits.

The Expansion of Charter Schools

Charter schools first appeared in Minnesota in 1990. By 2003, the number of states allowing charter schools had increased to 40, with approximately 2,700 schools serving 684,000 students.[79] Current estimates put the numbers at nearly 5,000 charter schools serving more than 1.5 million students.[80] By any measure, these figures show that charter schools have become a feature of many states' public educational systems. Given the fact that charter schools have enjoyed broad bipartisan support,[81] including federal funding through the Charter Schools Expansion Act, it is not surprising that their number and influence have increased since their introduction 2 decades ago.

The growth of charter schools has been accompanied by the evolution of charter school laws. Charters were established, at least in part, as a way to introduce market-driven education in a public-only context.[82] In return for some freedom from traditional regulation through state statutes and administrative codes, charter schools agree to accountability through performance contracts and parental choice. States have periodically examined this tradeoff to determine whether charter schools are both sufficiently autonomous and sufficiently accountable. In some instances, states have made statutory schemes more permissive by allowing new entities to authorize charters and by further relaxing other state controls. In other cases, states have increased their regulatory hold on charter schools by adopting more stringent standards for adoption, operation, renewal, and revocation.[83] Charter school proponents refer to such tightening of state control as regulatory "creep," a phenomenon they believe should be avoided.[84] However their actions are viewed, state policymakers clearly remain involved in determining how to fit charter schools into the public school system.

NCLB's Choice Provisions

A second recent and notable development involves the choice provisions codified as part of the No Child Left Behind Act. The reauthorization of NCLB, which was supposed to be complete in 2007, is on the legislative docket for Congress, though it is unknown when the House and

Senate will actually take up the matter. When it does, its members will examine the law's merits and shortcomings as they determine whether and how to revise its existing provisions. As matters currently stand, however, school choice is an integral part of NCLB. When the law was enacted, the U.S. Department of Education named four "pillars" as its foundation, one of which was "more choices for parents."[85] This "pillar" led to several school choice provisions—perhaps most notably as part of NCLB's accountability system, which imposes choice as a penalty for schools not making "adequate yearly progress" for two consecutive years.

"Adequate yearly progress" refers to a school's incremental progress toward NCLB's mandated goal of having 100% of students score at or above proficiency standards on state assessments in reading, math, and science by 2014. Students must be tested annually in Grades 3-8 and once during Grades 9-12. While states set the curricular standards and develop the assessments, both must be approved by the U.S. Department of Education. States also set progressively more stringent goals for schools each year (the annual AYP) as they target 100% proficiency in each subject.

Schools must annually report test scores to the public, including a comparison of scores disaggregated by race, socioeconomic status, gender, language, and disability. A school could be declared "in need of improvement" if it tests less than 95% of its student population or if too few students meet proficiency standards set for each assessment. Moreover, all goals must be met, not only for the student population as a whole, but also for each disaggregated group. For example, a school could be declared "in need of improvement" because only 90% of students learning English took the state's assessment. Likewise, if test scores revealed that all groups except children with disabilities had met the proficiency standards, the school would be deemed "in need of improvement" and the accountability provisions would apply.[86]

Penalties for failure to meet AYP are substantive. Schools designated "in need of improvement" for two or more consecutive years are subject to NCLB's choice provisions. Schools in such circumstances must notify parents of the situation and allow student transfers to other public schools that have met AYP. In addition, schools must set aside a portion of the funds received under NCLB to cover transportation costs for the students. If a school does not test enough students or student test scores do not demonstrate sufficient progress for a third consecutive year, NCLB funds must be made available to parents to allow them to purchase supplemental educational services (tutoring). When a school fails the standards for a fourth year, the district must take corrective action; if failure persists into a fifth consecutive year, the district must restructure the school. Restructuring may include converting the school to a charter school, if it is not one already. Moreover, the penalties are cumulative.

That is, parents with children entitled to supplemental educational services are also entitled to transfer to a school of their choice. In addition, if an entire school district is declared "in need of improvement" under NCLB for a fourth consecutive year, the state must take corrective action, with one suggested alternative being to permit students to transfer to another school. Finally, parents with children enrolled in schools deemed "persistently dangerous" must be given the option to choose another school regardless of how well or poorly students perform academically in the dangerous school.[87]

These NCLB provisions are significant as they represent the first federalized school choice program. They were controversial at the time of adoption and remain controversial now.[88] In fact, President Bush first argued for NCLB to include private as well as public school choice.[89] Under the bill he originally proposed, parents would have been given a voucher to attend any public or private school whenever a public school failed to perform at the required standard. Although private school choice did not survive the political process,[90] the fact that Congress embraced any form of school choice as means to school reform marks an important advancement of Friedman's market-based conception of school accountability. Whether current choice provisions will remain if NCLB is eventually reauthorized will reveal much about the country's commitment to and confidence in school choice as a tool to leverage educational improvement.[91]

The Impact of Parents Involved

Finally, as noted above, the Supreme Court's decision in *Parents Involved in Community Schools v. Seattle School District Number 1* will likely have significant impact on school officials' efforts to integrate student populations through controlled parental choice programs. Chief Justice Roberts concluded simply that, "the way to stop discrimination on the basis of race is to stop discriminating on the basis of race."[92] And yet, it is clear that the tie between race and opportunity has not yet been broken. Indeed, research documents the resegregation of America's schools along racial lines, with many more schools now more racially isolated than they were even a decade ago.[93] While Justice Kennedy's opinion holds out hope that policymakers may still pursue integrated education as a goal, the decision in *Parents Involved* severely restricts current efforts to do so. At the time of the decision, literally hundreds of programs existed across the country that used parental choice as an inducement to integrate. With the court's decision, those plans became subject to review to determine whether they might similarly be considered in violation of the Constitution.

Many consider the decision in *Parents Involved* to be a dramatic shift away from the promise of integrated education and equal educational opportunity espoused by *Brown*. Justice Breyer's dissent forcefully made this point when he concluded:

> Finally, what of the hope and promise of *Brown*? For much of this Nation's history, the races remained divided. It was not long ago that people of different races drank from separate fountains, rode on separate buses, and studied in separate schools. In this court's finest hour, *Brown v. Board of Education* challenged this history and helped to change it. For *Brown* held out a promise. It was a promise embodied in three Amendments designed to make citizens of slaves. It was the promise of true racial equality—not as a matter of fine words on paper, but as a matter of everyday life in the Nation's cities and schools. It was about the nature of a democracy that must work for all Americans. It sought one law, one Nation, one people, not simply as a matter of legal principle but in terms of how we actually live.... The last half-century has witnessed great strides toward racial equality, but we have not yet realized the promise of *Brown*. To invalidate the plans under review is to threaten the promise of *Brown*. The plurality's position, I fear, would break that promise. This is a decision that the court and the nation will come to regret.[94]

Justice Breyer's comment recognizes that the court's decision will require any school choice program that includes race-conscious provisions to determine whether its criteria are allowed. Programs similar to those in Seattle and Louisville are no longer permissible as a means to integrate public schools.

How then may integration be accomplished? Many consider Justice Kennedy's concurrence to be the roadmap for such an examination. Clearly Justice Kennedy wrestled with the issues laid bare by *Parents Involved*[95] and worried about the effects the decision would have on the racial composition of public schools. While ultimately invalidating the Seattle and Louisville choice programs and what he characterized as "crude" systems of classifying individual students by race,[96] he expressed the view that, "[t]his Nation has a moral and ethical obligation to fulfill its historic commitment to creating an integrated society that ensures equal opportunity for all of its children."[97] He listed six methods by which he believed such a goal could be accomplished consistent with the constitution: (a) "strategic site selection of new schools;" (b) "drawing attendance zones with general recognition of the demographics of neighborhoods;" (c) "allocating resources for special programs;" (d) "recruiting students and faculty in a targeted fashion;" (e) "tracking enrollments, performance, and other statistics by race";[98] and (f) "if necessary, a more nuanced, individual evaluation of school needs and student characteristics that might include race as a component."[99]

It remains to be seen to what extent this decision will curtail parental choice programs. Justice Kennedy does not explicitly name parental choice as one of the six factors, though the first (strategic site selection), the fourth (recruiting students and faculty), and the last (an individual examination of student characteristics including race as one factor among many) may be related to various choice initiatives. However, the court's decision could cause officials to dismantle existing race-conscious choice programs in order to avoid litigation on the issue. Alternatively, they may simply continue to allow parental choices without regard to impact on the racial composition of student populations.[100]

Not surprisingly, some litigation over the relationship of race and choice has emerged in the 5 years since *Parents Involved*. Three cases are of particular note. The first involved a challenge to an existing program, while the second and third could be construed as challenges to school districts' attempts to follow Kennedy's roadmap for addressing integration. First, Arkansas students and parents challenged a provision of the Arkansas Public School Choice Act of 1989,[101] which required that racial integration be preserved when approving any transfer between districts in the state's open enrollment program. The plaintiffs maintained that *Parents Involved* invalidated the provisions at issue. Although the court ultimately dismissed the case on other grounds, the case illustrates the impact of Parents Involved in reviewing longstanding choice programs that accounted for race in some manner.[102]

The second case involved a Pennsylvania school district's redistricting plan.[103] The district operated two high schools. Previously students had been able to choose between the two schools under some circumstances. When the district redrew attendance zones to balance the size of the two schools, students and parents sued. They alleged that the racial composition of the neighborhoods was inappropriately considered in the adoption of the redistricting plan. The federal district court directly applied *Parents Involved* to the situation and concluded:

> Regardless of whether Justice Kennedy's concurring opinion in Seattle is binding.... Seattle [*Parents Involved*] did not prohibit school districts from taking race into account as one of several factors that are considered ... [T]he District considered neighborhood demographics alongside numerous other goals that did not implicate race-equalizing high school populations, minimizing student travel, fostering educational continuity, and facilitating walkability.... [T]he mere fact that the District considered racial demographics in redistricting students in the Affected Area to attend Harriton

[High School] does not render the District's adoption of Plan 3R unconstitutional.[104]

The United States Court of Appeals for the Third Circuit affirmed that decision.[105]

The third case of note likewise considers zones of attendance, however, in this instance the zones directly related to the intradistrict choices available to students.[106] Unlike the programs in *Parents Involved*, this plan from Berkeley, California did not look at an individual child's race. Rather, the program divided the city into zones. Each zone was assigned a diversity index based on "the average household income in the neighborhood, the average education level of adults residing in the neighborhood, and the racial composition of the neighborhood as a whole."[107] When students applied for transfers within the district, the index was used to ensure diversity of each school's student body. All students from the same neighborhood, regardless of race (or income or educational level for that matter), had the same diversity index. The California Court of Appeals upheld the program. While the program was challenged under California law and therefore did not directly reference *Parents Involved*, it appears to exemplify Kennedy's suggestion to integrate schools by "drawing attendance zones with general recognition of the demographics of neighborhoods."

As these cases illustrate, policymakers are likely to continue to grapple with the application of Parents Involved. The effect of this landmark case on the efforts of states, school districts, and schools to provide integrated educational environments will undoubtedly be felt for many years to come.

The Impact of *Arizona Christian School Tuition Organization v. Winn*

Arizona Christian School Tuition Organization v. Winn is the most recent Supreme Court decision related to school choice. As noted above, it is important, not because it reached a decision on the merits of the Establishment Clause claim, but rather because the precedent will likely severely limit the opportunity to challenge any neovoucher program in a judicial forum. The court's five-member majority comprised of Chief Justice Roberts and Justices Kennedy, Scalia, Thomas, and Alito determined that the court had no jurisdiction to hear the case because the litigants lacked standing.

Standing refers to the requirement that anyone bringing a claim before the judiciary have a "case or controversy." Since the Constitution contains provisions that separate and balance the powers between the three branches of government, the fact that a taxpayer disagrees with some legislative enactment is typically insufficient to establish standing in a court of law. Instead, standing requires that the plaintiff has suffered some "injury in fact," meaning a violation of rights or privileges. The Supreme Court created an exception to this general rule in a 1968 case called *Flast v. Cohen*.[108] Recognizing that a violation of the Establishment Clause was an injury unto itself, the court determined that "taxpayer standing" would be sufficient to proceed to court if the litigant meets two criteria: (1) "the taxpayer must establish a logical link between that status and the type of legislative enactment attacked" and (2) "the taxpayer must establish a nexus between that status and the precise nature of the constitutional infringement alleged. Under this requirement, the taxpayer must show that the challenged enactment exceeds specific constitutional limitations imposed upon the exercise of the [legislature's] taxing and spending power and not simply that the enactment is generally beyond the powers delegated to [that body]."[109]

The question before the court in *Winn* was whether the plaintiffs challenging Arizona's tuition tax credits had standing. Arizona's program permitted the creation of school tuition organizations that distribute scholarships to students attending private schools, both religious and nonreligious. The tax code then permitted Arizona taxpayers to reduce their tax liability by donating to an school tuition organization.[110] Taxpayers could donate $500 per year per individual or $1,000 per year per married couple. Since the resulting tax credit financed religious school tuition with revenues that would otherwise have gone into the public coffers, challengers argued that the system violated the Establishment Clause.

The court never reached that allegation. Instead, Justice Kennedy writing for the court's majority, applied Flast's two-part inquiry and concluded that the taxpayers did not have standing to bring suit.[111] The court considered the tax credit different from an allocation or appropriation of state funds, instead concluding that the system merely permitted private individuals to donate private funds. In other words, the court likened the neovoucher program to a decision not to tax. As Kennedy explained:

> When the government declines to impose a tax ... there is no connection between the dissenting taxpayer and the alleged establishment. Any financial injury remains speculative. And awarding some citizens a tax credit allows other citizens to retain control over their own funds in accordance with their own consciences.[112]

The implications of the decision are substantial. In effect, *Winn* makes it practically, if not theoretically, impossible to challenge a neovoucher program on Establishment Clause grounds. Justice Kagan, with whom Justices Ginsburg, Breyer, and Sotomayor agreed, explained the ramifications of the majority's holding:

> The court's arbitrary distinction [between appropriations and tax credits] threatens to eliminate *all* occasions for a taxpayer to contest the government's monetary support for religion. Precisely because appropriations and tax breaks can achieve identical objectives, the government can easily substitute one for the other. Today's opinion thus enables the government to end-run *Flast's* guarantee of access to the Judiciary. From now on, the government need follow just one simple rule—subsidize through the tax system—to preclude taxpayer challenges to state funding of religion.[113]

Accordingly, state legislatures may be emboldened by the decision and determine that while vouchers have yet to garner much broad based political support, neovouchers may provide a more palatable approach to accomplishing the same end—state support for private school tuition. The decision is too recent to track its impact, but it seems likely that more states will follow Arizona's lead by enacting legislation to expand school choice through neovouchers.

DISCUSSION

As this examination illustrates, law shapes school choice in tangible and unmistakable ways. The work of legislators at federal, state and local levels defines and funds various choice options. The work of jurists and litigators considers whether those initiatives and their implementation are lawful. Whether through legislation or litigation, sources of law continually re-examine the balance struck between parens patriae—the state's interest in compelling and controlling education—and parents' individual liberty to make decisions for themselves and their children.

Of course, school choice is not limited to the United States, but also has a place in other countries' educational systems. David Plank and Gary Sykes report that school choice is gaining in popularity and operates to some extent in a number of countries including England, Chile, South Africa, the Czech Republic, China, Australia, New Zealand, and Sweden.[114] In fact, while not specifying school choice as it has come to be defined in the United States, the United Nations Universal Declaration of Human Rights asserts that "[p]arents have a prior right to choose the kind of education that shall be given to their children."[115] Of course, the particular contours of the choices available to parents in any country depend on the laws binding them.

It is therefore fitting to emphasize the fact that law not only defines and constrains parental choices, it is also a codification of collective values. With the input of their constituents, politicians and other policymakers debate the wisdom and effectiveness of various programs. Eventually decision makers ratify any compromises by making formal policy pronouncements. Each provision reflects the collective will and principles that survived the democratic, decision-making process. Even decisions about funding speak to what a body politic most values.

What values, then, do choice programs espouse? That question is at the heart of the debate surrounding school choice. The answer depends on the type of choice, its breadth, and the details of its operation. Does choice serve as an instrument to another deeply held commitment such as diversity or opportunity, or is choice itself the value?[116] Will school choice help the collective achieve the vision desired, or will it undercut the very values it intends to promote? If parental choice results in racially homogeneous schools, does that comport with or debase the concept of "public" schools? Likewise, if parents select a school or a curriculum that emphasizes science but omits art, are the children being sufficiently "educated" for the public? If parents have the predominant voice in educational policies through school selection and control of educational funds, how do schools then serve the childless portions of the electorate? Do schools serve only parents and children, or do they serve communities? These debates have long swirled around conceptions of parental choice.[117]

As such debates continue, whether in the form of reviewing current choice initiatives or considering the development of new forms of choice, law will play an inevitable role. This conclusion is unavoidable simply because law reflects the democratic processes created by the body politic. The creation and review of policy in the form of "law" is the means by which we collectively consider the relationship between the citizen and the state, between private choices and the public good. As Tyack and Cuban explain:

> In continuing the tradition of trusteeship of the public good, this engaged debate about the shape of the future, all citizens have a stake, not only the students who temporarily attend school or their parents. And this is the main reason that Americans long ago created and have continually sought to reform public education.[118]

Legislation and litigation are the products of our public struggle concerning the role of public education in a democratic society. Since the nation's founding, many have considered and continue to consider public education a necessary predicate for democracy to function.[119] That realization suggests that parents' choices will likely always be constrained by some measure of state control, maintaining the constant tension identified earlier between parens patriae and parents' rights to direct their children's education. How robust either principle is in relation to the other will depend on how particular forms of choice strike a balance between them. Legislation will continue to codify those balances and other choice arrangements, and litigation will continue to probe their consistency with existing constitutional and statutory requirements. The legislative and judicial activities reviewed here—in particular the four recent developments of charter school expansion, the advent and reauthorization of NCLB, the Supreme Court's decision curtailing the use of race in the Seattle and Louisville choice programs, and the court's limitation on religious challenges to neovouchers—demonstrate that the balance between parens patriae and parents' rights is in constant flux. Legislation and litigation are two tools that capture the status of that equilibrium at any given moment in time.

RECOMMENDATIONS

As policymakers undertake the daunting task of defining public education for current and future generations, it is likely that school choice will continue to play some role. Accordingly, the following recommendations are offered to officials to guide their work as they consider the implications of the choice initiatives established, the purposes they intend to serve, and the civic principles embedded by their adoption.

- Examine parental choice programs to ensure that they espouse the values of the communities they serve in a manner consistent with federal and state constitutional guarantees.
- Ensure that parental choice programs serve educational opportunity and equity rather than undercut them.
- Consider carefully the implications of any choice program, not only for those who "choose" but also for those who do not.
- Engage the research community not only to inform the debate about effectiveness of various options, but also to track the implications of the various choice programs undertaken.

CHAPTER 4

WHO CHOOSES SCHOOLS, AND WHY?

The Characteristics and Motivations of Families Who Actively Choose Schools

Natalie Lacireno-Paquet With Charleen Brantley

School choice has long existed in the United States, primarily through a family's ability to choose where to live or whether to attend a private school. In recent decades, federal, state, and local governments have become involved in organizing forms of school choice, so that available choices have grown significantly in variety and scope. These new or expanded choices include charter schools, vouchers, intra- and interdistrict choice, and magnet programs. These programs are frequently designed for a particular district or city, such as vouchers in Cleveland and Milwaukee, or controlled choice in Cambridge, Massachusetts, and Charlotte-Mecklenburg, North Carolina, and intradistrict and interdistrict choices in St. Louis. Many of these programs, such as magnets and vouchers, have roots in earlier racial desegregation efforts.

School choice is largely a state and local phenomenon. The only broad federally mandated policy on school choice can be found in the No Child Left Behind Act, which requires districts to allow parents or guardians of

Exploring the School Choice Universe: Evidence and Recommendations
pp. 65–88
Copyright © 2012 by Information Age Publishing

children in schools that repeatedly fail to meet Adequate Yearly Progress targets to choose a nonfailing public school in the same district.[1] There is also federal financial support for magnet and charter schools through competitive grant programs, as well as federally funded vouchers in the District of Columbia.[2]

Despite the growing range of options, in 2007 only an estimated 16% of children attended public schools of choice rather than their assigned school.[3] Yet the same source estimates that the parents of about 27% of all students in Grades 1 through 12 moved to their current neighborhood for its schools, which suggests greater exercise of choice than the 16% for students attending nonassigned schools. Between private schools, charter schools, magnet schools, and homeschooling, as well as the choice to remain in one's assigned or local school when other options are available, millions of American school children attend schools of choice.

In this chapter, we first examine data on the characteristics of choosers and their families, essentially asking who makes different kinds of choices. We then review the research on the motivations of choosers. Understanding these motivations is important for crafting policy. If choice were to be expanded dramatically, it would be useful to understand whether school choice functions according to theory. For example, the theory behind many choice programs is that choice engenders competition and competition leads to improvement. If this underlying theory of action doesn't work as expected, not only will choice programs not likely have desired outcomes, there might be negative consequences in terms of educational equity and racial or economic segregation.[4] Or, if choice played out in such a way that a lack of information led families to consistently choose lower performing schools, the intended goal of choice would not be met: schooling would not improve. Knowing the characteristics of choosers and their response to various design features is essential for policymakers to be able to design programs to ensure equity and access.

The Logic Behind School Choice

The historical roots of public policies addressing choice lie in early efforts to desegregate schools. For example, the court-ordered desegregation in St. Louis created two types of school choice there: interdistrict choice and intradistrict choice. African American students who were in segregated, poor quality schools could transfer to White suburban schools in other districts.[5] Also, students could choose one of the 27 newly created magnet schools within the district. In addition, the original purpose of magnet schools in many northern cities was to voluntarily desegregate schools.[6] Less praiseworthy were attempts in some southern states to defy racial desegregation orders through the provision of private-school vouchers to White students.

Although many modern day choice policies are characterized by language stressing choice and competition, many also continue to reflect explicit or implicit racial concerns. For example, the Cleveland voucher program provides funds to allow the district's mostly poor and African American students to attend private schools in the city. Backers of such programs assume that competition and the threat of losing students will spur the public schools to take new steps to provide low-income, African American children equal educational opportunities.[7]

Those who support school choice do so for diverse reasons, but there is widespread agreement among them that the ultimate goal is improved student learning or outcomes. Applying an economic rationale to schooling, choice policies adopt principles of the marketplace: If parents can choose among schools, schools will compete for students, and the competition will spur all schools to improve student learning in order to attract more parents and children. Of course, this logic depends on a number of assumptions that may or may not be correct, including that parents will choose the best school (frequently defined as academically superior), that there is abundant information on which to base a decision, and that competition can and will work as intended.

Education is a complex good or service, and thus what is "best" will have different meanings to different people.[8] Parents' priorities may not be to place their child in the highest achieving school, and such nonacademic priorities do not necessarily reflect irrational behavior. Parents may, for example, be looking for a good fit or a nurturing environment, a school with after-school care or a school similar to the one they attended. In addition, competing goals within public choice policies — the goal of equity versus the goal of competition, for example — may interfere with the workings of the idealized economic model, perhaps creating perverse incentives or unforeseen and unintended consequences, such as exacerbating racial and economic segregation of students.

In the real rather than the theoretical world, Hamilton and Guin note, several conditions are required for parental choice[9] to work well.[10] These authors contend that parents need to:

- have preferences about education and schooling and gather information about the schools available to their children;
- make trade-offs between the attributes of these schools;
- choose the school that best fits their preferences (p. 41).

What parents prefer regarding the education of their children is likely more than good test scores, though that is surely part of a set of preferences. Because choices about education do not happen in a vacuum, families make trade-offs between preferences and constraints. The supply of available schools also likely influences parental preferences and their ability to act on them. For example, many of the schools that parents might prefer can select the students they want and turn away others. This selection on the part of the school interacts with parents' actions and preferences and likely contributes to the patterns evident in choice outcomes.

Given the current policy environment, options and constraints, who chooses schools and who chooses what kinds of schools? The focus of the next section is on the characteristics of choosers. Following the section on characteristics, we review the research on the motivations for school choice, focusing on parents' use of information about schools, self-reported reasons for choice, and then motivations as revealed through behavior. We conclude the chapter with a brief review of the findings and some recommendations for policy.

REVIEW OF RESEARCH: CHARACTERISTICS OF CHOOSERS

To describe the profile of those who actively engage in choosing schools, we have opted to examine evidence about which groups choose each option (private schools, vouchers, charters, homeschooling, and others) most frequently. Specifically, we have identified patterns in (1) race/ethnicity (2) income or social class and (3) other factors, such as mother's education level. It is important to remember, however, that choice is constrained for most people. Such constraints may include money (for private school tuition or other fees), time (travel, distance), limited space availability, and the selective admissions process at many schools. Therefore, the picture sketched below of active choosers does not necessarily represent what the outcome might be if choices were more inclusive or more widely accessible.

Characteristics of Private School Students

Estimates from two National Center for Education Statistics surveys in 2007-2008 suggest that about 12% of American school children in Grades K-12 attend private schools,[11] with about 81% of all private school students attending schools with a religious orientation or purpose.[12] The percentage of students in private schools has remained relatively stable since 1993, experiencing an increase of two percentage points between 2003-04 and 2007-08.[13]

About 5.1 million students attend private schools, with 2.1 million of these attending Catholic schools, 1.9 million in other religious schools, and about 1 million in nonsectarian schools.[14] Behind these figures, there are some differences in private school enrollment by race, poverty status, and other demographic characteristics.

In terms of the demographic trends in private school enrollment, White, non-Hispanic students were a clear majority of both religious and nonsectarian private school students—about 73% of all religious private school students and 69% of nonsectarian private school students in 2007-08, compared to 9% and 11% Black, non-Hispanic, and 12% and 9% Hispanic.[15] Private religious schools are becoming more diverse, as the percentage of White students decreased and the percentage of Black and Hispanic students increased since 2003-04.[16] Looking at the population as a whole, enrollment rates in religiously affiliated private schools (the largest sector of the private school market) differed dramatically by demographic and family characteristics: parents' educational attainment (15% of all parents with a bachelor's or graduate degree enrolled their children in such schools; only 4% of those having only a high school diploma); family structure (10% of two-parent families; 5% of one-parent families); and poverty status (2% of those below poverty; 3% near poverty, and 12% of those classified as nonpoor).[17]

A smaller scale study of choice in several cities found similarities to the national research above.[18] Comparisons of public and private school students and their families have found, among other differences, that private school parents were more likely to be married, to have attended private schools themselves, and to be religious. In addition, private school parents rated different factors as more important in choosing a school, placing particular importance on values and on school culture, including environment and safety.

In general, then, most students in private schools are in church-related private institutions, though this percentage has been decreasing slowly over time. They are more likely to be White, non-Hispanic, and to come from homes in which there are two parents, where they would not be first-generation college students, and where the family income is well above poverty level. They are less likely to be students of color, to live in poverty, to have single-parent families, and to have a parent or parents with only a high school diploma.

Characteristics of Voucher Participants

Vouchers as a form of school choice typically consist of funds provided to parents or guardians to send a child to private school (or, in some cases, funds are provided directly to the school). There are publicly funded voucher or voucherlike programs, such as public scholarships or tax credit programs, as well as privately funded voucher programs. The design of these programs varies significantly. Some pay for all tuition fees, some pay partial tuition fees, some allow funds for religious schools, and some do not.

Similarly, it is difficult to neatly summarize the characteristics of voucher program participants. The U.S. Department of Education finds there are 24 programs operated in 14 states plus the District of Columbia that provide state financial assistance for students to attend private schools.[19] Data on voucher or voucherlike programs operated by states plus the numerous privately funded voucher programs are not collected in one place. In addition, each program has its own eligibility and benefits criteria. Thus some of the information presented below only represents the characteristics of students and families in particular voucher programs rather than across programs.

Most voucher programs, whether public or private, target low-income and minority students either directly or indirectly. For example, a number of voucher programs operate in a single city or district, usually areas that are very low performing and have concentrations of low-income and minority students, such as in Dayton, Ohio, and Washington, DC. Ohio's publicly funded Educational Choice Scholarship Program (Ohio EdChoice) provides scholarships to allow students in consistently low performing schools to attend nonpublic schools.[20] Not surprisingly, characteristics of voucher programs also vary widely. For example, Maine and Vermont have voucherlike programs dating back to the late 1800s that provide tuition for rural students living in areas without public schools, enabling them to attend public and nonreligious private schools elsewhere.[21] Many other programs operate in a single city or area, such as the Cleveland voucher program, or serve very particular groups of students, such as programs for students with disabilities in Arizona, Florida, Georgia, and Utah.

Voucher program participants are overwhelmingly poor and low-income, reflecting the fact that many programs purposefully target low-income students and families. For example, in the late 1990s the privately funded school voucher programs in San Antonio, New York City, Dayton, and Washington, DC, targeted low-income families, and indeed the average reported income of participants was quite low—about $9,000-$10,000 in the New York City program in 1998-99, and about $18,000 in the Dayton and Washington programs.[22] The publicly funded Milwaukee voucher program, which also targets low-income families, reported income data in its early years, 1991-1995, when the average family income for participants was about $12,000.[23] The Cleveland Scholarship Program, a publicly funded citywide voucher program gives priority to families with income below 200% of the poverty line.[24]

There is some evidence of higher female parental educational attainment among voucher users. In the Dayton, New York City, Cleveland, San Antonio, and Milwaukee programs, mothers of those who accepted vouchers had somewhat higher levels of education than did those who did not receive or others eligible but not participating in the programs.[25] Data from the national Children's Scholarship Fund also show that mothers of voucher users had slightly higher levels of education; voucher users' mothers were about seven percentage points more likely than eligible nonapplicants to have college degrees, but average family income for the voucher users was about $3,000 less.[26]

Various evaluation and research studies report that in addition to being primarily low income, the majority of voucher recipients are African American or Latino. This is not surprising considering that the programs are primarily in central cities where large percentages of the population are low income and minority. For example, 63% of Cleveland Scholarship recipients were minority in 2004; however, data for 2000-2001 indicate that about 81% of Cleveland public school students were minority.[27] In the privately funded Dayton voucher program, about 75% of the students were African American; in Washington, DC, 95% were African American; and in the San Antonio program, 96% were Latino.[28] The percentage of minority voucher recipients in Washington, DC, and San Antonio mirror the minority percentages of the public school population in those cities (95.5% minority each).[29] Data from the privately funded national Children's Scholarship Fund find that about 51% of its applicants are Black and another 19% are Hispanic or Latino.[30]

In general, based on data for voucher programs that are not geared specifically to students with disabilities, we find that students using vouchers—both publicly funded and privately funded—to attend private schools are primarily Black and Latino and primarily low income. These characteristics are likely directly related to program design and program location. The characteristics of the students attending private schools via vouchers differ quite dramatically from the general characteristics of private school students presented above. Given how the population of voucher participants differs from the general private school population, one might conclude that means-tested voucher policies have the potential to provide low-income and minority students with opportunities to attend private schools they may not otherwise been able to attend. Of course, nothing here addresses the issue of whether the schools voucher recipients attend are better than their public school options or whether they receive a better education.

Characteristics of Charter School Students

Currently, 40 states and the District of Columbia allow charter schools. In 2004-05, about 1.8% of all public school students attended charter schools and in 2009-2010 it is estimated that the percentage grew to 3.3%.[31] This percentage suggests that about 887,000 students were then enrolled in charters; that number has now risen to more than 1.3 million in a more recent estimate.[32]

Charter schools are not evenly distributed within states, and charter school laws do not generally target specific types of students, unlike many voucher laws and programs. Thus, there is more variation in who attends charter schools than in who uses vouchers. Reflecting perhaps the fact that 55% of charters are in central cities, compared with about 26% of traditional public schools, overall charter schools enroll a majority of students of color, with a national average of 32% Black, 24% Hispanic and 39% White students.[33] In traditional public schools, the percentages are 16% Black, 22% Hispanic, and 55% White.[34]

Because charter laws and patterns are not uniform, charter availability and enrollment trends vary both across and within states. Each state and region may have its own profile of a charter school chooser. While only about 3.3% of all public school students nationally attend charter schools, in some places, a large proportion of students attend charter schools— 61.5% in New Orleans, 38% in Washington, DC, 32% in Dayton, OH, 25% in Detroit, MI.[35]

There is also wide variation in enrollment patterns by race and other characteristics, depending upon the jurisdiction. Data from the National Charter School Research Project find that in 2008-09 school year, in 21 states, charter schools enrolled a higher percentage of minority students than traditional public schools (more than 5 percentage points higher); nine enrolled a similar percentage of minority students (within 5 percentage points); and in 10 states charter schools enrolled a lower percentage of minority students (more than 5 percentage points less).[36] Yet it is very important to pay attention to local context and enrollment patterns because overall state figures may mask whether charter schools increase segregation locally.[37]

Statistics on the poverty status of charter students present an equally mixed picture. Data from the 2008-09 school year indicate that 14 states have a higher percentage of students eligible for free and reduced-price meals enrolled in charter schools than are enrolled in traditional schools, four have similar percentages (within 5 percentage points), and 19 have charter students who are less likely to live in poverty than are traditional school students.[38]

National data on poverty also show changing patterns over time. The Digest of Education Statistics, with data from 2003-04, showed that, aggregated at the national level, 39% of charter schools have free and reduced-price meal populations of less than 15%, while only 22% of traditional public schools have free and reduced-price meals populations of less than 15%. In other words, a greater percentage of charter schools than traditional public schools have very low populations of poor students.[39] However, at the other end of the spectrum, the Digest also indicates that a higher percentage of charter schools serve very high concentrations of poor students. More specifically, in 22.5% of all charters, 75% of the student body is eligible for free and reduced-price meals; the comparable percentage of traditional public schools is 17.8%. By 2007-08, this pattern had changed somewhat, with only 10% of charter schools having a population of 0-25% free and reduced price lunch eligible students compared to 28% for traditional public schools.[40] On the other side of the free and reduced lunch price spectrum, 25% of charters had populations that were more than 75% eligible; compared to 19% of traditional public schools.

Given the data available we conclude that there is great diversity across the states in terms of the characteristics of charter school students. Because of this variation between and within states, it is impossible to say that the average charter school student is like X or Y. In some places charters appear to underenroll low-income and minority students compared with the general student population, but in others, the opposite is true. States where there are wide disparities in the racial or poverty enrollment between traditional and charter schools warrant further investigation into these patterns and the reasons for them.

Who Makes Other Choices?

There is much less research on the other forms of school choice, such as magnet schools, inter- and intradistrict choice, including choice via NCLB mandates, and homeschooling. Magnet schools and inter- and intradistrict choice are initiatives that predate charters and vouchers. The only recent data available on magnet schools, which are typically found in urban areas and large districts, come from the 2001-2002 Common Core of Data, which suggests that about 3% of all students attend magnet schools. However, that report offered no further data about magnet school students.[41]

Nor were the authors able to find recent estimates on the use of inter- and intradistrict choice programs, although in 1999 it was estimated that less than 1% of all school children exercised interdistrict school choice.[42]

It is estimated that about 27% of all families, especially White middle and upper class families, choose schools by virtue of choosing where to buy a home.[43] A later section of this chapter discusses this choice, but the authors were not able to find data on the characteristics of those who choose schools in this way.

Another, less common, public school option is school choice that is required to be made available to students in failing schools under the No Child Left Behind Act of 2001. Reports from the federal study of the NCLB Act shed some light on who is using the choice mandates.[44] The school choice mandate under NCLB requires districts to provide a choice for students who attended failing schools—that is schools that have failed to meet state targets on standardized tests—to attend another nonfailing school in the district. Districts are required to provide transportation to students who avail themselves of this choice. According to a federally funded study of NCLB, in the 2006-07 school year, almost 7 million students were eligible for choice under the NCLB mandate; and the number of students exercising the option was 45,000.[45]

Homeschooling represents yet another form of choice, one that Belfield and Levin call "perhaps the most radical reform of the U.S. education system ... the ultimate in privatization" because it completely removes education from the public realm, and little is known empirically about it.[46] Estimates of homeschoolers in 2007, from the National Household Education Survey, suggest that about 2.9% of all students aged 5-17 in the U.S. are homeschooled to some extent, with 84% of these students exclusively homeschooled.[47] The earlier NHES data, from 2003, comparing homeschoolers to students in public schools and private schools show some similarities and differences. Families who choose to homeschool tend to be larger, with 62% of them having three or more children, compared with 44% of other public and private school families. Homeschooled students are more likely to come from two-parent families than are public school students (80.8% compared to 69.5%), but the percentage is essentially the same as for private school students (80%).[48]

In 2007, homeschoolers were more likely to be White (77%) than all other students (58%), but they were closer to private school choosers (about 71%).[49] Lower percentages of Black and Hispanic students were homeschoolers compared to their size in the general school aged school population (4% and 10% respectively for homeschoolers, compared with 15% and 19% for traditional public school students). This same report estimated that in terms of family income, homeschooling families were less likely to be below the poverty line as is the general school population (about 12% compared to 19%). This marks a change from earlier data, when both homeschooled students and other students were about equally likely to be poor, at 19%.[50]

Parents of homeschooled students generally have more education than parents of public school students, but slightly less than parents of private school students. Another notable difference between homeschooled students and students in public or private schools is that home-schooled students are much more likely to live in the South.

The religious affiliation of homeschoolers is not proportional to that found among public or private school student populations.[51] Baptists are much more likely to homeschool than those of other religious affiliations and at a significantly higher percentage than their share of the public and private school market.

Summary of the Characteristics of Choosers

There is great diversity in the characteristics of choosers and choice program participants by type of choice, though some patterns do emerge from this review of the data. The exercise of choice appears to be growing. Users of means-tested vouchers are clearly more likely to be poor and minority, and they look quite different from the majority of private school choosers, who are White and not poor. Homeschoolers are like public school families in some ways, such as having similar income characteristics, but they are more like private schoolers in terms of race, and they are different from other choosers in terms of having larger families and in religion. There appears to be great variation in the characteristics of charter school students, and charter schools, as a group, appear to be increasing in their racial and ethnic diversity. Future research should continue to examine implementation results at the local level.

To know who is drawn to which choice option is one thing, but to know why is another. What motivates families to opt out of their neighborhood schools, engage in a possibly time-consuming search, and choose a school that may have additional costs?

REVIEW OF RESEARCH: MOTIVATIONS FOR CHOICE

Motivations of Active Choosers

In this section of the chapter we review research on parental motivations for school choice. We start by looking at how parents use information and what the information used by parents tells us about motivations, and then we examine their stated motivations or preferences in terms of choices actually made. Finally, we examine the behavior of choosers as indicative of preferences or motivations, as actions may speak louder than words about what one really values when it comes to schools and choices.

A note about some relevant complexities is in order before reviewing the research. A common, and commonly examined, assumption is that most parents will choose schools based on academic quality, although other factors such as religion may come into play. However, there is a difficulty with directly asking about "academic quality" as a motivator because the term means different things to different people. Hamilton and Guin suggest that parents' self-reports may "produce somewhat misleading conclusions,"[52] because they might offer socially appropriate answers (e.g., academic quality) rather than more honest ones (e.g., "I didn't want to drive my child across town to school every day").

Another common assumption about choice motivation rests on an economic theory of human behavior that presumes parents are "rational utility maximizers" who choose schools based on the best interests of their children.[53] A similar problem in analyzing motivation occurs here: a child's "best interests" like "academic quality," means different things to different people. Therefore, it is similarly unclear exactly what "best interests" might actually mean as a motivator.

Overview of the Research

Parents overwhelmingly say they value academics and characteristics of school quality (good teachers, good curriculum, high test scores, etc) when choosing schools.[54] In self-reports, such as in survey data and interview data, parents consistently cite academic quality to explain their decision to seek a school of choice and the particular choice they made.[55] However, such self-reports tend to have weaknesses, which include that respondents generally know what kinds of answers are socially acceptable and which are not. In addition, most studies of school choice reviewed here only look at active choosers and cannot answer the question of whether nonchoosers or nonactive choosers also value academic quality to the same extent.

Thus, some of the more interesting recent work looks at both what parents say they value and what they actually do—that is, what choices they actually make.[56] This research points to race and the socioeconomic composition of school student bodies as central factors in parents' choices. A complicating factor in interpreting the preferences that underlie choice behavior of families is that choice has to some extent been constrained by such things as lack of information, regulations regarding racial balance or program preferences for some types of students/families over others, and the ability of certain types of schools (private schools, some charters) to select their students. Research is also indicating that the social networks of parents plays a role in their choices, and choice "sets"—that is the schools they are even considering.

Most school choice options can be classified as "option demand" choices—that is where a student or his or her parent needs to actively select a nonassigned school in order to engage in school choice. Option demand programs include such choices as private schools, vouchers, charter schools, magnet schools, homeschooling, and inter- and intradistrict choices, and possibly even choosing a school through choosing where to live. Those who exercise option-demand choice are a self-selected group of students and families who exhibit motivation to obtain and evaluate information and then make an active choice of a nonassigned school. In the next section we review the research about how families use information in making their choices about schools. It is important to note that much of the research is somewhat dated, from the late 1990s and early-to-mid 2000s.

Use of Information and Searching Behavior

Studies examining how parents use different kinds of information in making school choices provide insight into the factors that parents deem important in their choices. For example, the fact that parents look at information about the racial composition of schools suggests that race plays a role in school choice. The fact that many parents use word-of-mouth or other social networks to gather information raises the possibility that parents trust people they know more than official sources of information, or that what parents are looking for in schools is hard to measure by test scores and statistical summaries about schools.

Recently, a study of parents who choose private schools in one county in Utah was conducted to understand the motivations for leaving public schools and choosing private schools.[57] The survey was a random 30% sample from eight different private schools. Parents were asked questions about why they left or never considered public schools and why they chose a particular private school. The top ranked reasons for both "exit" of the public system and "entry" into private schools were: quality of the curriculum, moral values, religious values, and quality of instruction. The survey results also indicate that some parents desired more challenging curriculum or more individualized attention. A small number of parents left in direct response to an incident or incidents in the public system.

One study covertly followed parents' use of information on a school choice information website.[58] This research examined the school factors or characteristics that parents used in their searches, and for those website users who provided some information about themselves, such as race and educational attainment, whether there were differences between those with college degrees and those without. These data on the obviously motivated, and perhaps the more advantaged (having Internet access in the late 1990s), show that individuals using the website to collect information on schools tended to look at student body characteristics most frequently, about 10 percentage points more than they looked at test scores and about 8 percentage points more than location. Also notable are the differences in search characteristics between those with and without a college education. College-educated searchers looked much more frequently at both student body composition and test scores and somewhat less frequently at location and the availability of basic programs.

More recent research on the search behavior of choosers compared to nonchoosers using the same Internet website on schools in Washington, DC, found those families who ended up in a choice school use the Internet search engine differently.[59] This study found that choosers use a two-stage decision making process: they first create their "choice set" through an editing process, then make in-depth comparisons of the options they are considering. While these findings are interesting, they may not be typical of all choosers, as the study combined an e-mail survey to those who left their e-mail addresses on the website (a minority of all users) with data on the information gathered by the users on the website. However, an earlier study on magnet school choice also identified the process of choice as having two stages. In that study, the first stage was creating a choice set through elimination: White families eliminated schools with high proportions of Black students, and Black families eliminated schools with high proportions of poor students.[60]

Research conducted in California examined different types of information-gathering techniques used by families who moved in order to gain access to particular schools and districts. The results were not inconsistent with the findings on the search behavior of Internet users.[61] Examining the school choices of mostly White families who bought a home in order to attend a particular school or district, it was found that parents made assumptions about the quality of schools from student body composition and sought to place themselves among peers of similar values and beliefs. The author calls these "status ideologies." Parents did not express concerns about the instruction or curriculum in the schools they avoided; rather they expressed concerns about the quality of the peers. These concerns linked perceived quality as being lower in schools with more low-income and minority students.

Other researchers have also tried to "observe" parents in their searching behaviors. For example, a study of how 48 parents in a Midwestern city made their choice decisions found that both higher and lower socioeconomic status parents make their choices in similar ways — that is, they use a similar process of gathering information about schools and eliminating or considering schools.[62] This research finds that while the processes are similar, the schools that get considered and that make up the "choice sets" of parents from different socioeconomic strata are very different. The primary way that parents learn about schools is through their social networks. Social networks are important regardless of the social class of the parents. What social networks do is present constrained choice sets of schools. Of particular note here is that lower income families tend to have more failing and less competitive schools in their choice sets. These ostensibly less desirable choice sets may, to some extent, be influenced by the customary attendance patterns of those attending feeder schools in earlier grades.

Other research also supports the importance of social networks in school choice.[63] Social networks appear to act as a filter, informing parents about which schools they can realistically consider. These networks can also inform parents and students about what choices are available, as in the first five years of the Milwaukee voucher program, where friends and relatives were the most frequently cited (about 51% of the time) sources of information on the program.[64] Social networks were also found to be influential in the earlier-cited study from California. Of the 36 parents who moved to their current home for the schools, only 25% visited the school for which they bought their home and only 9% had obtained any test score data before making the decision to move.[65] Respondents had relied primarily upon word of mouth and reputation, and the study's author found this information was not necessarily reliable.

In a 2005 survey of 800 parents who had made active school choices in three choice-rich cities (Milwaukee, Washington, DC, and Denver), the authors' findings are consistent with other research that word of mouth and social networks are important sources of information.[66] One notable difference is that the authors of the three-city study found that 85% of parents say they had visited a school under consideration. In the California home-buying study, while not perfectly comparable, the respondents had purposefully moved to their new homes for the schools but few had visited schools prior to their purchase.

Studies of different populations had similar findings about the use of information and lack of visits to schools under consideration.[67] One study of mostly low income, minority families making high school choices in Philadelphia found that while parents seemed aware of and involved in the choice of high schools, they gathered most of their information from word-of-mouth and personal contacts, and not all of the contacts had good information. Few parents visited the schools their children were considering, and most expressed preferences for schools that fit with their children's interests. Another study, of parents in Alberta, Canada, showed that among public school choosers, 36% reported that their social networks were the most influential source of information in their decisions, 28% said it was conversations with teachers, 18% visits to the schools under consideration, and 5% published test scores.[68] That said, 30% of them chose based on proximity to home and 16% on reputation.

A study of changes in the racial composition of magnet schools in Nashville, Tennessee also points to the importance of social networks.[69] For many White parents, the social networks were often linked to preschools. This study found that the social networks became less face-to-face and more online as the Nashville schools moved from being under court-ordered desegregation to unitary status.

Recent research also shows that having instructional and academic information about schools, which many choice programs provide (i.e. booklets on choice programs), is not necessarily sufficient to get families in large numbers to choose schools of high academic quality.[70] One study looked at the effect of providing information on schools of choice to parents of children attending schools serving primarily low- and middle-income families in Charlotte-Mecklenburg schools. In these schools, required to offer choice due to failing to make Adequate Yearly Progress under the No Child Left Behind Act, parents received information on the academic achievement of schools they were eligible to choose. This experiment on the effect of providing information to parents of students eligible for school choice found the proportion of parents choosing schools with higher academic achievement was 5 to 7 percentages points more than those not receiving the information.[71] Demographic information about schools appears to be a key factor parents consider in a variety of choice settings, even when other information directly related to academics is available.

In short, the research on the use of information points to the importance of social networks in getting information about schools of choice and evaluating schools. This research could be updated with explorations of the role of social media and the role of Internet in parents' access to information. However, the available research suggests the opinions of friends and others can be very influential, even though that informal information may not provide a good foundation on which to base educational choices. The research also seems to suggest that parents tend to go through a two-stage process in making the choice decision. The first is the elimination of possible schools, and second is the more in-depth examination of the schools remaining in the choice set. There is also some concern that some types of families, middle income and White, might have better access to the types of networks and information sources that provide more reliable information about schools and about how to get into good schools. Indeed, the research discussed here shows that higher income families do have social networks that lead them to consider different and higher achieving schools. It is apparent that parents use information on the composition of the student body in making decisions about which schools to avoid, but the reasons for doing so are not clear. Some parents may not want their children to be racially isolated, others may associate high minority concentrations with low quality, and others may have different reasons. However, this information is useful for policymakers to consider in constructing and designing choice programs that minimize the potential for resegregation.

Stated Reasons for Choice and Motivations of Active Choosers

In this section we look at the research on why parents say they chose the school they did and what factors were important in that choice. Like the research on choice behaviors, the research dates from the late 1990s and early-to-mid 2000s when choice was proliferating. This section includes studies of charter school choosers, voucher users, and those in controlled-choice districts. It is important to keep in mind that these studies generally ask parents after the fact about their choice. While we can assume that most survey and interview respondents will be honest, some people may be tempted to give socially acceptable responses or may try to justify their choice after the fact. In addition, many surveys provide a set of response choices rather than leaving the question open-ended for parents, which may limit responses and not accurately characterize the range of motivations that parents have.

In parental self-reports (surveys and interviews) of motivations for choice, academics are often the highest rated or most frequently cited reasons for choice.[72] A 1998 survey of more than 1,000 charter school parents in Michigan found that academic reasons (e.g., good teachers and academic reputation) were four of the five top rated reasons (with safety as the other) on a scale of 1 to 5.[73] One weakness with the survey is that it does not identify the information on which the parents based their choices. Parents may cite academic reasons, but whether they had any factual information about quality, for example, is unknown.

A similar study of charters in a different part of the country found consistent results.[74] Parents of more than 1,000 charter school students in Texas were surveyed and asked to rate the importance of five possible factors influencing their selection of schools: educational quality, class size, safety, location, and friends at the school. Between 93% and 96% of all parents, regardless of race, ranked educational quality as important or very important. (Some variation in responses by race and income was seen on the factors of safety, location, and friends. Low-income and Hispanic parents were more likely to rate safety as important or very important.) Interviews and focus groups with parents and students participating in the D.C. Opportunity Scholarship Program also suggests that academic and safety reasons, more specifically the search for a better education, and school safety were the most common motivators for participation.[75] Parents cited looking for better curriculum, religious education, and other more specific qualities of schools.

Another survey of charter school parents in Texas asked parents to rank six factors according to their importance in selecting the school of choice.[76] The six factors included test scores, discipline, school racial/ethnic characteristics, location, teaching of moral values, and safety. The highest ranked factor among parents of students in charters for not-at-risk students was teaching of moral values, but significant differences in first-choice rankings were evident by race: test scores for Whites (29%), teaching of moral values for Blacks (33%), and discipline for Hispanics (27.5%). These findings differ from the earlier Texas charter schools study that found academics as the highest rated factor (perhaps indicating that many parents do not equate "test scores" with "academics"). One potential source of this difference is that the respondents in the earlier charter school study were much more likely to be White, non-Hispanic (though the authors attempted to correct for this using weighting), while in the more recent study the racial composition of the sample had roughly equal numbers of each racial group.

One study of a controlled choice district with many magnet schools compared survey results from four groups of parents: those who chose magnet schools, those who chose integrated but nonmagnet schools, those who chose nonintegrated, nonmagnet schools, and those who did not actively choose any school.[77] Seventy-one percent of parents in the sample were active choosers, and White parents were somewhat more likely to be active choosers. Among those who actively chose schools, magnet school choosers rated academic reasons most highly; they also reported being less concerned about convenience and slightly more concerned about safety/discipline and values than parents who chose other options.

Students themselves seem to value academics when making school choices. One of the few studies to examine students' motivations for attending a choice school analyzed students' admission essays to five pilot high schools in Boston Public Schools. This study identified three main sets of reasons why students chose these pilot schools: academics, support, and school culture.[78] The category of academics in this study included factors such as a challenging curriculum (the most frequently coded reason), programs, and career and college preparation.

The evidence on the stated motivators for choice clearly points to academics and the search for a better education or a better educational fit as primary drivers behind seeking choice. However, in certain areas, such as urban areas, other reasons such as safety come into play as motivators. Next we examine the research on parents' actual choices, as they are indicative of preferences and motivations.

Behavior as Indicative of Motivations

While the stated reasons for choice are important to know and are informative to policymakers in designing choice programs, it is perhaps more telling to see how families actually behave in choice programs. Behavior can be indicative of motivation but also of access to choice and constraints on exercising choice. The research reviewed below points to race and poverty as important factors in how choice programs actually play out.

In a study of requests to magnet schools, it was found that White families tended to request transfers into schools with higher proportions of White students than the schools they were coming from, and similarly that minority families also requested transfers to magnets that had higher proportions of minorities.[79] These patterns were consistent even when school-level characteristics, such as type of magnet school, were controlled for. A more recent study in New York City shows that student body characteristics are a strong predictor of demand for high schools and high school programs.[80] In this study of the number of applicants per available seat in high school programs, it was found that schools or programs with higher percentages of Black students or high percentages of English Language Learners had lower demand. These results are consistent even when the academic achievement of the school is taken into account. This study, however, was unable to examine the demographics of the applicants.

One study of charter school parents first conducted a survey of their stated preferences, then examined how the stated preferences matched with the characteristics of the chosen charter schools.[81] The study found that, on average, charter school families went to charter schools with lower average test scores than their previous public schools. This held true even for those who listed test scores as the most important motivator for choice. While few parents in the survey chose the racial make-up of a school as a primary motivator, the authors found that the racial composition of schools was a strong predictor of the charter school chosen. These results are provocative: parents cite academics as primary but decisions are linked to race, suggesting that parents might be using race as a proxy for academic quality. Kleitz and colleagues remind us that even with clear preferences parents must choose from available schooling options and that real-life limitations also interact with preferences for choice.[82] For example, a parent without a car or accessible public transportation may be limited in the realistic set of schools from which she can choose, or families with two working parents may face limitations relating to after-school care that mediate the ability to achieve one's preference.

Research in a Colorado district found that parents tended to choose schools that were relatively close to their homes and that the schools parents chose to move their children out of were schools with high percentages of poor students and low test scores. However, there were other, higher achieving schools the parents could have chosen, suggesting perhaps that geographical distance is important.[83]

These studies are contradicted somewhat by another study, which seem to show behavior matching stated choice preferences.[84] The researchers examined four districts with varying degrees of available choices, asking how well parents' stated preferences match up to the characteristics of the schools they actually chose for their children.[85] Among New York City parents in the sample, those who actively chose a school tended to enroll their children in a school that was above the district mean on the main preference (e.g., test scores or some other characteristic cited by the parent); this relationship between preference and school characteristics was not evident for the nonchoosers in the study. The findings were similar in New Jersey, the other site in this study.

Other studies of how choice is playing out in an option-demand district have found that behavior is quite indicative of preferences and motivations.[86] The results also raise concerns about the differences between those who choose and those who do not engage in the choice process.[87] For example, in an experimental study on the impact of different types of information on choice, it was found that when presented with a simple summary of school performance and odds of admissions, parents in failing schools (NCLB-sanctioned schools) were less likely than might be expected to opt to choose another school.[88] However, among low-income families in non-NCLB-sanctioned schools, parents were more likely to choose highly selective schools when presented with information on the program and odds of admissions. The study also examined the role of school population characteristics on preferences and choices and the trade-offs parents make in terms of their preferences about student racial composition and test scores. They found that White parents valued schools with a mostly White population and Black families exhibited preferences for schools with higher Black student populations. In both cases, families balanced these preferences with their preferences for test scores. These findings are similar to other research on magnet schools and charter schools discussed above. What is clear from this work is that many parents and students make trade-offs among their preferences for things like location, guaranteed choice, student body composition and test scores and that access to information appears to aid in these considerations. It is also striking that there is a significant group of parents who are, as the authors say, "inert," in that they fail to actively engage in school choice even when it is widely available.

There appears to be fairly consistent evidence that when given the chance parents choose to avoid schools with high percentages of low income students, and that White parents avoid schools with high percentages of minority students. This and other evidence from various choice policies, including charter schools and controlled choice districts, gives some credence to the concern that school choice may lead to further segregation by race and class. However, some recent research suggests that we need to pay attention not just to the correlation between demographics and choice, but also to the influence of contextual neighborhood characteristics (i.e., transportation, disadvantage) and earlier schooling characteristics on the exercise of choice.[89]

Homeschooling

In this section we briefly examine the motivations for homeschooling one's children. Homeschooling is discussed separately because it is a choice to educate outside of traditional public and private schools. In the homeschooling arena, ideological concerns, such as religion and sheltering children from mainstream cultural influences, were typically found to be important motivators but are of perhaps declining influence.[90] Few studies have actually looked at why parents homeschool. Some information comes from the 2003 National Household Education Survey, which asked homeschooling parents to identify their primary reasons for homeschooling.[91] The three most often cited reasons were the school environment, reflecting concerns with such elements as safety, drugs, and peer pressure (85% of parents); the desire to provide religious or moral instruction (72%); and dissatisfaction with the instruction in schools (68%).

A study of parents involved with a charter school network that supports homeschoolers in California also found that being critical of or concerned about traditional public schools rated relatively high as a factor motivating homeschooling (15.77 out of 20), though in this particular survey being attracted to the particular charter organization was rated somewhat higher (16.47) and ideological reasons were also rated high (14.63).[92] More information comes from a recent study conducted in the southeast, which surveyed a nonrandom sample of homeschooling parents.[93] These findings suggest that homeschooling parents have a strong belief that they should be active in their child's education and, perhaps more importantly, that they also have the time, resources, and knowledge to do so. Consistent with the federal survey data, this study indicates that homeschooling parents have low confidence in the public schools' ability to educate their children and low opinions of public schools related to values and beliefs, ability to meet special needs, and teaching methods.[94] Indeed, the scale with items relating to parents' beliefs regarding public schools received the lowest mean rating out of the 11 total scales that included concepts such as personal beliefs about education and parents' self-efficacy in helping their children learn.

The choice to homeschool is quite different from choosing to send one's child to a nonassigned school. The evidence points to a strong distrust or dislike of traditional public schools' ability to teach their children, as well as concerns about the cultural and moral environment in public schools.

DISCUSSION AND ANALYSIS

The examination of the characteristics of participants in different types of choice programs suggests that those who make choices that are completely private, such as private schooling and homeschooling, tend to be different demographically than those who make choices through formal governmental or nongovernmental programs such as charter schools, magnets, and vouchers. Homeschool and private school students tend to be nonpoor and White; users of means-tested vouchers, on the other hand, tend to be minority and poor. The picture is more mixed for charter and magnet school students. The implications are that choice may be able to offer educational opportunities to low-income minorities in the small scale, such as vouchers and charters, but whether the same patterns of use would exist in large-scale programs has not been empirically determined. The mixed evidence across the states in terms of who participates in magnet and charter school choice also suggests that program design is very important in creating and constraining opportunities by race and class. It suggests that in and of itself choice does not necessarily provide greater educational opportunities to poor and minority students and, in fact, may exacerbate inequalities that already exist in education.

Parental choice for schools does not happen in a vacuum. It happens in multiple social, political, and cultural environments. The evidence points clearly to the prominent role played by social networks, word of mouth and informal information in choice. Parents seem strongly influenced by this type of information. Social networks appear to act as filters—not only about which schools are "good" and which are "bad" but which schools are part of a realistic choice set. It is unclear whether parents would rely less on word of mouth if other types of information were provided.

In terms of preferences or motivations for choice, it appears that some notion of academic quality is a key factor, though preferences and perceptions of quality appear to be influenced by race and other social factors. Kleitz and colleagues suggest that the preferences of parents for school choice do not differ by race, ethnicity, or social background and that all parents are seeking schools of educational quality.[95] Rather, they argue, the differences we see in actual choices by race are a result of "real world" context, options and limitations (p. 846). It may be that many parents want out of their assigned public school, perhaps thinking that any other school is better. Parents overwhelmingly say they are looking for a better education but much, though not all, of the research examined suggests that parents are paying more attention to the social and racial demographics of potential choice schools than they are to measures of academic quality. As Jacob and Lefgren note, "what parents want from school depends on the educational context in which they find themselves."[96] The evidence on behavior, or the way in which parents make their choices, doesn't match very well with what parents say are their preferences. This suggests that race and class play a key role and that parents may view the racial or peer composition of a school as a proxy for quality. This is not encouraging to those who view choice as a way to potentially eliminate the barriers to truly integrated schools. Indeed, Pallas and Riehl note, "[T]he evidence also suggests that there are valid concerns about whether school choice plans will increase the racial/ethnic separation of students, because parents tend to weigh demographic information about schools heavily and to make choice decisions that will not create social isolation for their children."[97]

RECOMMENDATIONS

Based on the review of the research, we make six recommendations:

- Policymakers need to carefully consider the intended target population to ensure that choice options adequately address needs and preferences.
- Policymakers need to design any choice program so as not to perpetuate or exacerbate segregation by race, ethnicity or income. Evi-

dence suggests that choice and particular design elements operate differently in different contexts. Therefore, thoughtful design requires looking beyond assumptions and theory to the evidence about how choice and particular design elements operate in practice.

- Public choice policies should address the constraints that target populations may have in potentially exercising their choices. For example, choice plans that are meant to encourage the exercise of choice among low-income families may not provide transportation, which is a significant barrier to participation.
- Both publicly and privately funded choice programs should work to ensure the wide dissemination of appropriate and useful information on programs, as informal information from social networks appears to be a powerful influence on parents' preferences and their ability to act on them.
- Since the Supreme Court has weighed in against the constitutionality of race-based student assignment policies, states and school districts need to find creative ways of ensuring that choice policies expand opportunities for those with the least access to choice and to quality schools.
- Further research in this area should examine the link between preferences and behaviors, perhaps exploring what factors help or hinder parents in acting on their preferences. This research especially should take into account contextual factors such as geographic location, constraints, and supply, to more fully understand the operation of choice. Policy may also benefit from research into the preferences of nonactive choosers.

CHAPTER 5

SCHOOL CHOICE AND ACCOUNTABILITY

Gregg Garn and Casey Cobb

Accountability, a term used extensively in the popular press and educational reform literature, is a fundamental principle of the school choice movement. However, the concept of accountability appears analogous to a Rorschach test: everyone sees something slightly different in the details. Educational researchers have long noted the lack of commonly defined terminology in the modern school choice and accountability movement, which dates from 1970. As early as 1974, Levin called attention to "the great diversity in the use of the word accountability."[1] Thus, our first task in this study was to review nearly 4 decades of research (1970-2007) and to distill it into a typology of four distinct accountability models: *bureaucratic, performance, market,* and *professional*. In early segments of this chapter, we define these forms, explore their evolution, and demonstrate how they are embedded in the school choice movement.

Having detailed the typology, we then move to examining the varied accountability systems inherent in several popular school choice options: vouchers and tax credits, charter schools, virtual/cyber schools, home schools, and inter- and intradistrict choice. After considering the impact of choice programs and their attendant accountability systems on district schools, we close by offering four practical recommendations for policymakers developing school choice accountability frameworks.

Exploring the School Choice Universe: Evidence and Recommendations
pp. 89–104

CLARIFYING ACCOUNTABILITY: A TYPOLOGY

Throughout recent decades, scholars have increasingly diversified the concept of educational accountability. In 1975, Browder completed an extensive review of existing accountability literature and concluded:

1. There were no commonly agreed upon definitions.
2. Accountability needed conceptual refinement. With no common framework, confusion abounded among such terms as *general accountability, institutional accountability* and *technological accountability.*
3. Accountability had become highly politicized. Various groups who might be held accountable attacked the concept and pounced on malfunctions in order to discredit it.[2]

In 1974, Levin identified four strands of accountability: (a) performance reporting, (b) technical process, (c) political process, and (d) institutional process.[3] In 1986, Kogan presented three education accountability models: (a) state or public control, (b) professional control, and (c) consumer control.[4] Two years later, Darling-Hammond posited five models of accountability: (a) political, (b) legal, (c) bureaucratic, (d) professional, and (e) market.[5] And in 1990, Kirst recognized six types of educational accountability: (a) performance reporting, (b) monitoring and compliance with standards or regulations, (c) incentive systems, (d) reliance on the market, (e) changing the locus of control, and (f) changing professional roles.[6] Our detailed review of these models uncovered substantive overlap, however, allowing us to synthesize them into four main types of accountability: bureaucratic, performance, market, and professional.[7] These four conceptions have appeared repeatedly in the school choice literature over the past 40 years and provide a useful lens for exploring the school choice movement.

Bureaucratic Accountability. Kirst described bureaucratic accountability as "monitoring and compliance with standards and regulations ... [with the] key accountability criterion [being] procedural compliance. Prominent examples include individualized education plans (IEPs) for handicapped children and targeting funds under Chapter 1 programs."[8] Darling-Hammond understood bureaucratic accountability as being embodied in "agencies of government which promulgate rules and regulations intended to assure citizens that public functions will be carried out in pursuit of public goals voiced through democratic or legal processes."[9] Cuban, however, underscored that an emphasis on meeting procedural requirements might not align with an emphasis on meeting the needs of students.[10] Because standards and regulations are often subject to legal challenge, the emphasis on compliance has resulted in the courts substantively shaping accountability requirements in bureaucratic accountability systems.

Performance Accountability. Rather than procedure, performance accountability is concerned with outcomes, with how schools and students perform. Levin's definition is "a periodic report of the attainments of schools and other educational units."[11] Kirst details the concept this way:

> Performance reporting includes such measurement techniques as statewide assessment, National Assessment of Educational Progress (NAEP), school report cards, and performance indicators, and it has some similarities to the audit report in business. In essence, performance reports assume that information per se will stimulate actions to improve education.... Also, state performance reporting can be used to monitor regulatory compliance for such state requirements as minimum graduation requirements.... This technique can be used to produce rewards as well as sanctions.[12]

The Federal Office of Educational Research and Improvement has defined performance accountability as "a set of indicators or statistics that provides information about how well schools are performing."[13] The current policy environment is dominated by performance accountability as brought on by federal and state mandates.

Market Accountability. According to Kirst, "[market] accountability occurs when consumers choose between schools, with the bad schools presumably closing if the pupils leave," although he cautioned that "choice restricted to the public sector may not be a powerful accountability device."[14] Darling-Hammond notes that in market accountability system,

> governments may choose to allow clients or consumers to choose what services best meet their needs; to preserve the utility of this form of accountability, government regulations seek to prevent monopolies, protect freedom of choice, and require that service providers give truthful information.[15]

Chubb and Moe, however, argued for redefining terms in the market place accountability model by maintaining that public schools are essentially a monopoly.[16] Students, they said, are forced into the local district school and enroll regardless of performance levels. They held that, in contrast, marketplace accountability must allow parents to choose among public and private schools, forcing schools to compete for students.

Professional Accountability. In professional accountability, experts in practice assume responsibility for setting and meeting standards of practice. According to Rivera, in this model, teachers as professionals (assuming competence and knowledge) are obligated to make decisions in a responsible manner and adhere to standards of professional practice. The process of peer review for tenure and dismissal ... is considered a professional accountability mechanism.[17]

Firestone and Bader offer a similar description:

Professionals are keepers of important values ... only they have the knowledge to determine if those values are being adequately met. From this perspective educators must show the value of their work to other educators, not to the public.[18]

Several common policies reflect this model of accountability, including, Kirst noted, "school accreditation, teacher-controlled boards for initial licensing of graduates from university teacher education programs and policies to devolve policy decisions to teacher-led school site councils."[19]

Systemic Interactions. Each of the four accountability models has particular strengths and weaknesses. As Kirst noted, they are not mutually exclusive, so that implementing multiple types simultaneously might compensate for the limitations of individual types.[20] Conversely, however, Kirp suggested that various models frequently conflict when they occur within the same accountability system:

Professionalism, legalism, bureaucratization, and politicization pull and tug against one another ... problems arise when one or another framework becomes too powerful—for instance, when legalism engulfs in procedural snarls questions that may either be unresolvable or better resolved less formally, when professionals deprive parents of effective voice in decisions concerning their children, or when bureaucratic rules undermine the exercise of wise professional discretion. Policy remedies take the form of redressing the balance among these frameworks.[21]

With the awareness that combinations of accountability models may work synergistically or antagonistically in practice, we turn next to examining accountability across the spectrum of school choice programs.

ACCOUNTABILITY IN POPULAR SCHOOL CHOICE PROGRAMS

The following discussion examines accountability types implicit in popular school choice programs: vouchers and tax credits; charter schools; virtual or cyber schools; home schools; interdistrict choice; and, intradistrict choice.

Vouchers and Tax Credits

In the 1950s, economist Milton Friedman first endorsed offering parents vouchers, funded by taxes, which they could use to send their children to any school.[22] He reasoned, as do many contemporary supporters, that school vouchers would create competition among schools for students, forcing schools to improve their services. However, the move from this theory to practice has uncovered significant implementation challenges. For example, it has proven difficult to determine an adequate and fair voucher amount because per-pupil costs vary significantly across and within private and public schools.

Support for taxpayer-financed vouchers remains relatively weak over-all.[23] According to the National Conference of State Legislatures only five states offer publicly funded voucher programs. Eligibility criteria typically include such factors as family income, disability, or area of residence.

Milwaukee and Cleveland are home to the most notable examples of publicly funded voucher programs. Both target low-income families. Presently Milwaukee's voucher plan provides $6,442 to approximately 21,000 students. Cleveland maintains two voucher programs, which collectively enroll about 7,300 students and offer up to $3,450 or $4,375 per student, depending on the program, tuition rates, and parent income. The Utah legislature passed a voucher program of $3,000 per student in 2007, but it was later repealed in a statewide referendum. In 2006, the Florida Supreme Court struck down the fledgling Opportunity Scholarship Program. The Washington, DC, voucher program was defunded in 2009.

Privately funded voucher programs are more prevalent than taxpayer-funded plans. Examples include Milwaukee's Partners Advancing Values in Education, the Educational Choice Charitable Trust in Indianapolis, the CEO Foundation of Connecticut, and the Children's Scholarship Fund. These programs typically operate in large city districts and are often sponsored by mayoral offices, private or religious organizations, or corporations. The monies are raised privately and distributed in most cases to economically needy families seeking nonsecular school choice options. The programs are thus targeted and limited in scope, much like the existing publicly funded voucher programs.

Tax credit programs operate very similarly to school vouchers. Under tax credit programs, education-related expenses are reimbursed through tax relief. Tax credits can be designed for individuals, parents or corporations, reimbursing them for education expenses or contributions to public schools or school tuition organizations.[24] Nine states currently support some form of tax credit program.[25]

In theory, school voucher and tax credit programs fall most directly under market accountability. In practice, however, vouchers can be highly regulated, invoking bureaucratic accountability that distances them from Friedman's free market conceptualization. Eligibility rules for low-income students or students with disabilities, caps on total student participation and voucher amounts, and other considerations suggest that these programs operate in quasi-markets. Vouchers for students attending public schools are subject to the same performance accountability standards required of those schools. Voucher programs that support enrollment at nonsecular schools are not influenced by performance accountability to the same extent.

Regulated voucher plans provide for some degree of the consumer-driven competition that market accountability intends to generate, since schools may compete for students' tuition dollars. However, the bureaucratic accountability embedded in voucher plan regulations is often a contested element. Voucher detractors believe that bureaucratic rules are necessary to provide a fair choice system and to ensure appropriate use of public funds. Voucher proponents, on the other hand, argue that many of the bureaucratic rules simply serve as undue protection for monopolistic public schools and that such overregulated environments are at odds with free market competition.

Free-market accountability, where an invisible hand weeds out poor quality schools and rewards high quality schools, does not appear to operate in the public-private school system in the current context. Vouchers have not been fully operational outside of a handful of programs that, for the most part, target low-income families. From an accountability perspective, bureaucratic forces are operating within the education marketplace.

Tax credits, however, seem less susceptible to bureaucratic influence than voucher programs. They arguably provide "the most indirect path of public money to private schools." As a result, suggest Huerta et al., "policymakers may feel less inclined to impose state regulations on private schools that enroll tax credit beneficiaries than on voucher recipients."[26]

Charter Schools

A charter school is a publicly funded alternative to district schools. Charters involve a contract between a district and the charter's organizer/s. In exchange for a broad waiver from bureaucratic accountability requirements, a charter school must achieve specific performance outcomes documented in its contract. Theoretically, the district renews a charter's contract if the school meets contractual goals and closes the school if it fails to meet goals.

The charter schools concept is credited to Ray Budde, a retired professor at the University of Massachusetts and author of a 1988 paper titled "Education by Charter: Restructuring Schools Districts."[27] The same year, Albert Shanker, then president of the American Federation of Teachers (AFT), also wrote about the charter concept in an influential piece in the *Peabody Journal of Education*.[28] Joe Nathan and Ted Kolderie introduced the idea to Minnesota state legislators in the early 1990s, resulting in the first charter school legislation in 1991.[29] The Center for Education Reform reports that as of September 2006, 40 states and Washington, DC, have charter school legislation, encouraging the creation of 5,400 schools serving 1.7 million children.[30]

Charter school accountability varies dramatically across and even within states, although all charter schools are grounded on performance accountability—that is, certain consequences occur when a charter meets or fails to meet its performance objectives. However, market accountability is also embedded in charters, since they provide families with a choice outside the district public schools and so involve some competition. Theoretically, bureaucratic accountability is not a part of charter school accountability. Because charter schools rely on public tax dollars, however, they must comply with a number of local, state and federal standards and regulations even though some are waived. How strongly bureaucratic accountability is monitored varies tremendously among contexts. And finally, charter schools offer the potential for professional accountability as well. Shanker's vision for charters included the notion of teachers holding one another to high standards of professional practice. Thus, it is conceivable that any charter might be subject to a variety of accountability models, with various models receiving varying degrees of emphasis.

Cyber/Virtual/Internet Schools

Clark defines a cyber school as an educational organization that offers K-12 courses through Internet or web-based methods.[31]

> Instruction is delivered through … prepackaged software programs, and teacher-directed distance learning or cyber learning where students receive either asynchronous or synchronous instruction via the Internet from a teacher or other instructor.[32]

Although online learning is becoming a common component of the American K-12 education system, a comprehensive online school is a 21st century choice innovation. Cyber schools have emerged only in the last few years, and their magnitude is still very small. There are a few virtual schools operated by school districts or states, but cyber schools are primarily authorized as an innovative branch of the charter school model. Estimates of Internet-based charter schools in January 2007 indicate 173 cyber schools are operating in 18 states.[33]

Even though the majority of cyber schools operate under a charter school agreement, the accountability mechanisms are less developed when compared with other reforms. At the inception of the virtual school reform, accountability expectations were almost exclusively market-based. Market-based accountability remains the accountability type. However, bureaucratic regulations for virtual schools are being developed in Ohio, Colorado, Pennsylvania, and California[34] (the states where this reform is maturing) due to financial scandals involving several virtual school operators. Unresolved issues remain regarding tracking student enrollment, monitoring instructional time, and developing fiscal accountability regulations.

Homeschooling

Isenberg reports that two separate issues drove the modern homeschooling movement, dating from its inception in the 1970s: concerns by religious parents about the moral standards of public schools and concerns by other parents about deteriorating academic standards.[35] The most current estimates by the National Center for Education Statistics put the number of homeschooled children at 1.5 million.[36] Every state allows homeschooling; however, state regulations vary tremendously in such areas as procedures for parents to inform the state of their intent to home school, qualifications for parents, student participation in state testing, and student performance evaluations.[37] Rudner found the great majority of homeschooled students are at the elementary level and come from non-Hispanic White, married families with higher levels of income and formal education when compared to national averages.[38] However, Welner and Welner, citing limitations in the data used by Rudner, argue homeschooled children are actually more diverse, ethnically and socioeconomically, than his study would suggest.[39]

In most states, accountability for homeschooling is based almost entirely on market accountability, since it is driven primarily by parental dissatisfaction with other schooling options. Isenberg notes that homeschooling has largely avoided bureaucratic accountability by actively opposing it: "fearing the possibility of state regulation, homeschooling interest groups succeeded not only in winning a legal status with minimal regulation but also in restricting the data that could be collected about homeschoolers."[40] The exceptions are the few states that require (and enforce) homeschool teachers to meet some basic requirements (a college degree, or state certification, for example), or that require homeschooled students to participate in statewide testing programs. Thus, bureaucratic, performance and professional accountability play a very minor role in accountability for children schooled at home.

Interdistrict Choice

Interdistrict choice plans offer options for students to attend public schools outside their home districts. Forty-two states have interdistrict choice policies.[41] Roughly 43% of the nation's districts permit transfers out to another district and 46% allow transfers in.[42]

Under interdistrict agreements, student participation is mostly voluntary. This stems from the 1974 Supreme Court decision in *Milliken v. Bradley,* which effectively stifled legally imposed, cross-district transfer programs. The two most common forms of interdistrict plans involve magnet schools and student transfer programs, which typically seek to encourage students to voluntarily move across district lines to reduce de facto racial segregation. Examples of the latter include Hartford's Open Choice program, Boston's Metropolitan Council for Educational Opportunity program, Rochester Urban-Suburban Interdistrict Transfer program, Milwaukee's Chapter 220 Voluntary Student Transfer Program, and the Choice is Yours Program in Minneapolis.

Interdistrict arrangements are determined on a case-by-case basis. Because pupil spending varies across districts, interdistrict programs are always complicated by fiduciary considerations and responsibilities. For instance, under some plans, a portion of a district's per-pupil funding follows the child; in other instances, such as some court-ordered desegregation plans, the state subsidizes a portion of the program's expenditures, including transportation costs.

Interdistrict choice is influenced primarily by market accountability, although markets can run the gamut from controlled markets to laissez faire ones. Local conditions can vary widely between those extremes, but interdistrict choice is most commonly offered in a modestly regulated environment.

Intradistrict Choice

Within-district school choice comes in many forms, with the two most common being specialty school programs and general open enrollment plans. Specialty school programs, also known as "nonneighborhood schools," include alternative, technical, thematic, and magnet schools, among others. Students are not typically assigned to specialty schools based on their family residence, but instead follow an admissions process. Admission can be on a first-come, first-served basis, or through lottery. In some instances, admission depends upon performance-based criteria, as in an engineering or performing arts school that requires mathematical or artistic acuity. Some districts seek or require balanced racial compositions across their schools, thus making race an admissions consideration.[43]

General open enrollment programs can occur at the entire district level ("choice districts") or at the student level on a case-by-case basis (individual student transfers). *Choice districts* represent situations where parents and students are free to choose, or at least to apply to, all schools in a district. Cambridge, MA, was one of the first districts to adopt this approach in 1981, followed by several other Massachusetts cities, Buffalo, NY, Montclair, NJ, Berkeley, CA, and New York City's formerly named District 4.[44] In many of these cases the districts are seeking racial redistribution and thus may regulate admission to the extent permitted by law. Such programs are often referred to as controlled-choice plans. *Individual student transfer* programs allow students to attend a school in their district other than their neighborhood-assigned or zone school. Districts with student transfer policies range in terms of their willingness to allow transfers; some districts openly endorse the policy while others reserve it for special situations only.

The number of students actively participating in open enrollment plans nationwide has been estimated around 4 to 5 million.[45] The No Child Left Behind Act choice option, although not explicitly limited as such, is a form of intradistrict school choice. It does not fall under the category of open enrollment, however, as only students in low-performing schools are eligible to transfer to another school.

In contrast to interdistrict forms of school choice, intradistrict plans tend to be more free-market based. Of the two basic intradistrict types, open enrollment relies more on market accountability; specialty schools, less so. For instance, magnet programs that are part of court-ordered or voluntary desegregation plans have some degree of bureaucratic accountability. Rules of admission, participation and resource allocation are part of the system. Even open enrollment policies, however, have some bureaucratic provisions, such as eligibility and transportation rules. Nonetheless, while "open enrollment" seldom is as open as it sounds, such policies are more viable within districts than across them.

School Choice Programs across the Accountability Typology

Table 5.1 below summarizes and illustrates the relative emphasis for each of the four accountability models on the various choice programs. This is by no means an exact science to show the relationship between accountability types and school choice programs. The purpose of Table 5.1 is to provide a basis for continued reasoned conversation on school choice and accountability.

The analysis summarized in Table 5.1 suggests that vouchers/tax credits, charter schools, cyber schools and intradistrict plans are strongly influenced by market accountability.[46] Vouchers, cyber schools, and home schools are less influenced by performance accountability, at least as judged by today's test-based accountability environment. It also appears that intradistrict, interdistrict, and charter plans invite the potential for the "most" accountability across the four types, and that home and cyber schooling invite the least. For the sake of comparison, district public schools appear as the last row in the table. Bureaucratic and performance accountability have much more influence in district schools than they do

Table 5.1. The Proposed Relationship Between Types of Accountability and School Choice Programs

Choice Program	Accountability Type			
	Bureaucratic Accountability	Performance Accountability	Market Accountability	Professional Accountability
Vouchers/tax credit	Both influential and not influential	Not influential	Strongly influential	Not influential
Charters	Influential	Influential	Strongly influential	Both influential and not influential
Cyber school	Both influential and not influential	Not influential	Strongly influential	Not influential
Home school	Not influential	Not influential	Influential	Not influential
Interdistrict	Influential	Influential	Influential	Influential
Intradistrict	Strongly influential	Influential	Strongly influential	Influential
District public	Strongly influential	Strongly influential	Both influential and not influential	Influential

in nearly every choice option, while market accountability has significantly less influence. To be sure, prior to No Child Left Behind Act, district public schools did not get penalized in any meaningful way for students who did not learn, who dropped out, or both.

All school choice forms discussed above reflect the influences of market-type accountability, although in practice educational markets often operate in quasi-regulated markets and bureaucratic influences often emerge in specific choice plans. Regulated or quasi-regulated markets are in play for current voucher plans, tax credits, many charter schools, some cyber schools, and many intra- and interdistrict enrollment plans. Regulated markets include, for example, controlled choice plans or voluntary choice plans designed to create more equitable opportunities for racially isolated or economically disadvantaged students. Less regulated plans, such as certain open enrollment programs, mimic laissez-faire markets more closely. An important point here is that school vouchers as envisioned by Friedman remain a theoretical concept that has not yet been fully realized in practice. Nevertheless, regulated vouchers, even with their participation and per-pupil funding restrictions, imply a degree of market accountability.

Accountability Constituents for School Choice Programs

All public schools have an obligation to our democracy and society writ large. The democratic entities that represent the greater polity include local governments, such as city councils and school boards, as well as state governments, such as legislative and executive branches and state agencies. Schools are also directly accountable to parents and the children who attend them. Table 5.2 illustrates how strongly each school choice model is accountable to its various constituents. Formal attempts to hold public schools accountable are done through these democratic entities, or constituents, which represent a particular citizenry. For instance, an elected school board is responsible for the quality of local schools and (in theory) represents the goals of its electing body.

Vouchers, charter schools, cyber schools, and home schools offer strong accountability directly to the parents and children (consumers), consistent with their market-based orientations. In theory, charter schools are also directly accountable to their local governing boards, state governing boards, or both; in practice, however, the level of accountability appears to vary on a state-by-state basis. For instance, charter school boards in Arizona are designed to serve their immediate school community (parents and students) and do not represent citizens in any particular town or city. Inter- and intradistrict plans offer accountability to the state and local

Table 5.2.   School Choice Accountability Strength by Constituency

Choice Program	Parent/Child	Accountability Constituency State Government/ Democratic Entity	Local Government/ Democratic Entity
Vouchers/tax credit	Strong accountability	Weak accountability	Weak accountability
Charters	Strong accountability	Moderate accountability	Moderate accountability
Cyber school	Strong accountability	Moderate accountability	Weak accountability
Home school	Strong accountability	Weak accountability	Weak accountability
Interdistrict	Moderate accountability	Strong accountability	Moderate accountability
Intradistrict	Moderate accountability	Strong accountability	Strong accountability

democratic entities, and to a lesser degree, families. Intradistrict plans offer the strongest accountability to local governing bodies that oversee them.

Two cautions apply to the judgments offered in Table 5.2. The first is that stakeholders with school choice experience may reasonably disagree with the assessments made based on their own experience. Because policies on any option vary widely across and even within states, a strong generalization will not apply to every instance. The second is that the three constituents we identify only begin to encompass stakeholders in what we would refer to as "the greater public good." Policy discussions should include a thorough exploration of how schools and school policies will advance accountability for greater societal goals.

Extending Notions of Accountability

At its core, accountability implies an obligation between debtor and debtee, between provider and constituent. It suggests that two parties enter a reciprocal relationship where a promised service is made in return for a payment of some type.[47] Bureaucratic, performance, and professional accountabilities all identify explicit criteria allowing for judgments about whether obligations have been met. School choice accountability presents a very different challenge. In the context of school choice accountability, payment can be construed as a student's enrollment at a school (and the tuition dollars that follow); the measure of whether a school has met its service or educational obligations can be considered the level of parents' satisfaction.

But this is only one way to look at accountability—as something imposed and assessed externally. Possibilities for accountability are not exhausted by the four models discussed here. For example, accountability can also be internal, as when teachers hold themselves accountable for students' learning or well-being.[48] In this case there is no external source holding teachers accountable. The distinction here is the difference between *being* accountable (internal) and being *held* accountable (external).

Moreover, accountability systems need not depend on the specific, explicit criteria required in bureaucratic, performance, and professional models. Instead, "goal-free" forms of accountability (to borrow a term from Michael Scriven's theory on evaluation) involve no predetermined or mutually agreed upon performance goals. Accountability to markets and to parents are goal-free in the sense that goals are not explicit; rather, they are in the minds, preferences, and utility functions of families—in other words, consumers—who make choices. Adam Smith's "invisible hand" dictates winners and losers in the educational marketplace while parents' school-related goals for their children remain either tacit, undocumented, or both.

Thus, although the accountability models discussed at length here wield widespread influence, policymakers are cautioned to remember that these four models do not exhaust the range of accountability possibilities. Not all accountability need be externally imposed; not all levels of satisfaction or dissatisfaction can be neatly correlated to specific, explicitly articulated criteria.

IMPACT ON TRADITIONAL PUBLIC SCHOOL DISTRICTS

Has school choice influenced the accountability of district public schools? Although causal claims are tenuous here, public school systems seem to have responded to the choice movement by offering or expanding their own choice options. At the very least one can ask whether market forms of accountability are showing up more explicitly in district public schools. District open enrollment plans, theme or specialty schools, and entire "choice districts" such as Cambridge, MA, offer examples where market accountability is manifest.

Charter schools were created to lessen the bureaucratic accountability on schools in exchange for increased emphasis on performance and market accountability. Some district schools are reinventing themselves or emerging under similar conditions. Adaptations of district public schools such as Boston's Pilot Schools, Oklahoma City's Enterprise Schools, and Connecticut's CommPACT Schools reveal charter-like characteristics, particularly with respect to their autonomous and deregulated environments. Yet on the whole, bureaucratic accountability remains strongly influential among school districts.

Performance accountability is the strongest form of accountability currently operating in district public schools, yet it did not derive from the choice movement. This form of accountability emerged from federal and state mandates requiring performance-based accountability systems. The federal No Child Left Behind Act dramatically increased the emphasis on student test score performance for all types of public schools. Finally, the influence of professional accountability has remained fairly constant in the context of district public schools.

CONCLUSIONS AND RECOMMENDATIONS

From a theoretical perspective, we have recommended elsewhere that multiple forms of accountability might collectively contribute to better educational accountability, all the while maintaining the "public" in our democratic schools.[49] Following a 5-year study of the Milwaukee voucher program, Van Dunk and Dickman suggested that the market-based program also had a "need for strict performance accountability … to allow choice to succeed in improving education."[50] There is some agreement, then, that multiple forms might be productively combined. However, policymakers need to be aware as well that multiple accountability models can also undermine at least free-market accountability, as Kirp noted.[51] For instance, bureaucratic and performance accountability could compromise the logic underlying free-market voucher systems. Restricting voucher participation by certain criteria or to meet racial balancing requirements (bureaucratic accountability) closes the open market. Likewise, holding private schools accountable to state performance standards by way of state testing (performance accountability) could dissuade their participation in a voucher system.

Policymakers would be wise to keep in view the forest, and not overly focus on the trees. For instance the preceding few sentences might suggest an argument for relying solely on market accountability, devoid of bureaucratic and performance influences. But if the larger policy objective is to reduce inequities in educational opportunities, releasing bureaucratic oversights gives up significant leverage to represent those who may not be served well by the market.[52]

Policymakers need to balance their concerns thoughtfully when creating an overall accountability system to ensure that its various components work in concert rather than in opposition to each other and that it attends to all constituents—parents and their children, of course, but also the taxpayer and society writ large. In sum, it is recommended that policymakers:

- Consider school accountability as something more than test performance or information for parents-as-consumers, the emphases reflected in the current prevalence of performance and market-based systems. Instead, shape accountability systems to examine whether schools are directly contributing to the greater societal good.
- When creating or judging school choice policies, consider local context. Choice policies and accountability systems vary widely across the United States and from one community or locale to another.
- Consider employing different types of accountability at different levels and in different combinations to hedge risk. Accountability systems that rely on a single accountability mechanism are susceptible to inefficiencies or inequities.
- When evaluating accountability systems, rely on empirical research. Possible future studies investigating the effects of various combinations of accountability types may be particularly useful.

CHAPTER 6

FUNDING FORMULAS, SCHOOL CHOICE, AND INHERENT INCENTIVES

Clive Belfield

This chapter reports on funding and financing of school choice across the United States. School choice includes a range of policy reforms, including: the promotion of private schools through vouchers and tuition tax credits; the introduction of charter schools; the liberalization of public school options within and across district boundaries; home-schooling; and deregulation to allow home-schooling options. These options may be contrasted with local public schools where places are allocated primarily based on residency and financing relies heavily on the local tax base. How school choice is financed will influence both its prevalence and its effectiveness in improving education as an alternative to local public schools.

This chapter examines how funding formulas and financing systems encourage or discourage school choice. We begin with a brief overview of funding mechanisms and the rationale for incentives. Because school choice reforms vary, we consider each variation, but our focus is primarily on charter schools. Charters illustrate many key issues that arise in other choice forms as well, and they are the most researched option. We draw on evidence from across the United States, although we pay particular attention to the Great Lakes states. Our discussion explores the impact of funding mechanisms on each of the school choice models.

Exploring the School Choice Universe: Evidence and Recommendations
pp. 105–123
Copyright © 2012 by Information Age Publishing

Our task here is not to argue for or against greater incentives but simply to describe how choice incentives are structured. We adopt the position that school choice is worth exploring a priori, but policymakers must be aware of all funding issues before deciding whether choice is feasible or practical in a particular situation. We do not investigate whether public schools are under- or overfunded against any social criteria. We focus only on issues of relative funding for school choice options and current public school spending.

We note that many claims regarding incentives for school choice reflect political, ideological, or self-interested predispositions rather than a dispassionate review of evidence.[1] Opponents of school choice argue that incentives are too generous and that local public schools are being undermined. Proponents argue that school choice options need greater incentives so that they can compete with local public schools. It is a challenge, however, to give a simple, universal, and uncontested response to the question of what constitutes optimal funding and appropriate incentives for school choice. In practice, funding and incentives can vary extensively. New options are not the same as the traditional public schools they compete with. Often they have different goals and serve different student populations, and the extent of such differences varies from state to state. Therefore, a raw comparison of per-student funding across choice schools and local public schools offers insufficient evidence to make a general determination about the strength of financial incentives. The correct incentive level for choice options depends on local circumstances.

FUNDING SYSTEMS FOR EDUCATION

Basic Principles

Much government funding for education is based on formulas tied approximately to student enrollments.[2] Student enrollment formulas start with an estimate of base foundational aid for regular instruction per child. Estimated foundation aid is then typically weighted to account for differences in educational costs using a cost-of-education index (at the national level, one such index is Taylor and Fowler, 2006).[3] Foundation aid also varies by grade level to reflect typical differences in class size and materials, such as laboratories and theaters.

The base amount is then augmented by two types of supplementary funding. One is student driven, such as supplements for special education, at-risk status, or limited English proficiency. The other is cost driven, reflecting the local economic conditions, historical service patterns, and transportation costs, and other particular circumstances (including court mandates). Duncombe and Yinger give a fuller account of how costs might differ according to geography, student disadvantage, and school size.[4]

In theory, such formulas seem straightforward: classify each student and decide on funding amounts per classification. These student-weighted formulas may be more equitable than allocations based simply on historical patterns. In practice, however, formulas are often extremely complicated. Students' needs vary substantively, as do district and school organizations and each change to the formula generates another layer of complexity. Also, per-student funding typically covers operating costs, with funding for facilities decided separately. As an alternative to funding based on per-student weights, categorical grants may be implemented, for special education budgets or for low-income students, for example.[5]

Funding allocated using such formulas comes from three public sources: federal, state, and local government. Of course, the tax base for each differs and so does its ability to raise revenue for particular education reforms. In addition, each level of government emphasizes a different element of the formulas's base amount, its student-driven components, and its cost-driven components. For K-12 schooling, the federal government primarily funds student-driven or cost-driven components. For example, Title I provides basic programs to help low-income or disadvantaged children meet state standards, and it also funds educational services for children with disabilities. Generally across the United States, state governments provide approximately 45% of education funding, local governments another 45%, and the federal government 10%. These proportions, however, vary significantly across states: in Minnesota, for example, the state provides almost three quarters of total funding.

Formulas to raise revenues for schools may be structured through foundation programs, guaranteed tax base programs, or a combination of the two.[6] And, some states have adopted legislation that significantly changes how revenues are raised for education, such as Proposal A in Michigan or Proposition 13 in California.[7] While this discussion is concerned with allocating revenue rather than raising it, it's worth noting that the structure of revenue-raising mechanisms may have some influence on school choice. Broadly, the greater the reliance on a single revenue source (the state, for example), the more likely it is that school choice options will be introduced. If there are multiple jurisdictions funding education, then these jurisdictions must all agree—or be mandated—to fund the school choice option to the same level as that for students in local public schools. The financial implications of school choice may differ across jurisdictions, however. For example, local districts incur costs when a student transfers in without extra funding, but the transfer is neutral from a state's perspective. Such was the case in Michigan. After Proposal A, schools were largely funded by a state sales tax (rather than property taxes), and the state was therefore able to unilaterally introduce more school choice options.

In principle, per-student funding need not be allocated only to students in traditional public schools. It could be allocated to any charter school directly, or to any private school student through a voucher system. It could also follow students across districts, or from school to school within a district. Even home-schooling parents might receive state funding through such mechanisms as tax breaks. If appropriate, per-student funding could be modified for each choice option using a cost-driven weight. For example, private schools might receive 75% of the funding provided for each public school student in the same district. Alternatively, contributions from each level of government might be modified: for example, charter schools might receive no local funds but more state funds.

The absolute generosity of the funding formula for various choices reflects incentives for choice options. Where funding is greater and restrictions on access are fewer, incentives for school choice are likely to be stronger, and more school choice options will be forthcoming for students.[8]

In thinking about incentives, it is important to realize that they influence choices only relatively—that is, they encourage one option in comparison with other options. Alternatives are implicit in any incentive structure, which intends to promote certain behaviors and choices. Often the alternative to the choice option is the local public school, but it need not be. For example, when we think about vouchers as an incentive to attend private school, often the assumed alternative is to attend the nearby public school. However, comparison of other alternatives may also be relevant; in a particular instance, it might be useful to compare charter school incentives with private school incentives. Because schools are (loosely) in competition with each other for enrollees, an incentive created for one type of school may often be thought of as a disincentive to another type. Hence, it may be helpful to think of a continuum of (strong and weak) incentives to zero incentives through to (weak and strong) disincentives. So, choice schools may receive: more than a sufficient share of funding (strong incentive); some funding but less than a comparable public school (weak incentive); zero funding (no incentive); or negative funding. That is, they may actually lose resources by attracting public school students (disincentive). Incentives can be thought of in relative or symmetrical terms: a strong incentive for one type of school represents a strong disincentive for the other types.

Challenges to Setting Funding Formulas

In principle, setting a funding formula to permit greater school choice appears straightforward. The first step is to calculate how much money—

for a student with a given set of characteristics—public schools spend or need to meet the state's education requirements (these are not necessarily the same). The second step is to make this amount available to any school, public or private. This would provide "equal incentives" for each type of school to serve students with a given set of characteristics, maximizing students' available choices.

However, fundamental trade-offs are often involved in implementation of funding formulas. For example, a formula may be designated "cost-plus," which requires schools to submit receipts and then reimburses their expenditures up to a fixed maximum. This case limits the possibility that a school will receive surpluses (or profits), but the school has no incentive to cut costs below the designated maximum.

Alternatively, the formula may be designed as "fixed price," which provides schools with a fixed amount of funding regardless of what they actually spend. The surplus goes as "profit" to the owner/manager of the school. In "fixed-price" cases, schools that are very efficient may reap very large profits—an economic imperative that cannot be eliminated. Once a school (or any enterprise) is allocated a fixed budget, it will seek ways to reduce costs and generate surplus (or profits). For example, Miron has described the cost-saving strategies used by education management organizations (EMO).[9]

Nor are these the only potential complications. There are several practical challenges to implementing a funding formula from its first step: identifying how much is being spent or should be spent. To begin, it is necessary to find a comparable local public school against which to compare a choice school. This comparison should be based on factors that influence costs, such as location, grade level, school size, and student characteristics. However, such comparison simply may not be possible: since one of the goals of school choice is to introduce educational options that did not previously exist, there may not be a comparable public school. In such cases, costs have to be calculated from a direct "bottom-up" assessment of a school's every need. Such assessment may be very expensive for a district to perform on a case-by-case basis.

Moreover, even if the goals of public and choice schools are the same, their costs may differ for several reasons. First, the regulations for choice schools may differ. For example, a private school may be exempt from collective bargaining rules for teachers, allowing it to pay teachers less (or hire teachers with different qualifications or skills). A looser set of regulations will give a school more freedom to make choices that may either increase efficiency or reduce costs. Second, various schools may differ substantively in teaching staff and facilities. Choice schools may be able to recruit teachers from a wider labor market than local public schools; they may be able to reduce salaries by hiring less experienced teachers or (in the case of religious schools) teachers who regard education as a vocation rather than an occupation. Local public schools, however, may have an advantage in terms of facilities, since they have access to public buildings and below-market rent; private or choice schools, on the other hand, may have to pay full market rent for any spaces they buy or lease.

Observable differences may also be evident in students. For example, choice schools may offer only elementary education, or may enroll fewer students with special educational needs. In cases where a school enrolls only students with characteristics associated with below-average cost, it is not efficient for it to be allocated average funding. When such characteristics can be observed, then the funding formula can account for them and provide each school with appropriately adjusted amounts. Ideally, choice schools should receive regular per-pupil funding for students with disabilities according to an independent cost estimate of required services for specific conditions (such as an Individualized Education Program). Some states (Pennsylvania, for example) offer extra incentives for charter schools to enroll students with disabilities, although they are typically for mild or moderate disabilities, which tend to be less costly to educate. In their recent review, Baker and Ferris estimate that, given the differences in the needs of the students they serve, charter schools in New York City should receive approximately $2,500 less in public funding compared to traditional public schools.[10]

Students, however, may differ in ways that are hard to observe. For example, a choice school may recruit students whose families are expressly committed to the mission of the school. These students may be "easier to teach" and so require fewer resources (for such services as remedial education or school counseling). Families may be required to contribute resources to the school. Such factors, though influential, cannot be incorporated into any choice funding formula because they cannot easily be described.[11]

Funding considerations also must include the effects of new options on existing enrollment patterns, which may potentially be large and with unpredicted budget consequences. For example, because they are not geographically limited, cyber-charter schools may grow to enormous size, fast outstripping their projected budget needs. Another possibility is found in the fact that some families may be sending their children to private school because of dissatisfaction with the local public school. If a high-quality charter school opens, parents may now choose to enroll their children there, so that their education becomes an additional public expense rather than a private one. A direct subsidy to a private school would have the same effect, so that cost for previously enrolled students would no longer be paid by their families, but by taxpayers. In short, new school choice funding formulas could create government educational obligations for millions of families who would otherwise have received no, or very limited, government funds. Creating school choice options has far-reaching ramifications for private as well as public schools, whose costs might also change significantly in the complex matrix of choice.

Finally, choice schools may have streams of revenue in addition to government subsidies. Therefore, even if an appropriate comparison with a local public school is possible and funding is determined, it is not certain that public taxes should provide full funding. For example, private schools charge fees to parents and may receive donations; similarly, charter schools may obtain grants from philanthropic agencies. Even when a private school accepts vouchers, it may continue to impose fees. Although policymakers may try to prevent such "topping-up," in practice it will be very difficult to enforce any rule against it. For example, schools might claim that fees are for services over and above regular instruction. In addition, such fees may be politically sensitive because a school may use them to restrict access to certain student groups. Yet, to withhold funding from choice schools because they have access to funding from other sources would discourage these schools from diversifying their revenues.[12]

FUNDING SYSTEMS FOR CHARTER SCHOOLS

Funding Mechanisms

Charter schools—publicly funded schools run by independent agencies and enterprises—illustrate the many challenges associated with school choice funding.[13] Functioning under a contract with a state or district authority, charters are often subject to similar, but slightly looser, regulations as local public schools. Some are former public or private schools that have converted to charter status; others are run by private, for-profit organizations called EMOs.

As is true in principle generally, devising a funding system for charter schools should be a straightforward task. It might seem that charter schools should receive the same amount of per-student funding as local public schools, from the same sources (federal, state, and local), and in the same proportions.[14] Yet, as noted above, there are several practical challenges.

For each state in the Great Lakes region, Table 6.1 describes the source of funding and the financing system for charter schools and how funds are allocated to them.

Even within this region, funding sources vary significantly. Some charters are funded by school districts (Illinois and Minnesota, for example),

Table 6.1. Financing System for Charter Schools: Great Lakes States

State	Funding From	System of Financing
Illinois	School district	Negotiated with sponsor school district and specified in charter, but 75%-125% of per-capita student tuition multiplied by the number of students residing in the district enrolled in the charter school.
Indiana	State	Charter schools receive 100% of the per-pupil funding that traditional schools receive.
Michigan	Charter authorizing body	One hundred percent of state and school district operations funding follows students, based on average school district per-pupil revenue, not to exceed a certain amount that rises from year to year based on state aid formula.
Minnesota	State	State portion of operations funding follows students, based on average state per-pupil revenue. School district portion of operations funding does not follow students.
New York	School district	School districts must provide 100% of a state-specified per-pupil funding calculation, although this amount may be reduced by agreement.
Ohio	State	A statewide base cost formula with adjustments, which includes a county-level cost of doing business factor.
Pennsylvania	School district	Funding follows students, based on average school district per-pupil budgeted expenditure of the previous year. For regional charter schools, funds come from the school district of a student's residence. Charter schools receive extra funding for special needs students.
Wisconsin	School district or state	Funding for a charter school authorized by a city, university or technical college is the sum of per pupil funding in the previous school year plus any revenue increase per pupil in the current school year times the number of students. Funding for a charter school authorized by a local school board is determined by negotiation between the two parties.

Source: ECS Charter School Profiles (www.ecs.org), retrieved February 8, 2011.

while others are funded by states (Indiana and Ohio, for example). These differences may reflect student demography. If charter schools enroll students from across school districts, it may be more appropriate to fund them at the state level rather than the district level. Generally, funding follows students, although the relationship varies across states and most states adjust their public school funding amounts. For example, in New York, there is some flexibility on charter school funds; in Wisconsin, the amounts may depend on which agency authorizes the charter school. Several key factors influence such adjustments.

First, charter schools often receive funds from nongovernment sources, including community groups and nonprofit charities.[15] These agencies may provide in-kind funds rather than money, so that their contributions do not appear in the school's formal accounting system. Based on a study of 10 charter schools in New York City in 2000-2001, Ascher et al. found a diverse array of supports for charter schools. Schools or district agencies provided such services as workshops. Charter school organizations assisted with information, networking, technical assistance, and political consultation.[16] Charter school authorizers provided legal assistance and information on accountability and operations. Nonprofit organizations provided funds for development. Finally, charter schools allied with nonprofit partners to provide instructional and operational services. Collectively, these supports may be a significant supplement to the funds from government agencies.[17] Baker and Ferris estimate that some New York charter schools may receive as much as $10,000 more per pupil than traditional public schools.

The key issue for funding charter schools is whether to subtract public funding to offset this additional outside funding or to allow charters full funding despite their outside funding, thereby allowing them to spend more than the local public school. The decision is a trade-off: either charter schools are penalized for successful external fund-raising, or they are allowed greater funding than local public schools.

Second, charter schools may be regulated differently than local public schools. Any schools operating in highly regulated systems will have higher costs: they must satisfy particular accountability rules and standards, including rules that may restrict their spending decisions (as when they must hire more expensive, certified teachers). Regulations can be structured either to support charter schools or to undermine them. For example, many states require school districts to provide in-kind services to charter schools, including transportation, classroom and library materials, extracurricular activities, personnel services, and school testing.[18] Transportation, in particular, is a significant fraction of total spending in school districts. Thus, it can be argued that charter schools that do not have to provide those services should receive less funding than regular public schools; when they receive full funding, they have a clear financial advantage.

However, charter schools typically also have short-term contracts with authorizing agencies (generally 3 or 5 years). If the agency deems that the contract has not been satisfied, the charter school may be closed. This threat imposes a risk on the charter school that is typically not imposed on public schools. In turn, risk imposes costs: teachers must be paid more to offset the higher probability of job loss; entrepreneurs will demand a higher profit or surplus to offset the possibility that the school may be prematurely closed. Yet, accountability mandates also apply to public schools: under No Child Left Behind, public schools failing to make Adequate Yearly Progress face sanctions that include possible closure. Therefore, the costs of a closure risk are similar across public and choice schools.

While external factors, such as whether the school operates in a low- or high-cost market, affect expenses, regulatory differences also can obviously produce cost differences between charter schools and local public schools.[19] Table 6.2 shows some regulations for charter schools in the Great Lakes states, indicating their variety.

The first column of Table 6.2 indicates whether charters must adhere to the local school district's collective bargaining agreement and hire teachers comparable to those in the local public school. Other personnel regulations might involve charters' requirements in relation to state retirement pension payments, or costs for in-service training or professional development. Because teacher salaries and benefits constitute a large part of the school budget, such regulations could result in significant cost differences between charters and public schools. In a number of states, no charter has to adhere to the local collective bargaining agreement (Illinois, Minnesota, and Pennsylvania, for example); in other states, only conversion charter schools must adhere to collective bargaining agreements (New York and Ohio, for example). Charter schools with greater flexibility on employment contracts might be able to save more than public schools on personnel.

The second column of Table 6.2 indicates which states in the Great Lakes states provide funds for facilities, another key area of cost differences.[20] Several researchers have identified shortfalls in funding for charter schools' facilities, in part because they do not have access to municipal bonds and because they cannot find facilities.[21] As Table 6.2 shows, state funding for charter facilities varies, and most often it is less than that available for local public schools.

A third cost differential area is charters' initial start-up costs.[22] Specifically, charter schools must secure a facility, purchase instructional materials, design a curriculum, hire educators, administrators, and possibly legal and financial experts, and advertise their services before opening.[23] For many of these services, public schools already have an operating pro-

Table 6.2.   Charter School Regulations

	School District Collective Bargaining Agreements	*Facilities Funds or Other Facilities Assistance*	*Start-Up or Planning Grants*
Illinois	No	Yes, for use of school buildings	Yes, based on student enrollment
Indiana	Yes, but may seek waivers	Yes, financing from local public improvement bond bank	No
Michigan	Yes, if local school board charters	No, but low cost financing arrangements possible	No
Minnesota	No	Yes, through state grants per student	Yes, for 2 years capped or per student enrollment
New York	Yes, if conversion charter	Yes, for use of vacant state buildings	Yes, through Charter School Stimulus Fund
Ohio	Yes, if conversion charter	Yes, through loans under the Facilities Loan Guarantee Program	Yes, from Community School Revolving Fund
Pennsylvania	No	Yes, for use of buildings approved by the state department of education	Yes, at state level
Wisconsin	Yes, if charter school is a district school	No	No

Source: ECS Charter School Profiles (www.ecs.org), retrieved February 8, 2011.

cedure. As the final column of Table 6.2 shows, only a few states provide start-up grants to help charters develop their procedures.[24] Additionally, some charter schools may lack the administrative staff needed to take advantage of federal and state grants to offset development costs.[25]

Such differences in sources and regulations will lead to different organizational forms. For example, if charter schools must meet certain educational standards to satisfy their contracts, they may underinvest in resources, such as libraries, that are not very clearly linked directly to achievement.[26] Alternatively, if charter schools must spend more on facilities and so have less money for staffing, they may hire less experienced or qualified teachers.[27] Most importantly, charter schools may be less likely to provide education for high-need populations.[28] As Miron and Nelson found, in Michigan many charter schools "specialize in low-cost, basic elementary education, with few students requiring special education services."[29] This decision is expressly motivated by incentives in the funding formula.

These issues are pertinent not only across public and charter schools, but also within the charter school sector. Perhaps the most notable feature of Table 6.2 is the significant variation in regulations across states. Charter schools are not uniform and so do not all incur the same costs. Using national data from 1999-2000, Bodine et al. have found significant differences among charter schools in teacher quality, student-staff ratios, length of the school day, and propensity to unionize.[30] An analysis of the 1999-2000 Schools and Staffing Survey by Fuller et al. revealed that conversion charter schools, which are more like traditional public schools, have greater access to public funding than do start-up charter schools.[31] As a result, conversion charter schools, on average, offer higher teacher salaries and employ more credentialed teachers and fewer part-time teachers. Miron found that EMOs may be better prepared to access capital funds than other types of charter schools.[32]

All of these differences may be attributable to the regulations across states, the types of students served, and the charter school's origin (conversion versus start-up school). Therefore, even if a district believes that it has funded one charter school optimally, the funding amount may not apply appropriately to other charter schools.[33]

Evidence on Optimal Funding for Charter Schools

We now turn to the evidence on whether charter schools—at least on average—are funded comparably to public schools.

Nationally, studies find that charter schools are funded at levels slightly below those for local public schools.[34] These studies typically look only at public funding, however, not total funding from all sources. Moreover, this overall conclusion may mask within-state differences. For New York, Huerta and d'Entremont reported that charter schools are underfunded relative to local public schools. However, the difference is probably small: Jacobowitz and Gyurko calculated that the disparity may be only 5%-10% of total public funding.[35] For Michigan, Miron and Nelson reported that although charter schools do receive less public funding, the types of students served by Michigan charters more than compensates for the difference.[36] For Indiana, Plucker et al. found no significant differences in how charter schools allocate resources.[37] The situation appears significantly different in Dayton, Ohio, where Hassel et al. studied the 2001-02 finances of ten community or charter schools. There, after adjusting for some enrollment and district characteristics, they found that the charters received over 25% less funding than local public schools.[38] And finally, in Philadelphia, charter school costs are higher, which may perhaps be because of contracts with EMOs.[39]

Unless there are regulatory caps on the number of charter schools, it may be appropriate to infer that where there are few charter schools, this must mean that there is not a sufficient incentive for them to open. That is, potential charter school entrepreneurs perceive that the returns to opening a school are too low. Similarly, in states where charter school growth has been fast, this indicates that the funding formula is sufficiently generous (or even overly generous).

FUNDING AND INCENTIVES FOR OTHER FORMS OF SCHOOL CHOICE

Many of the financing issues raised above in relation to charter schools are relevant to any form of school choice. Each form of school choice is different, however, and therefore this section highlights financing issues for three other choice models: private schools made available through voucher or tuition tax credits; interdistrict school choice; and home-schooling.

Vouchers and Private Schooling

School choice systems may promote private schooling. One such approach is to provide students with vouchers that provide funding directly to whichever school enrolls a student. As of 2011, there are three formal, publicly funded voucher programs operating across the United States: in Milwaukee, Wisconsin; Cleveland, Ohio; and statewide in Florida. A fourth program, in Washington, DC, began in 2004 but was stopped in 2010.

In 1990, Milwaukee introduced the nation's first voucher program: the Milwaukee Parental Choice Program. The program was initially limited to low-income families comprising no more than 1% of Milwaukee Public School students, but the cap was subsequently lifted. Initially only nonreligious schools could participate in the program, but this restriction, too, was lifted in 1998. As of 2011, 102 schools and 20,300 students were enrolled in the program. The voucher was initially $2,446 in 1990; in 2011, it had reached $6,442. In comparison, per-pupil funding for public schools across the state of Wisconsin was $10,550 (including transportation).

The Cleveland Scholarship and Tutoring Program was introduced in 1995. Children residing in the Cleveland Municipal School District received vouchers allowing them to attend any participating private school, with low-income families given preference. Again, the voucher amount was significantly below per-pupil funding in the local school district: for low-income families, the voucher amount was $2,250; for families with incomes above 200% of the poverty line, the amount was $1,875. Progressively, the maximum value of the voucher was raised o $3,450. Across Ohio, average per-student spending is now $10,510 in 2009-10.

The Florida Opportunity Scholarship Program was established in 1999: schools that receive a grade of F for 2 out of 4 years must either allow their students to move to another public school or provide them with a voucher to attend a private school. The voucher's value is up to $4,500 in comparison to public school funding of $6,300 (most recent year for comparison, 2006). Almost all the 1,400 participating students are in the high school grades. Finally, the D.C. Opportunity Scholarship Program, introduced in 2004 but stopped in 2010, was the first federal government initiative to fund K-12 education for low-income families residing in the DC public school district. In its final year, the Washington voucher amount was $7,500 in comparison to public school funding of $12,100.

These voucher programs are clearly new incentives for private schools, since they provide public funds for schools that would otherwise have none. However, in each program the value of the voucher is far less than the average per-pupil expenditure in the local school district (even if transportation costs are subtracted). Therefore, it is unlikely that these programs will expand school choice options significantly. These amounts simply are not a large enough incentive to attract existing private schools or to generate new ones. Of course, lesser voucher amounts may nevertheless be optimal from the governmental perspective. Providing vouchers to all private school students will inevitably benefit some families who would otherwise have paid for private schooling themselves; for these families, vouchers act as a straight subsidy and neither change behavior nor encourage an expanded set of school choice options. Thus, voucher funding requires a trade-off: without sufficient funding, schools will not accept vouchers; however, if the funding is too generous, too many families will receive windfall subsidies for going to private school. A low-value voucher may therefore expand school choice slightly, without generating a large fiscal deficit.

In some respects, funding for special education operates as a voucher system: student need is identified, and funding for it may be portable across public and private institutions. Individual evaluations determine that a student has particular needs (specified in an Individualized Education Plan); funds for services follow the child, so families may choose any institution capable of providing necessary services. The funding system in this case should be fairly straightforward. However, financial incentives do influence identification and placement rates: greater amounts of funding per child are associated with higher placement rates.[40] In most states, private institutions play only a very limited role in special education, although Florida has an explicit voucher program. Since 2001, its McKay program has been providing vouchers to children with disabilities so that they can attend private schools. In 2009-2010, total funding was $139 million across 20,930 students. But the values of the vouchers range from about $4,700 to $19,130, depending on the child's disabilities, with an average amount of $7,100. Thus, there is considerable variation in the resources a school might be allocated for each student.[41]

Tax codes offer another way to encourage private school choice. Specifically, states can provide tax exemptions either for private schools or for families' expenses for educational items. Such exemptions may be offered through taxable status, tax deductions or tax credits.[42] For example, private schools are considered not-for-profit and therefore do not have to pay taxes; they may also benefit from using church spaces, which provides a number of other tax incentives.

A tax policy that has recently grown more popular is the allowance of tuition tax credits, which permit families to subtract a portion of private school tuition costs from the amount of taxes they owe.[43] (Tax deductions work differently, allowing families to deduct some private schools costs from the amount of their taxable income.) Since 1997, seven states have enacted tuition tax credits for education (Arizona, Florida, Georgia, Illinois, Iowa, Minnesota, and Pennsylvania). Thus far, the credit amounts are often small (typically less than $1,000) and phased out as family income goes up. Nevertheless, they are another way in which the government may finance alternative school choices.

Homeschooling

Homeschooling is growing in popularity.[44] As is true for other school options, the rate of homeschooling varies significantly across states: as of 2004, home-schooling enrollments were estimated at 1,000 in Michigan (less than 0.1% of public school enrollment); 14,600 in Minnesota (1.7%); 23,900 in Pennsylvania (1.3%); and 21,300 in Wisconsin (2.4%). (These figures are likely to be underestimates, as the most recent national data (from 2007) indicates home-schooling has grown since 2004. Some of this variation undoubtedly reflects the incentives embedded in state and district policies.

Generally, home-schooling families receive no public funding for their children's education, so at first they may appear at a considerable financial disadvantage compared to families choosing other options. However, homeschoolers are allowed to use public school resources: in fact, they are entitled to use public school resources on a part-time or temporary basis, and legally they cannot be denied access to the public school system. Although data is sparse, it is believed that many homeschoolers do use public school resources, either temporarily or part time. Such use is most probably for expensive programs, such as sciences, and for physical education (which requires large spaces). Moreover, some homeschoolers enroll in cyber-charter schools, which means they receive direct support from the district or state. In additions, some states allow home-schooling families to claim increased tax credits and tax deductions. Whether these forms of support are sufficient to allow home-schooling families to offer adequate education is unknown; no research exists on the optimal resources needed for homeschooling.

As with other choice forms, the incentive to homeschool also depends on regulations that home-schooling families must satisfy: the more regulations, the higher the cost and the less desirable the option. Home-schooling regulations vary from state to state but may include notification to districts of the intent to homeschool; submission of plans for educating their children; and test taking. Still, these are far less burdensome that the regulations faced by public schools, charter schools, or private schools. Moreover, compliance with home-schooling regulations is unverified, and enforcement is often weak. In terms of regulations, then, homeschooling enjoys a greater incentive than choice or traditional public schools.

Calculating the optimal amount of public funding needed for home-schooling is difficult, however, because resources for homeschooling are very different from those for schools. For example, one of the parents (typically the mother) instructs the children, which means that parent does not work outside the home. Hence, the full "opportunity cost" for home-schooling families includes not only the loss of public school resources but also the parent's lost income. Estimating the lost income is difficult. While the parent's predicted earnings can be reasonably calculated, it would also be necessary to calculate the intrinsic rewards of teaching one's children (as opposed to working in an office, for example). Home-schooling parents may also acquire other resources at different prices than schools pay. For example, many home-schooling families draw on community resources, such as libraries and churches, for learning materials and curricula. As yet, no rigorous estimate of home-schooling costs to the state has been calculated.

A related form of home-based education is cyber schooling. In most states, cyber schools are funded just like charter schools, although they are perhaps closer to homeschooling. Importantly, cyber schools have operating costs that are substantially different from regular schools.[45] They do not, for example, incur transportation costs, although they often allocate students a laptop computer for home use.

As for other choice options, it is important to compare costs for cyber schools against costs for local public schools. One approach to financing cyber schools is to set funding as a percentage of regular funding and then progressively manipulate the percentage. In California, for examples, the cyber charter law initially set funding at 90% of that for regular schools, then later reduced the percentage to 70%. Subsequent revisions were tied to expenditures on "certified staff salaries and benefits" as well as on "instruction-related items." Homeschool cyber charters were expected to progress to a point where they spent at least 50% of their revenues on certified staff and salaries; nearly half of them failed to meet this threshold.

However, an additional funding issue in cyber schools is that they may have volatile enrollments that can create an insupportable funding commitment. An illustrative case is that of Western Pennsylvania Cyber Charter School. This school expanded enrollments to more than 1,000 within a few years of opening, but local school districts were unwilling to remit the per-pupil funds based on these enrollment claims, in part because the districts could not be certain that the students were part of their populations. Such situations are exacerbated when states have weak accountability systems for cyber schools.

Finally, a critical issue in evaluating how to fund these school choice options is the ability to ensure that a given amount of funding translates into a given quality of education. Given the paucity of research on the quality of either home-schooling or cyber-schooling, it is hard to establish what amount of public funding is optimal.

Interdistrict and Intradistrict School Choice

Finally, interdistrict and intradistrict school choice expands educational options for students while keeping them in traditional school systems. For example, in 1996 Michigan adopted an interdistrict choice program (Schools of Choice) that allows students to choose public schools outside their home district. School districts can determine whether to accept nonresident students, but they cannot prohibit their students from choosing a school in an alternative district. Approximately 80,000 students across the state are involved in the program.[46] Intradistrict, or "open enrollment," programs that allow students to choose among schools within a district are also becoming more common. For example, the Chicago Public School district offers students considerable choice.

It may be relatively easy to develop funding formulas for inter- and intradistrict choice. Every year, many thousands of students transfer across districts, with the fiscal consequences fairly easily absorbed.[47]

When education is funded at the local level, however, transfers can generate a significant strain on the local tax base if sufficient funds don't follow students from district to district. Also, the amount of funding per school within a district may vary (for magnet schools or remedial schools, for example). Such funding differences may be attributable to the factors considered above: differences in student populations, the use of particular resources, the prices of those resources, the availability of alternative funding sources (federal funding for magnet schools, for example), and services these schools might provide (transportation, for example). At the same time, intradistrict schools share the same administrative, managerial, and governance structures. Therefore, the absolute differences in costs may be smaller than for other forms of school choice.

CONCLUSION

Appropriate financial incentives are those that reward desirable outcomes and penalize undesirable outcomes. This is as true for education and school choice as for any other government service. Designing an incentive system, then, involves as a first essential step making decisions about which school choice reforms are desirable and which are not. Such decisions are beyond the scope of this chapter. Instead, the focus here has been to highlight various issues involved in designing funding formulas and financing mechanisms, given the assumption that incentives can be created to promote school choice.

While the issues are many, the central question is: Do choice schools receive enough public resources compared to traditional public schools to give them real incentive to offer students places? Simply, if the incentives are strong enough, more types of schools will emerge to offer more places.

Based on this review of the evidence we make the following recommendations for policymakers or funding agencies. As we show below, these recommendations may not always cohere with each other, creating a set of trade-offs.

- When funding school choice options, find the closest comparison school and examine the amount of resource that school receives. These comparisons should be made based on the characteristics of the students served, the location of the school, and the specific services that are being provided by the new school choice options.
- Recognize that school choice options will have different costs relative to traditional public schools. Costs also vary among various choice options (charter schools compared to homeschooling, for example). Such variation will exist even within a state. Policymakers

must appreciate these differences and consider the implications for funding allocations.

- Consider school funding in terms of opportunity costs. That is, a private school may receive a voucher worth more than it costs the school to educate that student. But the voucher program may still be a good policy decision for the state if the alternative—offering the student a place in a public school—would be more expensive.

The challenge is to try to fund school choice options equitably while recognizing real cost differentials. One approach is to directly investigate specific resources each school type requires and estimating their costing. Another is to examine the schools' year-end balances to see whether the choice incentives appear too strong or too weak. A third approach is to expand school choice options incrementally, progressively strengthening incentives to encourage more options and optimal choice conditions.

Other recommendations include:

- Take into account the full set of revenues that school choice options may have available.
- Consider directly the fiscal consequences of school choice, without a presumption that all schools should be funded equally.
- Mandate accountability and regularly monitor all forms of school choice (as well as traditional public schools).

A related set of recommendations are relevant for journalists, researchers and analysts who wish to compare funding across diverse forms of school choice:

- Realize that funding formulas are complex, with funding from many agencies and according to various rules.
- Do not relay on absolute differences in expenditures to determine whether choice schools are adequately funded. A full cost accounting is needed to see where choice schools may be spending more or less than regular public schools.
- Consider that choice schools will have lower unit costs if they do not offer such services as transportation and special education, but may have higher costs if they have no capital for facilities.
- Remember that schools with more flexibility will have lower unit costs.

CHAPTER 7

TEACHER QUALIFICATIONS AND WORK ENVIRONMENTS ACROSS SCHOOL CHOICE TYPES

Marisa Cannata

Teachers are vital to any school: academic success depends on high quality teachers providing high quality instruction. Indeed, teachers are the most important school resource for student learning.[1] Yet the impact of school choice on teachers and teaching has received less attention than other components of school operations. This chapter reviews what is known about teacher quality across types of schools and the impact of school choice on teachers' qualifications and work environments; it includes as well the little that is known about the impact of choice on the teaching labor market.

Because increasing school choice creates options for teachers as well as students, teacher qualifications and work environments might be expected to differ across school types. Traditionally, large districts serve as the single employer of teachers within a particular geographical area.[2] Teachers who want to work in a particular community have generally had to work for a certain district, which typically has had centralized hiring, staffing, and compensation policies. With little or no competition for teachers, many districts have had few incentives to create enticing work environments. However, increasing numbers of private schools and char-

Exploring the School Choice Universe: Evidence and Recommendations
pp. 125–146
Copyright © 2012 by Information Age Publishing
All rights of reproduction in any form reserved.

ter schools have increased the number of potential employers for whom teachers may work, introducing a competitive environment for traditional public school districts. Moreover, the employment options that choice schools present may vary not only in such practical criteria as salary but also in such areas as commitment to a particular educational philosophy or curriculum. Overall, choice schools may appeal to teachers on a variety of factors. Creating more schools of choice could thus alter dynamics in the teacher labor market.

The presence of various types of schools does not necessarily mean that they are competing for the same pool of teachers, however. Choice schools may differ in their teaching forces because of teacher characteristics or school characteristics, or both. Additionally, hiring practices in choice schools may differ, also contributing to a differentiated teaching force.

This chapter explores the question of how the increasing growth of school choice has affected the teaching force to date. Specifically, this research asks:

- *How do teacher qualifications compare across schools of choice and traditional public schools?* In answer to this question, information is provided across school types on teachers' certification status, educational level, selectivity of undergraduate college, and experience. Relevant data came from both existing research and original analyses.

- *Are schools of choice creating attractive work environments for teachers?* In answer to this question, both the results of recent research and new analyses offer a sketch of how teacher community, autonomy and influence, salary, and working conditions vary across traditional public schools and choice schools.

To the extent possible given scant existing research, this chapter also explores whether hiring practices appear to differ in public, private and charter schools and whether choice has affected the teaching force in terms of attrition, retention, and competition.

METHODS AND DATA SOURCES

Findings reported below are based on both a review of the existing literature on teachers in choice schools and on original analyses using the 2007-2008 Schools and Staffing Survey (SASS).[3] SASS is administered by the National Center for Education Statistics and is the largest national sample of teachers available. The 2007-2008 SASS surveyed 38,240 public and charter school teachers and 5,999 private school teachers, as well as their schools, principals, and districts.[4] The SASS sample includes teachers from every state and so can provide representative estimates at both the state and national levels. When school and district information is linked to the teacher survey, a rich set of contextual variables is available for comparison of teacher characteristics across settings.

More specifically, the analysis compares descriptive statistics of teacher qualification measures (certification, advanced degrees, teaching experience, and college selectivity) and work environments (salary, class size, hours worked, and overall satisfaction) using the SASS data.[5] Analyses are presented for all teachers in the SASS as well as for a subpopulation of teachers in urban schools. The distinction between groups is significant because schools of choice are clustered in urban areas, which tend to have less qualified teachers and less desirable working conditions.

One indicator of teacher quality used in this analysis is college selectivity because teachers with high general ability, as measured by high test scores, are more effective at raising student achievement.[6] The selectivity of the college from which a teacher graduated is a common indicator of general ability.[7] This analysis uses the selectivity rating of a teacher's undergraduate college, which is based on average test scores and other indicators of those admitted to the college, in Barron's Profile of American Colleges. Colleges labeled "highly competitive" or "most competitive" are considered highly selective in this analysis, while those labeled "less competitive" or "noncompetitive" are considered least selective. Colleges labeled "very competitive" or "competitive" are considered moderately competitive. Only the percentages who went to highly selective or least selective colleges are shown in the tables due to space considerations. Teachers who went to "special" schools, such as art colleges, that were not given a competitiveness rating were excluded from this analysis.

The definitions of other qualifications and work environment indicators in this analysis appear in the appendix, while definitions of the various types of choice schools appear below.

Types of School Choice

As types of school choice proliferate, clarifying terminology becomes a challenge. Existing literature on teachers in choice schools employs varied terms and inconsistent definitions for different types of schools. Some existing research uses fine-grained distinctions in its categories (as in the distinction between private independent day and boarding schools) while other studies use much more general categories. For these reasons, it is necessary to clarify terms employed in this study. The following paragraphs, then, describe and define the terms used in discussing choice schools; they also explore why teacher qualifications and work structures in choice schools may differ from those in traditional public schools.

A major characteristic of many choice schools is that they are private rather than public. In this study, the general term *private school* refers to all private schools.[8] Among private school teachers, distinctions are made among those teaching in *Catholic schools*, in *other religious private schools*, or in *nonreligious private schools*.[9] While all private schools share some similarities, there are reasons to consider each of these categories separately. All private schools may hire noncertified teachers, and they are free from district and state oversight. All also have freedom to define their goals and philosophy, possibly creating more enticing work environments. Perhaps most importantly, in addition to being exempt from state teacher certification requirements, private schools are also exempt from No Child Left Behind mandates for highly qualified teachers. Thus, private schools are not constrained by state or federal policy about whom they can hire.

On other measures, however, private schools may differ significantly among themselves. Many Catholic schools have a diocesan board or other governing hierarchy that supervises their operations, so that they lack the autonomy of many other private schools. In addition, because the mission of Catholic and other religious schools is tied to religious affiliations, these schools may attract or hire teachers from a pool of applicants somewhat different from the pool for nonreligious private schools. Another variance among private schools is participation in voucher programs. Unfortunately, the SASS data do not discriminate between private schools that do and do not accept voucher students. While some inferences about voucher schools may be made by examining the characteristics of private school teachers, it is not possible to directly compare voucher and nonvoucher private schools.

The term *charter school* refers to public charter schools.[10] When evidence on distinctions among charter schools (such as start-up or conversion schools) is available, differences are noted. A start-up charter school is a school that was newly created, while a conversion charter school is a school that previously operated as a traditional public or private school before converting to a charter school. Teacher qualifications and work environments in charter schools may be affected by greater flexibility in staffing policies. Moreover, charters may also design a school around a particular mission, creating the possibility that they will attract a different pool of teacher applicants. Further, charter schools usually have no collectively bargained contracts or other teacher union agreements, which may also influence teacher work environments and school staffing policies.

An important distinction among charters is that some are linked to homeschooling, as reflected in the categories *charter schools with a home-*

school focus and *charter schools without a homeschool focus.*[11] Non-classroom-based charters offer some information about teacher qualifications and work environments associated with homeschooling, about which little is known generally. However, for the purposes of this study, it is important to note that the data available pertain only to the teachers who oversee home-schooled students—it does not indicate the qualifications of the person/s directly providing instruction. (While 11 states require that a certified teacher supervise home-schooled students or approve their curriculum,[12] most of the instruction for home-schooled students is actually provided by nonschool personnel, such as a parent. Nine states place requirements on the parent, usually to have a high school diploma or equivalent.) It is also important to note that many home-schooled students are not enrolled in charter schools but are supervised or sponsored by a public school district, and so their experience is not reflected here. Also clouding the picture is that many charters are cyber or virtual schools rather than traditional home-based schools.[13] Given these variations, data presented in this study—which apply only to school-based personnel in charter schools—should not be considered an indication of the quality of instruction provided to all home-schooled students.

The terms *public school* and *public school choice* refer to any district-run, noncharter, public schools and choices; included here are magnet schools, district choice plans, and traditional public schools. Such an inclusive definition was necessary because earlier research rarely provides enough detail to determine whether these forms of public school choice were excluded from comparison groups designated "public schools." While charter schools are also publicly funded schools and are thus a form of school choice within the public sector, they are separately categorized and discussed because their operations and governance tend to be significantly different from that of the other schools grouped here.

The term *magnet school* refers to a public school that has a magnet program or that has a special program emphasis. Two characteristics of magnet schools may produce differences in their teacher qualifications and work environments. First, magnet schools often receive extra money from federal programs or foundations, which may help provide more resources or otherwise improve working conditions. Second, the special emphasis of a magnet school may serve as a unique attractor for high quality teachers or high quality principals, who then contribute to a positive school culture and foster a strong professional community. However, while magnet schools may thus have higher quality teachers self-select into them, their specialized focus may also repel teachers who do not agree with the mission. Thus, creating a new magnet program in an existing school or district may lead to teacher turnover. Because magnet school teachers remain part of the public school teaching force, other elements of the magnet school work environment may be less variable: a district may use the same salary schedule, union contracts, and staffing policies across all of its schools, including magnets.

District choice plans may include one of several types of public school choice. This may include open enrollment in which districts have a public school choice program that allows students to attend either their assigned school or another school in the same district or interdistrict choice programs which either allow their students to attend schools in other districts at no cost or allow students from other districts to attend their district at no cost. The competition for students induced by open enrollment or interdistrict choice may spur schools to focus on attracting and retaining high quality teachers. However, staffing practices in these districts and programs remain similar to those in traditional public schools because the districts retain a traditional governance structure. Indeed, some districts participate in open enrollment or interdistrict choice only because of state mandates. Due to the overlap in the districts with open enrollment interdistrict choice programs, this analysis is not able to distinguish between them.

The term *traditional public schools* refers to public schools offering no choice options. That is, the term refers to public schools that are neither charter nor magnet, in districts offering neither open enrollment nor interdistrict choice.

HOW DO TEACHER QUALIFICATIONS COMPARE ACROSS SCHOOLS OF CHOICE AND TRADITIONAL PUBLIC SCHOOLS?

Certification and Education

Previous literature indicates differences in the certification and education of teachers across private schools. Public schools have the most certified teachers (nearly all), followed by Catholic schools and then by other private schools.[14] Catholic elementary teachers are less likely to have a master's degree than public elementary teachers, but there is no such difference between Catholic and public secondary teachers.[15] A study focusing on magnet high schools, however, found that magnet school teachers have more education than Catholic school teachers.[16] Teachers in independent private schools, however, are more likely to have a master's degree than public school teachers.[17] An exception to this generality appeared in the Cleveland voucher program, where an evaluation found that public schools and participating private schools had equal numbers of certified teachers, but that the private school teachers had less education.[18]

Existing literature also finds that charter schools have fewer certified teachers and less educated teachers than public schools,[19] although the relative number of certified teachers varies among charter schools. Conversion charter schools have more certified teachers than start-up charters.[20] Among non-classroom-based charter schools, home-study schools have certified teacher rates similar to those in public schools; however, other non-classroom-based charter schools have fewer certified teachers.[21] The percentage of teachers with a master's degree also varies among charter schools, with some charter schools having high rates of teachers with advanced degrees and others having very few such teachers.[22]

The original analyses reveal that teachers in traditional public schools and in public choice schools have similar levels of certification and education (see Table 7.1). There is some evidence that teachers in urban magnet schools are more likely to have at least a master's degree than teachers

Table 7.1.   Percent Teachers With Certification or at Least a Master's Degree

School Type	All Schools			Urban Schools Only		
	Certified	Master's Degree	N	Certified	Master's Degree	N
Private (all)	51.4%**	38.0%**	5,999	51.4%**	40.6%**	2,334
Private, Catholic	71.32*	38.8*	2,379	66.9*	42.0	1,015
Private, other religious	40.8*	32.2*	2,426	44.9*	34.9*	852
Private, nonreligious	43.4*	46.1	1,194	40.0*	47.4	467
Charter (all)	84.6**	35.9**	1,237	82.4**	35.3**	685
Charter, no home-school focus	85.0*	35.2*	1,144	83.0*	35.1*	629
Charter, home-school focus	77.4*	49.7	93	74.3*	37.7	56
Public noncharter (all)	96.8	52.2	37,003	96.2	53.3	7,985
Magnet	96.1	55.0	2,810	96.5	56.9*	1,457
Public district choice	96.6	52.5	19,170	96.3	54.8	4,807
Traditional public	97.3	51.3	15,023	95.6	46.0	1,721

Note: Original analysis by the author using the 2007-08 Schools and Staffing Survey.
*Statistically significant difference from "traditional public" schools. **Statistically significant difference from "Public noncharter (all)" schools.

in traditional public schools. Teachers in private and charter schools, however, are much less likely to have certification or a master's degree than teachers in traditional public schools. This is also true when the sample is restricted only to urban schools. Charter schools, however, have more certified teachers than private schools. Interestingly, teachers in nonreligious private schools are equally as likely as teachers in traditional public schools to have a master's degree. This may reflect the presence of highly educated teachers in private independent schools noted in existing literature.[23]

With the exception of the rates of certification among charter schools with a home-schooling focus, these findings are consistent with the existing literature. A previous study on home-study charter schools in California found they have rates of certified teachers similar to those in public schools. While the new analyses presented here indicate charter schools with a home-schooling focus have relatively high rates of certified teachers, they still have fewer than traditional public schools. The difference may be due to differing regulations around homeschooling and charter schools. Eleven states require at least some of their home-schooled students to be supervised by a certified teacher, leading to high rates of teacher certification in these states. In other states, charter schools with a home-schooling focus may be caught between regulations governing homeschooling and those governing charter schools. Many home-schooling focused charter schools may be virtual or cyber schools. For example, Wisconsin does not require students in a home-based educational program to be instructed by a certified teacher.[24] Yet a recent court ruling found that instruction provided through a home-based virtual school under parent supervision violates teacher licensure requirements.[25]

Teaching Experience

Previous research has consistently found that charter school teachers have fewer years of experience than their peers in public schools.[26] Although many charter schools are new schools, the average years of experience of charter school teachers has stayed constant over time.[27] There is some indication, however, that experience levels vary by charter management organizations, with teachers in nonaffiliated charter schools having teachers with similar years of experience as those in traditional public schools.[28] Further, teachers in home-study-based charter schools have years of experience similar to those for teachers in other charter schools.[29] While little is known about the relative experience of magnet teachers and traditional public school teachers, there is evidence to suggest that teachers in multifocus magnet schools are more experienced

**Table 7.2.   Average Years of Total Teaching Experience
and Percentage of Teachers With More Than 3 years of Experience**

School type	All Schools		Urban Schools Only	
	Total Experience	Teachers With More Than 3 Years Experience	Total Experience	Teachers With More Than 3 Years
Private (all)	13.4	79.0%**	13.5	79.4%
Private, Catholic	15.2*	83.0	15.0	82.4
Private, other religious	12.5*	75.9*	12.8	78.3
Private, nonreligious	12.8	78.7*	12.5	77.0
Charter (all)	8.2**	66.2**	8.2**	67.6**
Charter, no home-school focus	8.2*	66.2*	8.2*	67.8*
Charter, home-school focus	8.8*	65.9*	7.7*	64.6*
Public noncharter (all)	13.7	83.4	13.7	82.1
Magnet	13.3	83.2	13.5	83.5
Public district choice	13.8	83.3	13.7	81.7
Traditional public	13.7	83.6	13.6	82.1

Note: Original analysis by the author using the 2007-08 Schools and Staffing Survey.
*Statistically significant difference from "traditional public" schools. **Statistically significant difference from "Public noncharter (all)" schools.

than teachers in single-focus magnet schools.[30] When making comparisons between private and public school teachers, Catholic school teachers have less experience than public school teachers, and non-Catholic private school teachers have even fewer years of experience than Catholic school teachers.[31]

According to the SASS data, teachers in charter schools, both with and without a home-schooling focus, have the fewest years of teaching experience across charter, private, and public schools (see Table 7.2). Among forms of public school choice, there is little difference in the experience levels of teachers. Overall, private school teachers have similar years of experience as noncharter public schools, but this masks variation within the private sector. Catholic schools have somewhat more experienced teachers while private schools with other religious affiliations have less experienced teachers. Teachers in non-Catholic and nonreligious private schools are less likely to be experienced teachers than teachers in traditional public schools, but these differences are not present when the sample is restricted to urban schools. Within urban schools, only charter schools have fewer experienced teachers than traditional public schools.

College Selectivity

The existing literature on the types of colleges from which teachers graduate indicates that generally, teachers in private schools and charter schools come from more selective colleges.[32] This is particularly true of teachers in private independent schools. Catholic school teachers, however, graduated from undergraduate colleges of similar selectivity as those attended by public school teachers.[33] Further, the overall findings for charter schools may mask variability among charter schools, as some charter management organizations appear to have teachers from less selective colleges.[34]

Table 7.3. Percentage of Teachers who Graduated From Highly Selective and Less Selective Colleges

School Type	All Schools		Urban Schools Only	
	Highly Selective College	Less Selective College	Highly Selective College	Less Selective College
Private (all)	15.4%**	20.5%**	16.9%**	20.12%**
Private, Catholic	8.4	25.0	8.5	25.9
Private, other religious	12.3*	21.3	16.3	18.2
Private, nonreligious	28.6*	13.6*	29.8*	14.4*
Charter (all)	10.7	22.1	11.3	20.9
Charter, no home-school focus	10.9	21.8	11.6	20.1
Charter, home-school focus	6.3	27.4	7.1	32.6
Public noncharter (all)	9.2	24.1	10.9	25.3
Magnet	13.3*	23.5	11.8	24.9
Public district choice	9.3	25.4	11.4	23.9
Traditional public	8.4	22.5	9.0	29.7

Note: Original analysis by the author using the 2007-08 Schools and Staffing Survey.
Estimates are not shown due to small sample size in subpopulation. *Statistically significant difference from "traditional public" schools. ** Statistically significant difference from "Public noncharter (all)" schools.

Table 7.3 reports original analyses that indicate notable differences in the selectivity of colleges from which teachers across various forms of school choice graduated. Teachers in nonreligious private schools are most likely to have graduated from highly selective colleges and the least likely to have graduated from less selective colleges. This is true among all schools and among schools in urban areas only. Otherwise, there were few differences in the percentage of teachers from various types of schools that graduated from highly selective or least selective colleges. Teachers in magnet schools and non-Catholic religious private schools were slightly more likely to have graduated from a highly selective college, but this difference was not significant when comparing only urban schools.

ARE SCHOOLS OF CHOICE CREATING ATTRACTIVE WORK ENVIRONMENTS FOR TEACHERS?

Working Conditions

One way schools of choice offer a unique work environment is by focusing on a particular school mission. As public schools must serve a diverse constituency, they are less able to define a specific school focus. Many charter schools, for example, cater to a specific educational niche and attract teachers who want to serve that niche. Indeed, studies of charter school teachers find they value the mutual selection process of school choice and want to work in a school that shares their goals or has like-minded colleagues.[35] Likewise, Catholic school teachers are often drawn to their schools because of an interest in the school's religious mission.[36]

Teachers may also be attracted to schools of choice because of the greater sense of community and collegiality than is found in traditional public schools. There is some evidence that charter, private, and magnet schools have higher levels of professional community than traditional public schools,[37] and that charters in particular attract teachers who want to work in an innovative atmosphere with a strong professional culture.[38] Other studies, however, have found more mixed results for the collegiality within choice schools[39]—which may be due to the lack of time for collaboration in some choice schools.[40] Although charter schools have slightly higher levels of professional community than public schools, in-school processes that lead to strong communities are similar in charter and public schools.[41]

Many forms of school choice, including private, charter, and magnet schools, give teachers more autonomy and independence within their classrooms.[42]This is not true for all schools of choice, however. Two studies of teachers in charter and public schools in Colorado find conflicting results in terms of the relative autonomy charter school teachers experience.[43]

There is mixed evidence about whether choice schools also offer teachers more influence in the schoolwide arena. Charter schools, private schools, and single-focus magnet school involve teachers in schoolwide decision making and curriculum.[44] Other studies, however, have found that teachers in charter and deregulated public schools did not necessarily have more influence on school governance and policy than their peers in traditional public schools.[45] Further, some studies have found charter school teachers actually have less influence over schoolwide decisions than public school teachers.[46]

Working conditions vary among different types of schools as well as among schools in the same sector.[47] Private schools consistently have smaller classes compared to public schools,[48] with the exception of private schools participating in Cleveland's private school voucher program, which had larger classes than the public schools.[49] Evidence concerning relative class size in charter and public schools is mixed,[50] perhaps because of differences between grade levels. One report suggests that charter schools have smaller elementary classes than public schools, but similar or larger class sizes in high schools.[51] The relative class size in magnet schools compared to nonmagnet public schools also varies depending on the grade levels in the school.[52] Non-classroom-based charter schools appear to have the largest student-teacher ratio, but teachers report spending an average of only 4.5 hours per month with each student.[53]

Besides class size, other working conditions vary among sectors. For example, charter teachers report greater dissatisfaction with the physical facilities than teachers in public schools.[54] Staff firing policies in charter schools may be very informal, and teachers may be unable to initiate grievance procedures on such important staffing concerns as being paid on time.[55] Charter school teachers are attracted to charter schools because they have safe environments, but they are typically critical of the amount of instructional materials or planning time provided.[56] Teachers in choice schools also work longer hours and have longer school years.[57] Particularly in private independent schools, teachers work long hours with many noninstructional duties.[58]

The original analyses using the SASS data indicate that there are few differences in the working conditions of teachers among forms of public school choice (see Table 7.4). The only difference is that teachers with departmentalized instruction (usually secondary school teachers) in magnet schools and in districts with enrollment public district choice plan have larger classes while teachers in traditional public schools have smaller classes. Teachers with self-contained classes (usually elementary

Table 7.4. Average Class Size and Average Hours Worked per Week

School Type	Class Size, Self-Contained Teachers	Class Size, Departmentalized Teachers	Hours Worked Per Week
Private (all)	17.1**	18.6**	47.8**
Private, Catholic	20.9*	23.4	49.2*
Private, other religious	15.4*	17.7*	46.3*
Private, nonreligious	15.5*	14.1*	43.4*
Charter (all)	21.9**	21.7**	53.0**
Charter, no home-school focus	21.8*	21.7	51.1*
Charter, home-school focus	23.4	21.5	50.1
Public noncharter (all)	20.0	23.7	51.6
Magnet	21.2	25.0*	51.9
Public district choice	20.2*	24.6*	51.6
Traditional public	19.3	22.5	51.5

Note: Original analysis by the author using the 2007-08 Schools and Staffing Survey. *Statistically significant difference from "traditional public" schools. **Statistically significant difference from "Public noncharter (all)" schools.

teachers) in districts with a public district choice plan also have some larger classes than teachers in districts with a choice plan.

More differences appear, however, in the working conditions of private and charter school teachers as compared to those of traditional public school teachers. Departmentalized teachers in charter schools and private schools have smaller class sizes than traditional public school teachers. Charter and Catholic school teachers in self-contained classes have larger classes than their peers in traditional public schools, while other private school teachers have smaller classes. In contrast to previous research findings on teachers in private independent schools, this analysis finds that teachers in private schools also work fewer hours per week than traditional public school teachers.

Salary and Satisfaction

Salaries also vary among the different types of schools (Table 7.5). Charter school teachers earn less than their peers in public schools with similar credentials and experience.[59] Although charter schools are less likely than districts to use a standard salary schedule, their salary structures are still quite similar to district salary schedules, with education and

Table 7.5.   **Average School-Related Earnings**

School Type	All Teachers	First Year Teachers	Teachers With 10-15 Years Experience
Private (all)	$34,361**	$24,300**	$35,549**
Private, Catholic	35,656*	25,468*	34,349*
Private, other religious	29,586*	21,468*	31,971*
Private, nonreligious	40,223*	28,504*	42,312*
Charter (all)	40,912**	35,579	46,151**
Charter, no home-school focus	40,860*	35,486	46,326*
Charter, home-school focus	41,884*	#	#
Public noncharter (all)	50,658	38,055	51,006
Magnet	52,895	41,108*	52,092
Public district choice	50,108	37,685	50,802
Traditional public	50,856	37,860	51,053

Note: Original analysis by the author using the 2007-08 Schools and Staffing Survey. #Estimates are not shown due to small sample size in subpopulation. * Statistically significant difference from "traditional public" schools. **Statistically significant difference from "Public noncharter (all)" schools.

experience being the largest contributors to a teacher's salary.[60] Other research suggests that charter schools have more flexibility to adjust to market conditions in the competition for teachers[61] or are more likely to experiment with merit pay.[62] Within the charter school sector, salaries and benefits may vary. Charter schools that converted from existing schools spend more per pupil on teacher salaries and benefits than newly created schools.[63] However, newly created charter schools are more likely than conversion charters to provide bonuses for teachers in certain subject areas or for teachers with National Board for Professional Teaching Standards certification.[64] Private school teachers earn the lowest salaries[65] and teachers in public schools cite pay and benefits as the reason they are not working in private schools.[66]

The original analyses show that teachers in charter and private schools earn lower salaries than do traditional public school teachers. However, average salaries mask differences due to real salary gaps and differences due to teacher experience levels.[67] As indicated in Table 7.6, charter school teachers also have less experience; thus it is not surprising that they earn lower salaries. It is more appropriate to compare the average salaries of teachers with common qualifications across school types. Among first year teachers, private school teachers continue to earn substantially lower salaries than public school teachers. First year charter

Table 7.6. Average Overall Satisfaction

School Type	Overall Satisfaction[1]
Private (all)	3.7**
Private, Catholic	3.6*
Private, other religious	3.7*
Private, nonreligious	3.6*
Charter (all)	3.4**
Charter, no home-school focus	3.4*
Charter, home-school focus	3.4
Public noncharter (all)	3.5
Magnet	3.4*
Public district choice	3.5*
Traditional public	3.6

Note: Original analysis by the author using the 2007-08 Schools and Staffing Survey. *Statistically significant difference from "traditional public" schools. **Statistically significant difference from "Public noncharter (all)" schools. [1]Overall satisfaction is the extent to which a teacher agreed (on a one-to-four scale) with the statement "I am generally satisfied with being a teacher at this school." 1 = *Strongly disagree*; 4 = *Strongly agree*.

school teachers, however, earn similar salaries to their peers in traditional public schools. Among experienced teachers, both charter and private school salaries continue to lag behind teachers in noncharter public schools. There is considerable variation in salaries among types of private schools, with teachers in nonreligious private schools earning about $7,000-$11,000 more than teachers in non-Catholic religious private schools.[68]

Overall, the existing literature indicates teachers across all schools appear satisfied with their school environments.[69] This may be due to self-selection as teachers seek out types of schools that can provide what they want.[70] Charter school teachers are satisfied with many aspects of their school, including their relationships with their colleagues, the professional environment, and the educational philosophy of their schools, but are dissatisfied with the facilities, the relationships with the district and union, and the lack of grievance procedures.[71]

Despite lower salaries, teachers in private schools report higher levels of overall satisfaction than their peers in traditional public schools, perhaps because of smaller class size or shorter hours evident in the SASS data.[72] Charter school teachers appear slightly less satisfied with their jobs as traditional public school teachers. There are also differences among forms of public school choice, with teachers in magnets expressing less satisfaction and teachers in districts with public district choice plans expressing more satisfaction than teachers in traditional public schools.

DO SCHOOLS OF CHOICE USE DIFFERENT HIRING PRACTICES THAN TRADITIONAL PUBLIC SCHOOLS?

Schools of choice and traditional public schools may use different hiring practices and so may recruit different teaching personnel. Overall, there is little research on the hiring practices of school leaders in choice schools, with only one study exploring how hiring preferences differ between charter and traditional public schools and finding few differences.[73] One notable difference is that charter school principals appear to place more importance on hiring teachers who are willing to take on extra responsibilities. Slightly more studies have compared charter and public school hiring processes and personnel practices. Charter school principals are more likely to experiment with personnel policies and use a wider array of recruitment strategies.[74] Charter school teachers are more likely than public school teachers to have had an interview at the school before they were hired; however, that interview tended to be only with the principal.[75] Charter school teachers also submitted a broader range of materials in their applications,[76] and charter school principals were willing to hire uncertified teachers if they had other desired attributes.[77] That willingness is somewhat surprising given the mandate for Highly Qualified Teachers in No Child Left Behind for both charter and public schools. Private schools, on the other hand, do not have such hiring restrictions, which may explain the finding that fewer private school teachers are certified.

WHAT IS THE IMPACT OF INCREASING SCHOOL CHOICE ON THE TEACHER LABOR MARKET?

Teacher Attrition and Retention

Previous research suggests that charter schools have higher attrition than public schools,[78] although one study suggests the difference may be due to characteristics of teachers and their schools.[79] The high turnover rate may also be a function of high dismissal rates, as charter schools dismiss a higher proportion of teachers than both public and private schools.[80] Private school teachers also have higher attrition than public schools, perhaps because they are more likely to plan on teaching for only a few years.[81]

There is mixed evidence about the fluidity of teachers' movement between school types when they move to new schools. Some evidence suggests that teachers are open to moving between schools of choice and a public school. Two thirds of teachers in private independent schools would consider working in a public school, and one third began their careers in a public school before moving to an independent school.[82] Teachers in public schools, however, were most likely to have spent their whole career in a public school, even though they considered teaching in a private school.[83] One study of teacher mobility in Florida found that teachers in both charter and public schools who move are more likely to move to a public school.[84] In Ohio, however, teachers who leave charter schools appear more likely to quit teaching altogether rather than move to another school.[85]

The Impact of School Choice on Traditional Public Schools

As schools of choice increasingly compete with traditional public schools for teachers, the teacher labor market might be affected. To date, however, there is little research on this important issue. Some evidence suggests that more private school competition for teachers results in higher teacher salaries and teachers who are more effective at raising student test scores.[86] Additionally, a study of teacher mobility between charter and public schools found that the pattern of movement between sectors leads to lower quality teachers in public schools and higher quality in charter schools, the apparent result of the lower quality teachers in charter schools being likely to move to public schools.[87] Another analysis of teacher mobility patterns across school type found that of all traditional public school teachers who moved schools, those who moved to charter schools were more effective in their schools than those who moved to another traditional public school.[88] Yet, school choice appears to have had little impact on district hiring and staffing practices. Two studies found that very few public school principals said that the introduction of charter schools impaired their ability to recruit or retain teachers or affected their teacher compensation structure.[89] Similarly, only 6% of public school principals said they changed their staffing policies due to charter school competition.[90] One explanation for the limited effect of charter schools on the teacher labor market may be that the labor is segmented so that most teacher applicants do not see charter schools as an alternative, as a study focused on one metropolitan area found.[91]

DISCUSSION

Both the existing literature and these original analyses find differences in the qualifications of teachers across private, charter, and public schools. Among private schools, Catholic school teachers appear most similar to teachers in traditional public schools, while the evidence on the qualifications of teachers in magnet schools is mixed. There are some differences among the qualifications of teachers in public school choice, but they do not tell a consistent story.

Determining whether schools of choice have higher or lower quality teachers than traditional public schools requires specifying criteria for quality. The most consistent criteria in the literature include having at least three years of experience and high general ability. Even on only these two measures, the relative quality of teachers in choice schools is unclear. While choice schools do tend to have more teachers who graduated from more selective colleges, and fewer teachers from less selective colleges, they also have more inexperienced teachers.

What explains these differences? One possible explanation is that choice schools, free from restrictions on teacher certification and hiring, attract a different pool of applicants. Individuals who graduated from highly selective colleges and want to teach may find themselves unable to obtain jobs in public schools without state certification; therefore, they apply to private schools. Another explanation is that private and charter school principals actively recruit and hire teachers from more selective colleges, altering the characteristics of their teaching force regardless of the composition of the applicant pool. That Catholic school teachers look more like public school teachers may point to the importance of hiring preferences. Like all private schools, Catholic schools are legally free to hire uncertified teachers. That they hire certified teachers from less selective colleges may reflect their hiring preferences or practices, which prioritize other teacher characteristics.

In terms of working conditions, private school teachers are the most satisfied with their jobs, despite having the lowest salaries. This may be partially due to the finding in this analysis that they also have smaller class sizes and work fewer hours. Contrary to expectations, charter schools have class sizes similar to those in traditional public schools. Overall, the analysis suggests that teachers in forms of public school choice and in traditional public schools have similar work environments.

There is limited evidence that charter schools use different hiring practices than public schools, although the extent to which these differences contribute to the qualification differences is not known. There is also little known about how school choice may be affecting the teacher labor market. The evidence that does exist indicates that public schools do not experience competition for high quality teachers and make few changes in staffing policies as a result. Although charter and private schools lose teachers at higher rates than public schools, there is no strong evidence about the place of schools of choice in teacher career patterns.

CONCLUSION AND RECOMMENDATION

The literature review revealed several gaps in existing research on teachers and teaching in schools of choice. First, there is little research on how hiring practices may differ among school types, whether the differences evident in teacher qualifications are due to teacher or school decisions, or whether these differences matter for student learning.[92] While there are a few studies of hiring and staffing practices in charter and public schools, a better understanding of how private and magnet schools select staff can promote a better understanding of school staffing across school types. Second, there is little evidence on whether competition from school choice affects the overall dynamics of the labor market. The research that does exist focuses on how competition affects salaries.

In addition, the amount of research across choice schools varies, with a great deal of recent research on charter schools and limited research on private schools, home schooling, magnet schools and programs, and other forms of public school choice. There is especially sparse research on teachers in homeschools or cyberschools. Because most home-school instruction is provided by nonschool personnel, no evidence on the relative quality of such instruction is available. There is similarly sparse information about the qualifications and work environment of teachers in private voucher schools. Most evaluations of publicly funded voucher programs focus on student achievement results, not on the internal school operations. An analysis of the instructional quality in private voucher schools as compared to that in public schools would provide better insight into achievement results.

These gaps point to future areas of research on teachers in choice schools. Additional work on how school choice is affecting the labor market could help to tease out whether differences in teacher composition across school types are due to teachers self-selecting into different types of schools or to different hiring practices across school types. For example, do principals in choice schools use different hiring criteria or processes? Do similar types of teachers apply to schools in multiple sectors? Do forms of public school choice have unique staffing structures in their districts? The relative amount and type of movement of teachers between schools of choice and traditional public schools can illuminate variations in teacher career patterns across school types as well as the degree of segmentation in the teacher labor market.

More work is also needed on teachers' motivations for choosing to work in a particular type of school. Given the variation in working conditions and salary across school types, it is probable that teachers select into schools with the work environments they most value. Public school teachers, for example, may come from a pool of applicants who value the high salary and job security a public school provides. Private school teachers, on the other hand, may come from a pool of applicants who are willing to trade a lower salary for a shorter workday and a school that shares their vision for education. It is not clear if teachers would be willing to move between school types if they would still be able to get either the working conditions or salary they want.

Finally, research on the extent to which increasing competition for teachers leads traditional public school districts or private schools to change existing staffing policies or hiring practices is also needed. Teachers are central to the operations and educational success of all schools. If school choice is to have a competitive effect on traditional public schools, then that should become apparent in school operations. While there are many potential changes a school or district could make, altering the teaching force and the work that teachers do is a potentially powerful method of responding to competitive pressures from choice schools. Understanding the impact of school choice on traditional public schools requires examining how school choice affects teachers, teaching, and the teacher labor market.

Based on these findings, it is strongly recommended that extensive additional research be conducted to fill the many existing knowledge gaps exposed in this study, especially regarding the question of how school choice affects the overall teacher labor market.

APPENDIX: MEASURES OF TEACHER QUALIFICATIONS AND WORK ENVIRONMENTS

Using teacher qualifications as indicators of teacher quality is problematic, as few qualifications are consistently linked to student performance. While teacher quality is an important component of student achievement, it is hard to isolate the effects of observed characteristics.[93] Despite this limitation, some qualifications are commonly used as indicators of quality. The common indicators employed in this study include teacher certification, educational level, years of experience, and college selectivity.

Teacher certification is an important measure as it is required of all public school teachers. In this analysis, teachers are considered certified if they have a regular or standard state certificate, advanced professional certificate, certificate issued after satisfying all requirements except the completion of a probationary period, or a certificate that requires some additional coursework, student teaching, or passage of a state test before regular certification can be obtained. Teachers with certificates issued to persons who must complete a certification program in order to continue teaching (previously labeled emergency certification) are not considered certified because the highly qualified teacher provision of the No Child Left Behind Act does not include emergency certifications as Highly Qualified and because teachers with less than full certification have lower performing students.[94] Teacher educational level indicates whether the teacher has a master's degree or more.

The years of experience criteria include the total years of full or part-time teaching the teacher has accrued, in public or private schools. The percentage of teachers in their first three years of teaching is included because some research suggests that teachers become more effective in their first three years.[95]

The measures of work environments include salary, class size, hours worked per week, and overall satisfaction. Teacher salary is the total school-related earnings during the regular school year. It is the sum of academic year base teaching salary, additional compensation earned for additional activities such as coaching or tutoring, and other income from school sources such as a merit pay bonus or state supplement. It does not include salary from teaching summer school or working in a nonschool job. Gaps in average teacher salaries between school types may exist even if all schools offer similar salaries to teachers with similar qualifications, because teaching qualifications vary among schools. For this reason, salaries are also compared for teachers with similar experience levels.

The average class size for teachers is reported separately for teachers in self-contained or departmentalized settings. A self-contained setting refers to teachers who instruct the same group of students most of the day in multiple subjects, most commonly in elementary schools. A departmentalized setting refers to teachers who have several classes of different students throughout the day. Departmentalized instruction is most prominent in secondary schools, where, for example, a math teacher may instruct five different groups of students in algebra during one day. For self-contained teachers, the class size is the number of students the teacher reported in an assigned class. For departmentalized teachers, the class size is the average of the number of students the teacher reported across all assigned classes.

The hours worked per week is a teacher-reported variable that indicates the total hours spent on teaching and other school-related activities during a typical full week. Overall satisfaction is the extent to which a teacher agreed (on a 1 to 4 scale) with the statement "I am generally satisfied with being a teacher at this school."

CHAPTER 8

EDUCATIONAL INNOVATION AND DIVERSIFICATION IN SCHOOL CHOICE PLANS

Christopher Lubienski

The concept of innovation has been closely tied to the push for school choice, serving as a key rationale for such choice plans as charter schools, vouchers and other alternatives to neighborhood-based school assignment. In particular, critiques of traditional public schooling arrangements have played upon the idea that governance by districts stifles creativity and entrepreneurial ingenuity in schools. Such critiques portray a "one-size-fits-all" public education system that neglects the needs of diverse communities and individual learners—presenting a serious equity issue. Hence, according to this thinking, education should be organized under competitive models to nurture new and different instructional approaches, resulting in a range of alternatives for families. Promoters hope that with a set of real options, parents will be able to make decisions based on different curriculum and instructional approaches, rather than on, say, the racial or social-class composition of schools.

Some choice reforms—policies and movements such as charter schools, vouchers, and open enrollment plans—are specifically designed to generate competition and thereby force innovation in schools. As a result of such focused efforts, innovation may appear, not only in the new

Exploring the School Choice Universe: Evidence and Recommendations
pp. 147–165

forms of schooling, but also within competing public schools. However, important questions then arise regarding these reforms:

- To what extent do various manifestations of school choice represent innovations in policy?
- How can school choice generate innovation?
- Where do those innovations occur, and what forms do they typically take?
- What factors encourage or inhibit innovation, and what are the consequences?

This review of research notes the dual goals of innovation and diversification of options. It finds that school choice is providing alternatives in some communities, but innovations generated by competitive forces are often focused in areas where they are least likely to improve equitable access to quality education. On the other hand, many useful innovations are emerging from sources not predicted by theories that focus on competition.

The first part of this review notes the promise of innovation, highlighting its significance, but also outlining some of the conceptual difficulties that emerge when we look more deeply into the concept with regard to education. Following this overview is a typology and survey of the types of innovations born of school choice, examined in light of its promoters' high expectations. The survey identifies areas where the most innovative practices are occurring, explores how such innovation may or may not provide new options for families, and examines factors that encourage or inhibit the generation and dissemination of educational innovation. Contrary to much of the simplistic rhetoric promoting choice as a sure route to innovation and improvement, a discussion of the structures and attributes unique to education demonstrates why it resists easy analogy to innovation in other fields. The concluding discussion suggests that the most beneficial innovations may emerge from professional, rather than competitive, impulses.

THE LOGIC OF INNOVATION IN SCHOOL CHOICE

There are many expectations and promises for school choice, including community empowerment, parental satisfaction, educational entrepreneurship, and, of course, higher achievement. But a central argument of the school choice movement has been that choice will both lead to and capitalize on beneficial innovation. That is, innovation has been promoted both as goal in itself and as a necessary condition for establishing environments and incentives that will inevitably lead to the ultimate goal of increased educational quality.

Choice advocates and theoreticians have been explicit in linking more marketlike structures in school choice plans to the opportunities and incentives required to generate innovation.[1] The thinking is that provider competition and liberated consumer choice is sure to generate widespread innovation in choice schools, a picture in direct opposition to that painted of public schools, which are characterized as imposing unnecessary constraints on creativity. Few have set out this logic as clearly as Nobel Laureate economist Milton Friedman, the intellectual author of the school choice movement, who argued that public education systems "repel the imaginative and daring," leading to an "excess of conformity."[2]

Nowhere is this perspective more evident than in the charter school movement, particularly in its early assessment of the potential of charters to serve as "laboratories" or "research and development" (R&D) centers for innovative educational practices. As John Flaherty argues: "One of the foremost arguments in favor of charter schools in public education is the increase in innovation that *will surely follow* [emphasis added] from the autonomy granted to charter schools."[3] Many expect that reforms harnessing competitive pressures to attract students will lead to a flowering of different program options from which families may choose.[4] Friedman, for instance, contended that choice systems will provide "many more choices, there will be a whole rash of new schools that will come into existence. The government schools will improve, and the private school system will improve."[5] This is because competition would produce a much wider range of alternatives—unless it was sabotaged by excessively rigid standards for approval. The choice among public schools themselves would be greatly increased. And most important, new sorts of private schools could arise to tap the vast new market.[6]

Thus, most of the legislation authorizing charters is explicit about the expectation that they will produce a flow of innovation in teaching and learning.[7] As Flaherty notes, the "search for innovative teaching methods was foremost on the minds of legislators."[8]

Similar expectations are also associated with other versions of school choice, since freedom from regulation is often equated with freedom to innovate. Such is the case with private schools. The Friedman Foundation—one of the leading champions of vouchers for sending children to private schools—argues that private schools produce superior outcomes because they are unregulated:

> Private schools are good largely because they are free to innovate. Forcing
> them to use the same standards as public schools, to take mandatory tests

based on curricula chosen by the state rather than parents or to comply with unnecessary red tape, is bad news.[9]

Other forms of school choice are also associated with innovation, but in different ways. For instance, virtual or cyber schooling, which is increasingly important in areas such as home schooling, is seen as an innovative delivery mechanism, though there is no particular expectation that it will deliver innovative content. Likewise, public school choice programs, such as magnet schools and open-enrollment plans, are considered innovative in expanding the options offered to parents, but are not necessarily considered a lever to force innovation in teaching and learning.

CONCEPTUAL ISSUES REGARDING INNOVATION AND SCHOOL CHOICE

For all of the certainty that innovative practices "will surely follow" from charters and other choice plans, the core concept of innovation is actually remarkably nebulous, and often conflated with other ideas. For instance, if a school is said to be "innovative," that could mean several different things. As commonly understood, the term could indicate that the school is (a) a result of a policy innovation, such as a school created by new legislation authorizing charter or alternative schools; (b) producing innovations, such as a school creating a new pedagogical approach; or (c) adopting innovations generated elsewhere, such as a school that borrows innovative models from other schools.[10] Moreover, people often speak of "innovation" when they are actually referring to *diversification* of options in a local context.

In fact, there are different established definitions of the concept, which may contribute to the confusion in its application to school choice. A common understanding, drawing on the primary meaning of the term, is that something must be new in order to be innovative.[11] That is, innovation is the act of creating something original—for example, in the case of schooling, a novel practice or approach. However, most "new" things draw from preexisting ideas or practices. Therefore, this purist definition slights innovations that are the result of combinations of previous practices, or ideas that have been transplanted from another field. Indeed, in some sense, any change represents innovation.

A more subjective conception classifies things as innovative if they are new to a local context.[12] However, this perspective ignores well-known problems with policy borrowing (that is, transplanting policies across contexts), while expecting each local community to reinvent the wheel is also a highly inefficient use of resources. Moreover, this subjective approach conflates the idea of *innovation* with *diversification*—an important consideration with regard to school choice. Even if "innovation" may refer to the creation of a new practice, something would *appear to be new* if it has not been seen before in a local context. And, indeed, creating new options for families is one of the primary themes of school choice in general, and one of the specific goals of innovation in particular. But a subjective focus on a local context can also dilute the larger push for producing new approaches by confusing the diffusion of practices with the creation of new ones. In fact, much of the argument advancing school choice acknowledges this distinction. For example, many of the laws authorizing charter schools see them as a mechanism to encourage "different and innovative teaching methods," indicating that reformers want both innovation *and* diversification of options.[13] Hence, innovations are anticipated not simply in organizational structures, but specifically in teaching and learning.[14]

Thus, the idea of innovation is itself vague, particularly in a politicized area such as school reform. Perspectives from economics and organizational theory provide some insights into the question of how change occurs, and how it may be distinct from "innovation." For instance, Rogers highlights the notion that a practice is innovative if it appears to be novel to people in local contexts.[15] Yet this perspective may blunt the push for new innovations overall by conflating the invention of a practice with its dissemination. For example, is opening a McDonald's restaurant in a town that previously had only a Wendy's an innovation? Most people would probably say no. Although some changes may appear to be innovations in a local context, they may represent nothing new in the broader scheme of things. Indeed, change alone is not innovation. As Daft and Becker observe: "Innovation is the adoption of something new; change is the adoption of something different."[16] Organizational theorists contend that true innovation involves "at least partly exogenous support or legitimization"[17]—an issue of "valuation," where marketplace value is an indicator of innovation.[18] Theories of management tend to equate innovation with invention, since organizations pursue innovations through research and development in order to gain a competitive advantage.[19] Similarly, economists note that innovation, unlike change, "presumes a net improvement"; from an economic perspective, innovation is something that produces improvements in efficiencies and outcomes, so if there has been improvement, then innovation must have occurred.[20] The industrial organization literature perceives innovation as the keystone in a process whereby inventions/innovations are commercialized and then propagated through the market largely by way of emulation.[21]

Regardless of the specifics of the meaning, the idea of encouraging innovation through competition in education, from the perspective of policymaking on this issue, presumes two prerequisites. First, innovations must be replicable—that is, what has been found to work in one school needs to be transferable to other schools. While this may seem obvious, inasmuch as school choice also encourages diversification and specialization, more successful practices may be unique (or uniquely effective) for a particular population or community, or may not be suited to more comprehensive models of schooling common in the district sector. Secondly, there must be some mechanism to facilitate the spread of a practice. Many market advocates argue that competitors will emulate successful practices. However, this also assumes that information about innovations is available to competitors, and that they are allowed to use them. Because of problems in this regard, some have argued that competition is not itself enough to encourage innovations, but that formal networks must be constructed to help in the dissemination of innovations.[22]

Discussions of innovation through school choice plans can be remarkably vague—partly because the nature of innovation can be unpredictable, but also because there is no consensus about what innovation means, especially in its difference from diversification. The next section pursues more clarity in the discussion by offering a typology of change that can be considered innovative to varying degrees. This typology draws on the empirical record of change and innovation evident in different school choice programs, and offers a brief overview of the types of innovation typical of various school choice models.

A TYPOLOGY OF INNOVATION FOR EXAMINING SCHOOL CHOICE

To better assess the logic applied to school choice—that competition will inevitably spark educational innovation and improvement—it is important to consider the different dimensions in and through which change may occur, so that we can weigh the extent that such changes might be considered innovations, a subset of change. These dimensions include the level at which innovation is perceived (school, district or classroom level, for example); the nature of practices thought to be innovative (marketing or pedagogical strategies, for example); and how innovations are prompted and nurtured by such choice mechanisms as charter schools, open-enrollment programs, inter- and intradistrict choice, voucher plans, and home schooling and virtual or cyber schooling. By examining these issues, we can better illuminate where changes are more substantive, more symbolic, or simply nonexistent—an important notion if we are to understand factors that nurture or inhibit innovations, and to design systems in which innovation is encouraged. As described in the concluding discussion, contrary to much of the simplistic rhetoric that promotes choice as inevitably leading to innovation and improvement, structures and attributes unique to education resist easy analogies about innovation drawn from other fields.

Levels of Innovation

A substantive discussion of educational innovation requires distinguishing among policies that conceptualize innovation as input and those that conceptualize it as intended outcome—or both. Policymakers may seek to promote improvements in schools by adopting innovative governance policies (as with charter schools), school funding (as with vouchers), or delivery mechanisms (cyber schooling)—all inputs at the *governance level*. Such changes may be ends in themselves, or may be intended to spur innovations more immediately evident to students—for instance, in a school's orientation or organization, or in the classroom. On the other hand, policymakers may seek to implement improvements directly at the classroom level—for example, by mandating a specific curriculum. However, school choice as a reform movement generally refrains from such top-down micromanagement. The assumption is that local actors (including parents and teachers) understand the individual needs and preferences of a child better than bureaucrats and policymakers.[23] Consequently, policymakers interested in choice focus instead on institutional levers for creating the optimal environment and structural incentives to compel schools to improve. Hence, in this thinking, classroom-level innovation is best encouraged through structural reforms, rather than specified by policymakers.[24]

After leveraging policy to produce changes in governance, a second and sometimes intermediate level is the local *school (or district)*. Institutional policies are typically targeted at precipitating improvements in schools. For instance, due to the competition generated in school choice systems, many schools have taken on a more entrepreneurial orientation, hiring business managers, cutting costs through contracting for services, or employing marketing campaigns. Freed from many school regulations, charter schools have a number of opportunities in this area, and many have pursued innovations in terms of new forms of organization, alternative employment practices, accessing private capital, or targeting niche markets.[25] While these might appear most obviously in individual schools, their significance is most notable in terms of aggregate effects. A single school may make internal changes in terms of how teachers are evaluated or how the school promotes itself, but the larger impact is in how other schools in that area respond in creating a range of new and, it would be hoped, improved options for families in the community.

In fact, it is expected that these changes will then have an impact in the *classroom*. Policymakers can change institutional arrangements and shape alternative structures and incentives for schools, and schools can respond to those factors in how they organize themselves and arrange their resources. But, without improvements in educational quality—a classroom-level concern—other institutional and organizational reconfigurations are only so much reformist posturing. As Richard Shavelson observes, "the real issue is whether what goes on in the classroom has substantially changed."[26] Indeed, reforms such as charter schools make this a central consideration. However, educational historians warn that classroom practice—what organizational theorists call the "technical core" of the educational enterprise—is the area most resistant to change.[27]

Nature of Changes

In addition to the known difficulty of effecting classroom change, there are several other reasons to believe that many changes presented as "innovations" in education may be more about appearance than essence—particularly in view of the enhanced incentives to pursue innovations in the new education marketplace of school choice. In view of the weight of demographic factors, the degree to which schools have a primary impact on student learning is questionable, and it is not clear that educational innovations can significantly enhance that effect.[28] Thus, because it is so difficult to increase student learning, instead of focusing on innovations in teaching and learning, schools often focus on marketing innovations to simply attract "better students." An "innovative" school may thus appear to have changed its impact on student learning when what has actually changed is the student body. Moreover, many parents are not particularly interested in sending their children to an "innovative" school, preferring instead schools that focus on traditional practices. Furthermore, in an area such as education, families are at an "informational disadvantage" relative to schools because of the complexity of the organizational processes involved.[29] Because of this asymmetry, it is relatively easy for schools to suggest innovation even when little or none is taking place.[30] This issue is exacerbated because of the rise of marketing in areas with more intensive school choice programs.

Therefore, it is important to consider the nature of changes and practices that are presented as innovations. Some innovations entail fundamental and sustained improvements in teaching and learning. For instance, computer assisted instruction that seeks to individualize education for different learners might be shown to improve academic outcomes. Innovations in systems and structures might also represent real change, but they may not automatically have the anticipated impact on teaching and learning—change might remain at the structural level. But innovations in symbols and marketing may become more common; such "innovations" may be of value more for their use in shaping perceptions of the educational enterprise, as with changing the name of a school or an administrative title, or the addition of school uniforms, or a school logo.[31]

Diversification and Innovation

As noted earlier, innovation should not be too easily equated with diversification. While creating more alternatives is important, and is certainly a coequal goal, it is important to note that innovation is a prerequisite for diversification. That is, innovation generates new options, whereas diversification extends the fruits of innovation into multiple local contexts, where families could then choose among different options. Thus, although innovation and diversification are closely related, they are distinctly different processes. Observers must take a big-picture perspective when considering innovation in schools in order to assess whether new practices are either initiated or replicated at a given school.

One question to consider is whether school choice is itself a prerequisite for, or a result of, innovation. If the former, then markets may be better suited for creating alternatives, since competitive forces generated through choice can spark innovations, which will lead to a greater diversity of options. But if, it is the latter—if choice results from innovation—then governments, capitalizing on research and development efforts, might more easily establish contrasting programs at different schools in order to offer families alternatives. That is, the state could provide diverse options, reflecting innovations already in existence. While further innovations may then transpire, the primary point in this scenario would be to offer alternatives.

This issue is illustrated in the example of charter schools, which were advanced as R&D centers for new practices and approaches in teaching and learning. The idea behind this thinking was that autonomy from direct state oversight, competition, and choice would generate innovations, and thus diversification in the form of new options for families. Although some ideas were truly novel, many charter schools quickly trended toward more familiar educational practices, and charter school "innovations" in teaching and learning were for the most part already evident in other schools (see below). Notably, this includes state-run schools of choice such as magnet schools, through which district-run schools were already using practices that were then considered "innovative" in charter schools. Consequently, the rhetoric around charter school innovations shifted, so that advocates saw them as "laboratories" or "greenhouses" where unique practices available elsewhere could be further developed. Later, some saw charters only as "showrooms" where new practices could be brought to local contexts, making them primarily delivery mechanisms, as opposed to development mechanisms. In this sense, it is not clear that greater innovation necessarily results from competitive choice systems. Instead, insofar as the "innovations" evident in charter school classrooms were already evident elsewhere, one could make the case that innovations were already occurring in larger state systems.

ASSESSING INNOVATION IN SCHOOL CHOICE MODELS

With these considerations in mind, a brief overview of practices in different school choice schemes suggests that innovations tend to vary somewhat by school type, and most often appear outside of the classroom.[32] Furthermore, few substantive innovations may be occurring in teaching and learning, but the paucity of good research on innovation in many of these models suggests that this topic is drastically understudied.

- Perhaps the model with the greatest level of innovation is *cyber schooling*, including blended models of online and face-to-face instruction that cut across not only instructional approaches but also public and private sectors. Cyber schooling, or virtual schooling, an innovation in content delivery, is particularly popular with home schoolers, although it has spread far beyond that audience. Numerous charter schools are cyber schools, and many other public and private schools use Internet delivery as a resource to varying degrees.[33] Cyber schooling affords parents additional opportunities to monitor children's work, and it gives administrators new means to employ, supervise and assess teachers.[34] Although there are many opportunities for further educational innovations in this respect, this new forum for schooling also presents significant accountability and resource challenges in some areas, such as questions of quality and training for teachers on the public payroll.[35]

- *Home schooling* is often associated with traditional family values, and frequently represents a reaction against overly modern curriculum and pedagogy, but it also offers the potential for developing great innovations in teaching and learning. Home schooling families are developing strong networks, and are even establishing "institutions," such as learning centers, to support learning in ways that parallel, but differ from, conventional schooling.[36] Home schooling is also blurring boundaries between different sectors, as charter schools and public school districts seek different ways of catering to this growing population.[37] However, the little useful research that has been done on this model strongly suggests that, despite its potential for innovation, most home schooling in fact focuses on traditional forms of pedagogy.[38]

- *Charter schools* are the choice model most explicitly tied to the idea of innovation. Because their substantial autonomy provides great opportunity for creativity, and because of the competitive pressures charters face, proponents have been clear in their expectations to see substantive innovations in charter classrooms.[39] However, research suggests that in charters—the most studied model in terms of innovation—most innovations are happening outside the classroom. For instance, charters have embraced alternative employment practices such as merit pay, and they have taken the lead in using marketing to attract students.[40] Yet larger scale studies indicate relatively few innovations in charter classrooms, with most practices tending toward familiar or traditional approaches.[41]

- *Magnet schools* may also have the opportunity to innovate, due to their distinctive missions, and often more homogenous community. However, since they may deal with more specific and sometimes more affluent students, opportunities to innovate may result more from demographics than school type. Still, there have been relatively few studies of innovation in magnet schools. In the early 1990s, over one third of magnets focused on a specific subject, and over one quarter had a unique pedagogical focus.[42] Teachers in magnet schools report greater levels of autonomy and less standardized curricula, but few substantive differences in classrooms compared to other schools.[43] Some magnet schools have attempted to reorient themselves to be more student centered, and in pursuit of this goal have adopted such practices as project-based learning.[44]

- *Intra- or interdistrict* choice plans are typically not geared specifically toward generating innovations, as are, say, charter school programs. Instead, they primarily allow for greater freedom of choice. Still, some research has suggested that some schools in such districts are pursuing information about parental decision-making practices—perhaps a form of administrative innovation.[45] In some instances, though, districts provide for the establishment of individual schools or sets of schools specifically for research and development, "to develop best practices and to be a catalyst for change that could be transferred to the rest of the system" (see below).[46] These efforts, brought about by professional impulses to improve, rather than to generate competitive incentives, have garnered some acclaim from across the political spectrum for the extent of their educational innovations.[47]

- *Vouchers for private schools* are advanced more with parental control, rather than innovation, in mind. However, private schools in voucher programs in many ways best approximate the theoretical conditions for producing innovations as outlined by market theorists: they are free of district regulation, must compete for students, and are held accountable to consumers largely on results. Yet, while the provoucher Friedman Foundation contends that "Private schools are good largely because they are free to innovate," there is virtually no evidence to suggest that private schools accepting vouchers are generally any more innovative—especially at the classroom level—than any other schools.[48] Although vouchers programs themselves might be considered to be innovative at the policy level, in fact, parents might very well pursue private education for their children largely because it is often associated with more traditional curriculum and instruction. Even on a wider scale, looking at public and private schools in general, the picture is quite mixed. Some progressive private schools (not the type to accept vouchers) are known to adopt nontraditional forms of curriculum and pedagogy,[49] but independent private schools are also the most conventional and often the most internally standardized.[50]

Thus, in general, there is a considerable amount of activity and change in and around schools, although differences in that regard do not appear to be strictly associated with school type or model. Instead, once again, evidence of substantive and symbolic innovation is clearer at policy and administrative levels, such as with employment and promotional practices, while evidence of new and different classroom practices is relatively sparse or, where it exists, often concentrated in the state sector—contrary to the logic of some competition-oriented reforms.

FACTORS THAT INHIBIT OR ENCOURAGE INNOVATION

In order to understand the patterns of innovation and conformity in different models of school choice, it is important to understand the sources of innovation, at least on a theoretical level. Then we can recognize how these do or do not play out in the real world of schooling and, more importantly, appreciate the obstacles to innovation that are inherent in different models, and in education itself.

How Innovations Emerge

Essentially, theorists point to two general sources of innovation. The first is driven by professional or social-benefit ideals; the second by marketplace incentives. Innovation can emerge from professional motivations where innovators seek to meet a social need or to advance the public good through improvements and inventions. An impulse toward such innovation is built into the norms of many professions.[51] Historically, advances in the field of medicine illustrate the desire to improve care for humanitarian reasons. In such instances, innovations are developed for the public good by nonprofit entities. However, in the current environment, there is some concern that introducing competitive incentives into traditionally nonprofit sectors—including education—can reorient or diminish such impulses.[52]

Of course, in the marketplace, competitive environments have generated innovations in many areas. In an arena focused on material gain, individuals and organizations pursue innovations in order to maximize profits and win competitive advantages. The market then rewards the most flexible and effective innovators who can provide consumers with higher quality options and lower costs. The need for ever-increasing innovation is woven into the fabric of markets, but support for it can take different shapes. Some markets, such as information technology, are structured to nurture small-scale, independent innovators; for example, many improvements in computers have been developed by people working in their basements (or a garage, in the case of Apple Computers). Other markets, like aerospace engineering, rely on larger corporate firms with access to considerable resources for R&D.[53]

In considering both professionalism and competition as sources of innovation, it is important to examine how each affects both the rate and the focus of innovation. Economists such as Gary Becker argue that competitive market incentives "would induce a more rapid rate of innovation into curriculum and teaching"—but to what end is not clear.[54] For instance, the competitive pharmaceutical industry directs a considerable amount of innovation toward profitable, but not necessarily widespread, problems.[55] Furthermore, it is not clear that markets necessarily produce a greater rate of innovation in education, since such incentives work better in some sectors than others, and it remains unclear what type of market education represents.[56]

Under these two models, different factors can be leveraged to encourage the development of substantive innovations in education. The market-based perspective emphasizes that competition provides structural incentives to compel schools to pursue new and better ways of teaching individual learners. Therefore, the focus in the market model is largely on enhancing effectiveness at the school and classroom level by structuring the external incentives to induce innovation, which in turn will enhance effectiveness at the school and classroom level. Eschewing the idea that schools might benefit from more resources, market advocates rely on competition and its threat of fewer resources to force schools to innovate. Consequently, teachers' qualifications become less important than their ability to think creatively in response to competitive pressures. But in this equation such creativity is also thought to require autonomy from external (i.e., district, union) regulations that leave little room for entrepreneurial activity.

In contrast, the social-benefit perspective acknowledges that education professionals are specially trained to deal with issues in schools. Therefore, they can be expected to seek solutions to problems by innovating, both because they are aware of a professional responsibility to do so and because better meeting students' needs is an intrinsically good thing to do. Still, while professionals may not be primarily motivated by financial gain, efforts to create and improve systems for meeting the needs of students require major resources—for instance, to support professional or curriculum development, or program creation and administration. Moreover, successful innovations can be elevated and disseminated as "best practices," but the possibility is easily undermined. Where there is a lack of professional autonomy, bureaucratic mechanisms often impose new practices on practitioners, irrespective of context and most often with thoroughly inadequate professional development.

While professional and market models for innovation differ widely in their assumptions and implementation, however, both face significant structural barriers to change inherent in the current educational environment and processes.

Impediments to Innovation

There are also many serious impediments to innovation in education under both market and professional models. Market advocates highlight one of the most serious challenges in publicly administered schools: the control exerted by the "education establishment"—the supposedly hegemonic alliance of school boards, bureaucracies, and teachers unions. Critics note that self-interested parties controlling education governance focus resources and efforts toward their own purposes, rather than toward improving the education of children. Indeed, although there is some interest from unions and education officials in reforming education, concerns about special interests cause many to suspect that such reforms are largely about further enriching and empowering the established inter-ests.[57]

While this is a strong and compelling critique, there is research indicat-ing that innovations have often resulted from government or bureaucratic intervention when choice-based systems were failing to generate innova-tions—indicating that competitive markets may also involve barriers to innovation.[58] Indeed, some of the most innovative educational practices in the United States are evident in district-run programs.[59] In fact, key aspects of public education, such as open access and public funding, defy the logic of purer market models, and the blunt application of markets in education may create *disincentives* for substantive educational innova-tion.[60] It appears that education markets embody incentive structures that corrupt market pressures to innovate, so that such markets might actually cause many schools to standardize curricula rather than inno-vate.[61] This is particularly true in cases where consumers have common goals for a service such as education (which are often reinforced through such standardized measures of quality as standardized tests).

Other challenges are found in characteristics of the current teaching force and profession. As market advocates correctly point out, under cur-rent arrangements, teachers do not own—and therefore cannot profit from—any innovations they develop, thereby undercutting the incentive to innovate. Additionally, new ideas about teaching children can be blocked by district and union regulations. Moreover, high rates of turn-over in the profession and a disproportionate share of inexperienced and unqualified teachers in poorer schools make it difficult to develop and sustain new pedagogies. On the other hand, it could be that less experi-enced teachers may be *better* situated to develop innovations, since their approach to teaching is not yet as established.

Other potential barriers to innovation are evident at the organizational level of the education enterprise. For instance, it could be that newer organizations, such as a newly established charter school, are not bound by previous practices and traditions, and thus are better positioned to develop and embrace alternative practices—an argument for new charter schools. But sociologists also point out that such organizations are more desperate to establish "legitimacy," and have to prove themselves in the marketplace—incentives to adopt established practices.[62] Indeed, there is some evidence that new schools established as alternative educational models quickly recognize pressures to conform to common methods of schooling.[63] (In fact, the greater autonomy offered as the remedy to escape standardization often serves instead as a device that allows schools to avoid at-risk students, as well as the educational innovations that could help those students.[64]) And as with teachers, schools generally do not own any innovations they develop. This is particularly evident in the contradictory position in which charter schools find themselves. Unlike district-run models, such as Boston's Pilot Schools, which are also designed as R&D centers to create innovations for other public schools, charter schools are expected to share any innovations they develop with the schools with which they compete. Private schools and education management organizations are in some ways better positioned to deal with the problem of owning and profiting from innovations, but this would mean using legal protections to withhold innovations from competitors.

The issue of scale also has implications for encouraging or inhibiting innovations. Reformers often highlight the importance of small, independent "mom and pop" schools as the best model for innovation in education, as local providers can pursue different ways of meeting the needs of individuals. Yet, because it is so difficult to observe instructional processes and measure learning outcomes in multiple small sites, questions about legitimacy and quality constantly plague such operations.[65] Furthermore, sizable organizations such as large school districts or private education management organizations have the institutional capacity to develop and nurture innovations by directing additional resources—what economists call "monopoly rents"—to R&D efforts *shielded from direct competition*. Larger organizations, however, have a greater interest in developing "process innovations" that reduce costs than they do in developing benefits to clients. While market theorists point to incentives for bureaucracies to be self-focused, the for-profit motive of the new education management industry suggests that different types of large educational organizations share an incentive to redirect the purpose of innovation away from students and toward organizations. In order to access savings from such innovations, education management organizations have an incentive to standardize their model. And, indeed, many claim that it is not just public school districts, but also private management companies that lead to "cookie-cutter" models of schooling.[66]

CONCLUSION: THE POTENTIAL FOR INNOVATION IN SCHOOL CHOICE

The question of innovation in education is significant because of the need to find new ways of reaching chronically underserved students. As critics correctly note, traditional approaches to education too often deny individual students and whole communities equitable access to quality educational opportunities. Innovation is a key mechanism for developing more effective ways of meeting the needs of diverse learners, and for improving the quality of education. Without substantive improvements in educational opportunities, parents may be more likely to choose schools based on criteria other than quality, such as the demographic characteristics of students at a school. But the question of how to encourage useful educational innovations has substantive implications for this issue. Contrary to the expectations of competition-based reform models, some of the more innovative practices—such as mentoring programs or the use of new technologies and manipulatives in mathematics—are emerging due to professional activity in the public sector. However, not only does it appear that choice itself is no panacea when it comes to further outcomes such as raising achievement,[67] but when competition is introduced as a significant factor in local education markets, schools, unfortunately, may recognize perverse market incentives to adopt symbolic innovations in areas such as marketing in ways that may further sort students.[68]

Indeed, the question of innovation is problematic because of the notable resistance to change traditionally exhibited by the education system in the United States. In fact, historians and others have highlighted not only the remarkable continuity of educational practices over the decades, but also the ability of the system to deflect and co-opt efforts to make substantive changes.[69] Partly this may be due to the ways that teachers and parents internalize and then replicate their own schooling experiences for the next generation, and in the process construct a defined notion of what "real" schooling should look like.[70] Moreover, the system is designed in such a way that constant reform can generate much activity at policy levels in terms of governance, accountability, or funding, while teachers still seem to hold a rather consistent view of what they need to do on a daily basis. In fact, as an institution, the education system is inherently conservative in terms of the pace of change. Although many—perhaps too many[71]—fads come and go, core practices remain remarkably similar through the years.[72] While this is rightly seen as a fault in the system in terms of its chronic failure to meet the needs of disadvantaged communities, it may also indicate that teachers focus on some stable learning goals rather than on every new instructional trend.

In any event, competition-based school choice reforms seek to reconfigure the institutional arrangements of schools in order to change the incentives that drive activity in schools. While such choice reforms have been quite successful in reshaping activity at the policy or administrative levels, they have been less so in terms of creating change at the key point in these organizations: in teaching. In fact, there is some evidence that public sector institutions have been at least as successful in promoting substantive educational innovations.[73] The main obstacle to educational innovation through market mechanisms is that education itself does not easily fit into a market model. Continued public participation in terms of governance and funding, and public values of open access and equity, represent quite a different set of values than in purer market models.

Additionally, the incentives for innovation are not necessarily comparable to what one finds in sectors that produce computers or cars. Indeed, in some markets, competition can generate standardizing tendencies, rather than incentives to innovate or diversify.[74]

Consequently, we are seeing somewhat of a retreat from the idea of innovation as a central goal for school choice—at least among more thoughtful reformers. While innovation was one of the most commonly cited goals earlier in the school choice movement, and particularly for charter schools, it may have served more of a symbolic service as a rhetorical device for advancing school choice reforms, rather than as a substantive goal. In fact, the idea has largely disappeared from much of the discourse around school choice, and some early advocates are now backtracking from their initial expectations about the ease of inducing innovations in education through school choice.[75]

More importantly, though, is the point that innovation is not automatically beneficial. While "innovation" has often been cited as a reason to embrace school choice, the autonomy and competitive incentives unleashed in school choice schemes can also lead to negative consequences, in view of the values commonly held for public education. School choice allows families to choose schools outside of traditional attendance areas that too often reflect race and class divisions. While it is possible that competition can ramp up effectiveness in schools and provide quality options for underserved students, it is also entirely possible that it might do precisely the reverse: competition might result in schools pursuing more effective marketing campaigns to attract already advantaged students, thus actually exacerbating racial and class divisions.[76] For example, the rise of marketing that has accompanied school choice programs has not been simply informational, but has often targeted specific groups, playing on race and class issues in ways that may further erode opportunities for equitable education.[77] Other opportunities for innovation created by the push for organizational autonomy may have similar detrimental effects, as when schools choose locations likely to attract more advantaged students.[78] That may be an innovation, but it is not necessarily desirable.

If reformers are serious, as they have said, about inducing greater rates of educational innovation in classrooms in order to better meet the needs of different students, it may be that the R&D capacity needs to be substantially reimagined. Simply replicating current practices in different communities may provide more choices, but it is far from clear that the act of choosing in itself leads to better education, or that more effective practices already exist for the many different underserved learners. Indeed, there is real concern that the families of students most in need of alternatives are often those least likely to take advantage of choice. Consequently, diversification is a worthy but insufficient goal without educational innovations to generate new and better ways of serving diverse learners. This review points to several considerations for encouraging substantive educational innovations:

- As with innovations in other sectors, educational improvement entails directing considerable resources into particular schools to develop and pilot specific new approaches to teaching and learning with different populations, rather than trying to do it on the cheap through the relatively simple restructuring of choice models.
- The development of innovations involves nurturing and shielding such efforts from immediate mandates and competitive pressures, rather than forcing schools representing new ideas to sink or swim in the educational marketplace.
- As noted, there are unique qualities around education that defy the easy application of basic market models. If markets are to be used effectively for organizing the production and distribution of education, more thought has to be given to the type of market reflected in education, such as the specific conditions that can best encourage innovation.
- Inability to routinely provide good information about school quality can motivate schools to choose symbolic action rather than substantive innovation; for markets to work effectively, informational "asymmetries" between producers and consumers need to be addressed. We cannot rely on competition alone to generate quality information for families. While many point to value-added modeling or parent information centers, non-market efforts such as rigorous school inspections (as in the United Kingdom) that provide parents with information on multiple dimensions of school quality can also be useful.
- Furthermore, governments are often better suited than independent market actors to provide a range of options for families. We know that professional activity in the state sector has often been more successful at generating innovations. It could also be that innovation will flow more from government generated choice plans such as magnet schools, where efforts are made to establish and sustain a range of options.

CHAPTER 9

SCHOOL CHOICE AND SEGREGATION BY RACE, ETHNICITY, CLASS, AND ACHIEVEMENT

**Roslyn Arlin Mickelson, Martha Bottia,
and Stephanie Southworth**

In the past 2 decades a range of school choice forms have become viable educational options for students in all 50 states and the District of Columbia. School choice is a complex, politically charged, imprecise concept that subsumes a vast array of practices across both the public and private education sectors. The various forms of public school choice include intradistrict magnets, a limited number of interdistrict options, charters, and public voucher programs. Private schools, private voucher programs, and home schooling comprise private sector choice options. Since the 1980s school choice has become more popular with local, state, and federal policymakers who draw upon market principles for restructuring education. Choice also appeals to parents and educators frustrated with the slow pace of school improvement in many low-performing urban schools, and to those whose belief systems hold that markets can provide more efficient education than the state.[1]

Exploring the School Choice Universe: Evidence and Recommendations
pp. 167–192
Copyright © 2012 by Information Age Publishing

Choice advocates expect that the implementation of various forms of choice will trigger broad-based gains in academic achievement and greater equity, both in the choice schools and their host school systems.[2] The public narrative about school choice rarely explores the effects of this reform for choice schools' racial, ethnic, socioeconomic status, and ability composition, nor does the debate examine the effects of the presence of choice options on the composition of the conventional schools in the district. This chapter synthesizes the educational and social science literature on these two questions.

Efforts to reform education through market principles have been circulating for decades.[3] Market principles involve competition, choice, deregulation, standards, accountability, and the individual pursuit of rational self-interest. Various choice options, along with efforts to privatize educational services and school management, reflect ideologies that seek to diminish the role of the state in public and private domains, to reassess the distinctions between private and public realms, and to advance market forces in the provision of essential social services including education. In theory, school choice will empower parents to match the needs of their children with an array of educational options, thereby maximizing the quality of their child's education. Deregulation and competition will foster innovation and reform among choice and nonchoice schools, and market forces ultimately will eliminate schools that do not provide the high quality education that parents demand.

Choice advocates gained important allies during the presidencies of Ronald Reagan and George H.W. Bush as the executive branch of the federal government renewed its focus on the ostensibly widespread shortcomings of public education.[4] Chubb and Moe's influential 1990 book *Politics Markets, and America's Schools*[5] brought additional attention and mainstream policy legitimacy to claims that school choice could be the "silver bullet" for school improvement. Since 2008, choice reforms, particularly charter schools, have received support from the Obama administration. Competition for the administration's signature educational reform initiative, *Race to the Top*, privileges applicants whose proposals include expansion of charters.[6]

As market-inspired school reforms gained momentum among conservative policymakers in federal and state governments, the continuing crisis in urban education, despite decades of compensatory education programs and desegregation efforts, led many parents of low-income students of color to consider choice reforms as an alterative strategy for improving their children's educational opportunities. In the 1980s choice in the form of vouchers gained traction in Milwaukee, home of the nation's first public voucher plan, through an alliance between ascendant political conservatives and powerful Black Milwaukee legislators, who together made common cause with parents frustrated over the failing Milwaukee Public Schools.[7]

Choice, Desegregation, and Segregation

Based upon the Supreme Court's ruling in *Brown* that racially segregated schools are inherently unequal, efforts to integrate public schools were rooted in the concept of equality of educational opportunity. School choice reforms were intimately involved in early desegregation efforts following *Brown*. However, school choice was not employed to foster integration or educational equity; in fact, the practice has roots in the south's notorious struggles against integration that followed the 1955 *Brown II* decision.[8] After the Supreme Court ordered school districts to end de jure segregation with all deliberate speed, in lieu of dismantling their dual systems Southern school districts devised "freedom of choice" plans that ostensibly allowed Black and White students to attend any school of their choice. Although in theory these plans would allow any student to attend the school of their choice, in practice, "freedom of choice plans" were a conscious strategy of resistance to desegregation.[9] These choice plans did nothing to desegregate public education because only a handful of Blacks enrolled in White schools, while no Whites enrolled in Black schools. Eventually the Supreme Court ruled that freedom of choice plans by themselves were not sufficient to achieve integration, and it approved other means, including busing.[10]

Decades later various forms of public school choice were reintroduced as reforms specifically designed to voluntarily desegregate public schools. Magnet schools, often located in low-income minority communities, offered specialized programs designed to attract suburban residents. Magnets operated as desegregation tools if they employed "controlled choice" pupil assignment plans that considered how an applicant's race contributed to the school's racial balance.[11]

Versions of controlled choice pupil assignment plans continue to be used in both mandatory and voluntary desegregation plans. However, in 2007 the Supreme Court held that the use of an individual student's race in pupil assignment plans, such as controlled choice magnets, was unconstitutional.[12] Although a majority of the justices recognized the importance of diversity and the avoidance of racial isolation in K-12 public schools, the court struck down particular aspects of the Seattle and Louisville student assignment plans because they relied too heavily upon only an individual applicant's race as an admission criterion.

The Seattle and Louisville decision left many school leaders and citizens confused about the future use of race in school assignments. While the court placed limits on the ability of school districts to take account of an individual student's race in school assignments, it did not—as is sometimes reported—rule out any and all consideration of race in student assignment. In fact, a majority of Justices explicitly left the door open for school districts to take race-conscious measures to promote diversity and avoid racial isolation in schools,[13] and even invited educators and citizens to collaborate creatively to design diverse schools. Justice Kennedy's opinion also endorsed specific strategies, including strategic siting of new schools and race-conscious recruiting of students and faculty.

The Supreme Court's affirmation of the centrality of diversity to educational equity and excellence aligns with social and behavioral science research that shows the demographic composition of schools is strongly related to the opportunities to learn within them.[14] Research indicates that socioeconomic status, racial and ethnic backgrounds, immigrant status, and achievement levels of other students in a school are factors significantly associated with that school's academic climate and the material differences in learning opportunities within it—especially students' access to qualified, licensed, and experienced teachers—which, in turn, affect the levels of equity and excellence in the school. Specifically, the preponderance of the evidence shows that racially and ethnically diverse schools and schools without concentrated poverty are likely to be positive learning environments for students from all ethnic backgrounds, socioeconomic levels, and academic potentials.[15] Asian and Latino immigrant students may be an exception to this pattern.[16] Diverse schools foster academic achievement, break the intergenerational transmission of racial misunderstanding and hostility, and prepare students for citizenship and work in a pluralistic democratic society that is part of a globalizing economy.[17] However, research suggests diverse schools can be resegregated by ability grouping and tracking.[18] The benefits from integrated schools are weakened when ability grouping and tracking deny students the opportunity to learn in diverse classrooms.[19]

Two trends related to the issues above are now clearly in evidence: school choice and its various options are increasingly popular reform strategies and America's schools are resegregating. In fact, racial isolation levels are rising to the levels of the 1970s.[20] These concurrent trends raise an important question: are school choice options promoting diversity, or are they instead contributing to segregation?

Definitions and Methods

The widespread growth of school choice and the length of time that many programs have operated are now sufficient to permit empirical examinations of the relationships between choice and various dimensions of diversity within and among schools, including race, ethnicity, socioeconomic status (SES), achievement, and ability composition. The present study uses this literature to investigate if the design and implementation of various choice options promote diversity or segregation in choice schools themselves as well as among the conventional schools in their communities. It is worth noting that the choice literature remains rife with methodological, measurement, and epistemological debates that reflect the intensely political and ideological nature of school choice policy.[21] The authors do not engage this debate itself; rather, they summarize the extant literature on the topics that met thresholds for high quality qualitative or quantitative research as articulated by the American Educational Research Association.[22]

Race and ethnicity are the first focus of this chapter. Contemporary racial and ethnic categories are socially constructed, historically contingent, and fluid.[23] Nevertheless, this chapter uses the conventional categories of American Indian, Asian, Black, Latino, and White to refer to major racial and ethnic groups, even though these designations cannot capture the dynamic aspects of America's demography or the ethnic variations within each major racial group. These variations include multiracial designations, identities that are increasingly embraced by younger people wishing to claim all aspects of their heritage.

The second focus of the chapter, SES, reflects a family's location in the social stratification hierarchy. Researchers often use free or reduced-price lunch status or parental educational attainment to indicate SES. Race and SES are highly correlated because people of color are disproportionately poor. The intersection of race and SES is especially relevant to how particular forms of choice affect school segregation, because many choice options are designed to target low-income children.

Most schools organize instruction by ability groups or academic tracks,[24] the third focus of this chapter. Although ability and achievement are related constructs, achievement refers to the performance of students, while ability captures whether a student has certain identified intellectual gifts or learning disabilities that entitles him or her to special education services. Certain choice options are designed to target students with disabilities or those who are gifted, again illustrating how the design of a choice option may contribute to the demographic composition of a school.[25]

This chapter summarizes the authors' survey and synthesis of existing research on how forms of school choice affect diversity in school composition—both within choice schools and in the host community's nonchoice public schools. The synthesis includes published journal articles, books, chapters in collections, and unpublished reports from scholars and from a variety of research institutions including agencies or departments of the federal government.[26] The breadth of the literatures on magnets, inter-district plans, vouchers, charters, private schools, and home schooling allows for an analysis only of major trends, rather than more nuanced findings. Whenever possible, findings from state and national studies are included; case studies are discussed if they illustrate a general point, or in some instances, if they are the only studies available on a particular topic.

The remainder of this chapter is organized into three sections. The first section addresses how school choice forms may or may not promote segregation by race and SES. The second section examines whether various forms of school choice foster segregation by ability or achievement. The final section summarizes the findings and offers policy recommendations.

SEGREGATION BY RACE, ETHNICITY, AND SOCIOECONOMIC STATUS

History and Background

At the same time that school choice reforms grew in popularity during the 1990s, the population of American students became more racially and ethnically diverse. During the last 2 decades, many of America's schools have resegregated by race, ethnicity and SES. The resegregation of American schools is a reversal of a trend toward greater desegregation that peaked at the end of the 1980s. At present, resegregation is growing in Southern and border states that were once largely desegregated. In the Northeast, Midwest, and West—regions that experienced less desegregation—segregation is taking on an ethnic complexity not seen before as the nation becomes increasingly multiracial.[27]

Asian students constitute the ethnic group most likely to attend an integrated school while Whites are the most likely group to attend a racially isolated one. Whites typically attend schools where only one out of five students comes from other racial groups. Roughly three fourths of Black and Latino students attend racially isolated minority schools. A majority of racially isolated Black and Latino neighborhood schools are also schools of concentrated poverty. This is important because the SES composition of schools is strongly predictive of its students' academic achievement. Racially isolated schools with high concentrations of poor students have very high dropout rates and very low achievement scores.[28]

Many factors contribute to the resegregation of America's schools. For one, as the relative size of the White population declines, students of color have fewer interracial contacts. Changing residential patterns—the spatial footprint of race and SES inequality—also contribute to resegregation. Federal court decisions and school district policies contribute as well. For example, in the 1990s, a series of Supreme Court decisions ending mandatory desegregation allowed many school districts to return to racially segregated neighborhood school-based assignment plans.[29]

Given the concurrence of resegregation with the increasing popularity of school choice, it becomes important to examine to what extent school choice may also be contributing to segregation by race, ethnicity, SES, and ability. The following sections address this question.

Choice Options and Segregation by Race, Ethnicity, and Socioeconomic Status

Magnet schools offer families a range of curricular and instructional options within a school system (intradistrict choice) and in rare instances, across school boundaries (interdistrict choice). As of 2009 about 3% of all public schools in the United States are magnet schools. They are located in 30 of the 50 states.[30] Common intradistrict magnet options are specialized schools (full magnets) or programs within schools (partial magnets). Magnets are characterized by their curricular themes (such as science and art) or pedagogic emphases (such as discovery learning) that are intended to appeal to students across ethnic and SES boundaries. Specialized magnet schools may employ selective admissions requirements (such as test scores or artistic performance). The designs of magnet schools are central to whether they promote diversity or contribute to resegregation by race, ethnicity, SES, or ability. Many magnets were designed to voluntarily desegregate schools through "controlled choice." Race-neutral intradistrict choice plans permit families to choose any school in the district and consequently, they produce diverse student bodies less often.

It is possible for a magnet to attract a diverse student body yet have an internal organization that produces second-generation segregation.[31] For instance, a diverse magnet school can be internally segregated by race, SES or achievement if it is a partial magnet or it uses academic tracking or ability grouping.[32] Schools with partial magnets or dual magnets (a school with two distinct magnet themes) can be quite diverse in terms of their overall SES, race, ethnicity, and achievement composition. However, the student population in the partial magnet can be strikingly different from the rest of the school.[33] In partial magnets, the magnet students can be isolated in classrooms and thereby have very little contact with the larger school population.

The most common forms of interdistrict choice plans are interdistrict open enrollment and interdistrict desegregation plans.[34] Interdistrict open enrollment plans allow students to transfer between school districts. Because they are guided by competitive market forces, interdistrict open enrollment policies are not designed specifically to address the needs of students in failing urban schools. Instead, the policies are intended to provide families with educational choices and to encourage competition among districts as a means of stimulating school improvement. In 2003, 487,000 students were enrolled in open enrollment plans permitted by 42 states and Puerto Rico. By 2007, almost all states had interdistrict open enrollment policies and almost half of all school districts (46%) accepted students from other districts. However, many suburban districts fearing inner city students will negatively affect their adequate yearly progress decline to accept transfer students from urban school systems.

Interdistrict—or metropolitan—desegregation plans enable students to cross over existing school district boundary lines for the purpose of voluntary racial, ethnic, and socioeconomic school desegregation. These equity-inspired plans are designed to remedy past race and class inequalities in educational opportunities. Interdistrict desegregation plans allow suburban students to attend schools, typically magnets, in urban areas and urban residents to attend schools in suburban districts. Interdistrict desegregation plans have been implemented in St. Louis, Hartford (CT), East Palo Alto (CA), Boston, Indianapolis, Milwaukee, Rochester (NY), and Minneapolis. Several plans (most notably St. Louis) grew out of federal mandates, while other plans originated in state court responses to desegregation or fiscal equity lawsuits. The Boston and Rochester plans were initiated through state and community efforts to avoid litigation. The eight plans provided transportation, incentives for receiving districts, and outreach for recruitment. The plans tend to be small, with between 500 and 10,000 student participants. Their enrollments have diminished over the last decades due to waning legal and political support for interdistrict school desegregation.

Charter schools are another public choice option shaped by the design of their enabling statutes. Between 1991 and 2007, forty states, the District of Columbia, and Puerto Rico have enacted charter school legislation. About 2.5% of public school children, roughly 1.4 million students, attend charter schools.[35] Jurisdictions with the greatest proportion of public school students in charter schools are the District of Columbia, with 35.4%, and Arizona, with 9.7%. The racial and SES composition of charters is affected both by legislation, which varies from state to state,[36] and by local and state demographics.[37] Varying legislation[38] leads to charters with diverse missions, pedagogical styles, and informal admission practices, all of which affect the schools' levels of diversity or segregation. The Obama administration's educational policies foster the creation of more charters.[39]

More than 80% of the charter schools have a theme or curricular focus such as math and science or the arts; students' academic needs (gifted and talented, special education); instructional approaches (Montessori, experimental learning), or ethnic themes (e.g., Afrocentrism). Preexisting schools may be converted to charters, as happened in Washington, DC, where the Catholic archdiocese converted seven Catholic elementary schools into charters.[40] By 2009, 26 states had Internet-based cyber charters, which blend home schooling with an Internet-based "virtual" school and serve over 105,000 students.[41]

Although they are limited in number, voucher programs are a controversial form of public school choice. Voucher programs are not designed to promote school diversity by race, SES, or ability. They consist of initiatives that "allow parents to use all or part of the government funding set aside for their children's education to send their children to the public or private school of their choice."[42] Most public vouchers are targeted at low-income students in urban schools, those attending failing schools, or students with disabilities.

During the last 2 decades, publically funded voucher programs had been authorized in Arizona, Colorado, the District of Columbia, Florida, Louisiana, Maine, Vermont, Ohio, and Utah, and Wisconsin. As of March, 2011 only the District of Columbia, Louisiana, Ohio, Utah, and Wisconsin offer students vouchers.[43] In 2002, there were 78 privately funded voucher programs open to low-income recipients in 38 states and the District of Columbia.[44] Because of the paucity of information about privately funded programs, this chapter focuses on publicly funded vouchers.

District-level public voucher programs for low-income students exist in Cleveland, Milwaukee, New Orleans, and Washington, DC. Milwaukee's program is the largest, serving 20,000 students in 2010.[45] In the wake of Hurricane Katrina, New Orleans enacted a district-level voucher program in 2008. It enrolled 630 students in the 2008-2009 school year.[46]

In theory, those holding vouchers can use them to gain entrance into any receptive private or public school; in practice, most vouchers recipients attend religious private schools.[47] The Supreme Court held in *Zelman* (2002) that public funds for vouchers could be used to pay for private education in parochial schools.[48]

Several statewide public voucher programs are also in place. Maine and Vermont provide vouchers to rural high school students whose communities have no secondary schools. Arizona, Florida, Ohio, and Utah offer special education voucher programs or vouchers for students in low-performing schools. Florida offers vouchers to low-income students.[49] In November, 2007, Utah voters defeated an expanded plan for a universal program that would have provided all students with tuition vouchers to attend a sectarian or secular private school of their choice.[50]

As of 2009, about 11% of all students in the United States attended private schools.[51] Secular private schools are less racially segregated than public schools because they draw their students from a broad geographic area. However, roughly 80% of private school students attend religious schools where levels of racial segregation are quite high.[52] In Catholic and other religious private schools, the levels of segregation are often equal or greater than the levels in nearby public schools. Roughly half of private schools are Catholic, another 28% are other religious—primarily conservative Christian denominations—and the remaining ones are secular.[53] Elite, secular private schools also tend to be segregated by SES.

Home schooling is a rapidly growing educational option that ranges from highly formal and structured to informal, child-centered, and flexible approaches to curricula and instruction.[54] In 2007 2.9% of school age children were home schooled.[55] Typically parents instruct their children in core subjects in their homes. They often join with other home schoolers in their communities for field trips to concerts and museums, foreign language instruction, organized sports, music and dance lessons, and social activities. Home schooling has become a social movement—a collective project with a history, well-developed social networks, and organizational and material supports.[56] In fact, Patrick Henry College, founded in 2000, caters to homeschooled students.[57]

Roughly 20% of those who practice home-based education draw upon the resources of local schools or virtual charter schools as a supplement. Notably, a number of home-schooled students attend traditional schools for long periods of their childhoods.[58] For example, during 2007 Senator John Edwards and his late wife Elizabeth home schooled their two younger children while he campaigned for the Democratic Party presidential nomination.

There are growing numbers of online and virtual schools available for home schoolers. Roberts reports more than 30 virtual schools representing both Christian and secular perspectives.[59] Virtual schools often blur the line between charter and home schooling. Several states have online charter schools that cater to home schoolers. Some states accept out-of-state students who pay tuition, thereby allowing students from one state to be "home schooled" in another state.[60]

Race, Ethnicity, and Socioeconomic Status Enrollment Patterns in Choice Schools

Because many choice schools are created to serve a particular population, their designs shape their demographics. Charter school students are more likely to be Black or Latino and less likely to be White or Asian than those who attend regular public schools.[61] In almost every state, the average Black charter school student attended a school with a higher percentage of Black students and a lower percentage of White students than her noncharter counterpart. Although Whites are less likely to attend charters than minority students, due to the disproportionately high enrollment of minority students in charter schools, White charter schools students are likely to go to school with more non-White students than Whites who attend regular public schools. An exception tends to be charters devoted to gifted education, which are disproportionately White.

Ethnic self-segregation is evident among many charter school populations. These trends are not due to White flight from charters, but to White, Black, Native American, and Latino parents who choose schools based more on their racial composition than on the relative academic quality of the charter school. Such parents often seek charter schools with a majority of students from their own race, even if the charter has lower test scores than the school their children exited.[62]

Racial segregation is also evident in voucher programs. In Florida the percentage of Black voucher recipients was much higher than the percentage of Blacks in the overall state population. A majority of students in voucher programs in Milwaukee, Cleveland, and Washington, DC, are Black.[63] However, Hanauer reported that 53% of voucher recipients in Cleveland were Black, compared with 71% of public school students.[64] Rural voucher recipients in Vermont and Maine, states with very small minority populations, are overwhelmingly White.

Approximately three fourths of private school children are White, 9.5% are Black, another 6% are Hispanic, 6% are Asian/Pacific Islander, and 0.7% is American Indian or Alaskan Native. Asians and White students are twice as likely to enroll in private school as are Blacks and Latinos, who despite being Catholic, have become less likely to enroll in private schools, including Catholic schools, in recent years. According to the National Center for Education Statistics, 85% of students enrolled in private schools are nonpoor (at or above 200% of the poverty threshold). One in four private schools serves wealthy, elite families. While most Catholic schools have some students who qualify for free or reduced-priced lunch, other types of private schools are much less likely to have low-income students.[65] Although elite, nonsectarian, private schools frequently offer a limited number of scholarships to less affluent students of color, middle- and upper-class White students are overrepresented in private school populations.

The nation's approximately 1.58 million home-schooled students represent 2.9% of the nation's school population.[66] A recent study predicts that by the end of 2011, the home-schooled population will grow to 2.04 million, or 3.8% of the K-12 student population. Home schoolers come from diverse SES, race, and ethnic backgrounds.[67] In 2007, about 3.9% of White students were home schooled compared to .08% of Blacks and 1.5% of Hispanic students.[68] This means that Whites were five times as likely as Blacks and three times as likely as Hispanics to be home schooled. Although homeschoolers hold a wide spectrum of political, ideological, religious, and educational beliefs,[69] a majority are Evangelical Christians.[70] Many home-schooling parents are religiously motivated to protect their children from what they perceive as secular humanism and other antireligious forces in public schools. In addition to the larger "Christian" majority, there is a much smaller "inclusive" camp within the home-school movement.[71]

Even though the above trends are documented, accurately describing the size and demographics of the home-school population is a difficult task because of the essentially private, largely unregulated nature of their education.[72] Existing studies suggest that home-schooling families are more likely to be English speakers, White, slightly more affluent, and more religious than the general population. In addition, these families are more likely to be larger, headed by two adults with postsecondary education, and more politically conservative than families that send their children to formal schools.[73]

Which Choice Designs Promote Race and Socioeconomic Status Segregation?

Local, state, and federal policies that govern various forms of school choice shape a particular option's likely contribution to school race and SES segregation or integration. Intradistrict magnets are designed to be more racially and socioeconomically diverse than their surrounding neighborhood schools.[74] They generate the voluntary desegregation of public schools by offering students alternatives to neighborhood schools, which most often have homogeneous race and SES compositions. Racially integrated magnet schools also tend to be diverse in terms of student SES.[75] Some school districts that once employed controlled choice magnet programs to satisfy court-mandated desegregation kept their magnet programs after being granted unitary status. But when Dade County, FL,[76] Charlotte-Mecklenburg, NC, and Nashville, TN,[77] changed the designs of their magnet programs and dropped controlled choice, magnet schools resegregation by race and SES followed.

While, in theory, open enrollment interdistrict choice plans could counteract the race and SES resegregation in urban schools by providing students with an opportunity to transfer to higher performing suburban schools, the evidence indicates open enrollment plans have not done so.

Almost every state and the District of Columbia have open enrollment plans, but the number of students involved in them is limited. Practical problems (lack of transportation) and structural limitations (receiving districts can choose not to participate or refuse to accept inner-city students) often render open enrollment plans more symbolic than genuine. In fact, open enrollment plans allow the more advantaged inner city students to transfer to relatively Whiter, more affluent school systems, thereby exacerbating race and SES inequality between districts.[78]

In contrast to open enrollment interdistrict choice plans, interdistrict desegregation plans were originally introduced to foster racial and SES integration. Interdistrict magnet plans reflect the reality that cities and their suburbs are spatially and politically integrated metropolitan areas with interdependent economies, workforces, utilities, and transportation systems.[79] For example, at its peak St. Louis's interdistrict plan involved almost 13,000 Black urban students in suburban schools and 1,500 White suburban students who attended urban magnets.[80] Boston's METCO plan enrolled about 3,300 students who attend 34 school districts in metropolitan Boston and four school districts outside Springfield.[81] Holme and Wells report that not only do interdistrict desegregation programs promote racial and socioeconomic diversity, but overall, urban and suburban residents, students, and educators participating in them grow to like them the longer the program continues. Despite the evidence of the relative satisfaction of parents, and their success in promoting race and SES diversity, metropolitan area interdistrict desegregation plans remain rare.[82]

Scholars find that intradistrict magnet schools increase interracial exposure, particularly in districts with mandatory desegregation plans.[83] For example, in San Diego, all participants tended to apply to magnet schools that had a higher percentage of White students than their neighborhood schools. Magnet programs increased the exposure of White and middle-class youth to non-Whites and low-income students because as more minority than White students applied to magnet schools, the magnets became more integrated, and the neighborhood schools became less segregated. McAuliffe reported that while the Los Angeles Unified School District's controlled choice magnet plan fostered greater integration in these schools, it triggered greater segregation of Whites and Asians who remained in the traditional schools.

The effects of magnet schools on the racial and SES composition of other schools in the host district also depend upon the demographics of a local community. Within a school district, the location of a magnet school in relationship to residential patterns is crucial to a magnet school's capacity to generate racial and SES diversity. Magnets could have a negative effect on desegregation if there are too many or if they are placed in

White neighborhoods.[84] Saporito reported that Whites were more likely to apply to magnet schools as the percentage of non-White students in their neighborhoods increased.[85] Minorities, however, were not more likely to apply as the percent of non-White students in their neighborhoods increased. He concluded that school choice among magnets in Philadelphia led to increases in economic and racial segregation in neighborhood schools. However, Archibald found that magnet schools did not increase economic segregation among schools. Economic segregation was prevalent in all districts whether or not they had magnet schools.[86]

Charter schools tend to have an overrepresentation of minority students (58%) compared to the general public school population (35%).[87] They also tend to be more racially segregated than the other public schools in their school systems.[88] There appear to be no significant differences in the socioeconomic compositions of both types of public schools.[89] The majority of charter schools are located in central cities where 65% of students are low-income, whereas in rural and urban fringe districts the proportion of low-income students drops to about 30%.[90] Although a majority of Black and Latino students in both regular and charter schools are low-income, slightly fewer low-income Blacks and Latinos attend charters in urban fringe and rural schools. Irrespective of a charter's location, relatively few White charter students are from low-income families.[91]

The evidence suggests that with few exceptions, charter schools tend to be places of racial isolation. Charter schools in most states enroll disproportionately high percentages of minority students. As a result, students of all races are likely to attend charter schools that have a higher percentage of minority students than their host district's other schools.[92] Whites who attend charters tend to go to a racially isolated White school. Segregation is worse for Black than for Latino students, but is very high for both. For example, Cobb and Glass found that Arizona's charter schools are significantly more racially segregated than the conventional public schools.[93] They reported that charter schools enrolled a considerably higher proportion of Black students than conventional public schools. Rapp and Eckes examined charter school enrollment data in the Common Core of Data. They concluded that although charter schools have the opportunity to be more racially integrated than nonchoice schools, they rarely are. Even when students have the flexibility to enroll in charters across conventional school district boundary lines, which would generate more diverse enrollments, students infrequently do so.[94]

Because there are relatively few charters in most school districts, it is unlikely that they affect the racial composition of the other schools in the host district.[95] Carnoy and his colleagues found that charters enrolled the more advantaged of the disadvantaged student population. In school districts where large proportions of the student population enroll in charters, like Washington, DC, it is possible that charters contribute to the concentration of most disadvantaged of the low-income students in the host district's conventional schools.[96]

By design, most public voucher programs are targeted at low-income students. The limited evidence available suggests that low-income students who have more knowledgeable and informed parents are the ones who take advantage of voucher plans. Witte found on average Milwaukee parents of voucher recipients had higher education levels but lower incomes than nonrecipients.[97] Similar results were found in Cleveland. Although incomes of voucher recipients and those who are eligible for vouchers did not significantly differ, twice as many mothers of voucher recipients completed college as the mothers of those who were eligible but who did not receive vouchers.[98]

Very little information is available about the SES and racial composition of the schools that accept vouchers. Available data suggest that vouchers do not promote racial desegregation. Sohoni and Saporito's analysis of national data revealed that attending neighborhood schools would foster more diversity than vouchers (and other forms of choice). Most voucher recipients are from low-income Black and Latino families, and those families tend to choose private religious schools that are frequently racially segregated.[99] There is evidence from Milwaukee that voucher students attended racially identifiable schools, although the schools may be less segregated than Milwaukee Public Schools.[100] Forster reported that urban voucher schools, while still segregated by race and SES, were somewhat less segregated than the other schools in the host district.[101] Because vouchers are sometimes equivalent only to partial funding for most private school tuition, families of recipients often must supplement the voucher in order to utilize them in private schools, something the poorest of low-income families cannot afford.[102]

The scarcity of reliable data complicates efforts to estimate vouchers' likely effects on the racial or SES composition of the public school systems from which their recipients exit. An earlier assessment of vouchers in Milwaukee found that choice has no effect on overall racial balance of the public schools.[103] At best, vouchers do not undermine or counteract trends toward greater racial and ethnic segregation. At worst, they slightly exacerbate them.

As noted above, private schools, the most widespread form of school choice, typically are segregated by race, ethnicity, and SES. Reardon and Yun[104] found that, overall, private schools are racially segregated and that racial segregation in the private sector contributes to segregation in the public sector. They conclude that segregation within the private sector does more to produce racially homogeneous schools than do patterns of segregation between public and private sectors.[105]

At all income levels Whites are more likely to enroll in private school than their Black, Latino, or Asian counterparts. On average, Whites are more racially isolated in private than in public schools, and they experience the most racial isolation in Catholic schools. Levels of Black-White segregation are greater within the private school sector than within public schools, and they are highest in Black Catholic schools. While, nationally, White enrollments are twice as large as those of minorities, in certain local markets Whites enroll in private schools at rates up to 10 times that of minorities. White enrollment rates in private schools are highest in school districts with the largest percent Black students. Latino-White segregation is greatest in public and Catholic schools and relatively lower in secular private schools. Latino public school students are more racially isolated than Black public school students, but those who attend private schools are more integrated than their peers in the public sector.[106]

Whether an intended or unintended consequence, home schoolers are segregated by race and SES because they learn among children who are almost always the same race and SES—members of their own family. Parents choose home schooling for a variety of complex and multidimensional reasons.[107] In some cases, parents are attracted to home schooling precisely in order to insulate their children from people in schools (students and educators) who are different in terms of religion, culture, behavior, and academic performance. Other parents choose to home school in order to celebrate and reinforce their own culture—Afrocentric home schoolers, for example.[108] Because home schoolers represent a relatively small portion of the overall student population and are widely dispersed geographically, there is little to no data about the practice's effects on the race and SES composition of the school systems the students would otherwise attend.

SEGREGATION BY ABILITY AND ACHIEVEMENT

History and Background

Racial, ethnic, and socioeconomic isolation are not the only forms of school composition affected by the design and implementation of school choice. Choice can also integrate academically gifted or learning-disabled students or isolate them from mainstream populations. Historically, for example, students with disabilities were segregated from other students in separate schools and classrooms. In 1975 the Education for All Handicapped Children Act[109] gave students with disabilities the right to an education in mainstream classrooms rather than in restrictive settings presented within separate classrooms and schools. Today many choice forms give special-needs students and their families the option to be mainstreamed or to attend selective programs or programs targeted to their educational needs.

Curricular tracking and ability grouping are widespread practices found in most schools. Tracking and ability grouping separate students by prior achievement or ability level, ostensibly in order to target instruction and curricula to their needs. However, because race and SES are correlated with school performance, ability grouping or tracking often result in segregation by race and SES—as well as by ability and prior achievement—even in schools that are racially diverse.[110] There is very little systematic research available about the role of tracking and grouping in the promotion of segregation by achievement level within choice schools.

Choice Options and Segregation by Ability and Achievement

Just as some forms of school choice may promote race and SES desegregation or segregation by virtue of their designs, a choice option also may promote segregation by ability or achievement. This segregation may occur when parents choose a magnet, voucher program, private, or charter school specifically designed for special-needs or higher ability students, or when educators "counsel" students away from certain schools.[111]

A magnet's student body can be academically diverse or segregated depending upon the school's design or theme. For instance, there is a long tradition of segregating gifted students into schools that require a selective exam for entry (for example, Boston's Latin School or San Francisco's Lowell High School). Certain charters segregate by student achievement or disability because they are designed to meet differing academic needs of specific student populations. They serve students along the achievement and ability continua: special education students, adjudicated youth, English language learners, teen parents and gifted and talented students.[112]

As McLaughlin and Broughman point out, private schools have a complicated relationship with special education. On the one hand, public school administrators regularly contract with the small number of specialized private schools to educate students with severe disabilities who cannot be adequately served in public schools. On the other hand, many private schools (especially elite, secular ones) have admission requirements that screen out low-ability students or low-performing students.

Only half of all private schools offer remedial reading and math, and very few offer special education services.[113]

Enrollment Patterns by Ability and Achievement in Choice Schools

Since many charters, magnets, vouchers, and private schools are designed for gifted, general, and special-needs students, it follows that such options will attract a particular type of student and, therefore, promote segregation by achievement or ability level. Choice options designated for gifted students, particularly schools that require certain test scores to enter, will therefore resegregate students by achievement. And because achievement is correlated with race, ethnicity, and SES, exam school students tend to be disproportionately populated by high ability White, Asian, and middle-class students.

Importantly, public charter schools and magnets are legally obligated to ensure that students with disabilities enjoy equal consideration for admission, though interpretation of the law varies by state.[114] However, special-needs students appear to have differential access to choice programs that target specialized populations. Miron, Nelson, and Risely found that Pennsylvania's charter schools had lower percentages of gifted students than conventional public schools.[115] Similarly, aside from the charter schools that explicitly focus on special-needs children,[116] charter schools tend to have smaller proportions of students who have disabilities requiring special educational services (8%) than district-operated regular public schools (11%).[117] In Michigan, for instance, special education enrollment in charter schools is about 3.7%, while the public school enrollment is 12.3%.[118] Other states report similar gaps in enrollments of special-needs students.[119] This may be because some charter schools steer and counsel parents of special-needs students in ways that dissuade them from enrolling their children in a particular charter school.[120] School policy may also affect the numbers of special-needs students who attend charter schools.[121] Lacireno-Paquet found that admissions criteria, college prep curriculum and transportation availability all affected the types of students who attended the charter school.[122] The actual percentages of special-needs students in charter schools may not be adequately assessed because some parents may hide the disability status of their children when applying to a charter school.[123]

Although some voucher programs target special-needs students, there is some evidence that voucher programs have not provided them with more attractive or accessible opportunities.[124] For example, in Cleveland, voucher recipients were more likely to come from higher achieving schools. The Cleveland schools that lost 17 or more students to vouchers all had test scores above the district's or the state's average.[125] The voucher students' exit may have reduced the mean achievement in the public schools they left and thereby increased the stratification of achievement within low-income Cleveland public schools, but the evidence is inadequate to definitively assess whether voucher programs affect the achievement composition of the public school systems voucher students choose to leave.[126]

Private schools are much less likely than public schools to provide services to children with disabilities.[127] This is the case in Catholic schools, the largest private system. The exceptions to this statement are the small number of private schools that specialize in teaching children with learning disabilities. Elite, nonsectarian schools frequently admit students by exam, thereby screening out those with academic weaknesses or special needs. About 6% of homeschooling parents cite health or special needs as a reason for homeschooling their children.[128] Overall, there are insufficient data to draw any conclusions about home schooling and diversity by ability.

Which Choice Designs Promote Segregation by Ability and Achievement?

Whether a choice school will mainstream or segregate students of varying abilities and achievement levels depends upon the school's theme, its design, and its resources. To illustrate, charter schools tend to have fewer special-needs students than other schools in the host district,[129] which may be explained by economies of scale. Charter schools tend to be smaller and have fewer resources than conventional public schools and therefore have fewer means to adequately educate special-needs students.[130] In some states, such as North Carolina, charter schools enroll a higher percentage of special education students than conventional public schools. However, their special education students are at the low end of the needs spectrum, and those with more severe needs appear to have been "counseled out."[131] Similarly, a report on Pennsylvania charter schools found that not only did charter schools enroll a lower percentage of special-needs students than conventional public schools, but many of the special education students enrolled either were speech or language disabled,[132] relatively easy conditions to accommodate.[133]

Academically selective magnets, charters, and private schools, by design, have high-achieving or gifted students. These selective schools may also affect levels of segregation by ability in conventional schools in the district. For instance, Neild examined effects of the presence of academically selective magnet schools on surrounding neighborhood schools in Philadelphia.[134] She found that academically selective magnets had very little effect on low-achieving, conventional schools. This is because the students within those schools were less likely to apply to the magnet schools. However, because academically selective magnets tended to draw more academically talented students from higher achieving schools, they reduced the sending school's overall achievement.[135] Dills reported similar results in a Washington, DC suburb. She estimated the effects of introducing an academically selective magnet school into a district and found that removing higher performing students from nonmagnet schools not only lowered the mean achievement of the sending schools, but also lowered the actual performance levels of the students in those schools.[136] Except for the 30% of charter schools that have gifted and talented themes,[137] there is little evidence that charter schools generally cream higher achieving students away from the host district's public schools.

DISCUSSION AND POLICY ANALYSIS

This chapter synthesized educational and social science research findings on the relationships of various forms of school choice to the racial, ethnic, SES, achievement, and ability composition of students within six choice options—intradistrict magnets, interdistrict desegregation plans, vouchers, charters, private schools, and home schooling—and how the composition of each option, in turn, affected the composition of the other conventional schools in local communities. Table 9.1 summarizes the chapter's findings. The cells in the table represent generalizations grounded in the research reviewed in the chapter. There are, of course, exceptions to most generalizations. When possible, the nuances that do not appear in the cell were captured in the more expansive discussions that appeared in previous sections of the chapter.

Discussion: Does Choice Foster Diversity?

Choice theory can be interpreted as sympathetic to diversity or as inherently unrelated to it. Some choice advocates believe market forces will break down the ethnic, racial, and socioeconomic barriers to school attendance that, at present, too often relegate many poor children of color to utterly failing urban schools. In contrast, others see the market principles underlying choice as theoretically unrelated to diversity; they are about quality. Market principles are not egalitarian; they are blind to race and SES. Adherents to market principles expect the discipline of

Table 9.1. Summary of Research Findings on Effects of Various Forms of Choice on Race, Ethnicity, SES, and Achievement Diversity Within Choice Schools and Between Choice Schools and Local Conventional Schools

Type of School Choice	Effects on Race and Ethnicity Diversity	Effects on SES Diversity	Effects on Ability and Achievement Diversity
Vouchers			
Within voucher school.	Segregation.	Segregation.	Insufficient information.
Between voucher school and conventional schools.	Effects unlikely due to limited number of students participating.	Effects unlikely due to limited number of students participating.	Some evidence that higher-achieving students leave higher-achieving urban schools for voucher schools.
Intradistrict Magnets			
Within magnet school or magnet program.	Diversity in full magnets; segregation in partial magnets.	Diversity, but less SES diversity in race-neutral plans.	Segregation in gifted and talented magnets.
Between magnet school/program and local nonchoice schools.	Increased conventional school diversity when magnets are not placed in white neighborhoods.	Inconclusive-Some studies show no effect. Other studies show increase in SES segregation.	Some evidence of segregation in high achieving conventional schools due to exit of high performers to gifted magnets.
Interdistrict Plans			
Within interdistrict plans.	Diversity if controlled choice desegregation plan.	Diversity if controlled choice desegregation plan.	Insufficient data to generalize.
Between interdistrict plans and local nonchoice schools.	Some evidence open enrollment resegregates schools in sending district.	Some evidence open enrollment resegregates schools in sending district.	Insufficient data to generalize.

(Table continues on next page.)

Table 9.1. (Continued)

Type of School Choice	Effects on Race and Ethnicity Diversity	Effects on SES Diversity	Effects on Ability and Achievement Diversity
Charters			
Within charter school.	Segregation.	Segregation.	Segregation in exam charters and for special-needs and gifted children.
Between charter schools and conventional schools.	Effects unlikely due to the relatively small number of charters in most school districts.	Effects unlikely due to the relatively small number of charters, and their comparable SES compositions to local conventional schools in district.	Lower proportion of student with disabilities in charter schools. Some evidence that charter schools cream higher-achieving students away from host district's public schools.
Private			
Within private school.	Segregation.	Segregation.	Segregation in schools for special-needs students.
Between private schools and local nonchoice schools.	Segregation.	Segregation.	Inconclusive due to contradictory findings.
Home Schooling			
Within home schools	Segregation.	Segregation.	Insufficient data.
Between home schools and local nonchoice schools.	Effects unlikely because home schooling represents a relatively small portion of the overall student population and they are widely dispersed geographically.	Effects unlikely because home schooling represents a relatively small portion of the overall student population and they are widely dispersed geographically.	Effects unlikely because home schooling represents a relatively small portion of the overall student population and they are widely dispersed geographically.

market mechanisms will foster improvement in underperforming schools or they will be closed because consumers (parents and their children) will not choose them.

The corpus of social science research about most forms of school choice is sufficiently large to evaluate their contribution to academic excellence, equity, racial, ethnic, and socioeconomic diversity. The empirical evidence synthesized in this chapter suggests that, overall, choice has not fostered greater diversity in magnets, vouchers, charters, or private schools nor systematically stimulated diversity in conventional schools.[138] In practice, choice schools and programs are as segregated, and in some instances, more segregated, by race, ethnicity, and SES than the other public schools in their local community. As designed and implemented, choice options have resulted in very little desegregation. The exceptions to this generalization are full magnet programs with controlled choice, some interdistrict magnet plans, and some secular private schools. Rarely do any of the other choice options offer students a racially, ethnically, or socioeconomically diverse educational experience. Moreover, some forms of choice also segregate students by ability and achievement. The reasons that most choice options are segregated by race, ethnicity, SES, and in some cases by ability are complex but four reasons emerged from the research findings.

Design of Choice Program. Many choice options are intended to serve a homogeneous population such as gifted, special-needs, or low-income children. Under these circumstances, the design of the choice school itself as established by statutes or school board policies, structures school segregation.

Schools Choosing Students. Choice schools informally select their pupils despite statutes and policies prohibiting selection. Some choice schools and programs discourage the parents of English language learners, children not identified as gifted, students with discipline problems, and special-needs children from enrolling in them. Private schools formally choose students from families that have resources to pay tuition, and even among those who can pay, private schools frequently select students through the use of an entrance exam.

Scarcity of Interdistrict Choice. Most choice options are confined within a school district's boundaries. If a district has high proportions of low-income and ethnic minority students, it is impossible to achieve race and SES diversity. Regionwide choice programs remain rare even though many interdistrict choice programs have been successful in fostering diverse schools.

Parental Preferences. Some parents of Native American, Black, Latino, White, and special-needs children consciously choose schools segregated by race or ability. Parents frequently believe they have chosen a better quality school for their child, but the evidence reviewed in this chapter indicates that they are often guided less by a school's academic reputation and more by its demographic profile. Parents appear to select a choice school with a student body similar to their own race, even if the choice school has lower test scores than their current school. The economic theory that proposes parents will choose better schools for their children is based on the unrealistic assumptions that everyone agrees what makes one school "better" than another and that parents have perfect information about their choice options. However, parents of children with different abilities or from various race and SES backgrounds may construct the concept of a "better" school in a range of ways, sometimes selecting schools where the background of the students is similar to their own. Even in cases where parents define "better" schools as having higher levels of student academic achievement (a common criterion for good schools shared by choice theorists), they may lack good information about the academic quality of specific schools. In such cases, many parents use a school's SES, race, and ethnic composition as a proxy for its academic quality and level of safety.

RECOMMENDATIONS

Although education policymakers cannot influence the composition of schools in the private sector, directly shape housing policy, or influence the rapid demographic transformation of the student population, if they wish to avoid continued segregation by race, SES, ability and achievement in public schools, they can restructure existing choice plans and design new ones to create genuine and realistic opportunities for diverse education.[139] They can, that is, accept Justice Kennedy's invitation to devise creative and comprehensive plans that take account of race as well as other diversity factors as part of a "nuanced, individual evaluation of school needs and school characteristics."[140] In addition, all public choice policy can be modified either to negatively sanction designs that segregate or to reward those that generate diversity. Publicly funded choice schools can be required to actively pursue racial, SES, and achievement representation. Recommendations for policymakers and other stakeholders who wish to pursue this goal include:

Redesign Current Choice Policies to Ensure Diversity

- Because unregulated school choice leads to de facto segregation by race, ethnicity, SES, and at times by achievement or ability, to foster diversity it is necessary to implement some form of controlled-choice admission plans based on combinations of residential census tracts, student achievement, and SES (and in some cases, race can be utilized as well).[141] Short of instituting controlled choice admission policies for entrance into choice schools and programs, policies that utilize carrots and sticks can incentivize the voluntary desegregation of choice options.

- Create new magnet schools and site them in integrated or inner-city communities, not White neighborhoods. Do not give neighborhood students preferences for admission to magnets.

- Given that most communities already have multiple metropolitan area-wide public services (e.g., water, power, sanitation, transportation, telecommunications, parks and recreation facilities, sports franchises, medical and public health systems, labor markets), and that well-designed interdistrict plans have proven to be popular and successful at fostering diverse schools, renew and expand regional areawide choice options that transcend school district boundaries.

- Initiate policies that reward suburban school systems for participating in interdistrict magnet plans and disincentivize their opting out of existing plans.

- Design public school vouchers so that they can only be used in diverse schools.

- Do not permit private schools segregated by race, ethnicity, SES, or ability to convert to charter schools.

- Avoid the use of informal admission criteria (for example, requiring parental volunteers), steering, counseling, and other practices that result in magnet and charter schools choosing students, not students choosing schools.

- Coordinate local school siting and admissions policies with local housing policies to create diverse communities that lead to public schools integrated by race, ethnicity, and SES. Efforts to create diverse choice schools without diverse residential communities will be as effective and long lasting as cleaning the air on one side of a screen door.[142]

Provide Transportation to Students and Enhanced Information to Parents

- Provide transportation to all students involved in diverse school choice programs.

- Provide comprehensive and accessible information to parents about the value of diverse schools and the opportunities such schools offer to all children.
- Dispel common stereotypes about schools with racial, SES, and disability diversity.

Increase and Enforce Accountability Among Choice Schools

- Hold charters and voucher schools to the same performance standards as public schools.
- Revise the accountability incentives so that those who operate choice schools are not motivated to shape their clientele in ways that exclude students deemed less desirable.
- Hold charter schools accountable for failing to meet the diversity standards of their establishment agreements.

Redesign Public/Private Sector Relationships to Foster Diversity

- Incentivize public/private sector collaborations with diverse home schooling groups, voucher programs, and cyber schools.
- Disincentivize public/private sector collaborations with home schooling groups, voucher programs, and cyber schools that are segregated by race, SES, ELL status, or ability (unless a program is designed especially to accommodate a special needs student population).

CHAPTER 10

THE COMPETITIVE EFFECT OF SCHOOL CHOICE POLICIES ON PUBLIC SCHOOL PERFORMANCE

David Arsen and Yongmei Ni

One of the most important arguments for market-based educational policies is that they create competition that will pressure schools to use their resources more efficiently. School efficiency, also referred to as productivity, is the extent to which educational inputs (such as teaching hours) produce desired student outcomes (such as achievement gains). Increased efficiency means attaining better student outcomes with the same inputs, or the same student outcomes with fewer inputs. Ever since Milton Friedman proposed a voucher system more than half a century ago, school choice proponents have maintained that the competition introduced by choice policies will spur improvements in traditional public schools (TPSs) and so benefit students who remain in them. This argument has been central to countless school choice policy debates in recent decades. This chapter surveys available evidence on this question. We do not address the large number of studies of student performance in choice schools (charter schools or voucher schools, for example), but focus instead on the effects of school choice competition on TPSs.

Exploring the School Choice Universe: Evidence and Recommendations
pp. 193–209

School choice advocates appeal to theories of market competition to predict how TPSs will respond to choice policies. According to this argument, TPSs ordinarily have little incentive to improve their efficiency because they operate in relatively monopolistic markets. If, however, policies offer parents and students expanded choices and tie funding to enrollment, then educators will have an incentive to increase their productivity by working harder and implementing previously neglected administrative and educational improvements. This theory predicts that more productive schools will prosper by attracting increased enrollment, while less productive schools will be forced to improve or shut down.

On the other hand, some predict that a more competitive system will not benefit all students, but rather will create both winners and losers relative to the status quo. Increased choice and competition could diminish the quality of at least some TPSs as choice schools draw away motivated students, funding, effective teachers, or all three. If highly motivated students were more active in choosing to attend choice schools, less motivated students would become clustered in increasingly disadvantaged TPSs. These schools in turn could have difficulty responding to the competitive challenge because of negative peer effects over which school administrators have limited control. Choice policies could also introduce inefficiencies associated with high levels of student or teacher mobility or through the underutilization of facilities in schools losing students. Given relatively fixed operating expenses in the short run, average per-pupil costs may increase in TPSs that lose students. If revenues decline faster than costs in these schools, they may be forced to cut programs, which could spur the loss of additional students and resources and trigger a downward spiral.

As school choice policies grow, it is increasingly important to gain a better understanding of the validity of these contrasting predictions, since, for the foreseeable future, most students will remain in the TPS system. Relevant studies have not been possible in the United States until recently, however, since they require sufficiently high rates of choice program participation over a long enough period to elicit TPS responses. Although a variety of school choice policies could potentially generate market pressures, we focus on vouchers and charter schools because they are the only choice policies for which the competitive impacts on TPS outcomes have been studied systematically.[1] In this early stage of research, the initial results are mixed and inconclusive.

To frame our discussion of the empirical research, the next section offers some conceptual observations on various ways competition might affect school outcomes. We argue that in principle, choice policies could generate positive or negative consequences for students remaining in TPSs. We also identify features of choice policies and local settings likely to affect the distribution of costs and benefits among various constituencies and some key methodological issues for researchers. Finally, we summarize the empirical research on the competitive effects of vouchers and charter schools, and we offer some concluding observations.

CONCEPTUAL BACKGROUND

Discussions of the competitive consequences of school choice are most often framed in terms of economic theories of how markets affect the behavior of consumers and suppliers. School choice policies are intended to create market incentives that change the behavior of both families (consumers) and schools (suppliers). Even in theory, however, these behavioral responses and hence the educational consequences of competition are uncertain.

Proponents of school choice typically anticipate that given the opportunity, students (and families) will select higher quality schools, generally defined as schools that more efficiently produce desired student outcomes. Thus, high quality schools, including new entrants to the market like charters, are expected to gain students and resources at the expense of low-quality schools. This drain on low-quality schools is expected to prompt them to improve their technical efficiency as administrators move employees to work harder and/or implement better educational practices or programs. Indeed, schools that attract choice students would provide administrators of other schools with useful information on how their practices or resource allocation could be improved. In addition, choice could generate improvements in allocative efficiency as students sort themselves across schools into more compatible groupings based on their learning needs and interests. Such groupings would allow educators in both choice and traditional public schools to better adapt instructional programs to their particular student bodies.

This theoretical conception entails three interrelated mechanisms through which choice and competition could affect student achievement and efficiency.[2] First, it presumes that students will shift from lower to higher productivity schools, thereby raising the education system's overall efficiency. Second, it involves a re-sorting of students across schools, which will generate peer effects on student achievement. Third, it presumes that TPSs will respond to competition in particular ways, although those expectations may or may not be realized. Consideration of each of these mechanisms highlights ways in which the systemic adjustments predicted by choice advocates are highly uncertain and contingent.

First, if school choice is to generate improvements in student outcomes, choices should be based on schools' academic quality. However, if parents choose schools for other reasons—student racial or socioeconomic composition, sports facilities, proximity to home—their choices may not pressure schools losing students to improve their academic performance. In fact, parents often lack good information on schools' academic quality, and in such situations they may well use more visible features, including student demographics, as a proxy for school quality.[3]

Second, the re-sorting of students under school choice policies will generate peer effects for the education of students who remain in TPSs. Proponents expect that choice policies will produce positive peer effects by fostering groupings of students in schools with more compatible learning needs. However, if parents select schools based on peer characteristics, choice could increase socioeconomic and ability stratification across schools, harming some students who remain in TPSs. This is a particularly likely outcome if low-achieving students benefit from interaction with higher achieving classmates and active choosers are disproportionately higher achieving. In such cases, peer effects could harm the education of disadvantaged students who become more concentrated in TPSs.

Finally, it is unclear that schools losing students will respond by improving their educational performance, either by implementing better educational practices or inspiring harder work among employees. Such responses are certainly possible, but so are a variety of other potential strategies. For example, administrators in TPSs may choose to cooperate with one another or with new entrants to the local education market. Alternatively, TPSs might work together to create barriers to some choices in order to restrict families' options and blunt the potentially damaging impact of competition. Then again, TPSs may simply adopt a passive stance, being content to let other schools draw away certain students. Among schools and districts that do compete, efforts to improve school quality constitute only one of a range of strategic actions (such as marketing, extracurricular programs, upgrading facilities), each with differing consequences for school efficiency. In short, TPSs are likely to respond to competition with diverse strategies, including some that are unlikely to improve educational outcomes. While all of these potential responses have been reported anecdotally, we have as yet an incomplete understanding of which responses are most prevalent—and why.[4]

Whatever the response of TPS educators to market-based reforms, they may need to overcome two additional sources of inefficiency that choice policies could introduce. First, school choice will increase student mobility. While low levels of mobility can be accommodated, high levels generate a turbulent educational setting that undermines teaching and learning. Second, choice may hinder efficiency in TPSs losing students, if they are forced to underutilize their capital facilities or personnel. Given relatively fixed operating expenses, average per-pupil costs could easily increase in TPSs losing students, at least in the short term.

CONDITIONING FACTORS

School choice policies initiate a complex set of adjustments among participants in educational systems that can have either positive or negative results. The likelihood of either depends on choice program design and on local circumstances. We call these conditioning factors. While the research literature yields disparate findings on the effects of choice and competition, attention to conditioning factors may help to provide coherence to apparently conflicting findings. Moreover, a better understanding of such factors can help shape policies that preserve the benefits of choice policies while minimizing the potential harm. This list of conditioning factors is illustrative, not exhaustive, attending to four primary categories: (1) financial arrangements, (2) regulations, (3) policy implementation, and (4) local settings.

Financial Arrangements

The nature of competition among schools depends critically on the link between student flows and school funding. If resources are not at stake, schools are unlikely to compete for students. Choice policies vary greatly in the share of per-pupil funding that schools lose when students depart. Moreover, it is difficult to know how high the stakes should be. If the loss of revenue when a student leaves is less than the marginal cost of educating that student, then the school actually benefits financially from declining enrollment. But if, on the other hand, revenues decline faster than costs when students leave, schools losing students have difficulty avoiding cuts to existing programs; still less are they able to marshal resources necessary to improve services.[5] One way for policy to address this tension is to phase in the full per-pupil funding loss over a period of years.

In addition, student funding must be adequately adjusted for higher cost students (such as secondary versus elementary, or special versus regular education students); otherwise, choice schools have an incentive to compete for the cheapest and easiest students to educate. Insofar as choice schools are successful in enrolling low-cost students and excluding high-cost students, they reduce their own average cost. They accomplish this not by increasing their efficiency, however, but by increasing the average cost for TPSs that continue to enroll high-cost students.[6] In order to diminish such negative externalities and promote efficiency, it is important that the revenues schools receive match the differential cost of providing educational services to different types of students.

Regulations

The regulations governing choice policies strongly influence the incentives and constraints that market participants face. The predicted benefits of school choice for nonchoosers apply only if students choose schools, not the other way around. To reduce the risk of harmful effects on students who remain in TPSs, rules prohibiting selective admissions practices at choice schools are therefore essential. But since every school has an incentive to admit some students while discouraging others from enrolling, compliance with admission rules must be monitored and enforced. Uniform admission procedures at choice schools decrease the opportunity to enroll or exclude students on the basis of cost or other student characteristics.

Regulations regarding curriculum, teacher preparation, or testing in choice schools narrow the scope for educational innovation, but they can also help to level the playing field for competition among schools.

Policy Implementation

How a choice policy is implemented also affects outcomes. For example, parents typically lack complete information on the quality of alternative schools, and all schools have incentive to present only favorable information. Policies that ensure that families receive information on application procedures and academic programs of available schools help parents make sound choices. Moreover, they help schools learn from one another and encourage widespread adoption of best practices.[7] Prospects for positive changes in TPSs are also enhanced when implementation involves moderately paced expansion of choice participation, technical assistance for schools in need of improvement, and rigorous oversight of the policy rules by public agencies.

Local Setting

A particular policy can elicit diverse effects in different states or across local districts. For example, the rate of population growth or decline in a region will strongly condition the competitive pressures of choice policies.

In rapidly growing areas, the competitive threat of choice policies is greatly muted. Public schools may even welcome the departure of students to alleviate enrollment pressure. In areas with declining population, however, choice is more likely to generate strong competitive pressure on TPSs, especially in states where districts lack the ability to raise additional funding locally. This combination of circumstances also poses the greatest risk that choice will touch off a downward spiral in at least some TPSs.

Another element of the local setting that affects choice outcomes is the degree of preexisting inefficiency in an area's public schools, which itself may be the result of the range of private or public school choices historically available. Similarly, the potential for choice policies to generate either positive or negative peer effects on students remaining in TPSs depends on the degree of preexisting racial and socioeconomic segregation. Finally, the prospect for school choice to spur improvement also clearly depends on the quality of administrative leadership. If leadership is weak, politically divided and subject to rapid turnover, a school or district will have limited capacity to respond effectively to competitive pressures.[8]

In sum, the competitive effects of school choice on students who remain in TPSs are conditional and uncertain. Further research is needed to clarify the competitive effects of specific policy features in conjunction with given local conditions in order to minimize the potential harmful effects of choice competition on some students. Many school choice advocates themselves acknowledge the potential risks that choice policies can pose for nonchoosers. When they nevertheless argue that every child will benefit from school choice, they are usually relying on the idea that "school productivity would increase sufficiently to swamp any negative allocative effects that some students might experience."[9] For this reason, empirical evidence of school choice competition generating improved TPS efficiency becomes important. We turn now to an evaluation of empirical research on this issue.

METHODOLOGICAL CHALLENGES IN ASSESSING COMPETITIVE EFFECTS

School choice policies are seldom implemented as controlled experiments, so scholars must rely on nonexperimental, statistical methods to assess competitive effects. Researchers usually try to identify a causal relationship across local areas between the level of competition and TPS student achievement. In order to do so, however, they must overcome some key methodological obstacles. These include the nonrandom nature of choice school location and choice student participation, and the challenge of accurately measuring the intensity of choice competition.

First, the availability of choice options is not randomly distributed across local communities, but rather is likely to be related to the performance of local public schools. It is reasonable to expect new schooling options to be disproportionately established in areas where families are least satisfied with local public schools. However, this poses a methodological problem. Suppose, for example, researchers observe that a lower level of public school quality correlates with a higher degree of competition. It is possible that low public school quality induced more choice options—or, alternatively, that competition lowered public school quality. To reliably estimate the competitive effect, therefore, researchers must address this chicken-and-egg problem with statistical procedures such as fixed-effect transformations or instrumental variable (IV) estimators.[10]

Second, students who participate in school choice may differ systematically from those who do not in terms of their past performance, socioeconomic background, parental motivation, and innate ability. By drawing certain students away, school choice might significantly change the student composition of conventional public schools. For example, if choice schools tend to draw lower performing students, the average achievement level of students remaining in TPSs would automatically go up, even without any competitive effect. To correct for potential biases associated with student self-selection, researchers can include extensive control variables representing student characteristics in their estimations. Alternatively, when multiyear, student-level data are available, researchers can control for unobserved student characteristics such as parental motivation and innate ability through fixed-effects transformations.

Finally, studies of competitive effects must devise suitable measures of the intensity of competition that TPSs experience. Many studies of private schools' competitive effects have used the percentage of total enrollment in an area attending private schools. Charter school studies have measured the level of competition by the number of charter schools within a given radius of public schools, the distance from a public school to the nearest charter school, or the share of public school students who have left to attend charter schools. None of these measures is perfect, however, and there is no consensus about which is most suitable. Moreover, all reflect the existence of multiple suppliers, not the intensity of competition or whether and how schools or districts compete.[11]

EVIDENCE ON THE EFFECTS OF CHOICE COMPETITION

With the proliferation of school choice programs in recent years, there has been a steady growth in studies of the competitive effects of vouchers and charter schools on TPS performance. As a backdrop for our review of this research, it is useful to note Belfield and Levin's survey of more than 40 studies of "traditional" forms of competition on TPSs. This includes competition between public and private schools as well as competition among public schools that is realized when households choose to live within a particular school district in an area (Tiebout choice).[12] Belfield and Levin conclude that these forms of competition produce at most small positive effects on student achievement and efficiency. On average, they found that an increase of one standard deviation in competition produces less than a 0.1 standard deviation increase in public school test scores.

Competitive Effects of Vouchers

Evidence of vouchers' competitive effects comes mainly from two publicly funded programs, one in Milwaukee and one in Florida. Established in 1990, the Milwaukee Parental Choice Program (MPCP) offers vouchers for students from low-income families to attend secular private schools. The program was expanded in 1995 to include religious private schools. The MPCP remains one of the largest and longest running voucher programs in the nation. The program's financial impact on Milwaukee public schools is muted by design; the district loses roughly 30% of state aid associated with each voucher student. In 1999, Florida adopted the "A-Plus" accountability system, which included the Opportunity Scholarship Program that allowed students in low-performing schools (those receiving F grades for 2 consecutive years) to receive vouchers to attend private schools.[13]

Hoxby's study of the MPCP found a substantial positive competitive effect of vouchers.[14] Analyzing school-level data, she compared changes in the average performance of fourth-graders prior to and after the widespread use of vouchers. She found that public schools with the highest percentage of voucher-eligible students had significantly higher increases in achievement than schools with fewer or no voucher-eligible students. In math, for example, the annual increase in test scores in the schools with the highest proportion of voucher-eligible students was 7 percentile points, compared to 5 and 4 percentile points in schools with few or no voucher-eligible students. She also found that productivity, measured as test scores per thousand dollars spent, increased faster in schools subject to the most competition.

While voucher advocates have broadly cited Hoxby's study, critics say it overstated competitive gains because it did not take into account changes in the mix of TPS students.[15] In a follow-up study of the MPCP, Chakrabarti refined Hoxby's method to include controls for student composition and likewise found greater improvement in test scores in schools facing greater voucher competition.[16] In another MPCP study, however, Carnoy and his colleagues used recent data and two alternative methodologies, including one based on Chakrabarti's work, and found "essentially no evidence that students in those traditional public schools in Milwaukee facing more competition achieve higher test-score gains."[17]

Evaluations of Florida's Opportunity Scholarship Program have shown more consistent results. In a 2001 study and a follow-up study with Winters, Greene compared test score gains in voucher-eligible schools (those receiving F grades) with schools graded A-D.[18] Both studies found that voucher-eligible schools made greater gains than other public schools. These conclusions have been challenged on a number of statistical grounds.[19] Using fixed-effects strategies, Chakrabarti compared changes in the performance of F and D schools before and after the voucher program and also found that F schools made greater performance gains.[20] In a separate analysis of Florida's vouchers, Figlio and Rouse also found some improvements in reading scores in voucher-threatened, low-performing schools. The authors reported, however, that the gains were largely explained by changes in student composition and the stigma of failure rather than pressure from voucher competition.[21]

However, the Florida Opportunity Scholarship Program voucher program's integral connection to the state's broader accountability system complicates efforts to distinguish the voucher component's competitive effect. Carnoy, Ladd and others have suggested that the observed performance gains in voucher-eligible schools represent responses to the state's grading of schools, rather than the small voucher component of the program, because similar patterns of test score changes have been observed in other states (such as North Carolina) that grade schools but do not have a voucher program.[22]

Recently, Greene and Winters estimated the competitive effects of a federally sponsored program that provides a $7,500 voucher to low-income students in Washington, DC.[23] Using data for 2003-04 and 2004-05, the years before and after the voucher program's implementation, the authors employed a series of multivariate regression models to measure the impact of the physical proximity to voucher schools on public school achievement, controlling for demographic characteristics and baseline school test scores. The authors found no impacts of the voucher program on student achievement in the district's public schools, but this is not surprising for the initial year of the program, and the longer term competitive effects may differ.

Taken as a whole, the U.S. evidence on vouchers' competitive effects remains extremely limited. The available evidence, however, neither refutes nor strongly supports the prediction that vouchers will improve

TPS outcomes. Estimates of positive competitive effects are hard to differentiate from the effects of the larger accountability system and appear sensitive to the use of stronger controls for student self-selection and other measurement issues. Existing evidence so far only hints at how specific features of voucher programs (funding arrangements, regulations, and implementation) could be structured in order to enhance the overall beneficial consequences of voucher competition.

Competitive Effects of Charter Schools

More evidence is available on the competitive effects of charter schools. Studies have focused on states such as Arizona, California, Florida, Michigan, North Carolina, and Texas, where charter school enrollment is sufficient to potentially generate competitive pressures on TPSs. Among these studies, the results are once again very mixed.

Researchers have found charter competition to have a positive impact on TPS student achievement in Florida, no effect in California, and a negative effect in Ohio. Each of these studies employed multiple measures of the degree of charter competition.

Sass analyzed student-level Florida data for Grades 3-10 over a 3-year period with fixed-effect regressions and found a small significant positive competitive effect on TPS math achievement, but no effect on reading. [24] Zimmer and Buddin also used student-level, fixed-effect regressions to analyze data from six large California school districts between 1997-1998 and 2001-2002 and found no significant effect of charter school competition. [25] Carr and Ritter employed a pooled time series regression analysis of Ohio data and found a slight negative competitive effect. [26]

Two studies of North Carolina yielded contrasting findings. Holmes, DeSimone, and Rupp report that TPSs facing competition increased their test scores by approximately 1%, or about one quarter of the average yearly growth. [27] Bifulco and Ladd, on the other hand, examined a student-level panel dataset for Grades 3-8 from 1996 to 2002 and found no significant competitive effects on reading or math scores in nearby TPSs. [28] Bifulco and Ladd attribute the different findings in the two studies to their ability to better control for shifts in student composition through the use of student-level data.

As in North Carolina, studies of Michigan have produced conflicting results. Hoxby analyzed trends in school-level performance between 1992-1993 and 1999-2000. She found that achievement and productivity in Michigan's TPSs increased once charter school competition reached at least 6% of district enrollment. [29] The estimated increase was largest in the 4th grade, about 2.4 scale points a year in reading and 2.5 scale points in mathematics. In the same study, Hoxby also found similar positive charter school competitive effects in Arizona. The major qualification in assessing Hoxby's findings is that she did not control for student composition and other school characteristics that may change as charter schools enter the educational system. Bettinger analyzed school-level Michigan data from 1996-1997 to 1998-1999, incorporating controls for student characteristics and the possibility that charter location is influenced by the performance of public schools. He found no significant competitive effect of charter schools on test scores in nearby TPSs.[30]

Both the Hoxby and Bettinger studies were conducted at a relatively early stage in the development of Michigan's charter schools policy. Using 11 years of school-level data, Ni was able to analyze the evolution of charter schools' competitive effect over time. She refined Hoxby's measure of charter competition and controlled for several student and school characteristics.[31] Based on multiple estimation strategies, including fixed effects, Ni's results show that charter competition exceeding 6% of district enrollment had a negative impact on student achievement and school efficiency in Michigan's TPSs. This effect is small or negligible in the short run, but becomes more substantial in the long run (after 6 years of sustained competition). In the long run, for schools in districts where charter schools have drawn away a significant share of students, charter competition decreases math and reading test performance in the range of 0.2 to 0.5 standard deviations.

So far, Texas is the only state in which two studies have found consistent positive charter school competitive effects, if modest ones.[32] Bohete used a pooled time series regression analysis on district-level data for 1996 to 2002 and found that a one percentage point increase in countywide charter school enrollment was associated with a 0.1 percentage point increase in district test pass rates. Booker and colleagues used student-level data over 8 years for Grades 4-8 in fixed-effects regressions and found that the presence of nearby charter schools generated a small but statistically significant increase in test scores (effect size < 0.1).[33]

The sensitivity of research findings to methodology is further illustrated by Imberman's recent study, which employed both fixed-effect transformations and IV estimates to examine the impact of charter schools on TPS achievement in an anonymous urban school district.[34] He found moderate gains in TPS test scores when using fixed-effect methods, but negative effects when using IV procedures.

While charter schools offer the best opportunity to study the competitive effect of school choice policies in the United States, thus far the available evidence fails to yield a clear and consistent set of findings. If anything, the weight of the research suggests that charter school competition is not a very consistent force in its impact on TPSs achievement in one way or another. Several studies find no effects. When statistically significant effects have been found, they are generally small.

Is it possible to identify patterns across studies that might account for the diversity of research findings? In principle, differences in findings could arise from differences in (1) research methodologies, (2) state charter school policies, or (3) state settings.

First, as noted above, a key methodological choice for researchers is how they measure the degree of competition. Yet a review of past studies indicates no clear relationship between findings and measures of charter competition. Indeed some studies find largely consistent results using multiple competition measures.[35] Alternatively, the units of analysis vary across the studies. However, there is no apparent relationship in competitive effect estimates between studies that employ student-level analyses versus those based on building- or district-level analyses.[36]

Second, the funding arrangements and regulations governing charter schools vary across states in ways that could significantly modify their competitive impacts on TPSs. In some states, for example, only part of per-pupil revenue follows students to choice schools when they leave their resident TPSs. In Michigan, however, where Ni found negative competitive effects, students take the full amount of school funding with them to charter schools, and local districts have no ability to increase local revenues to maintain their operations. Moreover, the state's per-pupil foundation levels have declined in real terms since 2002. Whether such policy features can help explain interstate differences in estimated charter school competitive effects has yet to be determined.

Third, state and local contexts, including the pace of overall enrollment growth or decline, appear to condition competitive effects. In states with growing enrollment, such as California, Florida, and Texas, traditional public schools are less likely to experience acute competitive pressure when students move to charter schools. If TPSs are overcrowded, charter schools can serve as a welcome "release valve" to ease enrollment pressure. By contrast, in states with declining student populations, charter school policies create more intense zero-sum competition for students and resources. Among states that have been studied, Michigan and Ohio have the slowest overall enrollment growth, and recent studies in both have found competition to have a negative effect on TPS performance.

International Experience

School choice policies in other countries provide insights from large-scale programs that have been in effect for many years, although caution is required in relating findings from different educational settings abroad to the U.S. context. On balance, the international evidence remains mixed. In the Czech Republic, Filer and Munich found that school districts facing significant competition from private schools, which are partially funded by the state, had greater success in getting their students into university than did other districts.[37] Gibbons, Machin, and Silva, studying primary schools in England that are funded largely by the central government, found that students with a wider range of public school choices achieved better academic outcomes.[38]

On the other hand, studies of national school choice policies in Chile and New Zealand have produced less favorable evidence on competitive outcomes. Hsieh and Urquiola's study of Chile found no evidence that choice improved average educational outcomes in public schools, while Carnoy and McEwan found that competition led to small achievement gains in metropolitan areas, but small negative effects in the rest of the country, where three quarters of Chile's primary students live.[39] In New Zealand, Ladd and Fiske found that competition reduced the quality of elementary student learning as perceived by teachers, and generated negative effects on other aspects of schooling, such as teachers' job satisfaction.[40]

Experience with both Chile and New Zealand's large-scale choice plans reinforces the concern that schools with large concentrations of disadvantaged students have difficulty competing for students and resources, as more advantaged students leave for better schools.[41] It also undercuts predictions that the implementation of larger scale voucher programs in the United States would generate greater improvements in TPS outcomes than current, small-scale programs. Taken as a whole, the international evidence has yet to establish consistent evidence that choice programs make educational systems significantly more productive than they otherwise would be.

Case Studies of Public School Responses to Competition

Case studies hold the promise of providing a more nuanced understanding of how traditional public schools respond to competition. While quantitative studies are suited to evaluate statistical links between choice competition and TPS achievement, so far they have not provided much insight into how public school operations change in response to vouchers or charter schools. Case studies offer the opportunity of looking inside the "black box" of school organizational practices. Do educators in TPSs subject to competition work harder, become more responsive to student needs, or change their curricula or instructional practices?

Not surprisingly, the findings from case studies of TPS responses to choice policies are extremely heterogeneous. While the quantitative literature points to variations in competitive effects across states, case studies remind us that school and district responses vary widely within states as well. Indeed, competition can spur multiple responses within given schools, with some having potential to improve academic performance, and others not. Case studies also generally reinforce the notion that choice policies elicit stronger responses among TPS administrators as their perception of the financial threat from new competitors increases.[42] It is less apparent from the case study literature, however, whether these competitive responses can be expected to improve student achievement or school productivity.

Competition from vouchers and charter schools may spur public school districts to open new schools, change school leadership or set higher performance goals. They may also encourage public school educators to be more solicitous of parents and attentive to their concerns. Other possible responses include launching marketing initiatives, or creating "add-on" programs, such as all-day kindergarten and extracurricular activities.[43] Or, a TPS may instead choose to vilify charter competitors or otherwise obstruct charter school openings and operations.[44] Thus far, however, there is little evidence that choice competition stimulates significant changes or innovations in TPS instructional practice.[45]

While case studies highlight the diversity of schools and districts' organizational responses (and nonresponses) to choice competition, we cannot gauge, using such studies, competition's overall impacts on school operations or quality. It is noteworthy, however, that careful quantitative research is beginning to cast doubt on whether key organizational changes anticipated by the school choice movement are indeed associated with improved student performance. Berands and colleagues, for example, find that their measure of innovation is negatively associated with learning gains (when other conditions are controlled for), while Zimmer and Buddin failed to find evidence that increased school autonomy is associated with improved student achievement.[46] So the question remains not only whether competition generates any systematic impacts inside the black box of school operations, but also whether observed changes are a good thing.

SUMMARY, IMPLICATIONS, AND RECOMMENDATIONS

Only recently have choice policies been implemented in the United States on a scale sufficient to potentially elicit competitive responses from public schools. As yet, existing empirical studies permit no firm conclusions regarding the effects of school choice policies on student achievement and efficiency in traditional public schools. While the research base is growing, it remains limited. Available studies neither refute nor strongly support the prediction that voucher and charter school competition will improve traditional public school performance. Among studies with suitable statistical controls, some find positive effects, others find negative effects, and some find no significant effects at all. The substantive effects of choice policy competition also appear modest. Among studies finding statistically significant effects, most indicate small effect sizes in the range of $(+/-)$ 0.1.

The research surveyed here suggests, rather than conclusively establishes, that competition from vouchers and charter schools is no more beneficial for TPS performance than competition from nearby private or public schools in environments with no choice policy. Indeed, Belfield and Levin's review of studies of these traditional forms of school choice shows a higher proportion of findings indicating statistically significant positive effects on TPS outcomes than is evident among existing studies of voucher and charter school competition.[47]

The accumulating evidence is, however, beginning to point to interesting differences across state settings. This diversity of findings is not surprising, as we suggested in our discussion of conditioning factors at the outset. Additional research is needed on how specific policy features (financial arrangements, regulations, policy implementation), and the characteristics of local settings influence the impacts of choice reforms on the public school system. This will require comparative analysis of state-level studies. Even within states, however, there is clearly a need for research that moves beyond estimating mean state-level competitive effects to more closely exploring the causes of variations in competitive effects across local communities. Such an undertaking could benefit from careful coordination with case study research. While evidence suggests that the effects of competition are not linear, we cannot translate that finding into useful guidelines for policy until we better understand the thresholds for beneficial or harmful competition, and the duration or trajectories of effects over time.

Finally, the absence of strong evidence that choice policies improve the efficiency of traditional public schools does not rule out other potential benefits of these policies, such as improved outcomes for active choosers, a better match between families' values and school programs, or expanded freedom to choose. Likewise, an overall evaluation would also consider the equity and social cohesion impacts of school choice policies.[48]

We recommend that policymakers exercise caution when assessing predictions that school choice policies will benefit students who are not active choosers, since the evidence in support of this claim is not yet strong or conclusive.

CHAPTER 11

THE IMPACT OF SCHOOL CHOICE REFORMS ON STUDENT ACHIEVEMENT

Gary Miron and Jessica L. Urschel

One of the most common—and most widely disputed—claims about school choice is that it will lead to improved student learning and performance on standardized tests. With growing interest in school choice and the expansion and improvement of state accountability systems, an increasing number of studies have taken up the question of whether student performance improves in the many school choice models relative to performance in comparable nonchoice schools. This chapter closely examines a wide range of evidence regarding school choice and its impact on student achievement.[1]

Studying student achievement in school choice is complicated by a number of factors. First, there is limited evidence for some types of school choice. There are six broad choice types used in this book: vouchers/ tuition tax credits, charter schools, homeschooling, interdistrict choice, and intradistrict choice (including magnet schools and open enrollment plans) and virtual schools. The scope of evidence on homeschooling, virtual schools, and varied forms of inter- and intradistrict choice programs is very limited.

Exploring the School Choice Universe: Evidence and Recommendations
pp. 211–236

Another factor that complicates a synthesis of research evidence on school choice is that considerable weaknesses appear in available data. In fact, a majority of the studies available on school choice are limited by the researchers' lack of access to student-level data and the unavailability of other evidence that can be linked from year to year. In recent years, studies of school choice have been aided by the expansion of state assessment programs under the No Child Left Behind Act, which now require testing in Grades 3 through 8. A growing number of states are also moving to value-added accountability models that require student-level data sets. While excessive testing and preparation for testing is clearly taking away from time for instruction, a substantial evidence base that researchers and evaluators can draw upon is also accumulating.

A third factor that overshadows the body of evidence on school choice is the predominance of partisan researchers and activist organizations that carry out the research. Especially in the areas of homeschooling, vouchers, and charter schools, the bulk of studies that find positive impacts in favor of school choice have been conducted by advocacy groups. That is not to say that research commissioned by advocacy groups will all result in positive findings. What we can see, however, is that not one study released by groups advocating for school choice found that school choice had a negative impact on student achievement. Given the role of advocacy and opposition groups in publishing research to justify their agenda, it is not surprising to find that the two most polarizing and widely disputed forms of school choice (vouchers and charter schools) have been the most studied.

In this chapter we attempt to summarize what is currently known about the impact of various forms of school choice on student achievement. Key questions addressed are:

- What is the relative scope and quality of empirical research on school choice and student achievement?
- What are the overall conclusions that can be drawn from empirical research on school choice and student achievement?

The purpose of this chapter is not to explore or explain the large differences in performance among diverse forms of school choice. Instead, we aim to provide answers to broad policy-related questions regarding whether the overall policies that promote school choice are likely to result in higher levels of student achievement. The next section details our methodology and addresses such issues as how student achievement can reasonably be measured, which existing studies merit serious consideration, how the quality of studies can be assessed, and how findings can be reasonably combined into a "bottom line" statement of overall impact.

Following the methods section we present our synthesis of evidence across multiple types of school choice.

METHODS

The process of synthesizing existing research is dependent on several key methodological decisions. Most important are the selection criteria for studies to be included in the analysis. That is, what characteristics make a study worth including? The selection criteria dealt with study design, quality issues, time limits, and/or geopolitical borders. The following discussion details selection criteria for this review as well as methods used to determine quality ratings and to synthesize findings. A discussion of limitations concludes this section.

Selecting Studies

In deciding which studies to include, we applied seven criteria.

1.   Presence of a technical report offering a clear account of analytical procedures used.
2.   Presence of aggregate analysis and conclusions. That is, we chose to exclude studies that would have required us to conduct our own analysis and draw our own conclusions based on others' data.
3.   Use of standardized tests to measure student achievement. Standardized test results, for example, often provide the only way to compare achievement across a wide range of charter and noncharter schools.
4.   Use of comparison groups. Any attempt to assess a given school's achievement impact requires some understanding of how choice students might have performed in the absence of choice schools. While randomized experiments with control groups are one of the most promising ways to determine impact, practical considerations have limited school choice researchers to observing "naturally" occurring comparison groups of nonchoice schools.[2] In cases where studies included a variety of research designs, we considered only the methodologically strongest design.
5.   Exclusion of duplicated studies. Only findings from the most recent study were included in cases where a particular author or group issued an update of earlier work using the same study design within the same location(s).

6. Exclusion of case studies or single school studies. These were excluded because it is unlikely findings can be reasonably generalized to the larger population of schools.

7. Exclusion of studies on school choice outside the United States of America. Although we recognize the importance of lessons that can be drawn from the experiences of other countries, we were concerned that we could not identify and consider a representative sample of international studies on school choice.

We considered and rejected two other selection criteria. First, we chose not to limit the time period because that would have resulted in few available studies for some choice models. And second, we chose not to exclude studies by advocacy or opposition groups, because doing so would have required making several difficult and subjective judgments. Instead, we have trusted that our quality rating methodology for weighting the evidence would—in part—reflect the inherent biases in research conducted by such groups.

Impact Ratings

For the purpose of our analyses, the key finding for each study was its assessment of impact on student achievement. It is important to bear in mind that impact is not necessarily synonymous with absolute achievement levels. For example, a magnet school with low test scores might still have significant positive impact if its students are gaining at a faster rate than similar students in other district schools. Conversely, a charter school with high test scores might have negative impact if its students are gaining more slowly than similar students in noncharter public schools. It is for this reason we considered comparison groups critical to assessing impact.

We assigned each study an impact rating according to the scale shown in Table 11.1. Positive values indicate that a study showed a particular school choice form to increase student achievement, and negative values indicate that it showed the model to decrease student achievement.[3]

Due to the wide variety of measures and methods employed across the studies, it would be difficult, if not impossible, to derive an overall "effect size."[4] Instead, we have systematically combined ratings of the studies' findings with an assessment of their design quality.

Assessing the Quality of the Studies

In a scheme similar to Scriven's weight and sum methodology,[5] each study was rated on six weighted dimensions of overall quality: research design, duration of study, controls, measures used, scope of the study,[6]

**Table 11.1. Scale for Impact Ratings of Studies
of Student Achievement in Diverse Forms
of School Choice**

Scale Value	Description
2	Positive overall impact
1	Slightly positive overall impact
0	Mixed impact or no difference
−1	Slightly negative overall impact
−2	Negative overall impact

and completeness of the technical report[7] (see Table 11.2). Assigned weights ranged from 0 to 10 points depending on the importance of the dimension; scores on each dimension were added to produce a rating of overall study quality. All ratings are based solely on information in technical reports or publications.

Out of a possible 32 points, high quality studies generally scored 20 or more. The very weakest and least rigorous studies typically had quality scores ranging from 3 to 10.

Because the values or variations within each dimension of study design are specific and concrete, the process of assigning scores was based on objective criteria. However, the total scores assigned for each dimension are subjective and reflect our judgments regarding the relative weight that each dimension should receive. For example, the overall study design can receive a maximum of 10 points, whereas the type of outcome measure is worth only 2 points. These judgments, though subjective, were informed by earlier syntheses of charter school research conducted by Miron and Nelson in 2001 and 2004.[8] The weighting system used here has evolved and become more elaborate to account for the characteristics of the broader field of school choice research.[9]

Given the wide variety of methodological rigor across studies, quality ratings are especially important in a synthesis of school choice research. Our approach includes studies with substantial limitations, but we give them less weight than other studies. We judged it important to include some of these less rigorous studies because they have attracted considerable attention and have been important in driving policy. By including them in our synthesis, we are able to present these weaker studies in a framework that allows readers to see the relationship between rigor and influence.

Table 11.2. Weighting Scheme for Quality Ratings of School Choice Studies on Student Achievement

Dimension	Values or Variations Within Each Dimension	Points	Total Possible Points
Research design	Randomized	10	10
	Matched students	8	
	Same cohorts	4	
	Consecutive cohorts	1	
	Cross sectional	0	
Duration of Study	More than 3 years of data	4	4
	2-3 years of data	3	
	1 year of data (cross-sectional)	0	
Controls	1 point for each of the following controls considered in the design: (i) family income, i.e., FRL; (ii) ethnicity; (iii) special education and/or LEP; (iv) starting performance level or use of gain score; (v) parents' education level; (vi) indicator of length of exposure	0-6	6
Measure of student performance	NPR, NCE, or scaled score	2	2
	Cut score (% meeting state standard)	1	
	General rating or grade	0	
Scope of the study	Scope is based on 3 separate scores related to (i) relative size of the population studied, (ii) number of grade levels covered, (iii) number of subjects included.		6
	Relative size of population studied: 3 points for large comprehensive studies, 2 points for moderately comprehensive studies, 1 point for small studies, and 0 points for very small studies.	0-3	
	Grade levels covered in the study (2 points for at least one grade at each of the three school levels; 1 point for at least one grade at two levels; 0 for at least one grade at one school level)	0-2	
	Subjects covered in study (1 for math and reading, 0 for one or neither)	0-1	
Completeness of the technical report	Technical report with clear and complete methods section	0-2	4
	Complete set of findings	0-1	
	Limitations of study included	0-1	
Total points			32

Combining Impact Scores and Study Quality Scores

The impact ratings can be combined to provide a single impact score. Rather than simply calculating a mean impact rating, however, we have calculated a weighted mean in which each study is weighted by quality.

Additionally, we have developed a method to map the impact and quality ratings for each study analyzed. In our maps, each study is charted on a horizontal axis according to its relative quality, and along a vertical axis according to its impact rating for a particular choice model. Impact ratings range from strongly negative to strongly positive, as Table 11.1 indicates. The results maps illustrate three important facets: (1) breadth and scope of available research, (2) overall quality of research, and (3) overall concentration of findings in terms of impact ratings.

Limitations

We are mindful of some important limitations in this synthesis of research on student achievement across diverse forms of school choice. First, any thorough evaluation of schools and school choice models should examine nonachievement outcomes, such as equity, student and family satisfaction and market accountability, curricular quality and relevance, and instructional effectiveness. Moreover, even when student achievement is the only concern, standardized test results are but one of many ways to assess it.

Like any review or meta-analysis, our portrayal of the existing literature is colored by the selection of studies for examination. We have made explicit the rules that guided our search for and selection of studies, and where possible, we sought to test our findings' sensitivity to these assumptions. Generally, we have been somewhat surprised at the paucity of studies of student achievement and the difficulty we had in obtaining some of the studies. As readers will see in the next section, we attempted to set out clear evaluative criteria and to apply them fairly to all studies reviewed.

STUDENT ACHIEVEMENT FOR VOUCHERS PROGRAMS

Since first being proposed in the 1950s by Milton Friedman,[10] vouchers have been discussed and debated widely. Publicly funded school voucher programs have been established in Milwaukee (as of 1991); Cleveland, Ohio (as of 1996); and Washington, DC (as of an act of the U.S. Congress in 2003). Some small, privately funded programs have also generated evidence regarding the effect of vouchers on student achievement in New York City; Dayton (OH); Washington, DC; and Charlotte (NC).[11]

In theory, we would have grouped tuition tax credit programs with vouchers because of their similar nature. However, because we could find no empirical studies examining academic achievement in tuition tax credit programs,[12] we focus here solely on voucher programs.

Figure 11.1 illustrates our findings for 15 studies across the various voucher programs. We grouped the studies based on the particular program, and assigned letter codes for each program accordingly. Our discussion also groups studies by specific programs. This chart provides an illustration of estimated impact and quality ratings for 15 studies completed during the past 14 years. A full list of the references for these studies in included in the endnotes.[13]

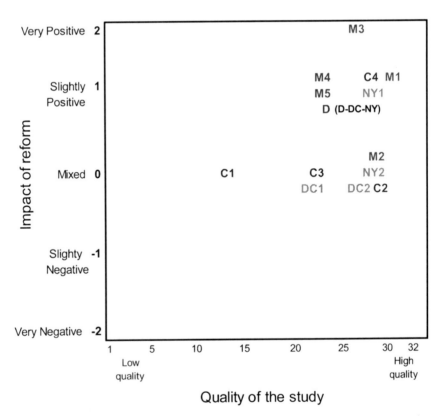

Figure 11.1.   Quality and impact ratings for 15 studies of student achievement in voucher programs.

Milwaukee. Milwaukee has the longest running voucher program in the nation. The program was started in 1991, and Witte and colleagues from the University of Wisconsin-Madison were contracted to evaluate the program.[14] Their evaluation used a host of demographic controls to match students from the Milwaukee Public School District. The final conclusion from their multiyear evaluation found that voucher students generally performed similarly to comparable students in math and reading.[15]

In 1996, Greene, Peterson, and Du analyzed the Milwaukee data and came to a different conclusion than Witte. Because the program had more applicants than spaces available, a lottery was used to randomly select students to be admitted into the program. When comparing scores of those students who were lottery winners against those of lottery losers, Greene, Peterson and Du found a significant difference in favor of the admitted and enrolled choice students in both math and reading. A more polished update of their findings was published in 1999.[16] Witte questioned their randomized approach on a number of grounds, including that some students who were refused subsequently enrolled in private schools, thereby biasing the control group through attrition, and potentially leaving the remaining control group with lower performing students.[17] Rouse was the third party to reanalyze the same data. She also used students from the lottery lists as a control group and found that voucher students were making gains in math but not in reading.[18] A study from 2011 by Cowen, Fleming, Witte, and Wolf (2011) found that the voucher students were more likely to obtain a higher level of educational attainment than their matched counterparts in the public school system.[19]

There were a number of limitations in all of these studies. While Witte and Rouse carefully presented detailed methods, rationales for decisions during the course of their analysis of data, and limitations in the interpretation of findings, this was not the case with the Greene, Peterson, and Du study.

Cleveland. The Cleveland voucher program was approved in 1995 and started operating in 1996. This program had a much smaller voucher amount available to help cover tuition at a private school than did the Milwaukee program, but it made available a larger number of vouchers.

The Ohio Department of Education hired Metcalf and colleagues from Indiana University to evaluate this program; the most recent publication led by Metcalf was in 2004 and found no real difference between voucher recipients and their comparison group.[20] In 2006, another group of evaluators led by Plucker released an updated report on the Metcalf work. The Plucker group added one more year of data and also altered some of the analysis techniques for imputing missing data. Its evaluation found that voucher students had made noticeable gains relative to the comparison groups after entry into middle school.[21]

In a 2006 study, Belfield[22] found no academic advantages for voucher users in second or fourth grade. Furthermore, his results did not vary after making adjustments for prior ability, intention-to-treat versus treatment effects, and dosage differences. Further, this study did not find differential effects for African American students as some of the other studies have found.

Similar to their work in Milwaukee, Greene and Peterson were quick to come up with their own analysis of the Cleveland results (see Greene, Howell & Peterson, 1997).[23] Their analysis of test data was limited to only two voucher schools, and they initially concluded that voucher students in those schools were making significant gains relative to a national norm. They updated the study in 1999 with additional years of data, at which point they found results to be mixed and in some cases negative. Nevertheless, the authors concluded that the program should be continued.[24] We have included only the second of their reports in our analysis, since both studies involved similar methods and authors, and the second reflected access to more data.

Washington, DC. The D.C. Opportunity Scholarship Program was the first federally funded private school voucher program in the United States. The U.S. Congress created the program in 2003, providing scholarships of up to $7,500 for low-income residents of the District of Columbia to send their children to local participating private schools. As with other voucher programs discussed, parents pay the difference between the voucher and the actual tuition costs. The U.S. Department of Education contracted a team of researchers led by Wolf to evaluate the program. The evaluation used a randomized controlled trial that compared students that received a place in a school via a lottery selection with students that did not. The two most recent reports from this evaluation conclude that there was no evidence of statistically significant differences in test scores between voucher recipients and students who applied but did not receive a voucher.[25]

In addition to this large, publicly funded voucher program, there is also a smaller, privately funded voucher program in Washington, D.C. An evaluation report after 1 year reported significant gains in math for African American students who switched to private schools in grades 2 through 5.[26] Unfortunately, no subsequent reports have been released on the student achievement results from this program.

New York City and Dayton, OH. A study of a privately funded voucher program in New York City[27] concluded that the program was resulting in significantly higher test results for African American voucher recipients, although no effects were seen for other ethnic subgroups. Krueger and Zhu[28] reanalyzed the data and found some serious shortcomings, including what they reported as exclusion of students and an inappropriate method for categorizing race. Their reanalysis indicated no effect favoring voucher students.

This program also was studied initially by some of the same persons involved in the studies of the New York and Washington, DC, private voucher programs. Findings from Dayton reported by West, Peterson, and Campbell[29] concluded that there were no differences between voucher recipients and nonrecipients. The one exception was for African American students, who gained more than similar non recipients.

Figure 11.1 illustrates that a moderate number of empirical studies have been completed on student achievement in voucher programs. Given the few voucher programs in the nation, however, the number of studies is surprisingly large. The figure also shows that most studies were of higher quality (with a mean quality rating of just over 25 points on a 0-32 scale). In fact, the quality ratings for the voucher research are considerably higher than the research for other areas of school choice. On the whole, the voucher studies suggest a moderate effect in favor of private schools that participated in the voucher programs; the weighted mean for the impact ratings was +0.62. It is important to note that 7 of the 15 studies had mixed findings, three of the seven with slightly positive findings had positive results only for African American students, and one study with slightly positive findings had positive results only for low performing students. None of the studies, however, indicated that vouchers were deterring learning for students who switched from public to participating private schools.[30]

STUDENT ACHIEVEMENT FOR HOMESCHOOLING

Research on the student achievement of homeschoolers has been the most difficult area of school choice to assess. Some of the obstacles are due to an inability to accurately count the home-school population, a lament well noted in home-school research. A more important difficulty that we encountered was locating and identifying studies that met our minimum inclusionary criteria. While there are many studies on home-schooling—as Ray's 2008 Annotated Bibliography[31] attests—not all examine academic achievement. Within the group that does, only a small percentage use standardized tests as the outcome measure.[32] Often, studies cited in home-schooling magazines or journals that appeared to have a rigorous design could not be obtained or located, even though they were cited by other home-schooling researchers.[33] Home-schooling research studies generally tended to cite the same literature and to include many dated works (20 years old or older); many were also doctoral dissertations.[34] Other studies lacked such important items as a technical report, so that we were unable to discern quality. A few studies with strong designs were compromised by sample bias, researcher bias, or both. As noted earlier, however, we chose to include the studies with obvious bias, although they are down-weighted when these biases affect the design, scope of the study, or the completeness of the technical reports. Given the biases and errors built in to the existing body of home-schooling research, it comes as no surprise to learn that, on the whole, studies find high academic achievement among homeschoolers.

The scope of studies on achievement within homeschooling is generally quite small. Because standardized tests are the comparison tool, population samples tend to be comprised of only those home-schooling families willing to have students tested. Often, researchers have obtained their samples through a testing center or a home-schooling advocacy group. In both situations, the fact that the sample misses families that are not active in advocacy groups or are unwilling to come in to test centers implies that it is not representative. This issue is more prominent in research on homeschooling than on other forms of school choice. Generalizability, therefore, is very limited. Common methodological issues include no demographic controls, no control groups, self-reported scores by the homeschooled students' parents, and nonreporting of poor scores.

We have included studies with sample biases because to exclude them would leave essentially no viable studies on homeschooling for analysis. Nevertheless, it is important to keep sample bias and methodological shortcomings in mind when considering the overall report from the field that academic achievement among homeschoolers is high. Routine standardized testing is not a part of the "set" curricula for homeschoolers in the way that it is for, say, public school students, who all are tested at multiple grades on a set schedule. The first time that many homeschoolers may take a standardized test is when they are preparing to enroll in college. Certainly, the characteristics of these children are different from those choosing not to pursue higher education, which leaves the field of home-school research with a large gap in its understanding of the students who are not tested or considered in these achievement studies.

Within the context of considerations detailed above, we found 19 studies on homeschooling and academic achievement that met our minimum selection criteria. Figure 11.2 charts them by their own report of impact and our rating of study quality. This figure provides an illustration of estimated impact and quality ratings for 19 studies completed during the past 26 years. A full list of the references for these studies is included in the end notes.[35]

In contrast to the graphs on the other forms of school choice, all the studies on home-schooling research are clustered in the upper left quad-

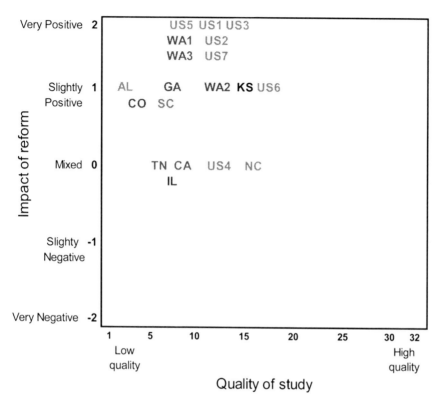

Figure 11.2.   Quality and impact ratings for studies of student achievement in homeschooling.

rant of the graph. Generally speaking, then, the body of home-schooling research on academic achievement is of low rigor and low overall quality.

As is apparent in Figure 11.2, we were unable to find any studies that found explicitly negative impacts of homeschooling on academic achievement. However, the quality of the research designs that produced such positive findings is low. Within our 0-32 point rating scheme, the overall mean quality score for the home-schooling research studies we included was 11.82, indicting fairly low design rigor. The highest quality rating for an individual study was 18, a score still only garnering slightly more than half the points available. The mean weighted impact rating for the studies was 1.35, indicating overall consensus among the researchers that home-schooling as a method of school reform has had a positive impact on those families that participate in testing.

One of the most widely cited studies in home-schooling literature that met our selection criteria was an older study by Ray (1997, 2000), who found home-schooled children scored at or above the 80th percentile on standardized tests.[36] Even though he used a relatively large sample and his results may be true for the population he included, his sample left out home-schooled students who do not take tests. His technical report is also a bit misleading when it claims random selection of participants. A closer reading of the report shows that he gained access to the population through the mailing lists of homeschool education organizations. He randomly selected from those mailing lists, not from the home-schooled population in general, leaving his work vulnerable to the same sample bias that runs through nearly all home-schooling research.

Ray has conducted much of the research in the field himself and is widely cited in nearly every study on homeschooling. He is the founder and president of National Home Education Research Institute, and he edits and publishes a journal about homeschooling, *The Home School Researcher*, in which many others have established their publishing record.[37]

Rudner's 1999 study of homeschoolers[38] is as frequently cited as Ray's work, though Rudner did not subsequently publish anything else on the topic. His original work was a large study that found home-schooled students scored in the 70th to 80th percentile on standardized tests. However, in addition to self-selection bias in his population, his sample was shaped by having been accessed through the testing center at Bob Jones University. Welner and Welner (1999)[39] argued that the results of the study suffer from limited generalizability. The same critique can be applied to Galloway's popular 1995 study showing homeschoolers' equal preparation for college, based on scores on the English subtest of the ACT. Her population sample came from an unnamed "large, private Christian University located in the Southeast,"[40] while her byline shows she was writing from Bob Jones University at the time. These two studies have served as foundational pieces in the field of home-school research, but their results reflect a largely White, Christian student population; reliance on them has skewed perceptions about homeschoolers and their performance on standardized tests. An increasing number of families of color are homeschooling, but they have been left out of nearly all empirical research on the topic.[41] In summary, some of the most widely cited studies in homeschooling seem to be subject to researcher and sample bias, although we incorporated them in our analysis.

While most of the research on homeschooling is conducted by researchers who are affiliated with or funded by organizations that advocate for homeschooling, the few studies conducted by researchers not connected with the homeschool establishment, such as Frost (1987) and

Belfield (2005) had mixed results. In general, homeschooled students scored higher on reading but lower than comparison groups on math. When demographic controls were introduced, there were no noticeable differences between groups in either reading or math.

STUDENT ACHIEVEMENT FOR INTERDISTRICT, INTRADISTRICT, AND MAGNET SCHOOL PROGRAMS

This section examines diverse forms of school choice found within the traditional public school sector, including inter- and intradistrict choice programs. Magnet schools, which are part of a federally funded program, are also considered in this section since they are a form of intradistrict choice that is overseen by the local district school board.

Magnet schools[42] have received less attention and inspired less controversy than the other forms of school choice, although they remain the a common school choice option. While charter school accountability has been a prominent topic in school reform literature over the last 15 years, a review of American Education Research Association conference programs reveals only one paper focusing on magnet schools from 1998 through 2006. Originally, magnet schools were devised as a strategy to decrease segregation in schools and as a response to violent protest against mandatory reassignment policies introduced in the mid-1970s.[43] Research literature on magnet schools is prolific in regard to nonacademic topics, including desegregation. However, relatively few isolate academic achievement and use standardized testing as a measure of success.

The majority of magnet school studies included in this analysis employ demographic controls, as any good study of school choice reform models should. Demographic controls are particularly important because such research is often subject to confounding variables. For example, parental involvement can be an interceding effect: parents who make the effort to research options and actively choose a school are likely to be more involved in a child's school life overall, contributing to higher academic achievement. Likewise, magnet schools tend to attract a greater percentage of students with high prior academic achievement, leaving nonmagnet schools in the district with more at-risk students and rendering comparisons incompatible. Therefore, it is critical to strong research design that a study includes a control for starting performance level or some other determination of a gain score.

Figure 11.3 maps the studies on magnet, intradistrict, and interdistrict choice schools that we analyzed. These three forms are grouped because too few studies met selection criteria in each category to allow for substantive individual analysis. For the combined forms, we identified 26 studies

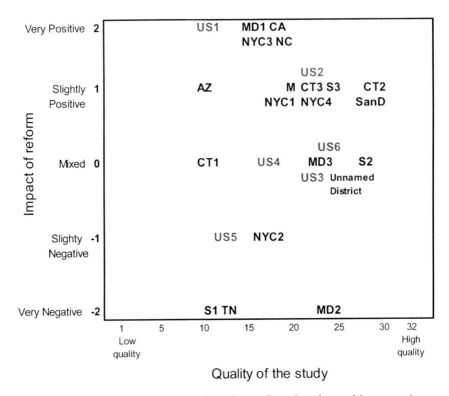

Figure 11.3. Quality and impact ratings for studies of student achievement in magnet or interdistrict choice schools.

of student achievement that were completed in the last 42 years. Figure 11.3 provides an illustration of estimated impact and quality ratings for these 26 studies. A full list of references for these studies is found in the endnotes.[44] Wide variety among the studies makes it important to consider them as a group. Some focused only on high school, while others focused on elementary or middle school levels. They also varied significantly in scope, from a single district to a national sample.

On average, these studies scored 19.19 on quality, although as Figure 11.3 indicates there was a significant spread in design quality as well as impact. Based on each study's perceived impact on student academic achievement, the overall impact rating for magnet schools is +0.45reflecting the general view that magnet schools have had a slightly positive impact on student achievement, as measured by standardized tests. The highest quality score was 29 points, which was earned by Bilfulco et al. (2009), Betts et al., (2006), and Ballou et al. (2006).[45]

Generally, studies discussed here tended to score high on design criteria. This is so in part because magnet school admission is typically decided by a lottery, in which many students submit a request to attend the school, and attendees are randomly selected from that pool (although sometimes preference is given to students in the school's surrounding neighborhood or to those with a sibling already admitted). Such an admission lottery facilitates random assignment for study design purposes. The target population is known (all students in the lottery pool), and the experimental and control groups are clear—the latter being the students who were not selected in the lottery. However, the two comparison groups are not exactly random or similar. Students are awarded entry by the school, but there is still a self-selection bias that remains because students (and their families) can and do reject admission. Our weighting scheme cannot account for this slightly-less-than-random design, but such accommodations were made by Ballou et al. (2006), Crain et al. (1992), and Heenber (1995).

Studies including a national sample tended to have only moderately high quality designs (Christenson et al., 2003; Gamoran, 1996), largely because they did not take advantage of randomization. Those two studies will be discussed below. Gamoran (1996)[46] is characterized by a large sample size and the use of the same cohorts to track student achievement over time. The study also used demographic controls and considered students' starting performance to determine value added. However, only 2 years of test data are used to draw conclusions. The data are also quite dated, from test years of 1988 and 1990. Also, only two grades were tested, implying limited generalizability to K-7 education. The study was published in 1996, indicating the need for new, rigorous research with wide scope and longitudinal data.

Another national study in our analysis was conducted in 2003 by Christenson and colleagues,[47] who were contracted by the U.S. Department of Education. The access to national data rendered a large sample size, but the data were limited to school-level information. Further, the analysis procedures highlight a difficulty in using national samples and standardized testing: individual states administer different standardized tests. This study addressed such incompatibility by converting multiple state tests to a common scale. As with the Gamoran study, this work has limited generalizability because it focused on only the elementary level.

The studies that could be included in our synthesis of evidence depict an overall slightly positive, comparison with public schools in terms of student performance on standardized tests.

STUDENT ACHIEVEMENT FOR CHARTER SCHOOLS

Charter schools have the largest number of studies examining student achievement of any of the six types. The mounting evidence is very welcome after so many years with few comprehensive evaluations or achievement studies. In 2001, Gill et al. found only three studies of charter schools that met their criteria for a summary of evidence.[48] In the same year, Miron and Nelson[49] found 15 studies of charter school achievement; in a 2002 update (published in 2004[50]), they identified only 17 studies for analysis. Thus, the total of 83 studies included here reflects significant growth in the field.

As the number of studies on charter schools has increased over the last 9 years, so, too, has the overall quality of the studies. There is a significant positive correlation between year of publication and quality ratings ($r = .23$, $p = .03$). There are five studies included in the analysis that utilize lotteries to employ a randomized design and there are now matched student designs for Arizona, California, Colorado, District of Columbia, Delaware, Florida, Idaho, Indiana, Pennsylvania, Tennessee, and Texas, as well as a multistate study by the Center for Research on Education Outcomes.[51] Older studies with weaker designs and few years of test data are being supplanted by studies with more rigorous designs and more years of data. Also, with the expansion of state testing systems to cover more grades, it is now easier for studies that rely on school level data to track cohorts or groups of students as they progress from grade to grade.

Figure 11.4 provides an illustration of estimated impact and quality ratings for 83 studies completed during the last 12 years that examine student achievement in charter schools. Full references for each study highlighted in the figure are listed in the endnotes.[52] Close examination of Figure 11.4 reveals that studies vary widely in impact reported and design quality. Overall, 30studies had positive findings, 23 studies had mixed findings, and 30 had negative findings. The mean impact rating for charters was +0.04. The weighted mean (adjusted for quality of studies) was +0.12. These findings indicate a mixed effect. Although not a strong or significant correlation, there is a slight tendency for the studies with more rigorous designs to conclude that charter schools were outperforming their comparison groups.

Over 80% of the charter studies are state studies. This is not surprising given that charter schools are a state-based reform model; 40 states and the District of Columbia have passed charter school laws, and more than 5,000 charter schools are now operating across the nation.[53] Fifteen of the studies look at multiple states or use national data sets.

Figure 11.4 illustrates the number and geographic variation of the studies, which is impressive relative to the other forms of school choice.

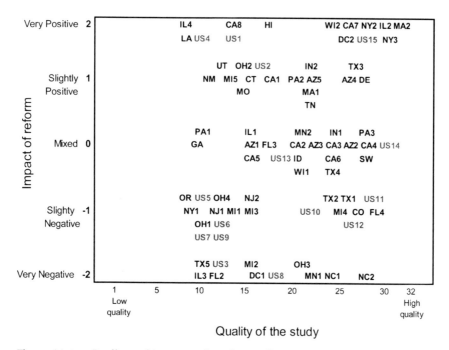

Figure 11.4.   Quality and impact ratings for studies of student achievement in charter schools.

There are some states which exhibit specific patterns. For example, all of the California studies either found mixed or positive results, while four out of the five Michigan studies and three out of the four Ohio studies produced negative results.

The impact ratings are more dispersed for charter schools than for the other forms of school choice we have examined. Similarly, quality ratings of the charter school studies vary widely. The mean quality rating is 19.16, much lower than that for district choice studies, virtually equivalent to voucher studies (19.19), and still much higher than that for home-schooling studies (11.44).

The unweighted average impact score across all studies was +0.04, suggesting that as a group the studies provide a mixed picture of the charter school effect. One possible explanation is that large gains or losses in some charter schools are offset by losses or gains in other charter schools, yielding a mixed achievement impact. A second possibility is that impact is consistent across charter schools, but small. That the impact ratings are widely dispersed suggests an explanation that gains and losses are frequently offset. The magnitude of change evidence from charter school studies is not substantial and those looking for the achievement gap to be closed will be disappointed.

STUDENT ACHIEVEMENT FOR VIRTUAL SCHOOLS

It is important to note that few studies have been completed on student achievement in cyber or virtual schools, which are typically charter schools, that until recently at least, catered to home-schooling families. For this reason, we have not created a separate chart to illustrate the relative quality and impact of the findings. In a 2003 study of California charter schools, Zimmer et al. (2003)[54] included some non-classroom-based charter schools and found that they had lower achievement scores than traditional public schools and other charters. In a 2002 evaluation of Pennsylvania charter schools, Miron et al.[55] similarly found that four virtual charter schools performed worse than or similar to comparison groups. A relevant study by the Center for Research on Education Outcomes (2011)[56] came out as our analyses for this chapter was concluding. The study looked at student achievement in Pennsylvania Charter Schools, which has the nation's largest concentration of virtual charter schools. One third of all charter school students in Pennsylvania are enrolled in virtual schools. The Center for Research on Education Outcomes study found that students in charter schools were making small gains in learning over time when compared with matched students in traditional public schools. While students in brick and mortar charter schools were slightly behind their matched peers, the students enrolled in virtual charter schools were making far smaller gains in learning over time.

SUMMARY OF FINDINGS

Overall, the existing research on school choice models and achievement provides a mixed picture, with some studies suggesting positive impacts and others indicating neutral or negative impacts. Except for the research on homeschooling, the inclusion of relatively lower quality studies did little to change the overall findings.

There were large differences across school choice type, both in terms of the amount of research available as well as the conclusions that can be drawn from the research. The entire body of the literature leads to the following key findings.

Vouchers and Tax Credits

- Given that few voucher programs exist, a relatively large number of studies on them are available. These studies focus on means-tested programs.
- The quality of the vouchers studies is reasonably high, with many relying on lottery lists to generate comparison groups of students.
- The results—on the whole—are slightly positive for means-tested voucher programs, particularly with regard to performance of African American students.
- There is an absence of empirical studies examining academic performance of students who are participating in the tuition tax credit programs.

Charter Schools

- The most studies are available on charter schools, with rapid growth in the literature appearing over the past 7 years.
- Design quality for research on charter schools varies considerably; for some half of the studies, relatively weak quality is due to the absence of—or inability to obtain—student-level data.
- Cumulative results from charter school research indicate that, on the whole, charters perform similarly to traditional public schools. Results from individual studies have remained mixed over time, even with the addition of newer and higher quality studies.

Homeschooling

- Relatively few studies exist.
- Most of the studies are especially weak in design quality.
- All findings are mixed or positive in favor of homeschooling.

Inter- and Intradistrict Choice Programs and Magnet Schools

- The quality of magnet school research is generally mixed, although the lottery lists from oversubscribed schools could facilitate more rigorous designs.

- Outside of magnet schools, there are very few studies of inter- and intradistrict choice programs.
- Overall findings were slightly positive.

Virtual Schools

- Only three studies could be found that considered student achievement results for virtual schools. All three studies focused on virtual charter schools.
- Students enrolled in virtual charter schools are making far smaller gains in learning over time relative to students in brick and mortar charter schools and relative to demographically similar students in traditional public schools.

Table 11.3 and Figure 11.5 facilitate comparison of findings across diverse choice models; together they summarize the total number of studies analyzed for each model as well as the impact and quality ratings in each category. Voucher studies had the highest overall quality ratings, and homeschooling the lowest. Impact ratings include not only the mean but also the weighted mean, which takes into account study quality. On average, homeschool studies had the most positive impact ratings, and charter schools the least positive—although still mixed. Figure 5 charts the general position of these four broad forms of school choice in terms of relative quality and impact. On the whole, we could discern no correlation between the studies' quality and their findings relative to choice's impact on student achievement.

Table 11.3.   Mean Quality and Impact Ratings Across Diverse Forms of School Choice Research

| Type of Choice | Studies (N) | Quality Rating (0 to 32 Scale) | | Impact Rating (+2 to -2 Scale) | | Weighted Mean Impact |
		Mean	SD	Mean	SD	
Voucher	15	25.33	4.17	0.60	0.63	0.62
Charter	83	19.16	6.27	0.04	1.28	0.12
Homeschool	19	11.44	3.88	1.20	.92	1.33
Intra-/inter-/magnet	26	19.19	5.70	0.42	1.24	0.45

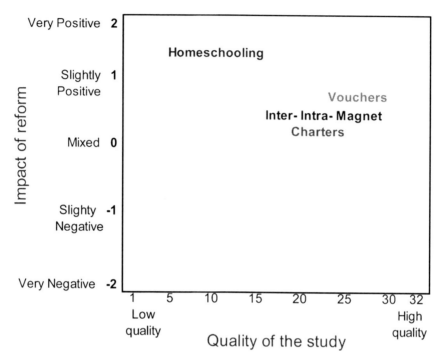

Figure 11.5.   Illustration of the overall findings across diverse forms of school choice.

Some Observations on the Findings

In considering import of the findings, we have been disappointed to note—especially relative to charter schools—that most of the media attention and public debate has focused on relatively weak cross-sectional studies. It appears that policy decisions are being shaped by research that does not merit the emphasis it is receiving.

As this analysis demonstrates, the research and evaluation literature has not yet produced clear and unambiguous factual statements about achievement across any of the key types of school choice. Thus, stakeholders must weigh the strengths and weaknesses of the evidence. Since it is unlikely that there will ever be a single definitive study, the most reasonable approach for interpreting the evidence is to conduct a meta-analysis or assemble a picture of the findings across the broad body of research, as we have done here.

Still, it is important to simultaneously remain aware that aggregating findings across types of school choice hides considerable differences.

Within all models, there are certainly successful choice programs and schools as well as seriously flawed ones. At a macro level this analysis can tell us what the body of research says and whether these school choice models are worthy of replication. Nevertheless, all forms of school choice could benefit from a better understanding of factors leading to success within particular schools or groups of schools.

A Cautionary Word on the Role of Advocacy Research

Given that school choice is a highly politicized issue, there are many attempts to influence policy with sensational claims about student achievement by advocacy or opposition groups. Typically, these claims allude to empirical research. Press releases with data charts and talking points appear in papers or on websites. Our review of the existing research had to weed through piles of these pseudo-studies/evaluations. Most were not included here because they lacked technical reports specifying the number of students and schools involved in a study or offering details on methodology. While technical reports may take many forms, the public should be aware that when one is not included, there is no way to determine whether the conclusions are justified or the findings can be verified and replicated.

Several advocacy studies of relatively high quality were included in this analysis. However, as with pharmaceutical companies doing rigorous research on their new drugs, findings that do not support the position of groups with a vested interest are less likely to be released, so that caution in interpreting significance of results is advisable.

RECOMMENDATIONS

The analysis detailed here yields two core recommendations for researchers and policymakers. The first is to improve research on school choice, and the second is to improve interpretation of school choice research.

Improve Research on School Choice

- Take care in creating comparison groups from lottery lists at choice schools. Selection bias may occur since some selected students may choose not to attend the choice school because of transportation or other barriers. The technique is promising, but researchers must still confirm and control for differences in the group of students who are accepted and those who are not.

- Consider using matched student designs, which are affordable and will be increasingly useful as state assessment systems improve and expand. Our analysis shows that studies using matched student designs often score high overall on quality ratings since they get more points for scope of study, demographic controls, completeness of technical reports than studies using other designs.

- Remember that impact can be adequately captured only with longitudinal designs. Thus, cross-sectional studies are most useful in assessing relative performance and describing the types of students enrolled in particular choice models.

- Promote more research on homeschooling, especially as increasing numbers of homeschoolers enroll in cyber schools.

- Promote research exploring differences across and within forms of school choice to help identify factors and conditions most likely to support successful school choice reforms.

- Clearly articulate research designs and methodologies, at the very least in an appendix or a Web document.

- Specify limitations and precautions that readers should consider when interpreting the findings.

Improve the Interpretation of Research on School Choice

- Remember that performance on standardized tests is only one of several important outcome indicators. Standardized tests are the easiest but not necessarily the best way to evaluate student learning.

- Be skeptical of sweeping conclusions drawn from the body of existing research; the range of findings and relative weakness of many studies does not support such claims. Remember that there simply are no definitive studies.

- Be aware that many commonly discussed and debated studies have weak research designs, as evidenced by their failing to meet our minimal selection criteria or, if included, by their quality ratings often being among the lowest.

- Consider the breadth of findings available regarding any single form of school choice, and when interpreting the research, remember the importance of study design, sample size, and the relevance of the comparison group.

- *Beware the press release.* Findings highlighted in press releases should be ignored if no technical report exists with details on the population studied or the study design used.
- When interpreting research, consider the source. Was the research funded or conducted by an advocacy group? Have the researchers ever released findings counter to their current results? Lead researchers of these studies typically have extensive experience, and the odds—for example, that someone would never have a finding that was in support of traditional public schools, or vice versa—speak loudly about the nature and purpose of their work.

CHAPTER 12

CONCLUSION

William J. Mathis and Patricia H. Hinchey

School choice approaches have been prominent for decades, and this is not likely to change anytime soon. The Obama administration's proposals for the reauthorization and administration of the Elementary and Secondary Education Act—as well as the criteria for competitive federal grants—promote the growth of various choice mechanisms. Charter school laws exist in 40 states and the District of Columbia, and advocates continue to press for expansion. Legislation promoting cyber schools, tax incentives, and choice-friendly "money follows the child" funding plans is regularly proposed in statehouses across the nation. Voucher policies and tax-credit-based 'neovoucher' policies also continue to expand, as do various forms of open enrollment policies. Choice is seen by policymakers as a means of advancing policy goals ranging from promoting integration to increasing school efficiency to increasing U.S. international competitiveness to facilitating the creation of a for-profit marketplace.

The chapters in this book examine how different approaches to school choice shape processes and influence outcomes. They describe the strengths and weaknesses of a varied menu of reform tools. They urge policymakers and other stakeholders to design, implement and assess school choice measures with caution because, while advocates make numerous assertions about the presumed benefits of school choice, the available research provides little or no high-quality research evidence to support these claims.

Exploring the School Choice Universe: Evidence and Recommendations
pp. 237–244
Copyright © 2012 by Information Age Publishing

In truth, research on the efficacy of various forms of school choice shows large variations in outcome associated with different types of school choice as well as by state and region. As a result any generalizations must be made with care. This is true in part because "school choice" policies differ widely not only in their many forms and goals, but also in the amount and type of supports and regulations, and in the state data available.

The research evidence reported in this book raises a number of important questions that should be answered before policymakers endorse the expansion of any given form of choice program.

- Does this form of choice advance equity or advance segregation?
- Does this form of choice spur innovation and improved school quality through competitive market effects?
- What is the full range of financial effects for different forms of choice?
- Is this form of choice funded at a level that is fair to all involved, including taxpayers?
- How does this form of school choice affect students in district public schools?
- Given that the major cost for any school is personnel, what effect does this form of school choice have on teacher recruitment and retention, teacher professionalism and training as well as on staffing ratios?
- In the long run, do children achieve at a higher level in schools using this form of choice than in district public schools?

In addition, the chapters point to a half-dozen issues confronting policymakers as they consider how best to approach school choice issues. We use this concluding chapter to highlight those issues and to offer a brief road map forward.

Issue 1: Conflicting Purposes of Education

In reviewing the underlying philosophical foundations of choice systems, Terri Wilson makes clear that the "public" goals of education can, and do, take on a wide variety of definitions. As a result policymakers should be explicit about the philosophical underpinnings of the policies they promote. For instance, the terms liberty, equity, justice, pluralism and democracy are widely embraced. But the weight placed on each of these values in school choice decisions can vary sharply and precipitate profound disagreements.[1] If the primary weight is placed on uncon-strained liberty, this will likely result in a different decision than the one that follows from an emphasis on equity.

There are large potential differences in the desired outcomes of educa-tion. Choice policies may nurture a consumer-oriented educational sys-tem or a society "with many satisfied individuals ... pursuing their self-interests," which maximizes liberty, Wilson notes. Or they may promote democracy and equity through "an active citizenry that creates the schools it thinks best through processes of democratic deliberation." Do we want policies that reify competition as the greatest good, but that tend to rein-force existing socioeconomic hierarchies? Or do we want greater equity across the American public and a more unified and engaged citizenry which will yield less 'creative destruction' from the marketplace? Policy options that lead to different goals can, of course, be pursued within a nonchoice framework; but many options are also available within a choice framework by selecting among choice policies and selecting among differ-ent ways of implementing those policies. Thus, rather than considering choice as a monolithic construct, the way the rules are written makes a great deal of difference.[2]

In state constitutional framings, the purpose of education is frequently defined as the broad advancement of civic virtue. This historical purpose for education stands in sharp contrast to the market-model consumer ori-entation of most school choice models. A move to such a system should be made deliberatively, with a full understanding of the shift in goals and likely outcomes. Without such overt deliberation about these issues, the outcome of the reform may be left to chance or to the vagaries of the day's social and economic forces. This is the antithesis of a sound and delibera-tive governmental decision making process.

Issue 2: Advancing Equity

Advocates of school choice often emphasize the goal of allowing stu-dents to escape failing schools, suggesting a goal of greater equity. How-ever, Mickelson and her coauthors report that to date, choice policies have served primarily to reinforce existing segregation by race, socioeco-nomic status, ability and achievement. There are several design factors in choice programs that contribute to such undesirable outcomes. Some pro-grams offer genuine options only to particular populations (bounded by geography and practicality) and some allow schools to choose their stu-dents. Moreover, while interdistrict choice programs appear to hold some promise in terms of addressing funding and segregation equity issues, if policymakers deliberately pursue these goals; in practice these plans often provide few if any meaningful choices. Similarly, while intradistrict choice can be built on the magnet school concept, deliberately designed to advance integration, in practice the design of such open enrollment policies includes no such nod to equity.

Overall, few school choice policies include design elements expressly intended to increase diversity. The disjunctions between rhetorical claims and actual practices demand careful examination.

Moreover, Lacireno-Paquet and Brantley show that peers, parents and schools make decisions whose effect is to *de facto* segregate. The single finding that applies most generally to all choice parents is that despite rhetoric about academics, White and non-White parents most often choose based on factors other than academic test scores. White parents avoid sending their children to schools with large concentrations of minorities, while minority parents avoid sending their children to schools with large concentrations of poor students. Garn and Cobb accordingly argue that assessment of specific plans must move beyond test performance and efficiency, and that the ubiquitous emphasis on "parents-as-consumers" must be replaced by an emphasis on ensuring that choice plans target the "greater societal good."

Choice programs can, of course, be designed in ways that offer significant new opportunities to families most in need. In designing equitable choice systems, however, policymakers must, as Julie Mead suggests, consider not only the fate of those students who choose new options but also the fate of those students who are left behind. An equitable policy must ensure desirable options for all students and find ways to avoid or counter past choice patterns leading toward segregation.

Issue 3: Competition, School Quality, and Innovation

A foundational claim for choice plans is that competition enhances school quality because schools must become more innovative in order to survive. This innovation was to arise out of decreased constraints on creativity plus a desire to maximize, or at least not lose, market share. Yet these hoped-for benefits of competition have not been realized. In fact, the evidence shows either no effect or effects that are too small to have meaningful policy implications. Lubienski explains why competition may not lead to classroom innovations: the very market-model purported to foster innovation may undermine it, as parents seek out tested, proven models over innovative ones. In contrast, innovation seems best nurtured by substantive investment in particular schools that are working to develop new strategies for specific populations. Indeed, policymakers must consider the possibility that government, rather than marketplace competitors, may be better positioned to nurture innovation by nurturing and sustaining a variety of innovative practices, free of immediate accountability consequences.

Similarly, Arsen and Ni report little evidence that competition has forced conventional public schools to increase their effectiveness and efficiency. Instead, research to date has produced weak and mixed findings.

Issue 4: Funding

The shift from a fairly standardized system of schools to a more decentralized and diverse set of funding recipients has given lawmakers a challenging new task. Charter school operators, in particular, are increasingly approaching legislatures to enhance their funding through a variety of mechanisms, such as "money follows the child" plans. Voucher and neovoucher policies raise complicated issues about allocating public dollars and about the fiscal impacts for taxpayers. Meanwhile, cyberschool operators are requesting greater access to students and to funding. Each funding decision raises volatile and controversial questions about the proper allocation and accounting of public funds.

Clive Belfield points to wide variability in funding formulas, the lack of transparency of funding (i.e., private grants may not always be visible), and difficulties associated with determining reasonable funding formulas and with comparing outcomes. Furthermore, funding and accounting systems for charter schools are not always comparable to conventional public schools within a given state. And fiscal, equity and programming issues are raised by perennial complexities such as the cost of special education services and whether the district of residence must pay.

Also unanswered is what should be done when a choice school operates with less spending. Should the public treasury pay the school at the lower amount or should the choice school keep the "profit"? What is the role of the state when such savings are realized by cutting salaries, increasing class size, cutting out physical education, or otherwise reducing services or opportunities? If private funds are subsidizing the school, how should these resources be considered in cost formulas?

Issue 5: Teaching and Teachers

Addressing similar issues, Marisa Cannata notes the dearth of information on the impact of choice on teachers and teaching. Some prominent charter school models require that teachers work longer hours. These models appear to lead to teacher burn-out. But Cannata points out the need for a great deal more research to determine how school choice policies affect the teacher labor market for choice schools as well as conventional public schools.

Similarly, given the potential of some choice models—particularly cyberschools—to be staffed by lesser qualified employees (at lower wages), empirical issues regarding teacher qualifications, evaluations and compensation have shot to the forefront of the policy agenda. Current policy advocacy focused on alternative teacher preparation and licensures, coupled with political movements to reduce the reach and power of teacher unions, have raised serious issues regarding the future of the teaching profession. New demands for upgrading the quality of the teaching force are heard at the same time that policies are proposed which lower or eliminate standards for teachers. A growing push is aimed at creating an easy-entry, easy-exit teaching force that is not consistent with the idea of teaching as a profession.

Issue 6: Effects on Achievement

The primary rationale for schools of choice is based on the broad claim that the quality of education will be improved through choice. Yet, Miron and Urschel conclude that the research and evaluation literature shows students participating in school choice generally performing at levels similar to students in district public schools. Some studies show slight detriments; some show slight benefits; Miron and Urschel conclude that none of the types of school choice has been found by the overall body of research to outperform district public schools.

This research is unevenly distributed across the various types of school choice, and greater clarity is found in some areas than in others. The strongest and most extensive body of research focuses on charter schools. "Cumulative results from charter school research indicate that, on the whole, charters perform similarly to traditional public schools," Miron and Urschel report. Few voucher programs exist and the research is thus, limited; but again the achievement outcomes are comparable to conventional public schools. Full-time cyberschooling and homeschooling are the areas where data collection and research are the weakest, given—for cyberschooling—that the practice is very new and—for homeschooling—the lack of standardized testing and, until recently, the large number of families that essentially homeschooled in secret. Inter- and intradistrict choice results are slightly positive but, again, the research base is quite small. Moreover, the latter two types of choice, while often addressed together, have very different legal foundations and restrictions and, thus, they may behave in different ways.

Miron and Urschel caution stakeholders to read claims about choice with a critical eye. Most specifically, readers should consider whether each report claiming substantive findings includes details on its methodology—and whether it is sponsored by an advocacy group that promotes or opposes choice initiatives.

Overall, even though school choice has seen its greatest growth over the past 20 years, these policies have not registered a pattern of test score improvements (or demonstrated substantial effect sizes) that would indicate sufficient potential to close the achievement gap or to improve outcomes. The existing evidence, however, also suggests that the most commonly measured achievement outcomes are not significantly lowered by school choice policies.

A ROADMAP GOING FORWARD

The book's contributors offer a vision of how research can inform a constructive discussion of how school choice might best create benefits for the public education system. School choice models have been endorsed in the majority of states, and both Democratic and Republican federal administrations have promoted various types of choice policies. Such systems have also been promoted by major foundations such as Broad, Gates and Walton.[3] This advocacy is premised on a competitive, market model of schools and of society. However, to date, test score improvement for choice schools has been unimpressive or nonexistent. At the same time, the United States has become more ethnically diverse while social and economic segregation has increased, funding inequities have remained largely unaddressed, and children's poverty rates continue to increase. Excepting only Mexico and Turkey, economic inequalities within the United States are now the greatest of any member of the Organization for Economic Cooperation and Development.[4]

In theory, choice plans can be shaped to ameliorate the problems documented by the authors of this book. This would require a commitment to democratic participation and to the careful and deliberate inclusion of equity-focused elements as part of choice policies. School choice systems can be implemented in different ways, and the nature of the operational decisions will go a long way toward determining the nature of the policies' outcomes.

- Choice rules can be written either (a) to reduce isolation by race, class, or special needs status, or (b) to have the consequence of becoming a vehicle for accelerating resegregation of our public school systems.

- Depending on the design and funding incentives, school choice reforms can either (a) promote innovation and the development of a diversity of options from which parents can choose, or (b) result in a stratified and noninnovative marketplace that appeals to consumers looking for a familiar yet exclusive option.
- School choice reforms have the potential either (a) to promote accountability, or (b) to facilitate the circumvention or avoidance of oversight.

In light of these highly disparate possible approaches and outcomes, it is incumbent upon policymakers to openly state the goals that the public school system should pursue and then, when considering school choice reforms, to carefully design, plan, implement, and evaluate these reforms. That is, policymakers would be wise to consider appropriate supports, such as transportation and diverse funding incentives, and to carefully construct safeguards to help the reform accomplish the identified goals of the public school system. Policymakers would also be wise to put in place requirements for transparency and accountability and to plan for evaluations of the reforms before expanding or rolling out new school choice programs.

In short, school choice, if carefully wielded by policymakers, has the potential to help accomplish important goals. To that end it is important that school choice not be treated as an a priori end in itself but rather as a testable way to address true problems and issues facing education and society.[5]

NOTES AND REFERENCES

CHAPTER 1: INTRODUCTION

1. Coons, J. E., & Sugarman, S. D. (1978). *Education by choice: The case for family control*. Berkeley, CA: Institute of Governmental Studies Press.

2. Hoxby, C. M. (2000). Does competition among public schools benefit students and taxpayers? Evidence from natural variation in school districting. *American Economic Review, 90*(5), 1209-1239.

3. Chubb, J. E., & Moe, T. (1990). *Politics, markets and America's schools*. Washington, DC: Brookings Institution.

   Hill, P., Pierce, L. C., & Guthrie, J. W. (1997). *Reinventing public education: How contracting can transform America's schools*. Chicago, IL: University of Chicago Press.

4. Auge, K. (2011). Douglas County's voucher charter school gets final OK. *The Denver Post*. Retrieved October 30, 2011, from http://www.denverpost .com/news/ci_18511245

   Note that this policy was subject to a court injunction as of late-2011, preventing the issuance of any vouchers.

5. For its international surveys of education systems, the Organisation for Economic Co-operation and Development (OECD) specifies that an institution is classified as private if it is (i) controlled and managed by a nongovernmental organization (e.g., a Church, Trade Union or business enterprise), or (ii) its Governing Board consists mostly of members not selected by a public agency. Given that many countries use private schools as a component of the system used to deliver compulsory level education, the OECD further divides private schools into two types: *Government-dependent private schools*, which receive more than half their funding from

Exploring the School Choice Universe: Evidence and Recommendations
pp. 245–347
245

government agencies or whose teaching personnel are paid by a government agency, and *Independent private schools*, which receive less than half their core funding from government agencies and whose teaching personnel are not paid by a government agency. These terms refer only to the degree of a private institution's dependence on funding from government sources; they do not refer to the degree of government direction or regulation.

6. Welner, K. G. (2008). *Neovouchers: The emergence of tuition tax credits for private schooling*. Lanham, MD: Rowman & Littlefield.

7. Welner, 2008 (see note 6).

8. Data for Figure 1.2 come from multiple sources:

Forster, G. (2005). *Using school choice: Analyzing how parents access educational freedom*. Indianapolis, IN: Milton and Rose D. Friedman Foundation.

Reeger, J. (2007, November 3). School-choice program helps kids attend private school. *Tribune-Review*.

Vasoli, B. (2007, May 29). Study: Educational choice saves money. *The Bulletin*. Retrieved July 28, 2012 from http://www.nje3.org/?p=55

Wilson, G. Y. (2002). *The equity impact of Arizona's Education Tax Credit Program: A review of the first three years* (1998-2000). Tempe, AZ: Education Policy Research Unit, ASU. Retrieved July 28, 2012 from http://nepc.colorado.edu/publication/the-equity-impact-arizonas-education-tax-credit-program-a-review-first-three-years-1998-

Welner, 2008 (see note 6).

Additional data sources were:

http://www.floridaschoolchoice.org/Information/CTC/files/ctc_fast_facts.pdf

http://www.floridaschoolchoice.org/Information/CTC/quarterly_reports/ftc_report_sept2011.pdf

http://www.azdor.gov/Portals/0/Reports/private-school-tax-credit-report-2010.pdf.

Estimates were made for the voucher numbers for 2005-06 and 2006-07.

9. The private school enrollment data for Figure 1.3 were obtained from the Condition of Education reports prepared by the National Center for Education Statistics: http://nces.ed.gov/programs/coe/tables/table-pri-1.asp. Fixed enrollment figures were not available for every year. Therefore, estimates were made based on the enrollment in previous and subsequent years.

10. Finn, C., Manno, B., & Vanourek, G. (2000). *Charter schools in action: Renewing public education*. Princeton, NJ: Princeton University Press.

Fuller, B. (Ed.). (2000). *Inside charter schools: The paradox of radical decentralization*. Cambridge, MA: Harvard University Press.

11. Miron, G., & Nelson, C. (2002). *What's public about charter schools?: Lessons learned about accountability and choice*. Thousand Oaks, CA: Corwin Press.

12. See

 Bulkley, K., & Wohlstetter, P. (Eds.). (2004). *Taking account of charter Schools: What's happened and what's next?* New York, NY: Teachers College Press.

 Lubienski, C. A., & Weitzel, P. C. (Eds.). (2010). *The charter school experiment: Expectations, evidence, and implications*. Cambridge, MA: Harvard Education Press.

13. The data for Figure 1.4 were obtained from the Common Core of Data, which is produced by the National Center for Education Statistics: http://nces.ed.gov/ccd/. Fixed enrollment figures were not available for every year. Therefore, estimates were made to fill in missing years based on the enrollment in previous and subsequent years.

14. NAPCS Press Release. (2011, December 7). Retrieved December 15, 2011, from http://www.publiccharters.org/pressreleasepublic/default .aspx?id=643

15. Grady, S., & Bielick, S. (2010). *Trends in the use of school choice: 1993 to 2007* (NCES 2010-004). Washington, DC: National Center for Education Statistics, Institute of Education Sciences, U.S. Department of Education. Retrieved November 2, 2011, from http://nces.ed.gov/pubs2010/2010004 .pdf

16. The data for Figure 1.5 were obtained from the Common Core of Data which is produced by the National Center for Education Statistics: http://nces.ed.gov/ccd/. Fixed enrollment figures were not available for every year. Therefore, estimates were made to fill in missing years based on the enrollment in previous and subsequent years.

17. The data for Figure 1.6 were obtained from the National Household Education Survey (NHES), which is administered by the U.S. Department of Education's National Center for Education Statistics (NCES). From this survey it was possible to obtain estimates of the percent of families that reported selecting a public school other than the one they were assigned to. From these estimates, we deducted the number of students enrolled in charter schools. Data from this survey have been reported in *Trends in the Use of School Choice: 1993 to 2007* (Grady & Bielick, 2010 [see note 16]).

18. http://nces.ed.gov/pubs2010/2010004/background.asp#f8

19. Grady & Bielick, 2010 (see note 16).

20. All the data points for enrollment in full-time virtual schools in Figure 1.7 are estimates. However, we believe that our approach set forth here pro-

vides a useful estimate of (a) when enrollment in these schools began, (b) the approximate growth trajectory, and (c) the current enrollment.

For the years from 1996-97 through 2007-08, the estimates are based on the annual EMO Profiles reports available from NEPC (http://nepc.colorado.edu/ceru-home). These data, however, cover only schools operated by for-profit education management organizations. Because much enrollment is through other entities, including state-operated institutions, we doubled the figures for each year based on the approximation that the enrollment in other forms of full-time virtual schools would be similar in overall size to the EMO-operated full-time virtual schools.

For the 3 years from 2008-09 through 2010-11, we used estimates set forth in the "Keeping Pace" reports prepared by the Evergreen Education Group (http://kpk12.com/reports/). If those Keeping Pace estimates are correct, it suggests that our multiple should be close to three (i.e., multiplying the for-profit EMO enrollment figure by two was very conservative).

21. Glass, G. V, & Welner, K. G. (2011). *Online K-12 schooling in the U.S.: Uncertain private ventures in need of public regulation.* Boulder, CO: National Education Policy Center. Retrieved December 3, 2011, from http://nepc.colorado.edu/publication/online-k-12-schooling

22. OECD. (2010). *Education at a glance 2010. OECD indicators.* Paris, France: Organisation for Economic Co-operation and Development.

23. OECD, 2010 (see note 23).

CHAPTER 2: NEGOTIATING PUBLIC AND PRIVATE: PHILOSOPHICAL FRAMEWORKS FOR SCHOOL CHOICE

1. By school choice, I refer to a wide range of programs and policies, including: open enrollment policies (both inter- and intradistrict), charter schools, cyber-schools, vouchers, tax credits and deductions, dual/ current enrollment in postsecondary education options, as well as homeschooling. Given the purposes of this chapter—a broader review of philosophical arguments that bear on school choice—I often refer to "school choice" of "schools of choice" in general terms. While choice policies certainly differ—and importantly so—from one another, a more comprehensive review of these differences is beyond the scope of this chapter.

2. Gary Fenstermacher contrasts the "in here," and "out there" aspects of the public and private.

Fenstermacher, G. (1997). On restoring public and private life. In J. I. Goodlad & T. J. McMannon (Eds.), *The public purpose of education and schooling* (pp. 55-71). San Francisco, CA: Jossey-Bass.

While the separation between public and private spheres of action remains central to most liberal theory, Fenstermacher also draws our attention to other traditions and understandings of these terms. Feminist thinkers, in particular, have argued that such a separation privileges public over private life, to the disadvantage of women who have historically been excluded by positions of public authority and power.

3. Lubienski, C. (2001). Redefining "public" education: Charter schools, common schools, and the rhetoric of reform. *Teachers College Record*, *103*(4), 634-666.

4. As many historians of education have detailed, this process was neither neutral nor without conflict. The seemingly "secular" curriculum of the public school system was saturated with Protestant religious sentiment, which helped to spur the creation of a separate—and largely Catholic—private school system. See,

   Tyack, D. (1974). *One best system*. Cambridge, MA: Harvard University Press.

   Kaestle, C. (1983). *Pillars of the republic: Common schools and American society, 1780-1860*. New York, NY: Hill and Wang.

5. Friedman, M. (1955). *The role of government of schooling, in economics and the public interest* (R. A. Solo, Ed.). New Brunswick, NJ: Rutgers University Press

   Friedman, M. (1962). *Capitalism and freedom*. Chicago, IL: University of Chicago Press.

6. Henig, J. R. (1994). *Rethinking school choice: Limits of the market metaphor*. Princeton, NJ: Princeton University Press.

7. Jencks, C. (1970). *Education vouchers: A report on financing elementary education by grants to parents*. Washington, DC: Centre for Policy Studies.

   It is also important to note that these later arguments were usually accompanied by actual—although modest—policy experiments, where Friedman's argument was—at least at the time—a conceptual one.

8. Viteritti, J. P. (1999). *Choosing equality: School choice, the Constitution and civil society*. Washington, DC: Brookings Institution.

9. Coons, J. E., & Sugarman, S. D. (1978). *Education by choice: The case for family Control*. Berkeley, CA: University of California Press.

10. As Joseph Viteritti argues, Coons and Sugarman, "saw choice as a vehicle through which families could select schools that revealed their own educational values," thus conceiving "parental empowerment in both political and economic terms."

    Viteritti, 1999, p. 56 (see note 8).

11. Armor, D., & Peiser, B. (1997). *Competition in education: A case study of interdistrict choice*. Boston, MA: Pioneer Institute.

12. Reese, W. (2005). *America's public schools: From the common school to 'no child left behind.'* Baltimore, MD: Johns Hopkins Press.

13. Chubb, J., & Moe, T. (1990). *Politics, markets and America's schools.* Washington, DC: Brookings Institution Press.

14. Jeff Henig provides an excellent analysis of why this volume became influential. As he argues, the re-emergence of choice as an idea and policy involved linking existing magnet schools to a rationale of choice and an alternative statement of market theory.

   Henig, 1994, pp. 64-66 (see note 6).

   In addition, Chubb and Moe's study won more attention because it presented a detailed model and linked this model to a broader theory of politics and democracy (Henig, 1994, 87).

15. For criticisms of choice, see

   Barber, B. (1997). Public schooling: Education for democracy. In J. I. Goodlad & T. J. McMannon (Eds.), *The public purpose of education and schooling* (pp. 21-32). San Francisco, CA: Jossey-Bass.

   Carnoy, M. (2000). School choice? Or is it privatization? *Educational Researcher, 29* (7), 15-20.

   For advocates of choice, see

   Hill, P. T., Pierce, L., & Guthrie, J. (1997). *Reinventing public education: How contract schools can transform American education.* Chicago, IL: University of Chicago Press.

   Nathan, J. (1996). *Charter schools: Creating hope and opportunity for American Education.* San Francisco, CA: Jossey-Bass.

16. While more extreme advocates of choice generally use the term "government schools," Christopher Lubienski details how a variety of choice advocates in Michigan used this language to broaden the possible definition of public schools.

   Lubienski, 2001, pp. 639-640 (see note 3).

17. Miron, G., & Nelson, C. (2002). *What's public about charter schools?: Lessons learned about accountability and choice.* Thousand Oaks, CA: Corwin Press.

18. Rotherham, A. J. (2003, April). Educational modernization and school choice. *Education Forum, 9.* Retrieved February 29, 2004, from http://www.educationforum.org.nz/upload/pdf/briefing_no_9.pdf

19. Lubienski, 2001, pp. 641-642 (see note 3).

20. Englund, T. (1993). Education for public or private good. In G. Miron (Ed.), *Towards free choice and market-oriented schools: Problems and promises* (pp. 27-44). Stockholm, Sweden: Skolverket.

21.   Labaree, D. F. (1997). Public goods, private goods: The American struggle over educational goals. *American Educational Research Journal, 34*(1), 39-81.

22.   For excellent examples of this kind of scholarship:

Henig, 1994 (see note 6);

Lubienski, 2001(see note 3);

Labaree, 1997 (see note 21).

23.   For the purposes of this review, I define "philosophical scholarship" broadly to include work in philosophy, political theory, and educational theory, as well as the different conceptual frameworks employed by scholars of school choice. While not formally "philosophy," the scholarship addressed in this review all addresses, in a variety of ways, conceptual and normative aspects of school choice.

24.   My use of the concept "liberty," here, is different from both the political meaning of "liberal" (a leftist, progressive, political orientation) and the academic meaning of "liberal" (a tradition of academic arguments that emphasize the importance of individual political rights). For the purposes of this review, I do not examine arguments of liberalism, per se, which is a diverse and complex field of scholarship in its own right. Instead, I group arguments for and against school choice, many made by scholars who could be termed "liberal theorists," into different frameworks: liberty, equity, justice, pluralism and democracy. Issues of liberalism appear in each of these frameworks, not just in arguments focused on issues of liberty. For a thoughtful overview of classical, contemporary and "affiliation" liberalism in relation to education, see

Feinberg, W., & McDonough, K. (2003) Liberalism and the dilemma of public education in multicultural societies. In K. McDonough& W. Feinberg (Eds.), *Education and citizenship in liberal-democratic societies.* Oxford, England: Oxford University Press.

25.   Commonly cited court cases include: *Pierce v. Society of Sisters, Wisconsin v. Yoder* and *Mozert v. Hawkins County Board of Education*.

26.   Pierce (1925), cited in Rosenblum, N. (2003). Separating the Siamese twins: Pluralism and school choice. In A. Wolfe (Ed.), *School choice: The moral debate* (pp. 79-103). Princeton, NJ: Princeton University Press.

27.   Judith Suissa offers a thoughtful critique of the very notion of a "comprehensive conception of the good" that underlies many liberal treatments of identity and difference in education. She argues that this assumption relies on a reductive and static conception of the complex and multi-faceted cultural values held by actual families. See

Suissa, J. (2010). How comprehensive is your conception of the good? Liberal parents, difference and the common school. *Educational Theory, 60*(5), 587-600.

28.   *Wisconsin v. Yoder*, 406 US 205 (1972).

29.   Galston defines this concept of liberty as "a robust though rebuttable presumption in favor of individuals and groups leading their lives as they see fit, within a broad range of legitimate variation, in accordance with what gives their life meaning and value."

Galston, W. (2002). *Liberal pluralism*. Cambridge, MA: Cambridge University Press.

30.   Galston, W. (1991) *Liberal purposes: Goods, virtues, and diversity in the liberal state*. Cambridge, MA: Cambridge University Press.

31.   While supportive of *Yoder* on grounds of parental rights, Callan ultimately deems the decision "morally unfortunate" because of the state's interest in the "prospective liberty" of children. In

Callan, E. (2006). Galston's dilemmas and *Wisconsin v. Yoder*. *Theory and Research in Education*, *4*(3), 263.

32.   Callan, 2006, p. 262 (see note 31).

33.   For example, while the rights of Old Order Amish parents to withdraw their children after eight years of school were upheld (*Wisconsin v. Yoder*), the rights of fundamentalist Christians to withdraw their children from participation in a given reading program were not (*Mozert v. Hawkins County Board of Education*).

34.   Kemerer, Goodwin and Ruderman, for instance, argue that education ought to respond to diverse conceptions of the good—exemplified in different choice alternatives—and that the "policies that best protect diversity and provide the greatest liberty are those that subsidize all reasonable approaches to education and allow families to choose freely among them" (p. 96).

Goodwin, R. K., & Kemerer, F. R. (Eds.). (2002). *School choice tradeoffs: Liberty, equity & diversity* (p. 96). Austin, TX: University of Texas Press.

35.   Merry, M., & Karsten, S. (2010). Restricted liberty, parental choice and homeschooling. *Journal of Philosophy of Education*, *44*(4), 497-514.

36.   Jonathan, R. (1997). Right and choices: Illusory freedoms. *Journal of Philosophy of Education*, *31*(1), 83-107.

37.   Viteritti, J. P. (2003). Defining equality: politics, markets and public policy. In A. Wolfe (Ed.), *School choice: The moral debate* (pp. 13-30). Princeton, NJ: Princeton University Press.

38.   It is not immediately clear, though, if this shift is due to a natural process of maturation or is instead the result of the political realities of instituting choice as a policy, which would demand an appeal to broader constituencies.

39. Wolfe, A. (Ed.). (2003). The irony of school choice: Liberals, conservatives, and the new politics of race. In *School choice: The moral debate* (pp. 31-51). Princeton, NJ: Princeton University Press.

40. Hill, P. T. (Ed.). (2002). *Choice with equity.* Stanford, CA: Hoover Institute Press.

41. Macedo, S. (2003). Equity and school choice: How can we bridge the gap between ideals and realities? In A. Wolfe (Ed.), *School choice: The moral debate* (pp. 51-69). Princeton, NJ: Princeton University Press.

42. Wolfe, 2003, p. 49 (see note 39).

43. *Brown et al. v. Board of Education of Topeka et al.* 347 U.S. 483 (1954).

44. Enrich, P. (1995). Leaving equality behind: New directions in school finance reform. *Vanderbilt Law Review 48*, 101-194

Viteritti, 2003 (see note 37).

Reich, R. (2006). *Equality and adequacy in the state's provision of education: Mapping the conceptual landscape* (A report prepared for Getting Down to Facts). Palo Alto, CA: Stanford University.

Brighouse, H., & Swift, A. (2009). Educational equality versus educational adequacy: A critique of Anderson and Satz. *Journal of Applied Philosophy, 26*(2), 117-128.

45. Reich, 2006, p. 7 (see note 44).

46. Minorini, P. A., & Sugarman, S. D. (1999). Educational adequacy and the courts: The promise and problems of moving to a new paradigm. In H. F. Ladd, R. Chalk, & J. S. Hansen (Eds.), *Equity and adequacy in education finance: Issues and perspectives* (pp. 175-208). Washington, DC: National Academy Press.

Ryan, J., & Heise, M. (2002). The political economy of school choice. *Yale Law Journal, 111*(8), 2043-2136.

47. As Rob Reich argues, "adequacy seems to press more lightly against parental liberty, for adequacy can be construed as to give wide latitude to parental liberty, so long as all children receive an adequate education."

Reich, 2006, p. 16 (see note 44).

48. Brighouse, H. (2000). *School choice and social justice.* Oxford, England: Oxford University Press.

49. Brighouse, H. (2004, November). What's wrong with privatising schools? *Journal of Philosophy of Education, 38*(4), 617.

50. Brighouse's connection between school choice and justice has been criticized from a variety of perspectives. Some theorists argue that Brighouse

overstates the realities of school choice proposals, and is too optimistic about their egalitarian potential. See

Foster, S. (2002). School choice and social justice: A response to Harry Brighouse. *Journal of Philosophy of Education, 36*(2), 291-308.

Others fault Brighouse for an over-regulation of choice principles, advocating instead for a fuller privatization of education. See

Tooley, J. (2003). Why Harry Brighouse is nearly right about the privatisation of education. *Journal of Philosophy of Education, 37*(3), 427-447.

51.   Gintis, H. (1995). The political economy of school choice. *Teachers College Record, 96*(3), 492-511.

Dwyer, J. G. (1998). *Religious schools v. children's rights*. Ithaca, NY: Cornell University Press.

52.   Ben-Porath, S. (2010). *Tough choices: Structured paternalism and the landscape of choice*. Princeton, NJ: Princeton University Press.

53.   Knight Abowitz, K. (2001). Charter schooling and social justice. *Educational Theory, 51*(3), 151-170.

54.   Knight Abowitz, K. (2008). Intergenerational justice and school choice. In W. Feinberg & C. Lubienski (Eds.), *School choice policies and outcomes: Empirical and philosophical perspectives* (pp. 79-98). Albany, NY: SUNY Press.

55.   Knight Abowitz, K. (2010). Qualifying my faith in the common school ideal. *Educational Theory, 60* (6), 683-702.

Knight Abowitz, K. & Karaba, R. (2010). Charter schooling and democratic justice. *Educational Policy, 24* (3), 534-558.

56.   Some of these alternate views of justice include communitarian conceptions of justice and ideals of justice as caring.

57.   Macedo, 2003 (see note 41).

58.   Macedo, S. (2003). Liberalism and group identities. In K. McDonough & W. Feinberg (Eds.), *Education and citizenship in liberal-democratic societies* (pp. 414-436). Oxford, England: Oxford University Press.

59.   While pluralism clearly plays a central role in many understandings of school choice, Nancy Rosenblum argues that pluralism has no inherent connection with school choice. She contends that the major arguments for choice—which she separates into performance, liberty and equality—do not rely on pluralism to justify choice.

Rosenblum, 2003 (see note 26).

60.   McConnell, M. W. (2001). Educational disestablishment: Why democratic values are ill-served by democratic control of schooling. In S. Macedo & Y.

Tamir (Eds.), *NOMOS XLIII: Moral and political education* (pp. 87-146). New York, NY: New York University Press.

61.   McConnell, 2001 (see note 60).

62.   Reich, R. (2002). *Bridging liberalism and multiculturalism in education.* Chicago, IL: University of Chicago Press.

63.   Reich cites Levinson as arguing against pluralist conceptions of schooling and McConnell as defending an overly broad version of pluralism. See

Reich, R. (2008). Common schooling and educational choice as a response to pluralism. In W. Feinberg & C. Lubienski (Eds.), *School choice policies and outcomes: Empirical and philosophical perspectives* (pp. 21-40). Albany, NY: SUNY Press.

Reich, R. (2007). How and why to support common schooling and educational choice at the same time. *Journal of Philosophy of Education, 41*(4), 709-725.

Levinson, M. (1999). *The demands of liberal education.* Oxford, England: Oxford University Press.

McConnell, 2001 (see note 60).

64.   Brighouse, 2000 (see note 48).

Gutmann, A. (1987). *Democratic education.* Princeton, NJ: Princeton University Press.

Callan, E. (1997). *Creating citizens: Political education and liberal democracy.* Oxford, England: Clarendon Press.

Levinson, 1999 (see note 63).

65.   All scholars do not share this focus on autonomy. In fact, certain critics argue that much of liberal theory is based on a falsely atomistic vision of the individual. See, e.g.,

Walzer, M. (1983). *Spheres of justice.* New York, NY: Basic Books.

66.   McConnell, 2001 (see note 60).

67.   Burtt, S. (2002). The proper scope of parental authority: Why we don't owe children an "open future"? In S. Macedo & I. M. Young (Eds.), *NOMOS XLIV: Child, family, and state* (pp. 243-272). New York, NY: New York University Press.

Merry, M. (2005). The ethics of identity. *Journal of Philosophy of Education, 39*(3), 564-567.

68.   Levinson, 1999 (see note 63).

69.   For example:

Levinson, 1999 (see note 63).

Macedo, S. (2000). *Diversity and distrust: Civic education in a multicultural democracy.* Cambridge, MA: Harvard University Press.

McDonough, K., & Feinberg, W. (Eds.). (2003). *Education and citizenship in liberal-democratic societies.* Oxford, England: Oxford University Press.

Wolf, P., & Macedo, S. (Eds.). (2004). *Educating citizens: international perspectives on civic values and school choice.* Washington, DC: Brookings.

Minow, M., Shweder, R., & Markus, H. (Eds.). (2008). *Just schools: Pursuing equality in societies of difference.* New York, NY: Russell Sage Foundation Press.

Minow, M. (2010). *In Brown's wake: Legacies of America's educational landmark.* Oxford, England: Oxford University Press.

70. Feinberg, W. (2006). *For goodness sake: Religious schools and education for liberal democracy.* New York, NY: Routledge/Falmer.

71. "Public schools, when working as they should, can provide the trust and understanding that can allow single-tradition religious schools at the educational margins."

Feinberg, 2006, p. 214 (see note 70).

See also, Feinberg, W. (1998). *Common schools/uncommon identities: National unity and cultural difference.* New Haven, CT: Yale University Press.

72. See

Levinson, 1999 (see note 63);

Macedo, 2000 (see note 69);

Levinson, M., & Levinson, S. (2003). "Getting religion:" Religion, community, and diversity in public and private schools. In A. Wolfe (Ed.), *School choice: The moral debate* (pp. 104-125). Princeton, NJ: Princeton University Press.

73. Gutmann, 1987 (see note 64).

74. Mathews, D. (2008). The Public and the Public Schools: the Coproduction of Education. *Phi Delta Kappan, 89* (8), 560-564.

75. Barber, 1997 (see note 15).

76. Pring, R. (2007). The common school. *Journal of Philosophy of Education, 41*(4), 503-522.

77. Brighouse, H. (2007). Educational justice and socio-economic segregation in schools. *Journal of Philosophy of Education, 41*(4), 575-590.

78. Pring, 2007, p. 504 (see note 76).

79. Brighouse, 2007 (see note 77).

Brighouse, H. (2005). *On education*. New York, NY: Routledge.

80. Macedo, 2000 (see note 69).

81. Meier, D. (1995). *The power of their ideas: Lessons for America from a small school in Harlem*. Boston, MA: Beacon Press.

82. Finn, C. E., Jr., Manno, B. V., & Vanourek, G. (2000). *Charter schools in action: Renewing public education*. Princeton, NJ: Princeton University Press.

83. Reich, 2007 (see note 63).

84. Waks, L. (2010). Dewey's theory of the democratic public and the public character of charter schools. *Educational Theory, 60*(6), 665-681.

85. Frankenberg, E., Lee, C., & Orfield, G. (2003). *A multiracial society with segregated schools: Are We losing the dream?* Cambridge, MA: Harvard University, The Civil Rights Project

86. Chubb & Moe, 1990 (see note 13).

87. Lubienski, 2001 (see note 3

88. Moses, M. S. (2002). The heart of the matter: Philosophy and educational research. *Review of Research in Education, 26*, 1-21.

89. Frankenberg, E., & Lee, C. (2003, September 5). Charter schools and race: A lost opportunity for integrated education. *Education Policy Analysis Archives, 11*(32). Retrieved November 30, 2007, from http://epaa.asu.edu/epaa/v11n32/

90. Brighouse, 2000 (see note 48).

91. McConnell, 2001 (see note 60).

92. Finn, Manno, & Vanourek, 2000 (see note 82).

93. Wilson, T. S. (2010). Civic fragmentation or voluntary association? Habermas, Fraser and charter school segregation. *Educational Theory, 60*(6), 643-664.

94. Fenstermacher, G. D. (2002). Should philosophers and educators be speaking to each other? *Educational Theory, 52*(3), 339-349.

Feinberg, W., & Lubienski, C. (Eds.). (2008). *School choice policies and outcomes: Empirical and philosophical perspectives*. Albany, NY: SUNY Press.

Moses, 2002 (see note 88).

95. For a philosophical approach to the issue of equality, see Howe, K. (1997). *Understanding equal educational opportunity: Social justice, democracy and schooling*. New York, NY: Teachers College Press.

Also, see the discussion of inequality that in part draws on Howe's work in Moses, 2002 (see note 88).

96.   Kenneth Strike takes a similar approach in asking what kinds of evidence
      we might need to evaluate charter schools against a standard of distribu-
      tive justice. He argues for the necessity of broader measures than standard-
      ized test scores for evaluating the aims of charter schools. See

      Strike, K. (2010). Charter schools, choice and distributive justice: What evi-
      dence do we need? *Theory and Research in Education, 8*(1), 63-78.

97.   Arsen, D., Plank, D., & Sykes, G. (1999). *School choice policies in Michigan:
      The rules matter.* East Lansing, MI: The Education Policy Center at Michi-
      gan State University.

98.   Howe, K. (2007). On the (in)feasibility of school choice for social justice. In
      D. Vokey (Ed.). *Philosophy of education 2006* (pp. 259-267). Urbana, IL: Phi-
      losophy of Education Society.

99.   Goodwin, R. K., & Kemerer, F. (2002). *School choice tradeoffs: Liberty, equity &
      diversity.* Austin, TX: University of Texas Press

      Levin, H. M. (1999). The public-private nexus in education. *American
      Behavioral Scientist, 43*(1), 124-137

      Levin, H. M. (2002, Fall). A comprehensive framework for evaluating edu-
      cational vouchers. *Educational Evaluation and Policy Analysis, 24*(3), 159-174.

100. Brighouse, H. (2008). Educational equality and the varieties of school
      choice. In W. Feinberg & C. Lubienski (Eds.), *School choice policies and out-
      comes: Empirical and philosophical perspectives* (pp. 41-60). Albany, NY: SUNY
      Press.

101. Kenneth Howe offers a critique of Brighouse's argument for targeted
      vouchers that emphasizes the larger political context that surrounds efforts
      to expand vouchers in the U.S. policy context.

      Howe, 2007 (see note 98).

102. Bulman, R., & Kirp, D. (1999). The shifting politics of school choice. In S.
      Sugarman & F. R. Kemerer (Eds.), *School choice and social controversy: Politics,
      policy and law* (pp. 36-67). Washington DC: Brookings Institution Press.
      Cited in Fusarelli, L. D. (2003). *The political dynamics of choice.* New York,
      NY: Macmillan.

      Also see, Plank, D., & Sykes, G. (2000). *The school choice debate: Framing the
      issues.* East Lansing, MI: The Education Policy Center at Michigan State
      University.

103. National Working Commission on Choice in K-12 Education. (2003,
      November). *School choice: Doing it the right way makes a difference.* Washing-
      ton, DC: Brookings Institution. Retrieved March 1, 2008, from http://
      www.brookings.edu/reports/2003/11education.aspx

CHAPTER 3: HOW LEGISLATION
AND LITIGATION SHAPE SCHOOL CHOICE

1. Traditional methods of legal research were employed by this study. Primary sources included constitutions, federal and state case law, statutes, and regulations. Secondary sources included books, law review and other articles related to choice as well as the web sites of major policy groups and organizations.

2. Goodlad, J. I., & McMannon, T. J. (Eds.). (1997). *The public purpose of education and schooling.* San Francisco, CA: Jossey-Bass.

3. Alexander, K., & Alexander, M. D. (2005). *American public school law* (6th ed.). Belmont, CA: Thomson West.

4. Garner, B. A. (Ed.). (1999). *Black's law dictionary* (7th ed.). St. Paul, MN: West Group.

5. Alexander & Alexander, 2005 (see note 3).

6. *Pierce v. Society of Sisters of the Holy Names of Jesus and Mary,* 268 U.S. 510, 45 S.Ct. 571 (1925).

7. *Pierce v. Society of Sisters of the Holy Names of Jesus and Mary,* 268 U.S. 510, at 534-535 (1923).

8. Some sparsely populated rural areas in Maine and Vermont also offered what might be considered a form of school choice. In those areas, if communities did not operate schools at a particular level, parents could enroll their children in neighboring school districts and the resident district would pay a form of tuition on behalf of the students. This practice was later expanded to allow enrollment in private nonreligious schools on the same basis. See 20-A M.R.S.A. § 5204 and 16 V.S.A. §821-822. These programs continue today.

9. *Brown v. Board. of Education of Topeka,* 349 U.S. 294, 301 , 75 S.Ct. 753, 757 (1955).

10. Viteritti, J. P. (1999). *Choosing equality: School choice, the Constitution, and civil society.* Washington, DC: Brookings Institution Press.

11. *Griffin v. County School Bd. of Prince Edward County,* 377 U.S. 218, 84 S.Ct. 1226 (1964).

12. *Green v. County Sch. Bd.,* 391 U.S. 430 (1968).

13. For more on this topic, see, for example: Hill, H., & Jones, J. E. (Eds.), (1993). *Race in America: The struggle for equality.* Madison, WI: The University of Wisconsin Press;

    Forman, J. (2005). The secret history of school choice: How progressives got there first. *The Georgetown Law Journal, 93,* 1287-1319;

Viteritti, 1999 (see note 10).

14. Friedman, M. (1955). The role of government in education. In R. A. Solow (Ed.), *Economics and the public interest* (pp. 123-44). New Brunswick, NJ: Rutgers Press.

15. Friedman, M. (1962). *Capitalism and freedom*. Chicago, IL: University of Chicago Press.

16. For a discussion of policy arguments supporting this use of choice, see

   Coons, J., & Sugarman, S. (1978). *Education by choice: The case for family control*. Berkeley, CA: University of California Press.

17. Metz, M. (1990). Magnet schools and the reform of public schooling. In W. Boyd & H. Walberg (Eds.), *Choice in education: Potential and problems* (pp. 123-147). Berkeley, CA: McCutchan.

18. Walberg, H. J., & Bast, J. L. (1993). School choice: The essential reform. *Cato Journal, 13*(1), 101-121.

19. Chubb, J. E., & Moe, T. M. (1990). *Politics, markets, & America's schools*. Washington, DC: The Brookings Institution.

20. See for example a discussion of Wisconsin's Chapter 220 Program, Wisconsin Legislative Fiscal Bureau. (2011). School Integration (Chapter 220) Aid, Informational Paper #27. Retrieved February 16, 2011, from http://legis.wisconsin.gov/lfb/Informationalpapers/27_school%20integration%20(Chapter%20220)%20aid.pdf

21. *Open Enrollment: 50-State Report*. Denver, CO: Education Commission of the States. Retrieved February 16, 2011, from http://mb2.ecs.org/reports/Report.aspx?id=268

22. Chubb & Moe, 1990, 217 (emphasis in original) (see note 19).

23. The National School Boards Association lists 13 currently operating voucher programs. Five programs serve cities (Milwaukee, Cleveland, New Orleans, Washington, DC, and Douglas County, CO) and six programs are limited statewide voucher programs for particular students (e.g., those with disabilities) in Arizona, Florida, Georgia, Ohio, Oklahoma, and Utah. Indiana and Louisiana have recently enacted statewide voucher programs for low-income students. To date, no state has approved and begun operation of a full scale statewide voucher program of the type Freidman envisioned. For details on existing programs, see Voucher Strategy Center, National School Boards Association. Retrieved July 27, 2012, from http://www.nsba.org/novouchers

24. Welner, K. G. (2008). *Neo vouchers: The emergence of tuition tax credits for private schooling*. Lanham, MD: Rowman & Littlefield.

25. Welner, 2008 (see note 24).

26. Tuition tax credits are different than tax deductions. Tax deductions reduce the amount of taxable income, while tax credits reduce the amount of taxes owed.

27. Brief of the National School Boards Association as Amicus Curiae in Support of Respondents, *Arizona Christian School Tuition Organization v. Winn*, — U.S. —, 131 S.Ct. 1436 (Sept. 22, 2010)(Nos. 09-987, 09-991).

28. Green, P. C., & Mead, J. F. (2004). *Charter schools and the law: Establishing new legal relationships*. Norwood, MA: Christopher Gordon.

29. Long, A. (2004). *Cyber schools*. Denver, CO: Education Commission of the States. Retrieved February 14, 2011, from http://www.ecs.org/clearing-house/51/01/5101.htm

30. *National Charter School Online Directory*. Washington, DC: Center for Education Reform, Retrieved February 14, 2011, from https://www.edreform.com/charter_directory/

31. Gordon, W. M., Russo, C. J., & Miles, A. S. (1994). *The law of home schooling*. Topeka, KS: National Organization on Legal Problems in Education.

32. Magnet School Assistance Program, 20 U.S.C. §7201-7213 (1994).

33. Charter School Expansion Act of 1998, Public Law 105-278, Oct. 22, 1998.

34. No Child Left Behind Act of 2001, Public Law 107-110, Jan. 8, 2002.

35. The Establishment Clause of the First Amendment reads: "Congress shall make no law respecting an establishment of religion ..." (U.S. Const. Amend. 1).

36. The Free Exercise Clause of the First Amendment reads: "Congress shall make no law . . prohibiting the free exercise [of religion] ..." (U.S. Const. Amend. 1).

37. An issue related to school vouchers is the provision of tax deductions or credits for those enrolling their children in private religious schools. The Supreme Court first upheld such a plan in *Mueller v. Allen*, 463 U.S. 388 (1983). A full discussion of such programs is beyond the scope of this review. For a discussion of these types of programs, see

Mawdsley, R. D. (2007). Tax exempt bond financing for religious educational institutions: What is required under the U.S. Constitution? *West's Education Law Reporter, 221*, 459-483.

38. Milwaukee: *Jackson v. Benson*, 578 N.W.2d 602 (Wis. 1998), *cert. denied* 119 S.Ct. 466 (Nov. 9, 1998);

Cleveland: *Zelman v. Simmons-Harris*, 536 U.S. 639, 122 S.Ct. 2460 (2002). The Washington, DC, program was created in 2004 after the Supreme Court's ruling in *Zelman*.

39. *Zelman v. Simmons-Harris*, 2002 (see note 38).

40.   See e.g., Green, P. C. (2001). Charter schools and religious institutions: A match made in heaven. *West's Education Law Reporter*, 1-18.

DeForrest, M. E. (2003). An overview and evaluation of State Blaine amendments: Origins, scope, and First Amendment concerns. *Harvard Journal of Law and Public Policy, 26*, 551-626.

41.   The "Religion Clause" reads: "No public money ... shall be appropriated to any religious worship, exercise, or instruction, or to the support of any religious establishment." (Article 2, Section 12, of the Arizona Constitution).

42.   The "Aid Clause" reads: "No tax shall be laid or appropriation of public money made in aid of any church, or private or sectarian school, or any public service corporation." (Article 9, Section 10, of the Arizona Constitution).

43.   *Cain v. Horne*, 202 P.3d 1178 (Ariz. 2009).

44.   See e.g., *Bush v. Holmes*, 919 So.2d 392 (Fla. 2006).

45.   *Kotterman v. Killian*, 193 Ariz. 273, 972 P.2d 606 (Ariz. 1999).

46.   *Arizona Christian School Tuition Organization v. Winn*, --- U.S. ---, 131 S.Ct. 1436 (2011).

47.   Green & Mead, 2004 (see note 28).

48.   *PLANS, Inc. v. Sacramento City Unified School District*, 319 F.3d 504 (9th Cir. 2003).

49.   Green & Mead, 2004 (see note 28).

50.   United States Department of Education (1995). *Religious expression in public schools*. Retrieved February 16, 2011, from http://www.ed.gov/Speeches/08-1995/religion.html

51.   *Bagley v. Raymond School Department*, 728 A.2d 127 (Me. 1999).

52.   *Eulitt v. Maine Dept. of Education*, 307 F.Supp.2d 158 (D. Me. 2004).

53.   *Locke v. Davey*, 540 U.S. 712, 124 S.Ct. 1307 (2004).

54.   Mead, J. F. (2002). Conscious use of race as a voluntary means to educational ends in elementary and secondary education: A legal argument derived from recent judicial opinions. *Michigan Journal of Race & Law, 8*, 63-149.

55.   *Parents Involved in Community Schools v. Seattle School District Number 1*, 127 S.Ct. 2738 (2007).

56.   See for example,

American Civil Rights Foundation v. Berkeley Unified School District, 90 Cal.Rptr.3d 789 (Cal. App. 1 Dist. 2009).

Doe ex rel. Doe v. Lower Merion School District, 665 F.3d 524 (3rd Cir. 2011).

57. *Murphy v. State of Arkansas*, 852 F. 2d 1039 (8th Cir. 1988).

58. *McDonough v. Ney*, 599 D. Supp. 679 (D.Me. 1984).

59. See for example, *State v. Schmidt*, 505 N.E.2d 627 (Ohio 1987).

60. *Wisconsin v. Popanz*, 112 Wis.2d 166, 332 N.W.2d 750 (Wis. 1983).

61. Wis. Stat. §118.15 (4).

62. *Council of Organizations about Parochiaid v. Governor*, 566 N.W. 2d 208 (Mich . 1997).

63. *Bush v. Holmes*, 919 So.2d 392 (Fla. 2006).

64. *Owens v. Congress of Parents, Teachers*, 92 P3d 933 (Colo 2004).

65. *Davis v. Grover*, Case No. 90-CV-25765 (Dane Cty. Cir. 1990); For a discussion see

Mead, J. F. (2000). *Publicly funded school choice options in Milwaukee: An examination of the legal issues.* Milwaukee, WI: Public Policy Forum.

66. *ACLU v. State of Wisconsin*, Complaint to the United States Department of Justice, June 7, 2011.

67. Mead, J. F. (1995). Including students with disabilities in parental choice programs: The challenge of meaningful choice. *West's Education Law Reporter, 101*(2), 463-496.

Green & Mead, 2004 (see note 28).

68. Letter to Lunar, 17 IDELR 834 (OSEP 1991); Letter to Evans, 17 IDELR 836 (OSEP 1991); Letter to Bina, 18 IDELR 582 (OSEP 1991); Letter to Bocketti, 32 IDELR 225 (OCR 1999); Letter to Gloecker, 33 IDELR 222 (OSEP 2000).

69. *Fallbrook Union Elementary School District*, 16 IDELR 754 (OCR 1990); *San Francisco Unified School District*, 16 IDELR 824 (OCR 1990); *Chattanooga Public School District*, 20 IDELR 999 (OCR 1993).

70. Letter to Lunar, 17 IDELR 834 (OSEP 1991); Letter to Evans, 17 IDELR 836 (OSEP 1991); Letter to Bina, 18 IDELR 582 (OSEP 1991); Letter to Bocketti, 32 IDELR 225 (OCR 1999); Letter to Gloecker, 33 IDELR 222 (OSEP 2000).

71. *San Francisco Unified School District*, 16 IDELR 824 (OCR 1990); Letter to Bocketti, 32 IDELR 225 (OCR 1999); Letter to Gloecker, 33 IDELR 222 (OSEP 2000).

72. See e.g.,

McKinney, J. (1992). Special education and parental choice: An oxymoron in the making. *West's Education Law Reporter, 76*, 667-677.

Mead, 1995 (see note 67).

Ahearn, E., Lange, C., Rhim, L., & McLaughlin, M. (2001). *Project search: Special education as requirements in charter schools, final report of a research study.* Alexandria, VA: National Association of State Directors of Special Education.

73.   When those parental choices would violate provisions of the law, it is less clear how to reconcile these principles. One situation in which such conflicts are most apparent involves charter schools designed specifically for children with disabilities and potential conflicts with IDEA's requirement that children with disabilities be educated with children without disabilities to the maximum extent appropriate. For a discussion of these issues, see

Mead, J. F. (2008). *Charter Schools Designed for Children with Disabilities: An Initial Examination of Issues and Questions Raised.* Alexandria, VA: National Association of State Directors of Special Education.

74.   Green & Mead, 2004, 26-29 (see note 28).

75.   See e.g.,

Shelby School v. Arizona State Board of Education, 962 P.2d 230 (Ariz. Ct. App. 1998);

Beaufort County Board of Education v. Lighthouse Charter School Committee, 516 S.E.2d 655 (S.C. 1999);

West Chester Area School District v. Collegium Charter School, 760 A.2d 452 (Pa. Commw Ct. 2000).

76.   *Johnson v. Burmaster*, 744 N.W.2d 900 (Wis. App., Dist. II 2007).

77.   *Johnson v. Burmaster*, 744 N.W.2d 900, at 909 (Wis. App., Dist. II 2007).

78.   See Wis. Stat. §118.40(8).

79.   Green & Mead, 2004, 1 (see note 28).

80.   National Charter School and Enrollment 2010. Washington, DC: The Center for Education Reform. Retrieved February 16, 2011, from http://www.edreform.com/_upload/CER_charter_numbers.pdf

81.   Vargari, S. (Ed.). (2002). *The charter school landscape*. Pittsburgh, PA: University of Pittsburgh Press.

82.   Finn, C. E., Manno, B. V., & Vanourek, G. (2000*). Charter schools in action: Renewing public education*. Princeton, NJ: Princeton University Press.

83.   Green & Mead, 2004 (see note 28).

84.   Finn, C. E., & Manno, B. V. (1998). The 12 labors of charters schools. *The New Democrat.* Retrieved February 16, 2011, from http://www.dlc.org/ndol_ci.cfm?kaid=110&subid=134&contentid=1554

85. *Four Pillars of NCLB.* United States Department of Education, Retrieved February 16, 2011, from http://www.ed.gov/nclb/overview/intro/4pillars.html

86. Public School Choice: Nonregulatory Guidance. (2009). Washington, DC: U.S. Department of Education. Retrieved February 16, 2011, from http://www.ed.gov/policy/elsec/guid/schoolchoiceguid.pdf

87. Public School Choice: Nonregulatory Guidance, 2009 (see note 86).

88. Sunderman, G. S. (2006). *The unraveling of No Child Left Behind: How negotiated changes transform the law.* Cambridge, MA: Civil Rights Project. Retrieved February 16, 2011, from http://dwot.org/nclb_unravel.pdf

89. Alvarez, L. (2001, May 4). On the way to passage, Bush's education plan gets a makeover. *The New York Times*, Section A, Column 1, 16.

   Kornblut, A. E. (2001, January 4). Bush ties school aid, test scores vouchers are downplayed; Kennedy sees room for a deal. *The Boston Globe*, pp. A1.

90. President Bush also championed a more modest federal voucher program as part of the aid package to the Gulf Coast following hurricanes Katrina and Rita. As with the NCLB voucher proposals, Congress refused to enact this part of his proposal.

91. The Obama Administration has proposed changes to the law, but public school choice remains a feature. The proposal features support for 3 types of public school choice: (1) "supporting effective charter schools"; (2) "promoting public school choice"; and (3) "Continuing the Magnet School Assistance Program." The proposal also retains conversion to charter schools as one of several "turnaround" strategies for chronically struggling schools.

   See *ESEA Reauthorization: A blueprint for reform.* Retrieved March 30, 2011, from http://www2.ed.gov/policy/elsec/leg/blueprint/index.html. In addition, in September 2011, Secretary of Education Arne Duncan informed states that waivers of the proficiency requirements of NCLB could be obtained from the Education Department if the state made commitments to high standards, rigorous assessment, and uniform accountability processes for all its schools. To date, the U.S. Department of Education has approved waiver requests from 33 states. See ESEA Flexibility. Retrieved July 27, 2012 from http://www.ed.gov/esea/flexibility

92. Orfield, G., & Lee, C. (2007). *Historic reversals, accelerating resegregation, and the need for new integration strategies.* Los Angeles, CA: The Civil Rights Project.

   Parents Involved in Community Schools v. Seattle School District Number 1, 127 S.Ct. 2738, at 2768 (2007).

93. *Parents Involved in Community Schools v. Seattle School District Number 1*, 127 S.Ct. 2738, at 2836 (2007) (Breyer, J., dissenting).

94. In fact, 64 *amicus curiae* (friend of the court) briefs were filed in conjunction with *Parents Involved*; 11 briefs supported the petitioners' view that the programs were unconstitutional, while 53 argued that the programs operated consistent with the constitution and should survive scrutiny.

95. *Parents Involved in Community Schools v. Seattle School District Number 1*, 127 S.Ct. 2738, at 2790 (2007) (Kennedy, J., concurring).

96. *Parents Involved in Community Schools v. Seattle School District Number 1*, 127 S.Ct. 2738, at 2797 (2007) (Kennedy, J., concurring).

97. Strategies listed as a-e in the text may be found at: *Parents Involved in Community Schools v. Seattle School District Number 1*, 127 S.Ct. 2738, at 2792 (2007) (Kennedy, J., concurring). Kennedy argues here that employing any one or combination of these strategies would be constitutionally permissible and would not require an application of strict scrutiny to be found so.

98. It should be noted that Kennedy cautioned that any use of race as part of a review of multiple factors prior to admission would still have to satisfy the dictates of strict scrutiny. That is, such a use of race would have to be necessary and narrowly tailored to a compelling state interest. Moreover, Kennedy's use of the modifying phrase—"if necessary"—also suggests that such a use would only be proper if other non- or less race-conscious means could be proven ineffective. *Parents Involved in Community Schools v. Seattle School District Number 1*, 127 S.Ct. 2738, at 2793 (2007) (Kennedy, J., concurring). For further discussion of the case and its various decisions, see, Green, P. C., Mead, J. F. & Oluwole, J. O. (2011). *Parents Involved*, school assignment plans, and the Equal Protection Clause: The case for special Constitutional rules. *Brooklyn Law Review, 76*(2), 503-567.

99. The Civil Rights Project (CRP) is attempting to track such effects by reviewing new reports, legislative enactments, and litigation. While the report does not make any claims that the measures tracked have been taken as a direct result of *Parents Involved*, the report details developments that both negatively and positively influence integration.

Tefera, A., Siegel-Hawley, G. & Frankenberg, E. (2010). School integration efforts three years after *Parents Involved*. The Civil Rights Project Retrieved March 31, 2011, from http://civilrightsproject.ucla.edu/legal-developments/court-decisions/school-integration-efforts-three-years-after-parents-involved/teferea-school-integration-three-years-after.pdf

100. Arkansas Code § 6-18-206.

101. *Hardy v. Malvern School District*, 2010 U.S. Dist. LEXIS 24609 (W.D. Ark. 2010)(Dismissing the case on sovereign immunity grounds without addressing the merits of the claim). See also, N.N. ex rel. *S.S. v. Madison Metropolitan School District*, 670 F. Supp.2d 927 (W.D. Wis. 2009) (Dismissing a case against a school district that had followed the racial balancing provisions of the state's urban/suburban transfer program.)

102.   *Student Doe 1 v. Lower Merion School District*, 2010 U.S. Dist. LEXIS 62797 (E.D. Pa. 2010).

103.   *Id.*, at slip op. 49-50.

104.   *Doe ex rel. Doe v. Lower Merion School District*, 665 F.3d 524 (3rd Cir. 2011), cert. denied 80 USLW 3551 (U.S. Jun 18, 2012).

105.   *American Civil Rights Foundation v. Berkeley Unified School District*, 90 Cal.Rptr.3d 789 (Cal. App. 1 Dist. 2009).

106.   *Id.*, at 792.

107.   392 U.S. 83 (1968).

108.   *Id.*, at 102-103.

109.   Arizona Revised Statutes Annotated §43-1089 (West. Supp. 2010).

110.   Justice Scalia, joined by Justice Thomas, wrote a concurrence explaining that he would have overturned *Flast*, a case he considers wrongly decided. *Arizona Christian School Tuition Organization v. Winn*, --- U.S. ---, 131 S.Ct. 1436, J. Scalia at 1449-50 (2011).

111.   *Arizona Christian School Tuition Organization v. Winn*, --- U.S. ---, 131 S.Ct. 1436, at 1447 (2011).

112.   *Id.*, at 1450, emphasis in original. Justice Kagan laid out two examples to illustrate what dissenting justices viewed as artificial distinction between appropriations and tax credits: "Suppose a State desires to reward Jews— by, say, $500 per year—for their religious devotion. Should the nature of taxpayers' concern vary if the State allows Jews to claim the aid on their tax returns, in lieu of receiving an annual stipend? Or assume a State wishes to subsidize the ownership of crucifixes. It could purchase the religious symbols in bulk and distribute them to all takers. Or it could mail a reimbursement check to any individual who buys her own and submits a receipt for the purchase. Or it could authorize that person to claim a tax credit equal to the price she paid. Now, really—do taxpayers have less reason to complain if the State selects the last of these three options? The Court today says they do, but that is wrong. The effect of each form of subsidy is the same, on the public fisc and on those who contribute to it. Regardless of which mechanism the State uses, taxpayers have an identical stake in ensuring that the State's exercise of its taxing and spending power complies with the Constitution" (at 1457).

113.   Plank, D. N., & Sykes, G. (2003). *Choosing choice: School choice in international perspective.* New York, NY: Teachers College Press

114.   United Nations Universal Declaration on Human Rights, Article 26. Retrieved February 16, 2011, from http://www.hrweb.org/legal/udhr.html

115.   See Mead, J. F. & Green, P. C. (2012). *Chartering equity: Using charter school legislation and policy to advance equal educational opportunity.* Boulder, CO:

National Education Policy Center. Retrieved March 21, 2012, from http://nepc.colorado.edu/publication/chartering-equity

116.   See e.g., Chubb & Moe, 1990 (see note 19).

Ascher, C., Fruchter, N., & Berne, R. (1996). *Hard lessons: Public schools and privatization*. New York, NY: The Twentieth Century Fund Press.

Hill P. T., Pierce, L. C., & Guthrie, J. W. (1997). *Reinventing public education: How contracting can transform America's schools*. Chicago, IL: The University of Chicago Press.

Engel, M. (2000). *The struggle for control of public education: Market ideology vs. democratic values*. Philadelphia, PA: Temple University Press.

Good, T. L., & Braden, J. S. (Eds.). (2000). *The great school debate: Choice, vouchers, and charters*. Mahwah, NJ: Erlbaum.

117.   Tyack, D., & Cuban, L. (1995). *Tinkering toward Utopia: A century of public school reform*. Cambridge, MA: Harvard University Press, 142.

118.   Goodlad & McMannon, 1997 (see note 2).

Cuban, L., & Shipps, D. (Eds.), (2000). *Reconstructing the common good in education: Coping with intractable American dilemmas*. Palo Alto, CA: Stanford University Press.

CHAPTER 4: WHO CHOOSES SCHOOLS, AND WHY? THE CHARACTERISTICS AND MOTIVATIONS OF FAMILIES WHO ACTIVELY CHOOSE SCHOOLS

1.   Little research has been conducted on who is making use of the choice provisions under NCLB though the available research suggests that not many parents avail themselves of the choice option. A federally funded evaluation of the program indicates that about 1% of eligible students make use of the program. See:

U.S. Department of Education, Office of Planning, Evaluation and Policy Development, Policy and Program Studies Service. (2009). *State and local implementation of the* No Child Left Behind Act, *Volume VII—Title I School Choice and Supplemental Educational Services: Final Report*. Washington, DC: Author.

2.   The D.C. Opportunity Scholarship program was federally funded from 2004-2009.

3.   Aud, S., Hussar, W., Planty, M., Snyder, T., Bianco, K., Fox, M., ... Drake, L. (2010). *The condition of education 2010 (NCES 2010-028)*.Washington, DC: National Center for Education Statistics, Institute of Education Sciences, U.S. Department of Education.

4.   See for example:

Schneider, M., & Buckley, J. (2002). What do parents want from schools? Evidence from the Internet. *Educational Evaluation and Policy Analysis, 24*(2), 133-144.

Gill, B. P., Timpane, M., Ross, K. E., Brewer, D. J., & Booker, K. (2001). *Rhetoric versus reality: What we know and what we need to know about vouchers and charters Schools.* Santa Monica, CA: RAND.

Henig, J. R. (1994). *Rethinking school choice: Limits of the market metaphor.* Princeton, NJ: Princeton University Press.

Saporito, S. (2003). Private choices, public consequences: Magnet school choice and segregation by race and poverty. *Social Problems, 50*(2), 181-203.

5.   Wells, A. S., & Crain, R. L. (1999). *Stepping over the color line: African American students in White suburban schools.* New Haven, CT: Yale University Press.

6.   One of the more common ways that districts throughout the South tried to resist desegregation was through "freedom of choice" plans. Black students were technically allowed to choose to attend White schools—or they could stay in their own, familiar schools. Given the threatening environment, these choice plans resulted in very little integration. The 1968 Supreme Court decision in *Green v. County School Board* (New Kent County, VA), struck down such a plan as clearly designed to perpetuate segregation.

Rossell, C. H. (2005, Spring). No longer famous but still intact: Magnet schools. *Education Next,* 44-49.

Henig, 1994 (see note 4).

7.   Chubb, J. E., & Moe, T. M. (1990). *Politics, markets and America's schools.* Washington, DC: Brookings Institution Press.

Moe, T. M. (2001). *Schools, vouchers, and the American public.* Washington, DC: Brookings Institution Press.

8.   Bulman, R. C. (2004). School-choice stories: The role of culture. *Sociological Inquiry, 74*(4), 492-519.

9.   The authors are well aware that many children do not live with parents, but with other caregivers. We use "parents" here only to streamline the text; we intend the term to include not only parents but a variety of others who assume parental responsibilities.

10. Hamilton, L. S., & Guin, K. (2005). Understanding how families choose schools. In J. R. Betts & T. Loveless (Eds.), *Getting choice right: Ensuring equity and efficiency in education policy* (pp. 40-60). Washington, DC: Brookings Institution Press.

11.   Grady, S., & Bielick, S. (2010). *Trends in the Use of School Choice: 1993 to 2007* (NCES 2010-004). Washington, DC: National Center for Education Statistics, Institute of Education Sciences, U.S. Department of Education.

12.   Broughman, S. P., Swaim, N. L., & Keaton, P. W. (2009). *Characteristics of private schools in the United States: Results From the 2007-08 Private School Universe Survey* (NCES 2009-313). Washington, DC: National Center for Education Statistics, Institute of Education Sciences, U.S. Department of Education.

13.   Grady & Bielick, 2010 (see note 11).

      Broughman, S.P., & Swaim, N.L. (2006). *Characteristics of private schools in the United States: Results from the 2003-2004 Private School Universe Survey.* Washington, DC: National Center for Education Statistics, U.S. Department of Education.

14.   Broughman, Swaim, & Keaton, 2009 (see note 12).

15.   Grady & Bielick, 2010 (see note 11).

16.   Grady & Bielick, 2010 (see note 11)

17.   Grady & Bielick, 2010 (see note 11).

18.   Teske, P., & Reichardt, R. (2006). Doing their homework: How charter school parents make their choices. In R. J. Lake, & P. T. Hill (Eds.), *Hopes, fears and realities: A balanced look at American charter schools in 2006* (pp. 1-9). Seattle, WA: University of Washington.

      Note the survey on which this research is based is also reported in Teske, P., Fitzpatrick, J., & Kaplan, G. (2007). *Opening doors: How low-income parents search for the right school.* Seattle, WA: University of Washington.

19.   U.S. Department of Education, Office of Innovation and Improvement (2009). *Education options in the states: State programs that provide financial assistance for attendance at private elementary or secondary schools.* Washington, DC: Author. Retrieved April 19, 2012, from http://www2.ed.gov/parents/schools/choice/educationoptions/educationoptions.pdf

20.   See Ohio Department of Education School Options: http://www.ode.state.oh.us/GD/Templates/Pages/ODE/ODEDetail.aspx?page=&TopicRelationID=667&ContentID=46634&Content=101804.

21.   U.S. Department of Education, 2009 (see note 19).

22.   Mayer, D. P., Peterson, P. E., Myers, D. E., Tuttle, C. C., & Howell, W. G. (2002). *School choice in New York City after three years: An evaluation of the School Choice Scholarships Program.* Princeton, NJ and Cambridge, MA: Mathematica Policy Research, Inc., and the Program on Education Policy and Governance, Harvard University. Retrieved April 19, 2012, from http://citeseerx.ist.psu.edu/viewdoc/download?doi=10.1.1.105.399&rep=rep1&type=pdf

Howell, W. G., & Peterson, P. (2000). *School choice in Dayton, OH: An evaluation after one year.* Cambridge, MA: Harvard University.

Wolf, P., Howell, W. G., & Peterson, P. (2000). *School choice in Washington, D.C.: An evaluation after one year.* Cambridge, MA: Harvard University.

23.   Witte, J. F. (2000). *The market approach to education: An analysis of America's first voucher program.* Princeton, NJ: Princeton University Press.

24.   Plucker, J., Muller, P. A., Hansen, J., et al. (2006). *Evaluation of the Cleveland scholarship and tutoring program: Summary report 1998-2004.* Bloomington, IN: Indiana University.

See also,

Ohio Department of Education. (2010). Cleveland Scholarship and Tutoring Program Fact Sheet. Retrieved from http://www.ode.state.oh.us/GD/DocumentManagement/DocumentDownload.aspx?DocumentID=98364

25.   Gill, B. P., et al., 2001 (see note 4).

26.   Campbell, D. E., West, M. R., & Peterson, P. E. (2003, November). *Participation in a national, means-tested school voucher program.* Paper prepared for presentation at the annual conference of the Association for Public Policy and Management, Washington, DC.

Martinez, V. J., Godwin, R. K., Kemerer, F. R., & Perna. L. (1995). The consequences of school choice: Who leaves and who stays in the inner city. *Social Science Quarterly, 76*(3), 485-501.

27.   Plucker et al., 2006 (see note 24).

U.S. Department of Education, National Center for Education Statistics. (2001). Common Core of Data, *Public Elementary/Secondary School Universe Survey,* 2000–01, and *Local Education Agency Universe Survey.* Washington, DC: Author.

28.   Howell & Peterson, 2000 (see note 22).

Wolf, Howell, & Peterson, 2000 (see note 22).

Peterson, P. E., Myers, D., & Howell, W. G. (1999). *An evaluation of the Horizon Scholarship Program in the Edgewood Independent School District, San Antonio, Texas: The first year.* Washington, DC and Cambridge, MA: Mathematica Policy Research and Program on Education Policy and Governance.

29.   U.S. Department of Education, National Center for Education Statistics, 2001 (see note 27).

30.   Campbell, West, & Peterson, 2003 (see note 26).

31.   U.S. Department of Education, National Center for Education Statistics (2007). *The Condition of Education 2007* (NCES 2007-064). Washington, DC: Author.

National Alliance of Public Charter Schools (n.d.) *Public Charter School Dashboard*. Retrieved March 27, 2011, from http://www.publiccharters.org/dashboard/schools/page/mkt/year/2010

32. National Alliance of Public Charter Schools. (2007). *Growth and Quality in the Charter School Movement: 2007 Dashboard*. Washington, DC: Author.

Aud et al., 2010 (see note 3).

33. U.S. Department of Education, National Center for Education Statistics, 2007 (see note 31).

34. Aud et al., 2010 (see note 3).

35. National Alliance of Public Charter Schools, n.d. (see note 31).

36. National Charter School Research Project. (2009). *State comparison data: Percentage of minority students*. Retrieved March 27, 2011, from http://www.crpe.org/cs/crpe/view/projects/1?page=yes&id=5&parent=1&question=4

37. Whether charter schools are leading to increased segregation in schools is beyond the scope of this brief. See the following sources, among others, for more on this debate:

Archbald, D. A. (2000). School choice and school stratification: Shortcomings of the stratification critique and recommendations for theory and research. *Educational Policy, 14*(2),214-240.

Betts, J. R., & Loveless, T. (Eds.). (2005). *Getting choice right: Ensuring equity and efficiency in education policy*. Washington, DC: Brookings Institution Press.

Frankenberg, E., & Lee, C. (2003). *Charter schools and race: A lost opportunity for integrated education*. Cambridge, MA: Harvard University.

Rapp, K. E., & Eckes, S. E. (2007). Dispelling the myth of "White flight": An examination of minority enrollment in charter schools. *Educational Policy, 21*(4), 615-661.

Renzulli, L. A. (2006). District segregation, race legislation, and Black enrollment in charter schools. *Social Science Quarterly, 87*(3), 618-637.

Teske, P., & Schneider, M. (2001). What research can tell policymakers about school choice. *Journal of Policy Analysis and Management, 20*(4), 609-631.

38. National Charter School Research Project. (2009). *State comparison data: Percentage of free/reduced price lunch students*. Retrieved March 27, 2011, from http://www.crpe.org/cs/crpe/view/projects/1?page=yes&id=5&parent=1&question=5 (see note 36).

39. Snyder, T. D., Dillow, S. A., & Hoffman, C. M. (2007). Table 97: Number and enrollment of traditional and public charter elementary and second-

ary schools and percentages of students, teachers, and schools, by selected characteristics: 2003-2004. *Digest of Education Statistics 2006* (NCES 2007-017).

Note that the data for Table 97 are estimates from the 2003-2004 Schools and Staffing Survey which somewhat underrepresented charter schools, affecting the estimates for charters in unknown ways.

40.   U.S. Department of Education. (2010). *Digest of Education Statistics* (online), Table 105. Number and enrollment of traditional public and public charter elementary and secondary schools and percentages of students, teachers, and schools, by selected characteristics: 2007-08 based on data from the National Center for Education Statistics, Schools and Staffing Survey (SASS), "Public School Questionnaire," 2007-08 and "Public Teacher Questionnaire," 2007-08. Retrieved March 27, 2011, from http://nces.ed.gov/programs/digest/d10/tables/dt10_105.asp

41.   U.S. Department of Education, National Center for Education Statistics. (2001-2002). *Common core of data (CCD), public elementary/secondary school universe survey.* Washington, DC: U.S. Department of Education, National Center for Educational Statistics.

42.   Henig, J. R., & Sugarman, S. D. (1999). The nature and extent of school choice. In S. D. Sugarman & F. J. Kemerer (Eds.), *School choice and social controversy* (pp. 13-35). Washington, DC: Brookings Institution.

43.   Aud et al., 2010 (see note 3).

44.   U.S. Department of Education, Office of Planning, Evaluation and Policy Development, Policy and Program Studies Service. (2007). *State and local implementation of the* No Child Left Behind Act, *Volume I—Title I school choice, supplemental educational services, and student achievement*, Washington, DC: Author.

U.S. Department of Education, Office of Planning, Evaluation and Policy Development, Policy and Program Studies Service (2009). *State and local implementation of the* No Child Left Behind Act, *Volume VII—Title I school choice and supplemental educational services: Final report*, Washington, DC: Author.

45.   U.S. Department of Education, 2009 (see note 44).

46.   Belfield, C. R., & Levin, H. M. (2005). *Privatizing educational choice: Consequences for parents, schools, and public policy.* Boulder, CO: Paradigm.

47.   Grady & Bielick, 2010 (see note 11).

48.   Princiotta, D., & Bielick, S. (2006). *Homeschooling in the United States: 2003 statistical analysis report*, NCES 2006-042. Washington, DC: U.S. Department of Education, National Center for Educational Statistics.

49.   Grady & Bielick, 2010 (see note 11).

50.   Tice, P., Chapman, C., Princiotta, D., & Bielick, S. (2006). *Trends in the use of school choice: 1993-2003*. Washington, DC: National Center for Education Statistics, U.S. Department of Education.

51.   Belfield, C. R. (2004). *Home-schooling in the US*. New York, NY: National Center for the Study of Privatization, Teachers College, Columbia University.

52.   Hamilton & Guin, 2005 (see note 10).

53.   Bosetti, L. (2004). Determinants of school choice: Understanding how parents choose elementary schools in Alberta. *Journal of Education Policy, 19*(4), 387-405.

54.   For example:

      Kleitz, B., Weiher, G. R., Tedin, K., & Matland, R. (2000). Choice, charter schools, and household preferences. *Social Science Quarterly, 81*(3), 846-854.

      Schneider, M., Teske, P., Marschall, M., & Roch, C. (1998). Shopping for schools: In the land of the blind, the one-eyed parent may be enough. *American Journal of Political Science, 42*(3), 769-793.

      Martinez, Godwin, Kemerer, & Perna, 1995 (see note 26).

      Witte, J. F. (1991). *First year report: Milwaukee parental choice program*. Madison, WI: University of Wisconsin.

55.   Schneider & Buckley, 2002 (see note 4).

      Miron, G., & Nelson, C. (2002). *What's public about charter schools?: Lessons learned about accountability and choice*. Thousand Oaks, CA: Corwin Press.

56.   Weiher, G. R., & Tedin, K. (2002). Does choice lead to racially distinctive schools? Charter schools and household preferences. *Journal of Policy Analysis and Management, 21*(1), 79-92.

57.   Bukhari, P., & Randall, E. V. (2009). Exit and entry: Why parents in Utah left public schools and chose private schools. *Journal of School Choice, 3*, 242-270.

58.   Schneider & Buckley, 2002 (see note 4).

59.   Buckley, J., & Schneider, M. (2003). Shopping for schools: How do marginal consumers gather information about schools? *The Policy Studies Journal, 31*(2), 121-145.

60.   Saporito, S., & Lareau, A. (1999). School selection as a process: The multiple dimensions of race in framing educational choice. *Social Problems, 46*(3), 418-429.

61. Holme, J. J. (2002). Buying homes, buying schools: School choice and the social construction of school quality. *Harvard Education Review, 72*(2), 177-205.

62. Bell, C. A. (2005). *All choices created equal? How good parents select "failing" schools.* New York, NY: National Center for the Study of Privatization, Teachers College, Columbia University.

63. Schneider, M., Teske, P., & Marschall, M. (2000). *Choosing schools: Consumer choice and the quality of American schools.* Princeton, NJ: Princeton University Press.

Bosetti, L., & Pyryt, M. C. (2007). Parental motivation in school choice: Seeking the competitive edge. *Journal of School Choice, 1*(4), 89-108.

64. Witte, 2000 (see note 23).

65. Holme, 2002 (see note 61).

66. Teske & Reichardt, 2006 (see note 18).

67. Neild, R. C. (2005). Parent management of choice in a large urban district. *Urban Education, 40*(3), 270-297.

Bosetti & Pyryt, 2007 (see note 63).

Smrekar, C. (2009). Beyond the tipping point: Issues of racial diversity in magnet schools following unitary status. *Peabody Journal of Education, 84,* 209-226.

68. Bosetti & Pyryt, 2007 (see note 63).

69. Smrekar, 2009 (see note 67).

70. Hastings, J. S., Van Weelden, R., & Weinstein, J. (2007). *Preferences, information, and parent choice behavior in public school choice.* Cambridge, MA: National Bureau of Economic Research.

Pallas, A. M., & Riehl, C. (2007, October 5). *The demand for high school programs in New York City.* New York, NY: Teachers College Columbia University. Paper prepared for the Inaugural Conference of the Research Partnership for New York City Schools, October 5, 2007.

71. Hastings, J., & Weinstein, J. M. (2008). Information, school choice, and academic achievement: Evidence from two experiments. *The Quarterly Journal of Economics, 123*(4), 1373-1414.

72. Stewart, T., Wolf, P. J., & Cornman, S. Q. (2005). *Parent and student voices on the first year of the D.C. Opportunity Scholarship Program.* Washington, DC: Georgetown University Public Policy Institute.

Miron & Nelson, 2002 (see note 55).

Kleitz et al., 2000 (see note 54).

Weiher & Tedin, 2002 (see note 56).

73. Miron & Nelson, 2002 (see note 55).

74. Kleitz et al. 2000 (see note 54).

75. Stewart, Wolf, & Cornman, 2005 (see note 72).

   Stewart, T., Wolf, P. J., Cornman, S. Q., & McKenzie-Thompson, K. (2007). *Satisfied, optimistic, yet concerned: Parent voices on the third year of the D.C. Opportunity Scholarship Program.* Washington, DC: Georgetown University Public Policy Institute

76. Weiher & Tedin, 2002 (see note 56).

77. Goldring, E. B., & Hausman, C. S. (1999). Reasons for parental choice of urban schools. *Journal of Education Policy, 14*(5), 469-490.

78. Doyle, M. C., & Feldman, J. (2006). Student voice and school choice in the Boston pilot high schools. *Educational Policy, 20*(2), 367-398.

79. Henig, J. R. (1990). Choice in public schools: An analysis of transfer requests among magnet schools. *Social Science Quarterly, 71,* 69-82.

80. Pallas & Riehl, 2007 (see note 70).

81. Weiher & Tedin, 2002 (see note 56).

82. Kleitz et al., 2000 (see note 54).

83. Theobald, R. (2005). School choice in Colorado Springs: The relationship between parental decisions, location, and neighborhood characteristics. *International Research in Geographical and Environmental Education, 14*(2), 92-111.

84. The different findings of this study may have been due to differences in the research design, in the types of choice studied, or possibly in the contexts of the studies.

85. Schneider, Teske, & Marschall, 2000 (see note 63).

86. Hastings, J. S., Kane, T. J., & Staiger, D. O. (2005). *Parental preferences and school competition: Evidence from a public school choice program.* Cambridge, MA: National Bureau of Economic Research.

   Hastings, Van Weelden, & Weinstein, 2007 (see note 70).

87. Hastings, Van Weelden, & Weinstein, 2007 (see note 70).

88. Hastings, Van Weelden, & Weinstein, 2007 (see note 70).

89. Lauen, D. L. (2007). Contextual explanations of school choice. *Sociology of Education, 80,* 179-209.

90. See for example:

Collom, E. (2005). The ins and outs of homeschooling: The determinants of parental motivations and student achievement. *Education and Urban Society, 37*(3), 307-335.

Bielick, S., Chandler, K., & Broughman, S. P. (2002). Homeschooling in the United States: 1999. *Education Statistics Quarterly,* 1-12.

91. Princiotta & Bielick, 2006 (see note 48).

92. Collom, 2005 (see note 90).

The scales used in the study's analysis were calculated by simply adding up responses to four questions or items that each had a 5-point scale, thus making the minimum value a 4 and the maximum a 20.

93. Green, C. L., & Hoover-Dempsey, K. V. (2007). Why do parents home-school? A systematic examination of parental involvement. *Education and Urban Society, 39*(2), 264-285.

94. Different from the federal survey, the Green and Hoover-Dempsey survey reports means for scales of items relating to parents beliefs about public schools, and their own abilities to educate their child, et cetera, rather than reporting how many parents rated a certain item as important.

95. Kleitz et al. 2000 (see note 54).

96. Jacob, B. A., & Lefgren, L. (2007, Summer). In low-income schools, parents want teachers who teach, in affluent schools other things matter. *Education Next,* 59-64.

97. Pallas & Riehl, 2007, p. 6 (see note 70).

CHAPTER 5: SCHOOL CHOICE AND ACCOUNTABILITY

1. Levin, H. (1974). A conceptual framework for accountability in education. *School Review, 82,* 363-364.

2. Browder (1975) cited in Kirst, M. (1990). *Accountability: Implications for state and local policymakers.* Washington, DC: U. S. Department of Education, Office of Educational Research and Improvement, Information Services.

3. Levin, 1974, p. 364 (see note 1).

4. Kogan (1986) cited in House, E. R. (1993). *Professional evaluation: Social impact and political consequences.* Newbury Park, CA: SAGE.

5. Darling-Hammond, L. (1988, Winter). Accountability and teacher professionalism. *American Educator,* 8-13, 38-43.

6. Kirst, M. (1990). *Accountability: Implications for state and local policymakers.* Washington, DC: U. S. Department of Education, Office of Educational Research and Improvement, Information Services.

7. Garn, G., & Cobb, C. D. (2001). A framework for understanding charter school accountability. *Education and Urban Society, 33*(2), 113-128.

8. Kirst, 1990, p. 8 (see note 6).

9. Darling-Hammond, 1988, p. 9 (see note 5).

10. Cuban, L. (1988). *The managerial imperative: The practice of leadership in schools.* New York, NY: New York University Press.

11. Levin, 1974, p. 364 (see note 1).

12. Kirst, 1990, pp. 7-8 (see note 6).

13. Cited by Rivera, M. J. (1994). Accountability and educational reform in Rochester, New York (Doctoral dissertation, Harvard University, 1994). *Dissertation Abstracts International.* (University Microfilms No. 9432425).

14. Kirst, 1990, pp. 9, 23 (see note 6).

15. Darling-Hammond, 1988, p. 10 (see note 5).

16. Chubb, J. E., & Moe, T. M. (1988). *What price democracy? Politics, markets and American schools.* Washington, DC: The Brookings Institution.

17. Rivera, 1994, pp. 9-10 (see note 13).

18. Firestone, W., & Bader, B. (1992). *Redesigning Teaclhing: Professionalism or Burelaucracy?* Albany, NY: State University of New York Press, 211-212.

19. Kirst, 1990, 10 (see note 6).

20. Kirst, 1990, 1 (see note 6).

21. Kirp, D. (1982). Professionalization as a policy choice. *World Politics, 34*(2), 137-174.

22. Friedman, M. (1955). The role of government in education. In R. A. Solow (Ed.), *Economics and the Public Interest* (pp. 123-44). New Brunswick, NJ: Rutgers Press.

    Freidman, M. (1962). *Capitalism and freedom.* Chicago, IL: University of Chicago Press.

23. See page 37 in: Rose, L. C., & Gallup, A. M. (2007). The 39th Annual Phi Delta Kappa/Gallup Poll of the Public's Attitudes Toward the Public Schools. *Kappan, 89*(1), 33-45.

24. Huerta, L. A., Gonzales, M. F., & d'Entremont, C. (2006). Cyber and homeschool charter schools: Adopting policy to new forms of public schooling. *Peabody Journal of Education, 81*(1), 103-139.

25. Center for Education Reform. (2011). Choice options state by state. Retrieved April 4, 2011, from http://www.edreform.com/

26. Huerta, Gonzales, & d'Entremont, 2006 (see note 24).

27. Budde, R. (1988). *Education by charter: Restructuring school districts, key to long term continuing improvement in American education.* Andover, MA: Regional Laboratory for Educational Improvement of the Northeast & Islands.

28. Shanker, A. (1988). Restructuring our schools. *Peabody Journal of Education, 65*(3), 88-100.

29. Nathan, J. (1998). *Charter schools: Creating hope and opportunity for American education* (2nd ed.). San Francisco, CA: Jossey-Bass.

30. Center for Education Reform. (2010, Fall). Quick facts: All about charter schools. Retrieved March 1, 2011, from http://www.edreform.com/index.cfm?fuseAction=document&documentID=1964

31. Clark, T. (2001). *Virtual schools: Trends and issues.* Report commissioned by the Distance Learning Resource Network, a WestEd Project co-sponsored by The Center for the Application of Information Technologies, Western Illinois University, October. Retrieved December 2, 2007 from http://www.wested.org/online_pubs/virtualschools.pdf,1

32. Huerta, Gonzales, & d'Entremont, 2006, 104-105 (see note 24).

33. Center for Education Reform, quoted in Leachman, S. (2007, September 16). Homework. *Daily Breeze* (Torrance, CA), 1A. Retrieved March 3, 2008, from ProQuest Newsstand database (Document ID: 1336514441).

34. Gartner, J. (2002). Online schools under scrutiny. Retrieved February 15, 2008, from http://www.wired.com/techbiz/media/news/2002/05/52207

35. Isenberg, E. J. (2007). What have we learned about homeschooling? *Peabody Journal of Education, 82*(2-3), 387-409.

36. National Center for Education Statistics. (2008). *1.5 million homeschooled students in the United States in 2007.* NCES Publication No. 2009030. Washington, DC: National Center for Education Statistics, U.S. Department of Education.

37. Home Schools Legal Defense Association. (2007). State home school laws. Retrieved December 1, 2007, from http://www.hslda.org/laws/default.asp

38. Rudner, L. M. (1999). Scholastic achievement and demographic characteristics of home school students in 1998. *Education Policy Analysis Archives, 7*(8). Retrieved December 1, 2007, from http://epaa.asu.edu/epaa/v7n8/

39. Welner, K. M., & Welner, K. G. (1999). Contextualizing homeschooling data: A response to Rudner. *Education Policy Analysis Archives, 7*(13). Retrieved December 1, 2007, from http://epaa.asu.edu/epaa/v7n13.html

40. Isenberg, 2007, p. 389 (see note 35).

41. Holme, J. J., & Wells, A. S. (2009). School choice beyond district borders: Lessons for the reauthorization of NCLB from interdistrict desegregation

and open enrollment plans. In R. Kahlenberg (Ed.), *Improving on no child left behind* (pp. 139-211). New York, NY: The Century Foundation.

42. NCES SASS, 2002, as cited in Holme and Wells, 2009 (see note 41).

43. The recent Supreme Court decision in *Parents Involved in Community Schools v. Seattle School District* and *Meredith v. Jefferson County Board of Education* deemed the practice of using race-based admissions unconstitutional. However some legal scholars believe Justice Kennedy's concurring opinion leaves the door open for interpretation.

44. Henig, J. R., & Sugarman, S. D. (1999). The nature and extent of school choice. In S.D. Sugarman & F. R. Kemerer (Eds.), *School choice and social controversy: Politics, policy and law.* Washington, DC: Brookings Institution.

45. Henig & Sugarman, 1999 (see note 44).

46. One could probably just as easily argue that school choice programs *foster* or *promote* certain types of accountability. Choice programs being *influenced by* or *promoting* certain accountabilities is likely an issue of semantics.

47. Cobb, C. D., & Rallis, S. F. (2008). District responses to NCLB: Where is the justice? *Leadership and Policy in Schools, 7*(2), 178-201.

48. Abelmann, C. & Elmore, R. F., with Even, J., Kenyon, S., & Marshall, J. (1999). *When accountability knocks, will anyone answer?* (CPRE Research Report No. RR-42). Philadelphia: PA. University of Pennsylvania, Consortium for Policy Research in Education.

49. Garn & Cobb, 2001 (see note 7).

50. Van Dunk, E., & Dickman, E. (2003). *School choice and the question of accountability.* New Haven, CT: Yale University Press, 21.

51. Kirp, 1982 (see note 21).

52. The debate over the effect of the educational marketplace on equity is highly ideologically charged. Some would argue that the market renders greater equity by providing opportunities for everyone (a level playing field, say, in the case of vouchers). Many others would argue educational equity cannot be reached via capitalist-oriented market forces, and in fact, such policies could result in greater inequities.

CHAPTER 6: FUNDING FORMULAS, SCHOOL CHOICE, AND INHERENT INCENTIVES

1. Vergari, S. (2007). The politics of charter schools. *Education Policy, 21*(1), 15-39.

2. Ross, K., & Levacic, R. (1999). *Needs-based resource allocation in education via formula funding of schools.* Paris, France: UNESCO.

3. Taylor, L., & Fowler, W. (2006). *Cost of wage adjustment index*. Washington, DC: NCES

4. Duncombe, W. D., & Yinger, J. (2007). Measurement of cost differentials. In E. Fiske & H. Ladd (Eds.), *Handbook of research in education finance and policy* (pp. 238-256). New York, NY: Routledge.

5. Picus, L. O., Goertz, M., & Odden, A. (2007). Intergovernment aid formulas and case studies. In E. Fiske & H. Ladd (Eds.), *Handbook of research in education finance and policy* (pp. 25-275). New York, NY: Routledge.

6. Picus, Goertz, & Odden, 2007 (see note 5).

7. McGuire, T. J., & Papke, L. E. (2007). Local funding of schools: The property tax and its alternatives. In E. Fiske & H. Ladd (Eds.), *Handbook of research in education finance and policy* (pp. 357-372). New York, NY: Routledge.

8. There is considerable evidence that schools respond in the same way that other businesses do: if their revenues go up they will try to provide more services. Therefore, if the public funding for private schools—through vouchers and tuition tax credits--is more generous, then the supply of private school places should increase. In an accounting sense, it does not matter to a school whether a particular level of funding comes from the state or the federal government.

9. Miron, G. (2008). Educational management organizations. In E. Fiske & H. Ladd (Eds.), *Handbook of research in education finance and policy* (pp. 475-496). New York, NY: Routledge.

10. Baker, B. D. & Ferris, R. (2011). *Adding up the spending: Fiscal disparities and philanthropy among New York City charter schools*. Boulder, CO: National Education Policy Center. Retrieved February 27, 2011, from http://nepc.colorado.edu/publication/NYC-charter-disparities

11. Recent evidence suggests that charter schools in New York enroll fewer English Language learners than traditional public schools. See

    Buckley, J. & Sattin-Bajaj, C. (2010). *Are ELL students under-represented in charter schools? Demographic trends in NYC 2006-2008*. New York, NY: National Center for the Study of Privatization, Teachers College, Columbia University. Retrieved February 27, 2011 from http://www.ncspe.org/publications_files/OP188.pdf

12. Of course, traditional public schools may draw on alternative sources of revenue (e.g., philanthropies or the business community); see

    Hansen, J. S. (2007). The role of nongovernmental organizations in financing public schools. In E. Fiske &H. Ladd (Eds.), *Handbook of research in education finance and policy* (pp. 314-331). New York, NY: Routledge.

13. For national numbers on whether charter schools receive the optimal funding, see

    Miron, G., & Urschel, J. L. (2010). *Equal or fair? A study of revenues and expenditure in American charter schools*. Retrieved February 24, 2011, from http://epicpolicy.org/publication/charter-school-finance

14. Augenblick, J., &Sharp, J. (2003). *How can we fund charter districts? The nuts & bolts of charter districts*. Denver, CO: Education Commission of the States.

    Anderson, A. B. (2004). *Charter schools in Washington State: A financial drain or gain?* Seattle, WA: Center on Reinventing Public Education.

15. Wohlstetter, P., Malloy, C. L., Smith, J., & Hentschke, G. (2004). Incentives for charter schools: Building school capacity through cross-sector alliances. *Educational Administration Quarterly, 40*(3), 321-365.

    Thomas B. Fordham Foundation. (2005). *Charter school funding: Inequity's last frontier*. Washington DC: Author.

16. Hassel, B. (1999). *Paying for the charter schoolhouse: Policy options for charter school facilities financing*. Washington, DC: Office of Educational Research and Improvement.

    Ascher, C., Cole, C., Harris, J., & Echazarreta, J. (2004). *The finance gap: Charter schools and their facilities*. New York, NY: New York University Institute for Education and Social Policy. Retrieved March 5, 2008, from http://steinhardt.nyu.edu/scmsAdmin/uploads/001/117/FinanceGap.pdf

17. In a follow-up study, Ascher et al. (2003) reported that of eight charter schools, two had for-profit institutional partners and four had nonprofit institutional partners.

    Ascher, C., Echazarreta, J., Jacobowitz, R., McBride, Y., & Troy, T. (2003). *Governance and administrative infrastructure in New York City charter schools: Going charter year three findings*. New York, NY: Charter School Research Project.

    The Krop and Zimmer (2005) sample of 153 start-up charter schools averaged $576 in private donations per pupil, but three schools received more than $10,000 per pupil. However, because these private funds are not clearly recorded in accountability systems it may be that they are understated. Also, schools may differ significantly in the amounts of private funding accumulated.

    Krop, C., & Zimmer, R. (2005). Charter school type matters when examining funding and facilities: Evidence from California. *Education Policy Analysis Archives, 13*(50). Retrieved March 5, 2008, from http://epaa.asu.edu/epaa/v13n50/

18. Osberg, E. (2006) Charter school funding. In P. Hill (ed.), *Charter schools against the odds: An assessment of the Koret Task Force on K-12*. Stanford, CA: Hoover Institution.

19. Carpenter, D. (2006). *Playing to type? Mapping the charter school landscape.* The Thomas B. Fordham Foundation. Retrieved March 5, 2008, from: http://www.edexcellence.net/doc/Playing%20to%20Type--Carpenter.pdf

20. Ascher, C., Echazarreta, J., Jacobowitz, R. McBride, Y., Troy, T., & Wamba, N. (2001). *Going charter; New models of support.* New York, NY: New York University Institute for Education and Social Policy. Retrieved March 5, 2008 from http://steinhardt.nyu.edu/iesp.olde/publications/pubs/charter/GoingCharter.pdf

21. Shaul, M. S. (2000). *Charter schools: Limited access to facility financing.* Report to Congressional Requesters. Washington DC: General Accounting Office.

Lacireno-Paquet, N., &Holyoke, T. (2007). Moving forward or sliding backward: The evolution of charter school policies in Michigan and the District of Columbia. *Education Policy, 21*(1), 185-214.

Merritt, E. T., & Beaudin, J. A. (2002). Finding a home. *American School & University, 75*(3), 330-33.

Krop, C. (2003). Charter school finances and facilities. In R. Zimmer, R. Buddin, D. Chau, G. Daley, B. P. Gill, C. Gaurino, ... D. J. Brewer (Eds.), *Charter school operations and performance: Evidence from California* (pp. 85-114). Santa Monica, CA: RAND.

22. Sullins, C. &Miron, G. (2005). *Challenges of starting and operating charter schools: A multicase study.* Kalamazoo: The Evaluation Center, Western Michigan University. Retrieved March 5, 2008, from http://www.wmich.edu/evalctr/charter/cs_challenges_report.pdf

23. Sugarman, S. (2002). Charter school funding issues. *Education Policy Analysis Archives, 10*(34). Retrieved from http://epaa.asu.edu/ojs/article/view/313

24. Public Sector Consultants, Inc. & MAXIMUS, Inc. (1999). *Michigan's charter school initiative: From theory to practice.* Lansing, MI: Michigan Department of Education. Abstract retrieved March 5, 2008, from http://epx.sagepub.com/cgi/content/abstract/17/3/317

General Accounting Office. (1998). *Charter schools: Federal funding available, but barriers exist.* Washington DC: Author.

25. Charter school operators most often cited training, technical assistance, and notification of their eligibility as factors helping them gain access to funds. Some may choose not to apply for federal or state grants because of the associated costs. Several states and the Department of Education have begun initiatives, such as alternative allocation policies, to help charter schools access federal funds.

26.   Wales, B, (2002). Libraries in charter schools: A content analysis. *Teacher Librarian, 30*(2), 21-26.

27.   Harris, D., & Plank, D. (2003). *Who's teaching in Michigan's traditional and charter public schools?* East Lansing, MI: The Education Policy Center, Michigan State University.

28.   Gill, B., Timpane, P. M., Ross, K. E., & Brewer, D. J. (2001). *Rhetoric versus reality: What we know and what we need to know about vouchers and charter schools.* Santa Monica, CA: RAND.

29.   Miron, G., & Nelson, C. (2002). *What's public about charter schools? Lessons learned about choice and accountability.* Thousand Oaks, CA: Corwin Press.

30.   Bodine, E., Fuller, B., González, M. F., Huerta, L. A., Naughton, S., Park, S., & Teh, L. W. (2008). Disparities in charter school resources: The influence of state policy and community conditions. *Journal of Education Policy. 23,* 1-33.

31.   Fuller, B., Gawlik, M., Gonzalez, E., & Park, S. (2004). Localized ideas of fairness: Inequality among charter schools. In K. E. Buckley & P. Wohlstetter (Eds.), *Taking account of charter schools: What's happened and what's next?* New York, NY: Teachers College Press.

32.   Miron, 2008 (see note 9).

33.   Krop and Zimmer examine the finances of charter schools in California. They find that funding amounts depend on charter school type. Specifically, conversion charter schools are more likely to take advantage of categorical aid than start-up charters; the latter type are more likely to rely on private donations. In California, 55% of conversion charter schools receive funding for transportation, 73% for Title I programs, and 83% for special education compared to 4%, 34%, and 67% of start-up charter schools.

Krop & Zimmer, 2005 (see note 17).

34.   Herdman, P. & Millot, M. D. (2000). *Are charter schools getting more money into the classroom? A Micro-financial analysis of first year charter schools in Massachusetts.* Seattle, WA: Center for Reinventing Education.

Nelson, H. F., Muir, E., & Drown, R. (2000). *Venturesome capital: State charter school finance systems.* Washington, DC: Office of Educational Research and Improvement, U.S. Department of Education.

Nelson, H. F., Muir, E., & Drown, R. (2003) *Paying for the vision: Charter school revenue and expenditures.* Washington, DC: Office of Educational Research and Improvement, U.S. Department of Education.

35.   In Delaware, average per-pupil revenue in charter schools was $8,821 as against $10,560 for comparable public schools. The main difference was in state aid: public schools received significantly more state aid than charter schools. Delaware charter schools spent a smaller proportion of their total

expenses on instruction, partially because they hired teachers with less experience and different qualifications.

Huerta, L. A., & d'Entremont, C. (2007. March). *Explaining how policy effects charter school quality, equity, and availability in New York State*. Paper presented at the American Education Finance Association Conference, Baltimore, MD.

Jacobowitz, R. & Gyurko, J. S. (2004). *Charter school funding in New York: Perspectives of parity with traditional public Schools*. Working paper. New York, NY: New York University Institute for Education and Social Policy.

36.   Miron and Nelson also describe how Michigan's elementary charter schools' expenditures differ from those of comparable-enrollment local districts. During 1995-1996, charters spent an average of 57% of revenues on instruction and 43% on support services; regular public schools spent 65% and 35% respectively. Charters' administrative expenditures were higher.

Miron & Nelson, 2002, pp. 43-44 (see note 29).

See also:

Prince, H. (1999). Follow the money: An initial review of elementary charter school spending in Michigan. *Journal of Education Finance, 25*(2), 175-194.

Anderson, P. L., Watkins, S. D., & Cotton, C. S. (2003). *The public school academy funding gap: Revenue disparities between "charter" schools and traditional public schools in Michigan*. Lansing, MI: Michigan Chamber Foundation.

37.   Plucker, J. A., Eckes, S., Chang, Y., Benton, S., Trotter, A., & Bradford, M. (2005). *Charter schools in Indiana: Overview, funding, and federal expenditures*. Bloomington, IN: Center for Evaluation and Education Policy.

38.   Hassel, B., Terrell, M. G., & Finn, C. E. (2004). *School finance in Dayton: A comparison of the revenues of the school district and community schools*. Thomas B. Fordham Institute. Retrieved March 5, 2008, from http://www.edexcellence.net/institute/publication/publication.cfm?id=330

39.   Gill, B., Zimmer, R., Christman, J. & Blanc, S. (2007). *State takeover, school restructuring, private management, and student achievement in Philadelphia*. Santa Monica, CA: RAND.

40.   Mahitivanichcha, K., & Parrish, T. (2005). The impact of fiscal incentives on identification rates and placement in special education: Formulas for influencing best practice. *Journal of Education Finance, 31*, 1-22.

41.   Moreover, the enrollment in this voucher program is modest: less than 20% of eligible students utilize the voucher. All information retrieved from the Florida Department of Education website.

42. No recent research has examined the value of tax exemptions for private schools.

43. Levin, H. M., &Belfield, C. R. (2005). *Privatizing educational choice: Consequences for parents, schools, and public policy.* Denver, CO: Paradigm.

44. Belfield, C. R. (2008). Home schooling. In E. Fiske & H. Ladd (Eds.), *Handbook of education finance in policy* (pp. 467-474). New York, NY: Routledge.

45. Huerta, L. & Gonzales, M.-F. (2004). *Cyber and home school charter schools: How states are defining new forms of public schooling* (working paper). New York, NY: National Center for the Study of Privatization, Teachers College, Columbia University. Retrieved March 5, 2008, from http://ncspe.org/publications_files/Paper87.pdf

46. Ni, Y. (2007). *The impact of charter schools on the efficiency of traditional public schools: Evidence from Michigan* (working paper). New York, NY: National Center for the Study of Privatization, Teachers College, Columbia University. Retrieved March 5, 2008, from http://ncspe.org/publications_files/OP145.pdf

47. Anderson, 2004 (see note 14).

CHAPTER 7: TEACHER QUALIFICATIONS AND WORK ENVIRONMENTS ACROSS SCHOOL CHOICE TYPES

1. Hanushek, E. A. (1996). School resources and student performance. In G. Burtless (Ed.), *Does money matter?* (pp. 43-73). Washington, DC: The Brookings Institution.

2. Merrifield, J. (1999). Monopsony power in the market for teachers: Why teachers should support market-based education reform. *Journal of Labor Research, 20*(3), 377.

3. The existing literature was identified by a search of electronic databases using a combination of keywords that identified the school type and teacher qualification or work environment. The references of the identified literature were also reviewed to identify additional relevant studies. Articles in scholarly journals, policy reports, and state evaluations were included. To be included in the literature reviewed, previous studies must have made some effort to either compare different forms of school choice or compare a type of school choice to a public school. Reports that presented data on one school type without making comparisons were not included.

4. SASS uses a complex sampling design with teachers clustered within schools. Sampling weights are used to produce nationally representative estimates for the population of public and private school teachers.

5. Chi-square tests were used to test the distribution of categorical measures among school types. Comparisons of means were used to analyze the differences for continuous variables. In the analyses, teachers in all private and all charter schools were compared with teachers in all public noncharter schools. In the detailed analyses, teachers in each type of school choice are compared to teachers in traditional public schools. An alpha level of .05 was chosen so that only differences where there is less than a 5% probability that the difference occurred by chance are noted as statistically significant. Because multiple comparisons are made for each variable (i.e., the educational level of traditional public school teachers is compared to both private and charter school teachers), a Bonferroni adjustment was made to limit the possibility of Type I errors.

6. Ferguson, R. F., & Ladd, H. F. (1996). How and why money matters: An analysis of Alabama schools. In H. F. Ladd (Ed.), *Holding schools accountable: Performance-based reform in education* (pp. 265-298). Washington, DC: Brookings Institution.

    Greenwald, R., Hedges, L. V., & Laine, R. D. (1996). The effect of school resources on student achievement. *Review of Educational Research, 66*(3), 361-396.

    Hanushek, E. A. (1971). Teacher characteristics and gains in student achievement: Estimation using microdata. *American Economic Review, 61*(2), 280-288.

    Rice, J. K. (2003). *Teacher quality: Understanding the effects of teacher attributes*. Washington, DC: Economic Policy Institute.

7. Ballou, D., & Podgursky, M. (1997). *Teacher pay and teacher quality*. Kalamazoo, MI: W.E. Upjohn Institute for Employment Research.

    Hoxby, C. M. (2002). Would school choice change the teaching profession? *Journal of Human Resources, 37*(4), 892-912.

8. In this chapter, private school teachers include any teacher included in the private school teacher data file in SASS.

9. The religious affiliation was obtained from the school survey.

10. Charter school teachers are defined as those teachers in schools that indicated they are a public charter school on the SASS school survey.

11. Charter schools with a home-school focus are those charter schools that indicated that they provide support to homeschool students.

12. Data obtained from database of state home-school laws at the Home School Legal Defense Association. Retrieved November 10, 2007, from http://www.hslda.org/laws/default.asp

13.   Huerta, L. A., Gonzalez, M.-F., & d'Entremont, C. (2006). Cyber and home school charter schools: Adopting policy to new forms of public schooling. *Peabody Journal of Education, 81*(1), 103-139.

14.   Kane, P. R. (1986). *Teachers in public and independent schools: A comparative study.* New York, NY: Teachers College, Klingenstein Center for Independent School Education.

Kane, P. R. (1987). Public or independent schools: Does where you teach make a difference? *Phi Delta Kappan, 69*(4), 286.

Cook, T. J. (2002). Teachers. In T. C. Hunt, E. A. Joseph, & R. J. Nuzz (Eds.), *Catholic schools still make a difference: Ten years of research: 1991-2000* (pp. 57-72). Washington, DC: National Catholic Association.

Schaub, M. (2000). A faculty at a crossroads: A profile of American Catholic school teachers. In J. Youniss & J. J. Convey (Eds.), *Catholic schools at the crossroads: Survival and transformation* (pp. 72-86). New York, NY: Teachers College Press.

15.   Cook, 2002 (see note 14).

Schaub, 2002 (see note 14).

16.   Bauch, P. A., & Goldring, E. (1996). Parent involvement and teacher decision making in urban high schools of choice. *Urban Education, 31*(4), 403-432.

17.   Kane, 1986 (see note 14).

18.   Plucker, J., Muller, P., Hansen, J., Ravert, R., & Makel, M. (2006). *Evaluation of the Cleveland Scholarship and Tutoring Program: Technical report 1998-2004.* Bloomington, IN: Center for Evaluation and Education Policy.

19.   Bomotti, S., Ginsberg, R., & Cobb, B. (1999). Teachers in charter schools and traditional schools: A comparative study. *Education policy analysis archives, 7*(22). Retrieved March 15, 2012, from http://epaa.asu.edu/epaa/v7n22.html

Burian-Fitzgerald, M., Luekens, M. T., & Strizek, G. A. (2004). Less red tape or more green teachers: Charter school autonomy and teacher qualifications. In K. Bulkley & P. Wohlstetter (Eds.), *Taking account of charter schools: What's happened and what's next?* (pp. 11-31). New York, NY: Teachers College Press.

Cannata, M., & Penaloza, R. (2010). *Comparing teacher characteristics, job choices, and teacher preferences by school type* (Working paper). Nashville, TN: National Center on School Choice.

Podgursky, M., & Ballou, D. (2001). *Personnel policy in charter schools.* Washington, DC: Thomas B. Fordham Foundation.

Texas Center for Educational Research. (2003). *Texas open enrollment charter schools: Sixth year evaluation*. Austin, TX: Author.

20. Guarino, C. (2003). Staffing in charter and conventional public schools. In R. Zimmer, R. Buddin, D. Chau, G. Daley, B. P. Gill, C. Gaurino, … D. J. Brewer (Eds.), *Charter school operations and performance: Evidence from California*. Santa Monica, CA: RAND.

21. Guarino, C., Zimmer, R., Krop, C., & Chau, D. (2005). *Non-classroom based charter schools in California and the impact of SB 740*. Santa Monica, CA: RAND.

22. Miron, G., Cullen, A., Applegate, B., & Farrell, P. (2007). *Evaluation of the Delaware charter school reform. Final report*. Kalamazoo, MI: The Evaluation Center, Western Michigan University.

23. Kane, 1986 (see note 14).

24. Data obtained from database at the Home School Legal Defense Association (see note 12).

25. ESchool News. (2007). Ruling puts state's virtual schools at risk. Retrieved December 7, 2007, from http://www.eschoolnews.com/news/top-news/?i=50953;_hbguid=b804746c-c3e9-4ca3-bf5b-428dd4c01a11&d=top-news

26. Burian-Fitzgerald, Luekens, & Strizek, 2004 (see note 19).

     Cannata & Penaloza, 2010 (see note 19).

     Guarino, 2003 (see note 20).

     Podgursky & Ballou, 2001 (see note 19).

     Texas Center for Educational Research, 2003 (see note 19).

27. Miron, Cullen, Applegate, & Farrell, 2007 (see note 22).

     RPP International. (1998). *A national study of charter schools: Second-year report*. Washington, DC: U.S. Department of Education. Office of Educational Research and Improvement.

     Texas Center for Educational Research, 2003 (see note 19).

28. Cannata & Penaloza, 2010 (see note 19).

29. Guarino, Zimmer, Krop, & Chau, 2005 (see note 21).

30. Bauch & Goldring, 1996 (see note 16).

31. Schaub, 2002 (see note 14).

32. Burian-Fitzgerald, Luekens, & Strizek, 2004 (see note 19).

     Hoxby, 2002 (see note 7).

Podgursky, M. (2008). Teams versus bureaucracies: Personnel policy, wage-setting, and teacher quality in traditional public, charter, and private schools. In M. Berends, M. Springer, & H. J. Walberg (Eds.), *Charter school outcomes* (pp. 61-79). New York, NY: Erlbaum.

33.   Baker, B. D., & Dickerson, J. L. (2006). Charter schools, teacher labor market deregulation and teacher quality: Evidence from the Schools and Staffing Survey. *Educational Policy, 20*(5), 752-778.

Kane, 1986 (see note 14).

34.   Cannata & Penaloza, 2010 (see note 19).

35.   Cannata & Penaloza, 2010 (see note 19).

Gross, B. (2011). *Inside charter schools: Unlocking doors to student success.* Seattle, WA: Center on Reinventing Public Education.

Johnson, S. M., & Landman, J. (2000). "Sometimes bureaucracy has its charms": The working conditions of teachers in deregulated schools. *Teachers College Record, 102*(1), 85-124.

Vanourek, G., Manno, B. V., Finn, C. E., Jr., & Bierlein Palmer, L. E. (1998). Charter schools as seen by students, teachers, and parents. In P. E. Peterson & B. C. Hassel (Eds.), *Learning from school choice* (pp. 187-212). Washington, DC: Brookings Institution Press.

Malloy, C., & Wohlstetter, P. (2003). Working conditions in charter schools: What's the appeal for teachers? *Education and Urban Society, 35*(2), 219-241.

Miron, Cullen, Applegate, & Farrell, 2007 (see note 22).

Miron, G., & Nelson, C. (2002). *What's public about charter schools? Lessons learned about choice and accountability.* Thousand Oaks, CA: Corwin Press.

36.   Cook, 2002 (see note 14).

37.   Cannata, M. (2007). Teacher community and elementary charter schools. *Education Policy Analysis Archives, 15*(11). Retrieved June 1, 2012, from http://epaa.asu.edu/ojs/article/view/59/185

Christenson, B., Eaton, M., Garet, M. S., Miller, L. C., Hikawa, H., & DuBois, P. (2003). *Evaluation of the magnet schools assistance program, 1998 grantees.* Washington, DC: U.S. Department of Education.

Royal, M., DeAngelis, K., & Rossi, R. (1997). *Teachers' sense of community: How do public and private schools compare? NCES 97-910.* Washington, DC: U.S. Department of Education, National Center for Education Statistics.

Goldring, E., & Cravens, X. (2008). Teachers' academic focus on learning in charter and traditional public schools. In M. Berends, M. Springer, & H. J. Walberg (Eds.), *Charter school outcomes* (pp. 39-59). New York, NY: Lawrence Erlbaum Associates.

38.   Malloy & Wohlstetter, 2003 (see note 35).

Vanourek et al., 1998 (see note 35).

39.   Bomotti, Ginsberg, & Cobb, 1999 (see note 19).

40.   Johnson & Landman, 2000 (see note 35).

41.   Goldring & Cravens, 2008 (see note 37).

42.   Cook, 2002 (see note 14).

Hoxby, 2002 (see note 7).

Nelson, C., & Miron, G. (2004). Professional opportunities for teachers: A view from inside charter schools. In K. Bulkley & P. Wohlstetter (Eds.), *Taking account of charter schools: What's happened and what's next* (pp. 11-31). New York, NY: Teachers College Press.

Miron, G., & Nelson, C. (2000). *Autonomy in exchange for accountability: An initial study of Pennsylvania charter schools.* Kalamazoo, MI: The Evaluation Center, Western Michigan University.

43.   Bomotti, Ginsberg, & Cobb, 1999 (see note 19).

Crawford, J. R. (2001). Teacher autonomy and accountability in charter schools. *Education and Urban Society, 33*(2), 186-200.

44.   Kane, 1987 (see note 14).

Bauch & Goldring, 1996 (see note 16).

Cook, 2002 (see note 14).

Miron & Nelson, 2000 (see note 42).

45.   Johnson & Landman, 2000 (see note 35).

46.   Bomotti, Ginsberg, & Cobb, 1999 (see note 19).

Crawford, 2001 (see note 43).

47.   Miron, Cullen, Applegate, & Farrell, 2007 (see note 22).

48.   Kane, 1987 (see note 14).

Gruber, K. J., Wiley, S. D., Broughman, S. P., Strizek, G. A., & Burian-Fitzgerald, M. (2002). *Schools and Staffing Survey, 1999-2000: Overview of the data for public, private, public charter, and Bureau of Indian Affairs elementary and secondary schools.* Washington, DC: U.S. Department of Education, Government Printing Office.

49.   Plucker et al., 2006 (see note 18).

50.   Fuller, B., Gawlik, M., Gonzales, E. K., Park, S., & Gibbings, G. (2003). *Charter schools and inequality: National disparities in funding, teacher quality, and student Support.* Berkeley, CA: Policy Analysis for California Education.

Texas Center for Educational Research, 2003 (see note 19).

Gruber et al., 2002 (see note 48).

Miron, Cullen, Applegate, & Farrell, 2007 (see note 22).

51.   RPP International, 1998 (see note 27).

52.   Christenson et al., 2003 (see note 37).

53.   Guarino, Zimmer, Krop, & Chau, 2005 (see note 21).

54.   Bomotti, Ginsberg, & Cobb, 1999 (see note 19).

Miron, Cullen, Applegate, & Farrell, 2007 (see note 22).

55.   Johnson & Landman, 2000 (see note 35).

56.   Miron, G. & Applegate, B. (2007). *Teacher attrition in charter schools*. Tempe, AZ and Boulder, CO: Education Policy Research Unit and Education and the Public Interest Center.

Miron, Cullen, Applegate, & Farrell, 2007 (see note 22).

Vanourek et al., 1998 (see note 35).

57.   Hoxby, 2002 (see note 7).

Johnson & Landman, 2000 (see note 35).

Malloy & Wohlstetter, 2003 (see note 35).

58.   Kane, 1986 (see note 14).

59.   Harris, D. (2006). Lowering the bar or moving the target: A wage decomposition of Michigan's charter and traditional public school teachers. *Educational Administration Quarterly, 42*, 424-460.

Miron & Nelson, 2000 (see note 42).

Texas Center for Educational Research, 2003 (see note 19).

60.   Gruber et al., 2002 (see note 48).

Harris, 2006 (see note 59).

61.   Podgursky, 2008 (see note 32).

62.   Gross, B., & DeArmond, M. (2010). How do charter schools compete for teachers? A local perspective. *Journal of School Choice, 4*(3), 254-277.

63.   Krop, C., & Zimmer, R. (2005). Charter school type matters when considering funding and facilities: Evidence from California. *Education Policy Analysis Archives, 13*(50), Retrieved March 15, 2012, from http://epaa.asu.edu/epaa/v13n50/

64.   RPP International, 1998 (see note 27).

65.   Cook, 2002 (see note 14).

Gruber *et al.*, 2002 (see note 48).

66.   Kane, 1986 (see note 14).

67.   Accurate comparisons of teacher compensation should also consider bene-fits because health and pension benefits are an important sources of total teacher compensation. See

Allegretto, S. A., Corcoran, S. P., & Mishel, L. (2004). *How does teacher pay compare? Methodological challenges and answers.* Washington, DC: Economic Policy Institute.

SASS provides information on the percentage of public districts and pri-vate schools that offer medical, dental, and life insurance and a retirement plan to teachers. While details on the size of the benefits are not available, private schools are less likely to offer each type of benefit than public school districts. Thus the salary differential for private school teachers is not ameliorated by higher benefits.

68.   Although not shown for space considerations, results are similar when the sample is restricted to urban schools. Data are available upon request.

69.   Bomotti, Ginsberg, & Cobb, 1999 (see note 19).

Guarino, 2003 (see note 20).

Schaub, 2002 (see note 14).

70.   Texas Center for Educational Research, 2003 (see note 19).

71.   Bomotti, Ginsberg, & Cobb, 1999 (see note 19).

Johnson & Landman, 2000 (see note 35).

Vanourek et al., 1998 (see note 35).

72.   Although not shown for space considerations, results are similar when the sample is restricted to urban schools. Data are available upon request.

73.   Cannata, M., & Engel, M. (in press). *Does charter status determine preferences? Comparing the hiring preferences of charter and traditional public school princi-pals.* Education Finance and Policy, 7(4).

74.   Grogan, E. & Youngs, P. (2008, March). *Teacher recruitment: How it is done, and who decides, in charter and traditional public schools.* Paper presented at the annual meeting of the American Education Finance Association, Nash-ville, TN.

Gross, 2011 (see note 35).

Podgursky & Ballou, 2001 (see note 19).

75. Liu, E. (2002, April). *New teachers' experiences of hiring in New Jersey.* Paper presented at the annual meeting of the American Educational Research Association, New Orleans, LA.

76. Liu, 2002 (see note 75).

77. Podgursky, 2008 (see note 32).

78. Harris, D. (2007). Should I stay or should I go? Comparing teacher mobility in Florida's charter and traditional public schools. *Peabody Journal of Education, 82*(2-3), 274-310.

Miron & Applegate, 2007 (see note 56).

Stuit, D., & Smith, T. (2009). *Teacher turnover in charter schools* (Working paper). Nashville, TN: National Center on School Choice.

Texas Center for Educational Research, 2003 (see note 19).

79. Gross & DeArmond, 2010) (see note 62).

80. Podgursky, 2008 (see note 32).

81. Cook, 2002 (see note 14).

Kane, 1986 (see note 14).

82. Kane, 1986 (see note 14).

Kane, 1987 (see note 14).

83. Kane, 1986 (see note 14).

84. Harris, 2007 (see note 78).

85. The Ohio Collaborative. (2003). *Conditions of teacher supply and demand in Ohio, 2003.* Columbus, OH: The Ohio Collaborative.

86. Merrifield, 1999 (see note 2).

Hoxby, C. M. (1994). *Do private schools provide competition for public schools?* (Working Paper No. 4978). Cambridge, MA: National Bureau of Economic Research.

Vedder, R., & Hall, J. (2000). Private school competition and public school teacher salaries. *Journal of Labor Research, 21*(1), 161.

Hanushek, E. A., & Rivkin, S. G. (2003). Does public school competition affect teacher quality? In C. M. Hoxby (Ed.), *The economics of school choice* (pp. 23-48). Chicago, IL: University of Chicago Press.

87. Harris, 2007 (see note 78).

88. Carruthers, C. (2009, March). *The qualifications and classroom performance of teachers moving to charter schools.* Presented at the conference of the National Center on School Choice, Nashville, TN.

89.   Buddin, R., & Zimmer, R. (2003). Academic outcomes. In R. Zimmer, R. Buddin, D. Chau, G. Daley, B. P. Gill, C. Gaurino, ... D.J. Brewer (Eds.), *Charter school operations and performance: Evidence from California* (pp. 37-62). Santa Monica, CA: RAND Corp.

   Cannata, M. (2011). Does charter competition impact principal behavior? In M. Berends, M. Cannata, & E. B. Goldring (Eds.), *School choice and school improvement* (pp. 177-191). Cambridge, MA: Harvard Education Press.

90.   Buddin & Zimmer, 2003 (see note 89).

91.   Cannata, M. (2011). Charter schools at the teacher job search. *Journal of School Choice, 5*(1), 111-133.

92.   Brewer, D. J., & Ahn, J. (2010). What do we know about teachers in charter schools? In J. Betts & P. T. Hill (Eds.), *Taking measure of charter schools: Better assessments, better policymaking, better schools* (pp. 129-152). Lanham, MD: Rowman & Littlefield Education.

93.   Hanushek, 1996 (see note 1).

94.   Betts, J. R., Rueben, K. S., & Danenberg, A. (2000). *Equal resources, equal outcomes? The distribution of school resources and student achievement in California*. San Francisco, CA: Public Policy Institute of California.

95.   Boyd, D., Lankford, H., Loeb, S., & Wyckoff, J. (2006). *Analyzing the determinants of the matching of public school teachers to Jobs: Estimating compensating differentials in imperfect labor markets*. Unpublished manuscript.

CHAPTER 8: EDUCATIONAL INNOVATION AND DIVERSIFICATION IN SCHOOL CHOICE PLANS

1.   Futurist Lewis Perelman concurs, noting that "'Choice' as a synonym for free markets—where consumers are free to choose and vendors are free to create and sell a variety of products and services—is undeniably essential to cure education's morbid productivity and festering irrelevance.... We need commercial choice and competition in education first to goad technical innovation—the profit motive is essential to reward the creation and provision of productive technologies. Profit-motivated competition also is necessary to provide quality control. Only markets can create the information needed to determine 'what works' economically."

   Perelman, L. J. (1993). *School's out: Hyperlearning, the new technology, and the end of education*. New York, NY: Avon.

   See also,

   National Governors' Association. (1986). *Time for results*. Washington, DC: Author.

Coulson, A. J. (1999). *Market education: The unknown history.* New Brunswick, NJ: Transaction.

Kolderie, T. (1993, November). The states begin to withdraw the 'exclusive.' *Changing Schools, 21,* 1-8.

2.   Friedman, M. (1962). *Capitalism and freedom.* Chicago, IL: University of Chicago Press. This thinking is echoed by Andrew Coulson, currently of the Cato Institute, in noting that "there is nothing in the public schools' procedure for selecting pedagogical methods that will ensure the continued use of effective approaches, that will tailor existing approaches to meet changing demand, or that will spur successful innovation and the development of new methods."

Coulson, A. J. (2002). Delivering education. In E. P. Lazear (Ed.), *Education in the twenty-first century* (105-145). Stanford, CA: Hoover Institution Press.

see also

Brandl, J. E. (1998). Governance and educational quality. In P. E. Peterson & B. C. Hassel (Eds.), *Learning from school choice* (pp. 55-81). Washington, DC: Brookings Institution Press.

Kolderie, T. (1994). Charters: An invitation to change. *Educational Leadership, 52*(1), 36.

Vanourek, G., Manno, B. V., Finn, C. E., & Bierlein, L. A. (1997). *Charter schools in action.* Indianapolis, IN; Washington, DC: Hudson Institute.

3.   Flaherty, J. F. (1995). Innovations: What are the schools doing? In R. G. Corwin & J. F. Flaherty (Eds.), *Freedom and innovation in California's charter schools* (pp. 63-73). Los Alamitos, CA: Southwest Regional Laboratory.

Fitzgerald, J. (1995). *Charter schools in Colorado.* Denver, CO: Colorado Children's Campaign.

Manno, B. V., Finn, C. E., Bierlein, L. A., & Vanourek, G. (1998, March). How charter schools are different: lessons and implications for a national study. *Phi Delta Kappan, 79,* 489-498.

RPP International. (2001). *Challenge and opportunity: The impact of charter schools on school districts (A report of the National Study of Charter Schools).* Washington, DC: Office of Educational Research and Improvement, U.S. Department of Education.

4.   Chubb, J. E., & Moe, T. M. (1990). *Politics, markets, and America's schools.* Washington, DC: Brookings Institution.

Hill, P. T. (1996, June). The educational consequences of choice. *Phi Delta Kappan, 77,* 671-676.

5. Friedman, M. (1994). The case for choice. In K. L. Billingsley (Ed.)., *Voices on choice: The education reform debate* (pp. 91-101). San Francisco, CA: Pacific Research Institute for Public Policy.

6. Friedman, M., & Friedman, R. (1980). *Free to choose: A personal statement.* New York, NY: Harcourt Brace Jovanovich.

    This thinking regarding choice, competition and innovation is reflected in the arguments for charter schools by a wide variety of advocates.

    Allen, J. (2001). Education by charter: The new neighborhood schools. In J. C. Goodman & F. F. Steiger (Eds.), *An education agenda: Let parents choose their children's school* (pp. 56-64). Dallas, TX: National Center for Policy Analysis.

    From, A. (1999, Fall). Where we stand: New democrats' 10 key reforms for revitalizing American education. *Blueprint.* Retrieved December 13, 1999, from http://www.dlc.org/blueprint/fall/1999/wherewestand.html

    Halpern, K., & Culbertson, E. R. (1994). *Blueprint for change: Charter schools.* Washington, DC: Democratic Leadership Council.

    Flake, J. L. (1999). *Profits and honor: Why for-profit education is a good Idea* (No. 99-16). Phoenix, AZ: Goldwater Institute.

    Hassel, B. C. (1999). Charter schools: A national innovation, an Arizona revolution. In R. Maranto, S. Milliman, F. Hess, & A. Gresham (Eds.), *School choice in the real world: Lessons from Arizona charter schools* (pp. 68-95). Boulder, CO: Westview Press.

    Kolderie, T. (1995). *The charter idea: Update and prospects, Fall 95.* Washington, DC: Center for Education Reform.

7. Lubienski, C. (2004). Charter school innovations in theory and practice: Autonomy, R&D, and curricular conformity. In K. E. Bulkley & P. Wohlstetter (Eds.), *Taking account of charter schools: What's happened and what's next?* (pp. 72-90). New York, NY: Teachers College Press.

    National Governors' Association. (1998). *Charter schools: Challenging Traditions and changing attitudes* (Issue Brief). Washington, DC: National governors' Association.

    SRI International, Powell, J., Blackorby, J., Marsh, J., Finnegan, K., & Anderson, L. (1997). *Evaluation of charter school effectiveness.* Sacramento, CA: Office of the Legislative Analyst.

    Surveys indicate that charter school founders also cite the possibility of innovation as one of the more attractive aspects of the model:

    Education Commission of the States & Nathan, J. (1995). *Charter schools: What are they up to?* Denver, CO: Author.

Anthes, K., & Ziebarth, T. (2001). *Collection of charter schools ECS statenotes.* Denver, CO: National Center for Governing America's Schools, Education Commission of the States.

RPP International & U.S. Department of Education. (1999). *The state of charter schools: Third-year report (National Study of Charter Schools).* Washington, DC: Office of Educational Research and Improvement, U.S. Department of Education, RPP International.

Berman, P., Nelson, B., Ericson, J., Perry, R., & Silverman, D. (1998). *A national study of charter schools: Second-year report.* Washington, DC: U.S. Department of Education, Office of Educational Research and Improvement.

Similarly, many teachers are drawn to the idea because of the possibility of experimenting or trying new models of curriculum and instruction:

Education Commission of the States & National Conference of State Legislatures (1998). *The charter school roadmap.* Washington, DC: Office of Educational Research and Improvement, U.S. Department of Education.

New Jersey Department of Education. (2001). *Report on charter school hearings.* Trenton, NJ: Author.

Vanourek, G., Manno, B. V., Finn, C. E., & Bierlein, L. A. (1998). Charter schools as seen by students, teachers, and parents. In P. E. Peterson & B. C. Hassel (Eds.), *Learning from school choice* (pp. 187-211). Washington, DC: Brookings Institution Press.

8.   Flaherty, 1995 (see note 3).

9.   Friedman Foundation. (2007). *The ABCs of school choice, 2006-2007 edition.* Indianapolis, IN: Author.

10.   Lubienski, C. (2003). Innovation in education markets: Theory and evidence on the impact of competition and choice in charter schools. *American Educational Research Journal, 40*(2), 395-443.

Miron, G., & Nelson, C. (2000). *Autonomy in exchange for accountability: An initial study of Pennsylvania charter schools.* Kalamazoo, MI: The Evaluation Center, Western Michigan University.

SRI International et al., 1997 (see note 7).

11.   Good, T. L., & Braden, J. S. (2000). *The great school debate: Choice, vouchers, and charters.* Mahwah, NJ: Erlbaum.

12.   Manno, Finn, et al. (see note 3).

13.   Lubienski, 2004 (see note 7).

14.   Lubienski, 2003 (see note 10).

see e.g., Clayton Foundation. (1997). *The Colorado charter schools evaluation, 1996*. Denver, CO: Colorado Department of Education.

15.   Rogers, E. M. (1995). *Diffusion of innovations* (4th ed.). New York, NY: Free Press.

16.   Daft, R. L. & Becker, S. W. (1978). *Innovation in organizations: Innovation adoption in school organizations*. New York, NY: Elsevier.

17.   Meyer, J. W. (1992). Innovation and knowledge use in American public education. In J. W. Meyer & W. R. Scott (Eds.), *Organizational environments: Ritual and rationality* (updated ed., pp. 233-260). Beverly Hills, CA: SAGE.

18.   Davies, P., & Adnett, N. (2007). *Knowledge creation in English schooling: The impact of school governance*. Stoke-on-Trent, UK: Institute for Education Policy Research, Staffordshire University.

      Wakeley, T. M. (1997). *Innovation, welfare, and industrial structure: An evolutionary analysis*. Aldershot, UK: Avebury.

19.   Hill, C. W. L., & Jones, G. R. (1989). *Strategic management theory: An integrated approach*. Boston, MA: Houghton Mifflin.

20.   Davies & Adnett, 2007 (see note 18).

      Lubienski, C. (2009). *Do quasi-markets foster innovation in education? A comparative perspective* (Education Working Paper No. 25). Paris, France: Organisation for Economic Co-operation and Development.

      See also Lake, R. J. (2008). In the eye of the beholder: Charter schools and innovation. *Journal of School Choice, 2*(2), 115-127.

21.   Jacquemin, A. (1987). *The new industrial organization: Market forces and strategic behavior*. Cambridge, MA: MIT Press.

      Shepherd, W. G. (1997). *The economics of industrial organization: Analysis, markets, policies* (4th ed.). Upper Saddle River, NJ: Prentice Hall.

22.   Lubienski, C. (2007). Marketing schools: Consumer goods and competitive incentives for consumer information. *Education and Urban Society, 40*(1), 118-141.

23.   Bast, J. L., & Walberg, H. J. (2004). Can parents choose the best schools for their children? *Economics of Education Review, 23*(4), 431-440.

24.   For instance, some may consider home schooling to be an innovation in terms of the form or format of teaching and learning at home. (Although many families use this vehicle to focus on un-innovative teaching methods; this is not necessarily a "bad" thing, since many families believe that schools have strayed too far away from tried-and-true methods.) But, in view of arguments regarding parental control or student achievement, policymakers have changed many of the institutional arrangements around home schooling in order to further encourage this practice—by lessening

reporting requirements, for instance, or mandating that local public schools accept homeschoolers in academic and extracurricular programs. Similarly, reforms such as inter- or intradistrict choice and charter schools represent substantial innovations of institutional arrangements within public-sector education. Charter schools, for example, have been widely heralded as policy innovations in that they represent a significant change in school governance: decentralizing authority, enhancing school autonomy, and elevating accountability to consumers. But unlike inter- or intradistrict choice plans, charter schools are themselves explicitly expected to then, in turn, create innovations "in teaching and learning."

Consortium for Policy Research in Education. (1998). Charter schools: Building blocks to success. *Spectrum: The Journal of State Government, 71*(2), 18-20.

Halpern & Culbertson, 1994 (see note 6).

Vanourek, Manno, et al., 1997 (see note 2).

Vouchers represent in some ways an even more dramatic innovation in the institutional arrangements of education, whereby students and public monies are redirected outside of the publicly governed sector. That institutional innovation is then expected to promote choice and competition, and a reorientation of organizations to be more consumer-centered; relatively few observers see vouchers (as opposed to charter schools) leading to innovations in teaching and learning.

25.   Technological innovations can also be important for sparking innovations in education, as when a number of public and private schools embrace a distance-learning component, for instance, in order to address an underserved demand.

26.   Jacobson, L. (1997, January). Charting the charters: As charter schools sweep the country, the big question for researches is: Do they work? *Teacher Magazine, 8,* 12-15.

27.   Tyack, D. B., Kirst, M. W., & Hansot, E. (1980). Educational reform: Retrospect and prospect. *Teachers College Record, 81*(3), 253-269.

Cuban, L. (1984). *How teachers taught: Constancy and change in American classrooms, 1890-1980.* New York, NY: Longman.

Cuban, L. (1992). Why some reforms last: The case of the kindergarten. *American Journal of Education, 100*(2), 166-194.

Tyack, D. B. (1974). *The one best system: A history of American urban education.* Cambridge, MA: Harvard University Press.

28.   Rothstein, R. (2004). *Class and schools: Using social, economic, and educational Reform to close the Black–White achievement gap.* Washington, DC: Economic Policy Institute.

29.   Meyer, 1992 (see note 17).

Cobb, C. W. (1992). *Responsive schools, renewed communities*. San Francisco, CA: ICS Press.

30.   Lubienski, C. (2007). School competition and the emergence of symbolism in a market environment. In C. F. Kaestle & A. E. Lodewick (Eds.), *To educate a nation: Federal and national strategies of school reform* (pp. 257-280). Lawrence, KS: University Press of Kansas.

31.   Lubienski, 2007, School competition ... (see note 30).

Lauder, H., Hughes, D., Watson, S., Waslander, S., Thrupp, M., & Strathdee, R. (1999). *Trading in futures: Why markets in education don't work*. Buckingham, England: Open University Press.

32.   Peter Weitzel provided invaluable research assistance for this section.

33.   Pape, L. (2006). From bricks to clicks: Blurring classroom/cyber lines. *School Administrator, 63*(7), 18-21.

Watson, J. (2007). *A national primer on K-12 online learning* (Electronic version). North American Council for Online Learning. Retrieved September 9, 2007, from http://www.nacol.org

34.   Tucker, B. (2007). *Laboratories of reform: Virtual high schools and innovation in public education* (Electronic version). Washington, DC: Education Sector. Retrieved September 9, 2007, from http://www.educationsector.org/research/research_show.htm?doc_id=502307

35.   Huerta, L., Gonzalez, M.-F., & d'Entremont, C. (2006). Cyber and home school charter schools: Adopting policy to new forms of public schooling. *Peabody Journal of Education, 81*(1), 103-139.

Watson, 2007 (see note 33).

36.   Gersen, W. (2003). The networked school. *Education Week, 23*(14), 30-31.

Robb, D. (2006). Don't call it school. *Teacher Magazine, 18*(3), 24-31.

37.   Lines, P. (2000). When home schoolers go to school: A partnership between families and schools. *Peabody Journal of Education, 75*(1), 159-186;

Huerta, L. A. (2000). Losing public accountability: A home schooling charter. In B. Fuller (Ed.), *Inside charter schools: The paradox of radical decentralization* (pp. 177-202). Cambridge, MA: Harvard University Press.

38.   See, e.g., Associated Press. (2008, January 15). Wisconsin at center of virtual schools debate. *Education Week, 27.* Retrieved from http://www.edweek.org/ew/articles/2008/01/15/17apvirtual_web.h27.html

Cai, Y., Reeve, J. M., & Robinson, D. (2002). Home schooling and teaching style: Comparing the motivating style of home school and public school teachers. *Journal of Educational Psychology, 94*(2), 372-380.

Ray, B. D. (2002). Customization through homeschooling. *Educational Leadership, 59*(7), 50-54.

39.   Brinson, D., & Rosch, J. (2010). *Charter school autonomy: A half-broken promise.* Dayton, OH: Thomas B. Fordham Foundation & Public Impact.

40.   Podgursky, M., & Ballou, D. (2001). *Personnel policy in charter schools.* Washington, DC: Thomas B. Fordham Foundation.

Triant, B. (2001). *Autonomy and innovation: How do Massachusetts charter school principals use their freedom?* Washington, DC: Thomas B. Fordham Foundation.

41.   Lubienski, 2003 (see note 10).

Good & Braden, 2000 (see note 11).

Miron, G., & Nelson, C. (2002). *What's public about charter schools? Lessons learned about choice and accountability.* Thousand Oaks, CA: Corwin Press.

Stout, R. T., & Garn, G. A. (1999). Nothing new: Curricula in Arizona charter schools. In R. Maranto, S. Milliman, F. Hess, & A. Gresham (Eds.), *School choice in the real world: Lessons from Arizona charter schools* (pp. 159-172). Boulder, CO: Westview Press.

42.   Steel, L., & Levine, R. E. (1994). *Educational innovation in multiracial contexts: The growth of magnet schools in American education.* Palo Alto, CA: American Institutes for Research.

43.   Hausman, C., & Brown, P. M. (2002). Curricular and instructional differentiation in magnet schools: Market driven or institutionally entrenched? *Journal of Curriculum and Supervision, 17*(3), 256-276.

44.   Viadero, D. (1996). School for thought. *Teacher Magazine, 7*, 18-20.

45.   Fossey, R. (1994). Open enrollment in Massachusetts: Why families choose. *Educational Evaluation and Policy Analysis, 16*(3), 320-334.

46.   Center for Education Research & Policy at MassINC, The Boston Foundation, & Center for Education Policy, U. of M., Amherst. (2003). *Mapping school choice in Massachusetts: Data and findings 2003.* Boston, MA: Center for Education Research & Policy.

47.   Meier, D. (1995). *The power of their ideas: Lessons for America from a small school in Harlem.* Boston, MA: Beacon Press.

Fliegel, S., & MacGuire, J. (1993). *Miracle in East Harlem: The fight for choice in public education* (1st ed.). New York, NY: Times Books.

Abramson, L. (2007). *A district where no two schools are alike.* Washington, DC: National Public Radio.

Manzo, K. K. (2007, November 14). Students in Boston's pilot schools outpacing others. *Education Week, 27*, 1, 14.

48. Friedman Foundation, 2007 (see note 9).

49. Neill, A. S. (1960). *Summerhill: A radical approach to child rearing*. New York, NY: Hart.

50. Chandler, L. (1999). *Traditional schools, progressive schools: Do parents have a choice?* Washington, DC: Thomas B. Fordham Foundation.

51. Kuttner, R. (1999). *Everything for sale: The virtues and limits of markets*. New York, NY: University of Chicago Press.

52. Duggan, M. (2000). Hospital market structure and the behavior of not-for-profit hospitals. *Rand Journal of Economics, 33*(3), 433-446.

53. Stiglitz, J. E. (1999). *Knowledge as a global public good*. Retrieved March 6, 2008, from http://www.worldbank.org/knowledge/chiefecon/articles/undpk2/w2wtoc.htm

54. Becker, G. (1999, September). *Competition*. Paper presented at the Address for the Heritage Foundation 25th Anniversary Leadership for America Lectures, Chicago, IL.

55. Drugs and money. (2001, September). *Multinational Monitor, 22*(4), 4.

56. Lubienski, C. (2006). School diversification in second-best education markets: International evidence and conflicting theories of change. *Educational Policy, 20*(2), 323-344.

57. Walberg, H. J., & Bast, J. L. (2003). *Education and capitalism: How overcoming our fear of markets and economics can improve America's Schools*. Stanford, CA: Hoover Institution Press.

58. Gauri, V. (1998). *School choice in Chile: Two decades of educational reform*. Pittsburgh, PA: University of Pittsburgh Press.

     Parry, T. R. (1997). How will schools respond to the incentives of privatization? Evidence from Chile and implications for the United States. *American Review of Public Administration, 27*(3), 248-269.

59. Tung, R., & Ouimette, M. (2007). *Strong results, high demand: A four-year study of Boston's pilot high schools*. Boston, CA: Center for Collaborative Education.

     Peirce, N. (2006, March 27). Boston's breakthrough schools. *Seattle Times*. Retrieved July 7, 2008, from http://community.seattletimes.nwsource.com/archive/?date=20060327&slug=peirce27

     Meier, 1995 (see note 47).

60. Lubienski, 2006, School diversification ... (see note 56).

     Smith, K. B. (2003). *The ideology of education: The commonwealth, the market, and America's schools*. Albany, NY: State University of New York Press.

61. Lubienski, 2006, School diversification ... (see note 56).

Lubienski, 2004 (see note 7).

62.   Meyer, J. W., & Rowan, B. (1992). Institutionalized organizations: Formal structure as myth and ceremony. In J. W. Meyer & W. R. Scott (Eds.), *Organizational environments: Ritual and rationality* (updated ed., pp. 21-44). Beverly Hills, CA: SAGE.

Meyer, J. W., Scott, W. R., & Deal, T. E. (1992). Institutional and technical sources of organizational structure: Explaining the structure of educational organizations. In J. W. Meyer & W. R. Scott (Eds.), *Organizational environments: Ritual and rationality* (updated ed., pp. 45-67). Beverly Hills, CA: SAGE.

63.   Carl, B. (1998, February). *Cause for optimism and caution: Michigan's charter school experience, disadvantaged youth, and the future of public education.* Paper presented at the annual conference of the Sociology of Education Association, Monterey, CA.

64.   Lubienski, C. (2005). Public schools in marketized environments: Shifting incentives and unintended consequences of competition-based educational reforms. *American Journal of Education, 111*(4), 464-486.

65.   Meyer, 1992 (see note 17). In contrast, computer technology innovations often have an end result in which innovations are obvious—a faster processor, or more capabilities, for instance.

66.   Lubienski, 2004 (see note 7).

67.   Abramson, 2007 (see note 47).

Braun, H., Jenkins, F., & Grigg, W. (2006). *Comparing private schools and public schools using hierarchical linear modeling* (No. 2006-461). Washington, DC: National Center for Education Statistics , U.S. Department of Education.

Braun, H., Jenkins, F., & Grigg, W. (2006). *A closer look at charter schools using hierarchical linear modeling* (No. NCES 2006–460). Washington, DC: National Center for Education Statistics, U.S. Department of Education.

Lubienski, C., Lubienski, S. T., & Crane, C. (2008, May). What do we know about school effectiveness? Academic gains in public and private schools. *Phi Delta Kappan, 89*(9), 689-695.

Lubienski, S. T., & Lubienski, C. (2006). School sector and academic achievement: A multilevel analysis of NAEP mathematics data. *American Educational Research Journal, 43*(4), 651-698.

Wenglinsky, H. (2007). *Are private high schools better academically than public high schools?* Washington, DC: Center on Education Policy.

68.   Lubienski, 2005 (See note 64).

Lubienski, 2007, Marketing schools ... (see note 22).

Sacchetti, M., & Jan, T. (2007, July 8). Pilot schools setting more hurdles. *Boston Globe*. Retrieved July 8, 2007, from http://www.boston.com/news/local/articles/2007/07/08/pilot_schools_setting_more_hurdles/?page=full

69. Finn, C. E. (1997, September/October). Learning-free zones: Five reasons why school reforms disappear without a trace. *Policy Review, 85*, 34-39.

Cuban, 1992 (see note 27).

70. Lortie, D. C. (1975). *Schoolteacher: A sociological study.* Chicago, IL: Chicago University Press.

Metz, M. H. (1990). Real school: A universal drama amid disparate experience. In D. E. Mitchell & M. E. Goertz (Eds.), *Education politics for the new century* (pp. 75-91). New York, NY: Falmer Press.

71. Ravitch, D. (2003, April). *Innovations in education: Does education really need more innovation in the age of scientifically based research?* Paper presented at the Office of Innovation and Improvement Innovations in Education Conference, Cambridge, MA.

72. Cohen, D. K. (1988). Teaching practice: Plus ça change.... In P. W. Jackson (Ed.), *Contributing to educational change: Perspectives on research and practice* (pp. 27-84). Berkeley, CA: McCutchan.

73. Lubienski, 2006, School diversification ... (see note 56).

74. Lubienski, 2006, School diversification ... (see note 56).

75. Hill, P. T. (2007, September 5). Waiting for the 'tipping point.' *Education Week, 27*, 26-27.

Kolderie, 1993 (see note 1).

Kolderie, T. (2003). *Evaluating chartering: Assessing separately the institutional innovation.* St. Paul, MN: Education Evolving, Center for Policy Studies, Hamline University.

76. Lauder et al., 1999 (see note 31).

Wells, A. S. (1993). *Time to choose: America at the crossroads of school choice policy.* New York, NY: Hill and Wang.

Saporito, S. (2003). Private choices, public consequences: Magnet school choice and segregation by race and poverty. *Social Problems, 50*(2), 191-203.

Frankenberg, E., & Lee, C. (2003). *Charter schools and race: A lost opportunity for integrated education.* Cambridge, MA: The Civil Rights Project, Harvard University.

Elacqua, G. (2004). *School choice in Chile: An analysis of parental preferences and search behavior* (Occasional paper). New York, NY: National Center for the Study of Privatization, Teachers College, Columbia University.

Schneider, M., & Buckley, J. (2002). What do parents want from schools: Evidence from the Internet. *Educational Evaluation and Policy Analysis, 24*(2), 133-144.

Ni, Y. (2007, April). *School choice and social stratification: An application of hierarchical linear models.* Paper presented at the annual conference of the American Educational Research Association, Chicago, IL.

Garcia, D. R. (2008, July). Academic and racial segregation in charter schools: Do parents sort students into specialized charter schools? *Education and Urban Society, 40*(5), 590-612.

Garcia, D. R. (2008). The impact of school choice on racial segregation in charter schools. *Educational Policy, 22*(6), 805-829.

77. Lubienski, 2005 (see note 64).

Lubienski,2007, Marketing schools ... (see note 22).

Lubienski, C. (2006). Incentives for school diversification: Competition and promotional patterns in local education markets. *Journal of School Choice, 1*(2), 1-31.

78. Lubienski, C., Gulosino, C., & Weitzel, P. (2009). School choice and competitive incentives: Mapping the distribution of educational opportunities across local education markets. *American Journal of Education, 115*(4), 601-647.

Gulosino, C., & Lubienski, C. (2011). Schools' strategic responses to competition in segregated urban areas: Patterns in school locations in metropolitan Detroit. *Education Policy Analysis Archives, 19*(13). Retrieved March 15, 2012, from http://epaa.asu.edu/ojs/article/view/829/913

CHAPTER 9: SCHOOL CHOICE AND SEGREGATION BY RACE, ETHNICITY, CLASS, AND ACHIEVEMENT

1. The synthesis of research reported in this chapter was supported by grants to the first author from the American Sociological Association, the Poverty & Race Research Action Council, and the National Science Foundation (REESE 06-0562). The authors thank Jason Giersch for his research assistance.

2. Available empirical evidence does not support claims that school choice triggers gains in academic achievement or educational innovations in non-choice schools. Other chapters in this volume address this issue in greater detail.

Also see Borsuk, A. J. (2007). Choice may not improve schools, study says. *Milwaukee Journal Sentinel.* Retrieved October 26, 2007, from http://www.jsonline.com/story/index.aspx?id=678202

Braun, H., Jenkins, F., & Grigg, W. (2006). *Comparing private schools and public schools using hierarchical linear modeling* (No. 2006-461). Washington, DC: National Center for Education Statistics, U.S. Department of Education.

Burgess, S., & Briggs, A. (2010). School assignment, school choice, and social mobility. *Economics of Education Review, 29*, 639-649.

Carr, M., & Ritter, G. (2007). *Measuring the competitive effect of charter schools on student achievement in Ohio's traditional public schools* (Occasional paper No. 146). New York, NY: National Center for the Study of Privatization, Teachers College, Columbia University.

CREDO. (2009). *Multiple choice: Charter school performance in 16 states*. Center for Research on Educational Outcomes. Palo Alto, CA: Stanford University.

Dodenhoff, D. (2007, October). Fixing the Milwaukee public schools: The limits of parent driven reform. *Wisconsin Policy Research Institute Report, 20*(8). Thiensville, WI: Wisconsin Policy Research Institute. Retrieved March 6, 2008, from http://www.wpri.org/Reports/Volume%2020/Vol20no8/Vol20no8p1.html

Lubienski, C., & Lubienski, S. (2006). *Charter, private, public schools and academic achievement: New evidence from NAEP mathematics data*. New York, NY: National Center for the Study of Privatization in Education, Teachers College, Columbia University.

Lubienski, S., & Lubienski, C. (2005, May). A new look at public and private schools: Student background and mathematics achievement. *Phi Delta Kappan, 86*(9), 696-699.

Nelson, F. H., Rosenberg, B., & Van Meter, N. (2004, August). *Charter school achievement on the 2003 National Assessment of Educational Progress*. Washington, DC: American Federation of Teachers.

Ni, Y. (2012, March). The sorting effect of charter schools on student composition in traditional public schools. *Education Policy, 26* (2),215-242.

For an alternative perspective, see

Walberg, H.J . (2007). *School choice: The findings*. Washington, DC: The Cato Institute.

3. Apple, M. (2006). *Educating the "right" way: Markets, standards, God and inequality*. New York, NY: Routledge.

Carl, J. (1997) Unusual allies: Elite and grass-roots origins of parental choice in Milwaukee. *Teachers College Record, 98*, 266-286.

Cookson, P. W., Jr. (1994). *School choice: The struggle for the soul of American education*. New Haven, CT: Yale University Press.

Chubb, J., & Moe, T. (1990). *Politics, markets, and America's schools*. Washington, DC: Brookings Institution.

Coons, J. E. & Sugarman, S. (1978). *Education by choice: The case for family control*. Berkeley, CA: University of California Press.

Godwin, R. K., & Kemerer, F. R. (2002). *School choice tradeoffs: Liberty, equity and diversity*. Austin, TX: University of Texas Press.

Pedroni, T. (2007). *Market movements: African American involvement in school voucher reform*. New York, NY: Routledge.

4. Emblematic of this renewed attention was *A Nation at Risk* (1983, Washington, DC: National Commission on Excellence in Education). This federal report indicted public schools for failing to educate students and thereby compromising the nation's economic and military capacities. For a critical analysis of *A Nation at Risk* see:

    Carol Ray, C., & Mickelson, R. A. (1993). Restructuring students for restructured work: The economy, school reform, and noncollege-bound youth. *Sociology of Education, 66*(1), 1-23.

5. Chubb & Moe, 1990 (see note 3).

6. U.S. Department of Education. (2009). States open to charters start fast in race to the top (Press release). Retrieved June 1, 2012, from http://www2.ed.gov/news/pressreleases/2009/06/06082009a.html

    U.S. Department of Education (2009). *Race to the Top Program Executive Summary*. Washington, DC: Author. Retrieved April 19, 2011, from http://www2.ed.gov/programs/racetothetop/executive-summary.pdf

7. Carl, 1997 (see note 3).

    Fuller, H., & Mitchell, G. A. (1999). *The impact of school choice on racial and ethnic enrollment in Milwaukee private schools*. Current Education Issues. Milwaukee, WI: Institute for the Transformation of Learning, Marquette University

    Pedroni, 2007 (see note 3).

8. *Brown v. Board. of Education of Topeka*, 349 U.S. 294, 301 , 75 S.Ct. 753, 757 (1955).

    Kluger, R. (1975). *Simple justice*. New York, NY: Random House.

9. Godwin & Kemerer, 2002 (see note 3).

10. The fiction that southern states' "freedom of choice" tactics would ever desegregate schools consistent with *Brown* was laid to rest by the Supreme Court's decisions in *Green v. County School Board*, 391 U.S. 430 (1968), in which it ordered school districts to eliminate segregation "root and branch." Later in *Swann v. Charlotte-Mecklenburg*, 402 US (1971), the court permitted the use of busing as a remedy for *de jure* segregation.

11. Alves, M. J., & Willie, C. V. (1987). Controlled choice assignments: A new and more effective approach to school desegregation. *Urban Review, 19*(2), 67-87.

12. *Parents Involved in Community Schools v. Seattle School District Number 1, et. al.,* 551 U.S. 701 (2007). *Parents Involved in Community Schools v. Seattle School District Number 1,* 127 S.Ct. 2738 (2007).

Ryan, J. (2007). *Guest Blogger: Seattle schools and Bakke.* Retrieved June 28, 2007, from http://scintegration.blogspot.com/2007/06/guest-blogger-seattle-schools-and-bakke.html

13. Ali, R., & Perez, T. (2011, December). *Guidance on the voluntary use of race to achieve diversity and avoid racial isolation in elementary and secondary schools.* Washington, DC: U.S. Department of Justice, Civil Rights Division and U.S. Department of Education, Office for Civil Rights.

Civil Rights Project & NAACP Legal Defense and Education Fund. (2007). *Still looking to the future—Voluntary K-12 school integration: A manual for parents, educators, and advocates.* New York, NY: NAACP Legal Defense Fund.

Ryan, 2007 (see note 12).

Parents Involved in Community Schools v. Seattle School District Number1, et al., 551 U.S. 701, Opinion of Justice Kennedy, 10, 18 (2007).

14. Since 2005 Mickelson and Bottia have surveyed and synthesized the literature on the effects of school and classroom composition on educational outcomes. As of this writing they have entered synopses of 500 articles, chapters, and other research reports on the effects of school and classroom composition on educational outcomes into a searchable database available at: http://Spivack.uncc.edu.

15. The evidence supporting this generalization is vast. A full listing of the relevant literature is beyond the scope of this chapter. Several synthetic works provide an overview of this literature. For example, in 2010 *Teachers College Record* published three special issues that presented new research on the effects of school and classroom composition on educational outcomes.

Brief of 553 Social Scientists as Amici Curiae in support of respondents *Parents Involved in Community Schools v. Seattle School District Number 1, et al.,* 551 U. S. (2007).

Linn, R., & Welner, K. (2006). *Race-conscious policies for assigning students to schools: Social science research and the Supreme Court cases.* Washington, DC: National Academy of Education.

Mickelson, R. A. (2008). Twenty-first century social science research on school diversity and educational outcomes. *Ohio State Law Journal, 69,* 1173-1228.

Mickelson, R. A., & Bottia, M. (2010). Integrated education and mathematics outcomes: A synthesis of social science research. *North Carolina Law Review, 87,* 993-1089.

Pettigrew, T. F., & Tropp, L. R. (2006). A meta-analytic test of inter-group contact theory. *Journal of Personality and Social Psychology, 90*(5), 751-783.

Also see three recent special issues of *Teachers College Record* that present new research on the topic. They are available at:

http://www.tcrecord.org/Issue.asp?volyear=2010&number=4&volume=112

http://www.tcrecord.org/Issue.asp?volyear=2010&number=5&volume=112

http://www.tcrecord.org/Issue.asp?volyear=2010&number=6&volume=112

16.   Goldsmith, P. A. (2003). All segregation is not equal: The impact of Latino and Black school composition. *Sociological Perspectives, 46* (1), 83-105.

Portes, A., & Hao, L. (2004). The schooling of children of immigrants: Contextual effects on the educational attainment of the second generation. *Proceedings of The National Academy of Sciences of the USA, 101*(33), 11920-11927.

17.   Brief of 553 Social Scientists as Amici Curiae in support of respondents *Parents Involved in Community Schools v. Seattle School District Number 1,* et al., 551 U. S. (2007)

Linn & Welner (see note 15).

Pettigrew & Tropp, 2006 (see note 15).

18.   Meier, K. J., Stewart, J. J., & England, R. E. (1989). *Race, class, and education: The politics of second generation discrimination.* Madison, WI: University of Wisconsin Press.

Mickelson, R. A. (2001). Subverting *Swann*: First- and second-generation segregation in Charlotte, North Carolina. *American Educational Research Journal, 38*(2), 215-252.

Wells, A. S., & Crain, R. L. (1994). Perpetuation theory and the long-term effects of school desegregation. *Review of Educational Research, 64,* 531-556.

19.   Lucas, S. (1999). *Tracking inequality.* New York, NY: Teachers College Press.

Lucas, S. (2001). Effectively maintained inequality: Education transitions, track mobility, and social background effects. *American Journal of Sociology, 106,* 1642-1690.

Oakes, J. (2005). *Keeping track: How schools structure inequality* (2nd ed.). New Haven, CT: Yale University Press.

20.   Orfield, G., & Frankenberg, E. (2008, January). *The last have become first. Rural and small town America led the way on desegregation.* Los Angeles, CA: Civil Rights Project at the University of California.

Orfield, G., & Lee, C. (2002). The resurgence of school segregation. *Educational Leadership, 60*(4), 16-20.

Logan, J. (2004). *Resegregation in American public schools? Not in the 1990s.* Providence, RI: Brown University, Lewis Mumford Center for Comparative Urban and Regional Research.

Logan, J. Minca, K., & Adar, S. (2012). The geography of inequality: Why separate means unequal in American public schools. *Sociology of Education, 85,* 287-301.

21.   For example, with respect to measuring achievement growth in charter schools see:

Greene, J. P., Forster, G., & Winters, M. A. (2003). *Apples to apples: An evaluation of charter schools serving general student populations* (Education Working Paper No. 1). New York, NY: Center for Civic Innovation at the Manhattan Institute.

also see CREDO, 2009 (see note 2).

Carnoy, M., et al. (2005). *The charter school dust-up: Examining the evidence on enrollment and achievement.* Washington DC: Economic Policy Institute.

For measuring the effects of private schools on segregation see:

Greene, J. P. (2005). Choosing integration. In J. Scott (Ed.), *School choice and diversity: What the evidence says* (pp. 27-41). New York, NY: Teachers College Press.

Yun, J., & Reardon, S. (2005). Private school racial enrollments and segregation. In J. Scott (Ed.), *School choice and diversity: What the evidence says* (pp. 42-58). New York, NY: Teachers College Press.

22.   American Educational Research Association. (2006). Standards for reporting on empirical social science research in AERA publications. *Educational Researcher, 36*(6), 33-40.

23.   Omi, M., & Winant, H. (1994). *Racial formation in the United States.* New York, NY: Routledge.

Snipp, C. M. (2003). Racial measurement in the American census: Past practices and implications for the future. *Annual Review of Sociology, 29,* 563-568.

24.   Oakes, 2005 (see note 19).

25.   Student ability is typically not considered a demographic characteristic of a school. The authors include academic ability in the list of demographic characteristics because a) certain forms of choice are specifically designed

to attract gifted or learning disabled students and b) the ways that disabilities and giftedness are socially constructed result in correlations between students' race and SES and these designations of ability.

26.   See, for example, American Educational Research Association, 2006 (see note 22).

27.   Orfield, G., & Lee, C. (2006). *Racial transformation and the changing nature of segregation*. Cambridge, MA. The Civil Rights Project at Harvard University.

Orfield & Frankenberg, 2008, (see note 20).

28.   Orfield, G. (2005). Introduction. The Southern dilemma: Losing Brown: Fearing Plessy. In J. C. Boger & G. Orfield (Eds.), *School resegregation: Must the South turn back?* (pp. 1-28). Chapel Hill, NC: University of North Carolina Press.

Orfield & Lee, 2006 (see note 27).

Swanson, C. A. (2004). Sketching a portrait of public high school graduation: Who graduates? Who doesn't? In G. Orfield (Ed.), *Dropouts in America: Confronting the graduation rate crisis* (pp. 13-40). Cambridge, MA: Harvard Education Press.

Schott Foundation. (2010). Yes we can: *The Schott 50 State Report on Public Education and Black Males*. Cambridge, MA: Schott Foundation for Public Education.

29.   Dreier, P., Mollenkopft, J., & Swanstrom, T. (2004). *Place matters: Metropolitics for the 21st century.* Lawrence, KS: University Press of Kansas.

Orfield, 2005 (see note 28).

30.   NCES. (2010). Table 2. Number of public elementary and secondary schools, by school type, charter, magnet, Title I and Title I school wide status and state or jurisdiction: School year 2008-2009. Retrieved April 19, 2011, from: http://nces.ed.gov/pubs2010/2010345.pdf

31.   Meier, Stewart, & England, 1989 (see note 18).

Wells & Crain, 1994 (see note 18).

32.   West, K. C. (1994). A desegregation tool that backfired: Magnet schools and classroom segregation. *The Yale Law Journal, 103*(8), 2567-2592.

Mickelson, 2001(see note 18).

33.   West, 1994 (see note 32).

Mickelson, 2001 (see note 18).

34.   Holme, J., & Wells, A. S. (2009). School choice beyond borders: Lessons for the reauthorization of NCLB from interdistrict desegregation and open

enrollment plans. In R. Kahlberg (Ed.), *Improving on no child left behind: Getting education reform back on track*. Washington, DC: Century Foundation.

Ni, Y. (2007, April). *School choice and social stratification: An application of hierarchical linear models*. Paper presented at the annual conference of the American Educational Research Association, Chicago, IL.

Ryan, J., & Heise, M. (2002). The political economy of school choice. *Yale Law Journal, 111*(8), 2043-2136.

35.   Institute of Educational Sciences. (2010). *Trends in use of school choice. 1993-2007*. NCES 2010-004. Retrieved from http://nces.ed.gov/pubs2010/2010004/intro.asp

CREDO, 2009 (see note 2).

Frankenberg, E., Siegel-Hawley, G., & Wang, J. (2010, February). *Choice without equity: Charter school segregation and the need for civil rights standards*. Los Angeles, CA: University of California, Civil Rights Project/Proyecto Derechos Civiles.

36.   Ryan & Heise, 2002 (see note 34).

Frankenberg, E., & Lee, C. (2003). *Charter schools and race: A lost opportunity for integrated education*. Cambridge, MA: The Civil Rights Project at Harvard University.

37.   Carnoy et al., 2005 (see note 21).

38.   Frankenberg & Lee, 2003 (see note 36).

39.   U.S. Department of Education, 2009, States open to charters ... (see note 6).

40.   Labbé, T. (2007, November 6). Church decides to convert 7 schools. *Washington Post*, B01.

41.   Brady, K. P., Umpstead, R., & Eckes, S. (2010). Unchartered territory: The current legal landscape of public cyber charter schools. *Brigham Young University Education and Law Journal, 19*, 191-274.

Rotherham, A. J. (2006, April 7). Virtual schools, real innovation. *New York Times*, p. A27.

42.   The Friedman Foundation for Educational Choice. (2008). *ABC's of school choice: 2007-2008* (6th ed.). Indianapolis, IN: Author.

43.   National Conference of State Legislatures. (2011). *Publicly funded school voucher programs*. Denver, CO: Author. Retrieved June 1, 2012, from http://www.ncsl.org/default.aspx?tabid=12942

Turkque, B., & Murray, S. (2009, May 7). Obama offers compromise on D.C. tuition vouchers. *Washington Post*, p. B01.

44. United States General Accounting Office. (2002). *School vouchers: Characteristics of privately funded programs.* Washington, DC: Author.

45. Wisconsin Department of Public Instruction. (2011). *Milwaukee parental choice program.* Number of Choice Students Enrolled by School 2010. Retrieved April 19, 2011, from http://www.dpi.state.wi.us/sms/choice.html

    National School Boards Association. (n.d.). Voucher Strategy Center. Retrieved April 19, 2011, from http://www.nsba.org/novouchers

46. National School Boards Association, n.d. (see note 45).

47. Dillon, S. (2007, June 22). Voucher use in Washington wins praise of parents. *The New York Times.* Retrieved March 6, 2008, from http://www.nytimes.com/2007/06/22/washington/22vouchers.html

48. *Zelman v. Simmons-Harris,* 536 US 639 (2002).

49. Harris, D. N., Herrington, C. D., & Albee, A. (2007). The future of vouchers: Lessons from the adoption, design, and court challenges of Florida's three voucher programs. *Educational Policy, 21*(1), 215-244.

50. Pyrah, J. (2007, November 7). Voters reject vouchers. *Daily Herald* (Provo, UT). Retrieved June 1, 2012, from http://www.heraldextra.com/news/voters-reject-vouchers/article_4068c190-e0c0-5837-9b22-7913a08fb5f9.html

51. U.S. Department of Education, National Center for Education Statistics (2009). *The condition of education 2009* (NCES 2009–081), Indicator 32. Washington, DC: Author.

52. Reardon, S. F., & Yun, J. T. (2002). *Private school enrollments and segregation.* Cambridge, MA: Harvard Civil Rights Project.

    U.S. Department of Education, National Center for Education Statistics (2008). Number of private schools, students, and teachers (headcount), by school membership in private school associations: United States, 2007–08. Retrieved June 1, 2012, from http://nces.ed.gov/surveys/pss/tables/table_2008_14.asp

53. Reardon & Yun, 2002 (see note 52).

    U.S. Department of Education, National Center for Education Statistics, 2008 (see note 52).

54. Apple, M. (2006). Godly technology: Gender, culture, and the work of homeschooling. *Social Analysis, 50*(3), 19-37.

    Roberts, S. (2007). Homeschooling. In S. Mathison & E. W. Ross (Eds.), *Battleground schools: An encyclopedia of conflict and controversy* (pp. 313-319). New York, NY: Greenwood/Praeger.

    Stevens, M. (2001). *Kingdom of children: Culture and controversy in the homeschooling movement.* Princeton, NJ: Princeton University Press.

55. U.S. Department of Education, National Center for Education Statistics. (2009). *The condition of education 2009* (NCES 2009-081), Indicator 6. Washington, DC: Author.

56. Apple, 2006, Godly technology … (see note 54).

Stevens, 2001 (see note 54).

57. The mission statement of Patrick Henry College identifies itself as an institution of higher education that caters to Christians and homeschoolers:

High school students. (n.d.) Patrick Henry College website. Retrieved June 1, 2012, from http://www.phc.edu/High_School_Students.php

58. Belfield, C. R., & Levin, H. M. (2005). *Privatizing educational choice: Consequences for parents, schools, and public policy.* Boulder, CO: Paradigm.

59. Roberts, 2007 (see note 54).

60. Rotherham, 2006 (see note 41).

61. Carnoy et al., 2005 (see note 21).

Cobb, C., & Glass, G. (1999). Ethnic segregation in Arizona charter schools. *Education Policy Analysis Archives, 7*(1). Retrieved from June 1, 2012, from http://epaa.asu.edu/epaa/v7n1/

Frankenberg, Siegel-Hawley, & Wang, 2010 (see note 35).

Garcia, D. R. (2010). Charter schools challenging traditional notions of segregation. In C. Lubienski & P. Weitzel (Eds.), *The charter school experiment: Expectations, evidence, and implications* (pp. 109-121). Cambridge, MA: Harvard Education Press.

Garcia, D. R. (2008, July). Academic and racial segregation in charter schools: Do parents sort students into specialized charter schools? *Education and Urban Society, 40*(5), 590-612.

Garcia, D. R. (2008). The impact of school choice on racial segregation in charter schools. *Educational Policy, 22*(6), 805-829.

Miron, G., Urschel, J., Mathis, W., & Tornquist, E. (2010, February). Schools without diversity: Educational management organizations, charter schools, and the demographic stratification of the American school system. Boulder, CO: National Educational Policy Center. Retrieved June 1, 2012, from http://nepc.colorado.edu/publication/schools-without-diversity

Ni, 2012 (see note 2).

U.S. Department of Education, National Center for Education Statistics. (2009). Table 3. Percentage distribution of students, by sex, race/ethnicity, school type, and selected school characteristics: 2007–08. Retrieved April 19, 2011, from http://nces.ed.gov/pubs2009/2009321/tables/sass0708_2009321_s12n_03.asp

Powers, J. M. (2009). *Charter schools: From reform imagery to reform reality.* New York, NY: Palgrave Macmillan.

RPP International. (2000). *The state of charter schools 2000: Fourth year report.* Washington DC: US Department of Education.

62.   This finding is important because it speaks to the accuracy of arguments that parents choose charters because of their superior academic potential.

Bilfulco, R., & Ladd, H.F. (2007). School choice, racial segregation, and test score gaps: Evidence from North Carolina's charter school program. *Journal of Policy Analysis and Management, 26*(1), 31-56.

Garcia, 2010 (see note 61).

Rapp, K. E., & Eckes, S. E. (2007). Dispelling the myth of "White flight": An examination of minority enrollment in charter schools. *Educational Policy, 21*(4), 615-661.

Renzulli, L. A., & Evans, L. (2005). School choice, charter schools and white flight. *Social Problems, 52*(3), 398-418.

Weiher, G. R., & Tedin, K. (2002). Does choice lead to racially distinctive schools? Charter schools and household preferences. *Journal of Policy Analysis and Management, 21*(1), 79-92.

Saporito, S. (2003). Private choices, public consequences: Magnet school choice and segregation by race and poverty. *Social Problems, 50*(2), 181-203.

Booker, K., Zimmer, R., &Buddin, R. (2005). *The effect of charter schools on school peer composition.* Santa Monica, CA: RAND.

63.   Harris, Herrington, & Albee, 2007 (see note 49).

Fuller & Mitchell, 1999 (see note 7).

Carnoy et al., 2005 (see note 21).

Hanauer, A. (2002, January). Cleveland school vouchers: Where the students go. *Policy Matters Ohio.* Retrieved March 6, 2008, from http://www.policymattersohio.org/pdf/WhereStudentsGo.pdf

64.   Hanauer, 2002 (see note 63).

65.   Fairlie, R. (2006, February). *Racial segregation and the private/public school choice.* New York, NY: National Center for the Study of Privatization in Education, Teachers College, Columbia University.

Reardon & Yun, 2002 (see note 52).

66.   U.S. Department of Education, National Center for Education Statistics. (2009). Table A-6-1. Number and percentage distribution of all school-age children who were homeschooled and homeschooling rate, by selected characteristics: 1999, 2003, and 2007. Retrieved April 19, 2011, from http://nces.ed.gov/programs/coe/2009/section1/table-hsc-1.asp

Ray, B. (2011). *Homeschool population report 2010*. Salem, OR: National Home Education Research Institute.

67.   U.S. Department of Education, National Center for Education Statistics, 2009, Table A-6-1 (see note 66).

Ray, 2011 (see note 66).

68.   U.S. Department of Education, National Center for Education Statistics, 2009, Table A-6-1 (see note 66).

69.   Sampson, Z. C. (2005, December 11). Home schools are becoming more popular among Blacks. *New York Times*, p. A34.

70.   Cooper, B., & Sureau, J. (2007). The politics of home schooling. *Educational Policy, 21*(1), 110-131.

71.   Roberts, 2007 (see note 54).

Apple, 2006, Godly technology ... (see note 54).

Stevens, 2001 (see note 54).

72.   Princiotta, D., & Bielick, S. (2006). *Homeschooling in the United States: 2003 statistical analysis report*, NCES 2006-042. Washington, DC: U.S. Department of Education: National Center for Educational Statistics.

U.S. Department of Education. (2004). *Issue brief: 1.1 million home schooled students in the United States in 2003* (NCES 2004-115). Washington DC: Institute of Educational Sciences.

73.   U.S. Department of Education, 2004 (see note 72).

74.   Cobb, C., & Glass, G. (2009). School choice in a post-desegregation world. *Peabody Journal of Education, 84*, 262-278.

McAuliffe Straus, R. (2010). Measuring multi-ethnic desegregation. *Education and Urban Society, 42*, 223-242.

Rickles, J., & Ong, P. (2005). The integrating (and segregating) effect of charter, magnet, and traditional elementary schools: The case of five California metropolitan areas. *California Politics & Policy, 9*(1), 16-38.

Sohoni, D., & Saporito, S. (2009). Mapping school segregation: Using GIS to explore racial segregation between schools and their corresponding attendance areas. *American Journal of Education, 115*, 569-600.

75.   Harris, D.N. (2006). *Lost learning, forgotten promises: A national analysis of school racial segregation, student achievement and "controlled choice" plans*. Washington, DC: Center for American Progress.

76.   Arcia, E. (2006). Comparison of the enrollment percentages of magnet and non-magnet schools in a large urban school district. *Education Policy Analysis Archives, 14*(33), 1-13.

77.   Mickelson, R. A., & Southworth, S. (2005). When opting out is not a choice: Implications for NCLB's transfer option from Charlotte, North Carolina. *Equity and Excellence in Education, 38*, 249-263.

Smrekar, C., & Gamoran, A. (2007, April). *Expanded (or exclusive) magnet school policy: Issues of equity and diversity in Nashville, TN.* Paper presented at the meeting of the American Educational Research Association. San Francisco, CA.

78.   Holme & Wells, 2009 (See note 34).

Koedel, C., Betts, J., Rice, L. & Zau, A. (2009). *The social cost of open enrollment as a school choice policy* (Working paper). New York, NY: National Center for the Study of Privatization, Teachers College, Columbia University. Retrieved June 1, 2012, from http://economics.missouri.edu /working-papers/2009/WP0910_koedel.pdf

79.   Bilfulco, R., Cobb, C. D., & Bell, C. (2009). Can interdistrict choice boost student achievement? The case of Connecticut's interdistrict magnet school program. *Educational Evaluation and Policy Analysis, 31*(4), 323-345.

Dillon, E. (2008). *Plotting school choice: The challenges of crossing district lines.* Washington, DC: Education Sector.

Dreier, Mollenkopft, & Swanstrom, 2004 (see note 29).

Holme & Wells, 2009 (See note 34).

Reback, R. (2008). Demand (and supply) in an inter-district public school choice program. *Economics of Education Review, 27*, 402-416.

Ryan & Heise, 2002 (see note 34).

80.   Wells, A. S., & Crain, R. (1997*). Stepping over the color line: African American students in White suburban schools.* New Haven, CT: Yale University Press.

81.   Massachusetts Department of Education. (n.d.). *Metco program.* Retrieved November 28, 2007, from http://www.doe.mass.edu/metco

82.   Holme & Wells, 2009 (see note 34).

Ryan & Heise, 2002 (see note 34).

83.   Bifulco, R., Ladd, H., & Ross, S. (2009). Public school choice and integration evidence from Durham, North Carolina. *Social Science Research, 38*, 71-85.

Clotfelter, C., Ladd, H., & Vigdor, J. (2008). School Segregation under color-blind jurisprudence: The case of North Carolina. *Virginia Journal of Social Policy and the Law, 16*(1), 46-86.

McAuliffe Straus, 2010 (see note 74).

Rossell, C. (2003). The desegregation efficiency of magnet schools. *Urban Affairs Review, 38*(5), 697-725.

also see,

Betts, J. R., Rice, L. A., Zau, A. C., Tang, Y. E., & Koedel, C. R. (2006). *Does school choice work? Effects on student integration and achievement.* San Francisco, CA: Public Policy Institute of California.

Smrekar, C. (2000). Magnet schools and the pursuit of racial balance. *Education and Urban Society, 33*(1), 17-35.

84.   Rossell, 2003 (see note 83).

Sohoni & Saporito, 2009 (see note 74).

85.   Saporito, 2003 (see note 62).

86.   Archibald, D.A. (2004). School choice, magnet schools, and the liberation model: An empirical study. *Sociology of Education, 77*(4), 283-310.

87.   U.S. Department of Education, National Center for Education Statistics. (2010). *Trends in the use of school choice, 1993-2007.* Washington, DC: National Center for Education Statistics, Institute of Education Sciences, U.S. Department of Education. Retrieved June 1, 2012, from http://nces.ed.gov/pubs2010/2010004/tables/table_4.asp

88.   Frankenberg, Siegel-Hawley, & Wang, 2010 (see note 35).

Garia, 2010 (see note 61).

Garcia, 2008, Academic and racial segregation … (see note 61).

Garcia, 2008, The impact of school choice … (see note 61).

Powers, 2009 (see note 61).

89.   Carnoy et al., 2005 (see note 21).

90.   U.S. Department of Education, National Center for Education Statistics NCES. (2001). *Characteristics of the 100 largest public elementary and secondary school districts in the United States 2000-2001.* Retrieved March 6, 2008, from http://nces.ed.gov/pubs2002/100_largest/methodology.asp

91.   Carnoy et al., 2005 (see note 21).

92.   Frankenberg & Lee, 2003 (see note 36).

Frankenberg, Siegel-Hawley, & Wang, 2010 (see note 35).

Garcia, 2010 (see note 61).

93.   Cobb & Glass, 1999 (see note 61).

Cobb& Glass, G, 2009 (see note 74).

94.   Rapp & Eckes, 2007 (see note 62).

95.   Powers, 2009 (see note 61). Powers examined the results from 14 years of charter school reforms in California. She found charter schools did not

ameliorate racial segregation in public education and may have exacerbated existing patterns of school segregation.

96. Carnoy et al., 2005 (see note 21).

97. Witte, J. F. (1998). The Milwaukee voucher experiment. *Educational Evaluation and Policy Analysis, 20*(4), 229-251.

98. Campbell, D. E., West, M. R., & Peterson, P. E. (2005). Participation in a national, means-tested voucher program. *Journal of Policy Analysis and Management, 24*(3), 523-541.

99. Reardon & Yun, 2002 (see note 52).

Sohoni & Saporito, 2009 (see note 74).

100. Witte, J.F. (2000). *The market approach to education: An analysis of America's first voucher program.* Princeton, NJ: Princeton University Press.

101. Forster, G. (2006, October). *Freedom from racial barriers: The empirical evidence on vouchers and segregation.* Indianapolis, IN: Milton and Rose D. Friedman Foundation

102. Zimmer, R., & Bettinger, E. P. (2008). Beyond the rhetoric: Surveying the evidence on vouchers and tax credits. In H. F. Ladd & E.B. Fiske (Eds.), *Handbook of research in education finance and policy* (pp. 301-315). New York, NY: Routledge.

103. Fuller & Mitchell, 1999 (see note 7).

104. The section of the chapter on private schools draws heavily from the comprehensive report on private school racial enrollments and segregation by Sean Reardon and John Yun (Reardon & Yun, 2002 [see note 52]). Their report used primary data from the 2000 Common Core of Data, the 1997-98 Private School Survey, the October Current Population Survey from 1998-2000, and the 1990 School District Data Book. Jay P. Greene disputes their findings that private schools are more segregated than public ones because he believes their comparison of segregation in public and private schools is conceptually flawed in several ways (Greene, 2005 [see note 21]). The authors of this chapter find Reardon and Yun's approach to estimating comparative levels of segregation in public and private schools to be conceptually and methodologically superior to the one proposed by Greene.

105. Reardon & Yun, 2002 (see note 52).

106. Reardon & Yun, 2002 (see note 52).

107. Roberts, 2007 (see note 54).

Levin, H. M., & Belfield, C. R. (2003). The marketplace in education. *Review of Research in Education, 27*, 183-219.

Apple, 2006, Godly technology ... (see note 54).

108. Sampson, 2005 (see note 69).

109. Public Law 94-142 (1975) . Education for All Handicapped Children Act.

110. Lucas, 1999 (see note 19).

Wells, A. S., & Holme, J. J. (2005). No accountability for diversity: Standardized tests and the demise of racially mixed schools. In J. C. Boger & G. Orfield (Eds.), *School resegregation: Must the South turn back?* (pp. 187-211). Chapel Hill, NC: University of North Carolina Press.

Oakes, 2005 (see note 19).

Welner, K. (2001). *Legal rights, local wrongs: When community control collides with educational equity.* Albany, NY: University of New York Press.

111. Welner, K., & Howe, K. (2005). Steering toward separation: The policy and legal implications of "counseling" special education students away from choice schools. In J. Scott (Ed.), *School choice and student diversity: What the evidence says* (pp. 93-111). New York, NY: Teachers College Press.

112. Center for Education Reform. (2007). *Annual survey of America's charter schools.* Retrieved October 1, 2007, from http://www.edreform.com/_upload/cer_charter_survey.pdf.

113. McLaughlin, D. H., & Broughman, S. (1997). *Private schools in the United States: A statistical profile, 1993-94.* Washington, DC: U.S. Government Printing Office.

114. Welner & Howe, 2005 (see note 111).

115. Miron, G., Nelson, C., & Risley, J. (2002). *Strengthening Pennsylvania's charter school reform: Findings from the statewide evaluation and discussion of relevant policy issues.* Kalamazoo, MI: The Evaluation Center.

116. U.S. Department of Education. (1998, November). *Charter schools and students with disabilities: Review of existing data.* Washington, DC: Office of Educational Research and Improvement. U.S. Department of Education.

117. Garcia, 2010 (see note 61).

RPP International, 2000 (see note 61).

118. Miron, G., & Nelson, C. (2002). *What's public about charter schools?: Lessons learned about accountability and choice.* Thousand Oaks, CA: Corwin Press.

119. Welner & Howe, 2005 (see note 111).

120. Reback, 2008 (see note 79).

Welner & Howe, 2005 (see note 111).

121. Lacireno-Paquet, N. (2004). *Policy regimes and markets: The impact of state policies on charter schools' service to disadvantaged students* (doctoral dissertation). New York, NY: Columbia University.

122.   Lacireno-Paquet, 2004 (see note 121).

123.   Miron & Nelson, 2002 (see note 118).

124.   Cullen, J. B., & Rivkin, S. G. (2001, February). *The role of special education in school choice*. Presented at the annual meeting of the NBER Economics of School Choice Conference, Boston, MA.

125.   Hanauer, 2002 (see note 63).

126.   Powers, J. M., & Cookson, P. W., Jr. (1999). The politics of school choice research: Fact, fiction and statistics. *Education Policy, 13*(1), 104-123.

       Levin, H. M. (1998). Educational vouchers: Effectiveness, choice, and costs. *Journal of Policy Analysis and Management, 17*(3), 373-392.

127.   Corwin, R. (2007). School choice. In S. Mathison & E. W. Ross (Eds.), *Battleground schools: An encyclopedia of conflict and controversy* (pp. 539-548). New York, NY: Greenwood/Praeger.

128.   U.S. Department of Education, National Center for Education Statistics, 2009 (see note 55).

129.   Fuller, B., Gawilk, M., Gonzales, E., & Park, S. (2003). *Charter schools and inequality: National disparities in funding, teacher quality and student support* (PACE Working Paper 03-2). Berkeley, CA: Policy Analysis for California Education.

130.   Welner & Howe, 2005 (see note 111).

131.   Welner & Howe, 2005 (see note 111).

132.   Welner & Howe, 2005 (see note 111).

133.   Miron Nelson & Risley, 2002 (see note 115).

134.   Neild, R. C. (2004). The effects of magnet school on neighborhood high schools: An examination of achievement on entering freshmen. *Journal of Education for Students at Risk, 9*(1), 1-21.

135.   Neild, 2004 (see note 134).

136.   Dills, A. K. (2005). Does cream-skimming curdle the milk? A study of peer effects. *Economics of Education Review, 24*(1), 19-28.

137.   Burgess & Briggs, 2010 (see note 2).

       Cobb & Glass, 2009 (see note 74).

       Gruber, K. J., Wiley, S. D., Broughman, S. P., Strizek, G. A., & Burian-Fitzgerald, M. (2002). *Schools and Staffing Survey, 1999-2000: Overview of the data for public, private, public charter, and Bureau of Indian Affairs elementary and secondary schools*. Washington, DC: U.S. Department of Education, Government Printing Office.

       Miron, Urschel, Mathis, & Tornquist, 2010 (see note 61).

Sohoni & Saporito, 2009 (see note 74).

138.   For an alternative approach to the research evidence on these questions,
       see Walberg, 2007 (see note 2).

139.   Koretz, D. (1996).Using student assessments for educational accountability.
       In E. A. Hanushek & D. W. Jorgenson (Eds.), *Improving America's schools:
       The role of incentives* (pp. 160-193). Washington DC: National Academy of
       Sciences.

140.   *Parents Involved in Community Schools v. Seattle School District Number 1*, et. al.
       551 U.S. 701, Opinion of Justice Kennedy, 10 & 18, (2007)

       Civil Rights Project & NAACP Legal Defense and Education Fund, 2007
       (see note 13).

141.   For example, in December, 2007 a California Superior Court upheld the
       Los Angeles Unified School District's use of student race as an admissions
       criterion for controlled-choice magnet programs established for the pur-
       poses of desegregating the school district. The LAUSD's use of individual
       student race is permissible under the Constitution of California, upon
       which the original 1981 desegregation decision is based.

       Landsberg, M., & Rubin, J. (2007, December 12). Admissions policy for
       L.A. Unified magnet schools is upheld. *Los Angeles Times*, p. B1.

142.   The authors adapted Jean Anyon's metaphor about school reform that
       originally appeared in her book *Ghetto Schooling* (New York, NY: Teachers
       College Press, 2001).

CHAPTER 10: THE COMPETITIVE EFFECT OF SCHOOL CHOICE POLICIES ON PUBLIC SCHOOL PERFORMANCE

1.   So far, very little research has appeared on the competitive impacts of
     homeschooling or "cyber" schools. Intradistrict choice programs typically
     elicit only minor competitive effects, since they do not alter the funding
     available to district administrators. Interdistrict open enrollment policies
     carry stronger financial incentives than intradistrict choice, but their com-
     petitive impacts on TPS outcomes have received very little scholarly atten-
     tion.

2.   Hsieh, C. T., & Urquiola, M. (2003). *When schools compete, how do they com-
     pete? An assessment of Chile's nationwide school voucher program* (NBER Work-
     ing Paper No. 10008). Cambridge, MA: National Bureau of Economic
     Research.

     Ladd, H. F. (2002). School vouchers: A critical view. *Journal of Economic Per-
     spectives, 16*(4), 3-24.

3.   Fiske, E. B., & Ladd, H. F. (2000). *When schools compete: A cautionary tale*. Washington, DC: Brookings Institution Press.

     For a review of research see Chapter Four of this volume, "Who Chooses Schools, and Why?" by Natalie Lacireno-Paquet and Charleen Brantley.

4.   Ni, Y., & Arsen, D. (2010). The competitive effects of charter schools on public school districts. In C. A Lubienski & P.C. Weitzel (Eds.), *The charter school experiment: Expectations, Evidence, And Implications*. Cambridge, MA: Harvard Education Press.

5.   Goldhaber, D., Guin, K., Henig, J. R., Hess, F. M., & Weiss, J. A. (2005). How school choice affects students who do not choose. In J. R. Betts & T. Loveless (Eds.), *Getting choice right: Ensuring equity and efficiency in education policy* (pp. 101-129). Washington, DC: Brookings Institution Press.

6.   Arsen, D., Plank, D., & Sykes, G. (1999). *School choice policies in Michigan: The rules matter*. East Lansing, MI: Michigan State University.

7.   Hastings, J. S., & Weinstein, J. M. (2007). *Information, school choice, and academic achievement: Evidence from two experiments* (NBER Working Paper No. 13623). Cambridge, MA: National Bureau of Economic Research.

8.   Goldhaber, Guin, Henig, Hess, & Weiss, 2005 (see note 5).

9.   Hoxby, C. M. (Ed.). (2003). School choice and school productivity: Could school choice be a tide that lifts all boats? In *The economics of school choice* (pp. 287-342). Chicago, IL: University of Chicago Press.

10. Fixed-effect transformations eliminate most attributes of public schools and communities that influence the likelihood of choice schools setting up, including unobserved attributes. Use of fixed-effect methods, however, typically requires researchers to have several years of data for their sample schools. Instrumental variable (IV) estimators represent an alternative strategy. Suitable instrumental variables should be related to the degree of choice competition, but have no impact on unexplained student achievement (i.e., they should be external to student achievement). However, truly external IVs are very hard to find in school choice research. Using weak IVs that do not satisfy both assumptions is problematic, since a slight correlation between the IVs and the measure of choice competition could cause larger bias than estimates using no IVs.

11. Belfield, C. R., & Levin, H. M. (2002). The effects of competition on educational outcomes: A review of the US evidence. *Review of Educational Research, 72*, 279-341.

12. Belfield & Levin, 2002 (see note 11).

13. In 2006, the Florida Supreme Court ruled the private school option of the Opportunity Scholarship Program unconstitutional. Students assigned to a failing school are no longer offered the opportunity to enroll in a private school. However, they can still attend a higher-performing public school.

In addition, there are two other voucher programs in Florida: the McKay Scholarship voucher program targeted to the disable students that started in 1998, and the Florida Tax Credit (FTC) Scholarship program, which started in the 2002-03. The law provides tax credits for contributions to nonprofit scholarship funding organizations that award scholarships to students with limited financial resources. So far, most research has focused on the OSP. Evidence on the effects of the other two voucher programs is very limited.

14. Hoxby, 2003 (see note 9).

15. Ladd, H. F. (2003). Comment on Caroline M. Hoxby: School choice and school competition: Evidence from the United States. *Swedish Economic Policy Review, 10*, 67-76.

16. Chakrabarti, R. (2008). Can increasing private school participation and monetary loss in a voucher program affect public school performance? Evidence from Milwaukee. *Journal of Public Economics, 92*(5-6), 1371-1393.

17. Carnoy, M., Adamson, F., Chudgar, A., Luschei, T. F., & Witte, J. F. (2007). *Vouchers and public school performance: A case study of the Milwaukee parental choice program*, 2. Washington, DC: Economic Policy Institute.

18. Greene, J. P. (2001). *An evaluation of the Florida A-Plus accountability and school choice program*. New York, NY: Manhattan Institute for Policy Research, Center for Civic Innovation.

     Greene, J. P. & Winters, M. A. (2003). *When schools compete: The effects of vouchers on Florida public school achievement* (Education Working Paper No. 2). New York, NY: Manhattan Institute for Policy Research, Center for Civic Innovation.

19. Camilli, G., & Bulkley, K. (2001). Critique of 'An Evaluation of the Florida A-Plus Accountability and School Choice Program.' *Education Policy Analysis Archives, 9*(7).

     Chakrabarti, 2008 (see note 16).

20. Chakrabarti, R. (2003). *Impact of voucher design on public school performance: Evidence from Florida and Milwaukee voucher programs*. Ithaca, NY: Cornell University.

21. Figlio, D. N., & Rouse, C. (2006). Do accountability and voucher threats improve low-performing schools? *Journal of Public Economics, 90*(1-2), 239-255.

22. Carnoy, M. (2001). *School vouchers: Examining the evidence*. Washington, DC: Economic Policy Institute.

     Ladd, 2002 (see note 2).

23. Greene, J. P., & Winters, M. A. (2006). *An evaluation of the effect of D.C.'s voucher program on public school achievement and racial integration after one year* (No. SCDP-06-01). New York, NY: Manhattan Institute for Policy Research.

24. Sass, T. (2006). Charter schools and student achievement in Florida. *Education Finance and Policy, 1*(1), 91-122.

25. Zimmer, R., & Buddin, R. (2009). Is charter school competition in California improving the performance of traditional public schools? *Public Administration Review, 69*(5), 831-845.

26. Carr, M., & Ritter, G. (2007). *Measuring the competitive effect of charter schools on student achievement in Ohio's traditional public schools* (Occasional paper No. 146). New York, NY: National Center for the Study of Privatization, Teachers College, Columbia University.

27. Holmes, G. M., DeSimone, J., & Rupp, N. (2003). *Does school choice increase school quality?* (NBER working paper no. W9683). Cambridge, MA: National Bureau of Economic Research

28. Bifulco, R., & Ladd, H. F. (2006). The impacts of charter schools on student achievement: Evidence from North Carolina. *Education Finance and Policy, 1*(1), 50-89.

29. Hoxby, 2003 (see note 9).

30. Bettinger, E. (2005). The effect of charter schools on charter students and public schools. *Economics of Education Review, 24*(2), 133-147.

31. Ni, Y. (2009). The impact of charter schools on the efficiency of traditional public schools: Evidence from Michigan. *Economics of Education Review, 28*(5), 571-584.

32. Bohte, J. (2004). Examining the impact of charter schools on performance in traditional public schools. *The Policy Studies Journal, 32*(4), 501-520.

33. Booker, K., Gilpatric, S., Gronberg, T., & Jansen, D. (2008). The effect of charter schools on traditional public school students in Texas: Are children who stay behind left behind? *Journal of Urban Economics, 64*(1), 123-145.

34. Imberman, S. A. (2008). *The effect of charters schools on non-charter students: An instrumental variables approach* (No. 149). New York, NY: National Center for the Study of Privatization, Teachers College, Columbia University.

35. Bifulco & Ladd, 2006 (see note 28).

     Sass, 2006 (see note 24).

36. While it is reasonable to take schools as the unit of analysis because the hypothesized competitive effect focuses on the organizational response of schools, student-level data are ideal to fully account for the student self-selection problem.

37. Filer, R., & Munich, D. (2003). Public support for private schools in post-communist central Europe: Czech and Hungarian experiences. In D. Plank & G. Sykes (Eds.), *Choosing choice: School choice policies in international perspective* (pp. 196-222). New York, NY: Teachers College Press.

38. Gibbons, S., Machin, S., & Silva, O. (2006). *Choice, competition and pupil achievement* (No. 129). New York, NY: National Center for the Study of Privatization, Teachers College, Columbia University.

39. Carnoy, M., & McEwan, P. (2003). Does privatization improve education? The case of Chile's national voucher plan. In D. Plank & G. Sykes (Eds.), *Choosing choice: School choice policies in international perspective* (pp. 24-44). New York, NY: Teachers College Press.

    Hsieh & Urquiola, 2003 (see note 2).

40. Ladd, H. F., & Fiske, E. B. (2003). Does competition improve teaching and learning? Evidence from New Zealand. *Educational Evaluation and Policy Analysis, 25*(1), 97-112.

41. Ladd, H. F., & Fiske, E. B. (2001).The uneven playing field of school choice: Evidence from New Zealand. *Journal of Policy Analysis and Management, 20*(1), 42-63.

    McEwan, P. J. (2004). The potential impact of vouchers. *Peabody Journal of Education, 79*(3), 57-80.

42. Hess, F. M. (2002). *Revolution at the margins: The impact of competition on urban school systems.* Washington, DC: Brookings Institution Press.

    Hess, F. M., Maranto, R., & Milliman, S. (2001) Small districts in big trouble: How four Arizona school systems responded to charter competition. *Teachers College Record, 103*(6), 1102-1124.

    Wells, A.S. (1998). *Beyond the rhetoric of charter school reform: A study of ten California school districts.* Los Angeles, CA: UCLA Charter School Study.

43. Arsen, Plank, & Sykes, 1999 (see note 6).

    Rofes, E. (1998). *How are school districts responding to charter laws and charter schools? A study of eight states and the District of Columbia.* Berkeley, CA: Policy Analysis for California Education.

44. Hess, Maranto, & Milliman, 2001 (see note 42).

45. Arsen, Plank, & Sykes, 1999 (see note 6).

    Bulkley, K., & Fisler, J. (2003). A decade of charter schools: From theory to practice. *Educational Policy, 17*(3), 317-342.

    Hess, 2002 (see note 42).

Lubienski, C. (2003). Innovation in education markets: Theory and evidence on the impact of competition and choice in charter schools. *American Educational Research Journal, 40*(2), 394-443.

46. Berends, M., Goldring, E., Stein, M.,& Cravens, X. (2010). Instructional conditions in charter schools and students' mathematics achievement gains. *American Journal of Education, 116,* 303-335.

Zimmer, R., & Buddin, R. (2007). Getting inside the black box: Examining how the operation of charter school affects performance. *Peabody Journal of Education, 82*(2-3), 231-273.

47. Belfield & Levin, 2002 (see note 11).

48. Levin, H. M. (1998). Educational vouchers: Effectiveness, choice, and costs. *Journal of Policy Analysis and Management, 17*(3), 373-392.

Levin, H. M. (2002, Fall). A comprehensive framework for evaluating educational vouchers. *Educational Evaluation and Policy Analysis, 24*(3), 159-174.

CHAPTER 11: THE IMPACT OF SCHOOL CHOICE REFORMS ON STUDENT ACHIEVEMENT

1. This study is the fourth time we have conducted such an synthesis of evidence on school choice. The first two times we conducted this analysis (Miron & Nelson, 2001; and Miron & Nelson, 2003) we focused on only charter schools. In 2008, we expanded our synthesis of evidence to cover diverse forms of school choice (see Miron, Evergreen, & Urschel, 2008). The current study considers an additional 60 studies that were added since we last updated this analysis in 2008.

Miron, G., & Nelson, C. (2001) *Student academic achievement in charter schools: What we know and why we know so little* (occasional paper No. 41). New York, NY: National Center for the Study of Privatization in Education, Teachers College, Columbia University. Retrieved May 31, 2012, from http://ncspe.org/publications_files/590_OP41.pdf

Miron, G., & Nelson, C. (2004). Student achievement in charter schools. In K. Bulkley & P. Wohlstetter (Eds.), *Taking account of charter schools* (pp. 161-175). New York, NY: Teachers College Press.

Miron, G., Evergreen, S., & Urschel, J. L. (2008). *The impact of school choice reforms on student achievement.* Boulder, CO: National Education Policy Center. Retrieved June 20, 2011, from http://epsl.asu.edu/epru/documents/EPSL-0803-262-EPRU.pdf

2. Inasmuch as many school choice programs have schools that are oversubscribed and regulations that require students to be selected at random from their waiting lists, randomized experiments ought to be possible, in principle. However, waiting lists often are not audited over time and are

insufficient for the construction of a good randomized experiment since they are often out of date, contain an accumulation of names over a number of years, and often cannot be readily produced when requested.

3.   Readers should bear in mind that our 5-point scale might understate the variation in impacts found across studies.

4.   See, e.g., Light, R., & Pillemer, D. (1984). *Summing up: The science of reviewing research*. Cambridge, MA: Harvard University Press.

Hedges, L., & Olkin, I. (1985). *Statistical methods for meta-analysis*. Orlando, FL: Academic Press.

5.   Scriven, M. (1981). The "weight and sum" methodology. *American Journal of Evaluation, 2*(1), 85-90.

6.   A large comprehensive study (3 points) requires more than 25 schools (school as unit of analysis) OR more than 1,000 students (if student is unit of analysis). A moderately comprehensive (2 points) requires between 11 and 25 schools, *or* 121-1,000 students. A small study (1 point) is defined by 5-10 schools *or* 50-120 students, and a very small study (0 points) considers 2-4 schools *or* fewer than 50 students. Studies with only one school are not included.

7.   Replication and verification are facilitated when there is a complete technical report. In interpreting findings, we generally perceive studies with comprehensive technical reports to be more credible. Some studies are most rigorous with randomized assignment, but they lose points due to the completeness of the technical report. It was surprising to us to see how many studies had weak or incomplete technical reports. Some of these had sparse details on methods and only reported on a restricted range of findings. Common in the weaker technical reports was that no mention was made of caveats or limitations that readers should taken into consideration.

8.   Miron & Nelson, 2004 (see note 1.)

9.   The scores assigned in the weighting scheme have also benefited from input from colleagues at the Western Michigan University Evaluation Center, where the weighting scheme has been vetted and opened up to public input in connection with two presentations (one in 2005 and one in 2008). An illustration of how the scores are calculated and assigned can be seen in the appendices for this chapter, which are available on line at http://nepc.colorado.edu/files/Appendices_A-D.pdf.

10. Friedman, M. (1955). The role of government in education. In R. O. Solo (Ed.), *Economics and the public interest* (pp. 123-144). New Brunswick, NJ: Rutgers University Press.

11. We have not included research on the earliest voucher pilot program from Alum Rock, California, which was started in 1972 because of their compli-

cations in implementing the program and also because the published research on this program did not yield specific results regarding the academic achievement of students taking advantage of the voucher.

12. Zimmer & Bettinger also confirm that they could not find any research on tuition or education tax credits and student achievement.

Zimmer, R., & Bettinger, E. (2008). Beyond the rhetoric: Surveying the evidence on vouchers and tax credits. In H.F. Ladd & E.B. Fiske (Eds.), *Handbook of research in education finance and policy* (pp. 447-466). New York, NY: Routledge.

13. The full list of references for Figure 11.1 are included below. Most of the studies are city or district specific. Further details about the quality and impact rating for each study can be seen in the appendices for this chapter which are available on-line at http://nepc.colorado.edu/files/Appendices_A-D.pdf

C1 [Cleveland]—Greene, J. P., Howell, W. G., & Peterson, P. E. (1999). *An evaluation of the Cleveland voucher program after two years.* Cambridge, MA: Harvard University, Program on Education Policy and Governance.

C2 [Cleveland]—Metcalf, K. K., Legan, N. A., Paul, K. M., & Boone, W. J. (2004, October). *Evaluation of the Cleveland scholarship and tutoring program: Technical report 1998-2003.* Bloomington, IN: Indiana University, School of Education.

C3 [Cleveland]—Belfield, C. (2006). *The evidence on education vouchers: An application to the Cleveland Scholarship and Tutoring Program* (Occasional Paper 112). New York, NY: National Center for the Study of Privatization, Teachers College, Columbia University.

C4 [Cleveland]—Plucker, J., Muller, P., Hansen, J., Ravert, R., & Makel, M. (2006). *Evaluation of the Cleveland Scholarship and Tutoring Program: Technical report 1998-2004.* Bloomington, IN: Center for Evaluation and Education Policy.

D [Dayton]—West, M.R., Peterson, P.E., & Campbell, D.E. (2001, August). *School choice in Dayton, Ohio after two years: An evaluation of the Parents Advancing Choice in Education scholarship program.* Cambridge, MA: Program on Education Policy and Governance, Harvard University

D-DC-NY [Dayton, District of Columbia, & New York]—Howell, W. G., Wolf, P. J., Campbell, D. E., & Peterson, P. E. (2002). School vouchers and academic performance: Results from three randomized field trials. *Journal of Policy Analysis and Management, 21*(2), 191-217.

DC1 [District of Columbia]—Wolf, P., Gutmann, B., Puma, M., Rizzo, L., & Eissa, N. (2007). *Evaluation of the DC Opportunity Scholarship Program: Impacts after one year.* Washington, DC: Institute of Education Sciences, U.S. Department of Education.

DC2 [District of Columbia]—Wolf, P., Gutmann, B., Puma, M., Kisida, B., Rizzo, L., Eissa, N., & Carr, M. (2010, June). *Evaluation of the DC Opportunity Scholarship Program*. Washington, DC: U.S. Department of Education (NCEE 2010-4018).

M1 [Milwaukee]—Rouse, C. (1998). Private school vouchers and student achievement: An evaluation of the Milwaukee Parental Choice Program. *Quarterly Journal of Economics, 113*(2), 553-602.

M2 [Milwaukee]—Witte, J. F. (1998). The Milwaukee voucher experiment. *Educational Evaluation and Policy Analysis, 20*(4), 229-251.

M3 [Milwaukee]—Greene, J. P., Peterson, P. E., & Du, J. (1999). Effectiveness of school choice: The Milwaukee experiment. *Education and Urban Society, 31*, 190-213.

M4 [Milwaukee]—Lamarche, C. (2008). Private school vouchers and student achievement: A fixed effects quantile regression evaluation. *Labour Economics, 15*, 575-590.

M5 [Milwaukee]—Cowen, J. M., Fleming, D. J., Witte, J. F., & Wolf, P. J. (2011, March). *Student attainment and the Milwaukee Parental Choice Program*. Fayetteville, AR: School Choice Demonstration Project.

NY1 [New York]—Mayer, D. P., Peterson, P. E., Myers, D. E., Tuttle, C. C., & Howell, W. G. (2002). *School choice in New York City after three years: An evaluation of the school choice scholarships program* (No. 8404-045). Princeton, NJ: Mathematica Policy Research.

NY2 [New York]—Krueger, A.B., & Zhu, P. (2004). Another look at the New York City voucher experiment. *American Behavioral Scientist, 47*(5), 658-698.

14. A number of annual reports were issued to the Wisconsin State Legislature, but because these analyses were superseded by subsequent reports, we have only considered the most recent analysis, which was summarized in a refereed article published by John Witte in 1998. See

    Witte, J. F. (1998). The Milwaukee voucher experiment. *Educational Evaluation and Policy Analysis, 20*(4), 229-251.

15. Witte, J. F., 1998 (see note 14),

16. Greene, J. P., Peterson, P. E., & Du, J. (1999). Effectiveness of school choice: The Milwaukee experiment. *Education and Urban Society, 31*, 190-213.

17. Witte, J. F. (1999). The Milwaukee voucher experiment: The good, the bad and the ugly. *Phi Delta Kappan, 81*, 59-64.

18. Rouse, C. (1998). Private school vouchers and student achievement: An evaluation of the Milwaukee Parental Choice Program. *Quarterly Journal OF Economics, 113*(2), 553-602.

19.   Cowen, J. M., Fleming, D. J., Witte, J. F., & Wolf, P. J. (2011, March). *Student attainment and the Milwaukee Parental Choice Program*. Fayetteville, AR: School Choice Demonstration Project.

20.   Metcalf, K. K., Legan, N. A., Paul, K. M., & Boone, W. J. (2004, October). *Evaluation of the Cleveland scholarship and tutoring program: Technical report 1998-2003*. Bloomington, IN: Indiana Center for Evaluation & Education, Indiana University.

21.   Plucker, J., Muller, P., Hansen, J., Ravert, R., & Makel, M. (2006). *Evaluation of the Cleveland scholarship and tutoring program: Technical report 1998-2004*. Bloomington, IN: Center for Evaluation and Education Policy.

22.   Belfield, C. (2006). *The evidence on education vouchers: An application to the Cleveland Scholarship and Tutoring Program* (Occasional paper 112). New York, NY: National Center for the Study of Privatization, Teachers College, Columbia University.

23.   Greene, J. P., Howell, W. G., & Peterson, P. E. (1997). *An evaluation of the Cleveland scholarship program*. Cambridge, MA: Program in Education Policy and Governance, Harvard University

24.   Greene, J. P., Howell, W. G., & Peterson, P. E. (1999). *An evaluation of the Cleveland voucher program after two years*. Cambridge, MA: Harvard University, Program on Education Policy and Governance.

25.   Wolf, P., Gutmann, B., Puma, M., Kisida, B., Rizzo, L., Eissa, N., & Carr, M. (2010, June). *Evaluation of the DC Opportunity Scholarship Program* (NCEE 2010-4018). Washington, DC: U.S. Department of Education.

26.   Wolf, P. J., Howell, W. G., & Peterson, P. E. (2000). *School choice in Washington, D.C.: An evaluation after one year*. Cambridge, MA: Harvard University, Program on Education Policy and Governance.

27.   Mayer, D. P., Peterson, P. E., Myers, D. E., Tuttle, C. C., & Howell, W. G. (2002). *School choice in New York City after three years: An evaluation of the school choice scholarships program* (No. 8404-045). New York, NY: Mathematica Policy Research.

28.   Krueger, A., & Zhu, P. (2004).Another look at the New York City school voucher experiment. *American Behavioral Scientist, 47,* 658-698.

29.   Peterson, P. E., West, M. R., & Campbell, D. C. (2001). *School choice in Dayton, Ohio after two years: An evaluation of the Parents Advancing Choice in Education Scholarship Program*. Cambridge, MA: Harvard University, Program on Education Policy and Governance Occasional Paper, PEPG 01-04.

30.   Based on his extensive review of the research evidence on school vouchers, Carnoy concluded that "vouchers' effects on student achievement are almost certainly smaller than claimed by provoucher researchers. Although programs in many cities were designed to be like randomized-trial medical experiments—with high validity and reliability—common problems in

implementation may have compromised validity and produced misleading results. Moreover, the results are marked by broad inconsistencies across grades, academic subjects, and racial groups. See

Carnoy, M. (2001). *School vouchers: Examining the evidence.* Washington, DC: Economic Policy Institute.

31. Ray, B. D. (2008). *Home centered learning annotated bibliography* (17th ed). Salem, OR: National Home Education Research Institute.

32. Several studies on home schooling have pointed to the inadequacy of standardized testing in measuring the success of home-schooled students, e.g.,

Meehan, N. & Stephenson, S. (1994). *Homeschooling in the United States; A review of recent literature.* (ERIC Document Reproduction Service No. ED 424 922).

Burns, J. (1999). *The correlational relationship between homeschooling demographics and high test scores.* (ERIC Document Reproduction Service No. ED 439 141).

Collom, E. (2005). The ins and outs of homeschooling: The determinants of parental motivations and student achievement. *Education and Urban Society, 37*(3), 307-335.

Ray, B. D. (2000). Home schooling: The ameliorator of negative influence on learning? *Peabody Journal of Education, 75*(1&2), 71-106.

Rudner, L. M. (1999). Scholastic achievement and demographic characteristics of home school students in 1998. *Education Policy Analysis Archives, 7*(8). (ERIC Document Reproduction Service No. ED 435 709)

Therefore, a portion of the field has focused on alternative measures of student success, such as first year college GPA (Jones, P., & Gloeckner, G. [2004]. First-year college performance: A study of home school graduates and traditional school graduates. *The Journal of College Admission, 183,* 17-20; Sutton, J. P. & Galloway, R. S. [2000]. College success of students from three high school settings. *Journal of Research and Development in Education, 33*(3), 137-146); perceptions of college admissions officers (Ray, B. D. [2001]. *Home education in Ohio: Family characteristics, academic achievement, social and civic activities, and college admissions officers' thoughts.* Salem, OR: National Home Education Research Institute); self-confidence (Sheffer, S. [1995]. *A sense of self: Listening to homeschooled adolescent girls.* Portsmouth, NH: Boynton/Cook); leadership skills (Montgomery, L. R. [1989]. The effect of home schooling on the leadership skills of home schooled students. *Home School Researcher, 5*(1) 1-10); and adulthood characteristics (Ray, B. D. [2004]. Homeschoolers on to college: What research shows us. *The Journal of College Admission, 185,* 5-11; Knowles, J. G., & Muchmore, J. A. [1995]. Yep! We're grown-up home-school kids—And we're doing just fine, thank you! *Journal of Research on Christian Education, 4*(1), 35-56).

334 NOTES and REFERENCES

33. State department reports fell into this category. We saw Arizona Department of Education (1989). *Students taught at home: 1989 average grade equivalents*; North Carolina Division of Non-Public Education (1989). *North Carolina home school nationally standardized achievement test results 88-89 school term*; Arkansas Department of Education (1988); and Tennessee Department of Education (1987). Home school student test results: 1986 and 1987. These were reported often but we could not locate those reports anywhere. The major researcher citing these studies, Klicka, also did not have them any longer (Ridley, V.N., legal assistant to Christopher J. Klicka, Esq., personal communication, December 18, 2007).

34. Some examples are Rakestraw, J. F. (1987). *An analysis of home schooling for elementary school-age children in Alabama* (Unpublished doctoral thesis). University of Alabama, Tuscaloosa.

    Delahooke, M. M. (1986). *Home educated children's social/emotional adjustment and academic achievement: A comparative study* (doctoral dissertation). Los Angeles: California School of Professional Psychology.

    Tipton, M. (1990). Untitled, unpublished MA thesis for Antioch University.

35. The full list of the references for Figure 11.2 are included below. Most of the studies are state-specific. These are identified by their 2 letter state abbreviation. Studies that are national or cover more than one state are identified as "US." Further details about the quality and impact rating for each study can be seen in the appendices for this chapter which are available on-line at http://nepc.colorado.edu/files/Appendices_A-D.pdf

    AL—Rakestraw, J. (1988, December). Home schooling in Alabama. *Home School Researcher, 4*(4), 1-6.

    CA—Delahooke, M. M. (1986).Home educated children's social/emotional adjustment and academic achievement: A comparative study. *Dissertation Abstracts International, 47* (2), 475A. (UMI No. 8608759).

    CO—Jones, P., & Gloeckner, G. (2004). First year college performance: A study of home school graduates and traditional school graduates. *The Journal of College Admission, 183,* 17-20.

    GA—Gray, D. W. (1998). *A study of the academic achievements of home-schooled students who have matriculated into post-secondary institutions.* (Doctoral dissertation, University of Florida, Sarasota, 1998). *Dissertation Abstracts International, 59*(021).

    IL—Frost, E. A. (1987). A descriptive study of the academic achievement of selected elementary school-aged children educated at home in five Illinois counties. (Doctoral dissertation, Northern Illinois University, 1987). *Dissertation Abstracts International, 48*(7), 1589A.

KS—Duvall, S. F., Delquadri, J. C., & Ward, D. L. (2004). A preliminary investigation of the effectiveness of homeschool instructional environments for students with attention-deficit/hyperactivity disorder. *School Psychology Review, 33*(1), 140-158.

NC—Boulter, L. T. (1999). *Academic achievement in home school education.* Salisbury, NC: Catawba College.

SC– Galloway, R. A. S. (1995, April). *Home schooled adults: Are they ready for college?* Paper presented at the annual meeting of the American Educational Research Association, San Francisco, CA.

TN—Holder, M. A. (2001).*Academic achievement and socialization of college students who were homeschooled.* Unpublished doctoral dissertation, The University of Memphis. (UMI No. 3829894).

US1—Ray, B. D. (1990). *A nationwide study of home education: Family characteristics, legal matters, and student achievement.* Salem, OR: National Home Education Research Institute.

US2—Ray, B. D. (1997). *Strengths of their own: Home schoolers across America academic achievement, family characteristics, and longitudinal traits.* Salem, OR: National Home Education Research Institute.

US3—Rudner, L. M. (1999). Scholastic achievement and demographic characteristics of home school students in 1998. *Education Policy Analysis Archives, 7*(8), 1-33.

US4—Belfield, C. R. (2005). Home-schoolers: How well do they perform on the SAT for college admissions? In B.S. Cooper (Ed.), *Home schooling in full view: A reader* (pp. 167-177). Charlotte, NC: Information Age.

US5—Clemente, D. F. (2006). *Academic achievement and college aptitude in homeschooled high school students compared to their private-schooled and public-schooled counterparts* (UMI No. 3218862). Unpublished doctoral dissertation, Regent University, Virginia Beach.

US6—Qaqish, B. (2007). An analysis of homeschooled and non-homeschooled students' performance on an ACT mathematics achievement test. *Home School Researcher, 17*(2), 1-12.

US7—Ray, B. D. (2010). Academic achievement and demographic traits of homeschool students: A nationwide study. *Academic Leadership: The Online Journal, 8*(1).

WA1—Richman, H. B., Girten, W., & Snyder, J. (1990). Academic achievement and its relationship to selected variables. *Home School Researcher, 6*(4), 9-16.

WA2—Wartes, J. (1990). Recent results from the Washington homeschool research project. *Home School Researcher, 6*(4), 1-7.

US3—Witt, V. L. (2005). A comparison and descriptive analysis of home-school reading and vocabulary scores to the national average. *Dissertation Abstracts International, 65*(01), 1696. (UMI No. 3174333).

36.   Ray, B. D. (1997). *Strengths of their own: Home schoolers across America—Academic achievement, family characteristics, and longitudinal traits.* Salem, OR: National Home Education Research Institute.

Ray, 2000 (see note 32).

37.   Further widely cited reports by Cisek, G. J. (1991). Alternative assessments: Promises and problems for home-based education policy. *Home School Reseacher, 7*(4), 13-21; Lyn Boulter from Boulter, L., & Macaluso, K. (1994). Individualized assessment of home schooling education. *Home School Researcher, 10*(2), 1-6; Rhonda Galloway from Galloway, R. A., & Sutton, J. P. (1995). Home schooled and conventionally schooled high school graduates: A comparison of aptitude for and achievement in college English. *Home School Researcher, 11*(1), 1-9; Wartes, J. (1987). Report from the 1986 home school testing and other descriptive information about Washington's home schoolers: A summary. *Home School Researcher, 3*(1), 1-4. Other well-known homeschool researchers not studying academic achievement also made their public reputation known through *Home School Researcher*, such as Marlee Mayberry and J. Gary Knowles. In this analysis, Qadish (2007) is sourced from *Home School Researcher.*

38.   Rudner, 1999 (see note 32).

39.   Welner, K. M., & Welner, K.G. (1999). Contextualizing homeschooling data: A response to Rudner. *Education Policy Analysis Archives, 7*(13). (ERIC Document Reproduction Service No. EJ 588 923).

40.   Galloway, R. A. S. (1995, April). *Home schooled adults: Are they ready for college?* Paper presented at the Annual Meeting of the American Educational Research Association, San Francisco, CA.

41.   Cooper, B. S., & Sureau, J. (2007). The politics of homeschooling. *Educational Policy, 21*(1), 110-131.

Welner & Welner, 1999 (see note 39).

McDowell, S. A., Sanchez, A. R. & Jones, S. S. (2000). Participation and perception: Looking at home schooling through a multicultural lens. *Peabody Journal of Education, 75*(1&2), 124-146.

42.   In this section, we use the words "magnet schools" consistently, but we intend that term to also include interdistrict and intradistrict forms of school choice. We know the terms are not synonymous, but to use each term individually throughout the section would be laborious for the reader. If we were to put each of these forms of school choice into their own sections, the sections would be so small as to be not worth reporting. Finally,

intradistrict choice also goes by the name of "open enrollment" in the research literature, and that is also included in this section.

43.   For a discussion of this aspect of magnet schooling, see

Fuller, B., Burr, E., Huerta, L., Puryear, S., & Wezler, E. (1999). *School choice: Abundant hopes, scarce evidence of results*. Berkeley, CA: Policy Analysis for California Education.

44.   The full list of the references for Figure 11.3 are included below. Most of the studies are state-specific. These are identified by their 2 letter state abbreviation. Many of the studies are for unnamed schools districts. Studies that are national or cover more than one state are identified as "US". Further details about the quality and impact rating for each study can be seen in the appendices for this chapter which are available on-line at http://nepc.colorado.edu/files/Appendices_A-D.pdf

AZ [Arizona]—Strogen, J. (2007). *The implications of open enrollment on student achievement, parent leadership, and demographics in elementary schools.* Unpublished doctoral dissertation, Arizona State University.

CA [Arizona]—Goldschmidt, P., & Martinez-Fernandez, J. F. (2004, December). *The relationship between school quality and the probability of passing standards-based high-stakes performance assessments.* Los Angeles, CA: National Center for Research on Evaluation, Standards, and Student Testing, University of California, Los Angeles.

CT1 [Connecticut]—Beaudin, B. (2003). *Interdistrict magnet schools and magnet programs in Connecticut: An evaluation report.* Hartford, CT: Connecticut State Department of Education, Division of Evaluation and Research.

CT2 [Connecticut]—Bilfulco, R., Cobb, C. D., & Bell, C. (2009). Can interdistrict choice boost student achievement? The case of Connecticut's interdistrict magnet school program. *Educational Evaluation and Policy Analysis, 31*(4), 323-345.

CT3 [Connecticut]—Esposito, C. L., & Cobb, C. D. (2008). *Estimating the school level effects of choice on academic achievement in Connecticut's magnet, technical and charter schools.* New York, NY: National Center for the Study of Privatization, Teachers College, Columbia University.

M [Unnamed Midwestern district]—Archbald, D. (1995). A longitudinal cohort analysis of achievement among magnet students, neighborhood school students, and transfer students. *Journal of Research and Development in Education, 28*(5), 161-169.

MD1 [Maryland]—Larson, J. C., & Allen, B. A. (1988). *A microscope on magnet schools: 1983-1986. Volume 2: Pupil and parent outcomes.* Rockville, MD: Montgomery County Public Schools, Department of Educational Accountability.

MD2 [Maryland]—Adcock, E. P., & Phillips, G. W. (2000, April). *Account-ability evaluation of magnet school programs: A value-added model approach.* Paper presented at the Annual Meeting of the American Educational Research Association, New Orleans, LA.

MD3 [Maryland]—Yu, N Y., Li, Y. H., Tompkins, L. J., & Modarresi, S. (2005, April). *Using the multiple-matched-sample and statistical controls to exam-ine the effects of magnet school programs on the reading and mathematics perfor-mance of students.* Paper presented at the annual meeting of the American Educational Research Association, Montreal, CA.

NC [North Carolina]—Okpala, C. O., Bell, G. C., & Tuprak, K. (2007). A comparative study of student achievement in traditional schools and schools of choice in North Carolina. *Urban Education, 42*(4), 313-325.

NYC1 [New York City]—Eagle, N., & Ridenour, G. (1969). Differences in academic performance and report card grades between "open enrollment" and "matched home" elementary school children, after one and two years. *Urban Education, 4*, 115-123.

NYC2 [New York City]—Crain, R. L., Allen, A., Thaler, R., Sullivan, D., Zellman, G., Little, J. W., & Quigley, D. D. (1992). *The effects of academic career magnet education on high schools and their graduates.* Berkeley, CA: NCRVE.

NYC3 [New York City]—Crain, R. L., Heebner, A. L., & Si, Y. (1992). *The effectiveness of New York City's career magnet schools: An evaluation of ninth grade performance using an experimental design.* Berkeley, CA: National Center for Research in Vocational Education.

NYC4 [New York City]—Heebner, A. L. (1995). The impact of career mag-net high schools: Experimental and qualitative evidence. *Journal of Voca-tional Education Research, 20*(2), 27-35.

SanD [San Diego]—Betts, J. R., Rice, L. A., Zau, A. C., Tang, Y. E., & Koe-del, C. R. (2006). *Does school choice work? Effects on student integration and achievement.* San Francisco, CA: Public Policy Institute of California.

S1 [UnnamedSouthern district]—Dickson, B. L., Pinchback, C. L., & Ken-nedy, R. L. (2000). Academic achievement and magnet schools. *Research in the Schools, 7*(1), 11-17.

S2 [UnnamedSouthern district]—Ballou, D., Goldring, E., & Liu, K. (2006). *Magnet schools and student achievement.* New York, NY: National Cen-ter for the Study of Privatization, Teachers College, Columbia University.

S3 [UnnamedSouthern district]—Ballou, D. (2007). *Magnet schools and peers: Effects on mathematics achievement.* Unpublished paper. Retrieved April 24, 2011, from http://www.eric.ed.gov/ (ED504971)

TN [Tennessee]—Institute for Assessment and Evaluation. (2006). *Knox County magnet schools evaluation.* Knoxville: Author, University of Tennessee.

US1 [national or multistate]—Blank, R. K., Dentler, R. A., Baltzell, D. C., & Chabotar, D. (1983). *Survey of magnet schools: Analyzing a model for quality integrated education.* Washington DC: U.S. Department of Education.

US2 [national or multistate]—Gamoran, A. (1996). Student achievement in public magnet, public comprehensive, and private city high schools. *Education Evaluation and Policy Analysis, 18*(1), 1-18.

US3 [national or multistate]—Lee, D., Coladarci, T., & Donaldson, G. A., Jr. (1996, April). *Effects of school choice on academic commitment and achievement: Evidence from NELS: 88.* Paper presented at the annual meeting of the American Educational Research Association, New York, NY.

US4 [national or multistate]—Christenson, B., Eaton, M., Garet, M. S., Miller, L. C., Hikawa, H., & DuBois, P. (2003). *Evaluation of the magnet schools assistance program, 1998 grantees.* Washington: U. S. Department of Education, Office of the Under Secretary.

US5 [national or multistate]—Archbald, D. A., & Kaplan, D. (2004). Parent choice versus attendance area assignment to schools: Does magnet-based school choice affect NAEP scores? *International Journal of Educational Policy, Research, & Practice, 5*(1), 3-35.

US6 [national or multistate]—Esposito, C. L. (2010). *School type and mathematics achievement: A comparison of secondary schools using the Educational Longitudinal Study of 2002 data set* (Unpublished doctoral dissertation). University of Connecticut.

Unknown district—Engberg, J., Epple, D., Imbrogno, J., Sieg, H., & Zimmer, R. (2011). *Bounding the treatment effects of education programs that have lotteried admission and selective attrition.* Retrieved May 3, 2011, from http://www.ncspe.org/list-papers.php.

45. Bilfulco, R., Cobb, C. D., & Bell, C. (2009). Can interdistrict choice boost student achievement? The case of Connecticut's interdistrict magnet school program. *Educational Evaluation and Policy Analysis, 31*(4), 323-345.

Betts, J. R., Rice, L. A., Zau, A. C., Tang, Y. E., & Koedel, C. R. (2006). *Does school choice work? Effects on student integration and achievement.* San Francisco, CA: Public Policy Institute of California.

Ballou, D., Goldring, E., & Liu, K. (2006). *Magnet schools and student achievement.* New York, NY: National Center for the Study of Privatization, Teachers College, Columbia University.

46. Gamoran, A. (1996). Student achievement in public magnet, public comprehensive, and private city high schools. *Education Evaluation and Policy Analysis, 18*(1), 1-18.

47.   Christenson, B., Eaton, M., Garet, M. S., Miller, L. C., Hikawa, H., & DuBois, P. (2003). *Evaluation of the magnet schools assistance program, 1998 grantees.* Washington, DC: U. S. Department of Education, Office of the Under Secretary.

48.   Gill, B., Timpane, P. M., Ross, K. E., & Brewer, D. J. (2001). *Rhetoric versus reality: What we know and what we need to know about vouchers and charter schools.* Santa Monica, CA: RAND.

49.   Miron & Nelson, 2001 (see note 1).

50.   Miron & Nelson, 2004 (see note 1.).

51.   Center for Research on Education Outcomes. (2009). *Multiple choice: Charter school performance in 16 states.* Palo Alto, CA: Author.

52. The full list of the references for Figure 11.4 are included below. Most of the studies are state-specific. These are identified by their 2 letter state abbreviation. Studies that are national or cover more than one state are identified as "US." Further details about the quality and impact rating for each study can be seen in the appendices for this chapter which are available on-line at http://nepc.colorado.edu/files/Appendices_A-D.pdf.

AZ1—Mulholland, L. (1999, March). *Arizona charter school progress evaluation.* Tempe, AZ: Morrison Institute for Public Policy, Arizona State University.

AZ2—Solmon, L. C., Paark, K., & Garcia, D. (2001). *Does charter school attendance improve test scores? The Arizona results.* Phoenix, AZ: Golwater Institute, Center for Market Based Education.

AZ3—Solmon, L. C., & Goldschmidt, P. (2004). *Comparison of traditional public schools and charter schools on retention, school switching and achievement growth* (Policy Report: No. 192). Phoenix, AZ: Goldwater Institute.

AZ4—Garcia, D. R., Barber, R., & Molnar, A. (2009). Profiting from public education: Education management organizations (EMOs) and student achievement. *Teachers College Record, 11*(5), 1352-1379.

AZ5—Garcia, D. R., Barber, R., & Molnar, A. (2009). Profiting from public education: Education management organizations and student achievement. *Teachers College Record, 111*(5), 1352-1379.

CA1—Raymond, M. E. (2003). *The performance of California charter schools.* Palo Alto, CA: CREDO: Hoover Institution, Stanford University.

CA2—Rogosa, D. (2003). *Student progress in California charter schools, 1999-2002.* Palo Alto, CA: Stanford University.

CA3—Zimmer, R., Buddin, R., Chau, D., Gill, B., Guarino, C., Hamilton, L., … Brewer, D. (2003). *Charter school operation and performance: Evidence from California.* Santa Monica, CA: RAND.

CA4—Zimmer, R., & Buddin, R. (2006). Charter school performance in two large urban districts. *Journal of Urban Economics, 60,* 307-326.

CA5—EdSource. (2007). *California's charter schools: Measuring their performance.* Mountainview, CA: Author.

CA6—Toney, A. N., & Murdock, D. (2008). *Charter school performance in Los Angeles Unified School District: A district and neighborhood matched comparison analysis.* Los Angeles, CA: California Charter Schools Association.

CA7—Woodworth, K. R., David, J. L., Guha, R., Wang, H., & Lopez-Torkos, A. (2008). *San Francisco Bay Area KIPP schools: A study of early implementation and achievement. Final report.* Menlo Park, CA: SRI International.

CA8—Toney, A. N. (2009, January). *A longitudinal analysis of charter school performance in Oakland Unified School District.* Los Angeles, CA: California Charter Schools Association.

CO—Carpenter, D. M., II, & Kafer, K. (2009). *The state of charter schools in Colorado.* Denver, CO: Colorado Department of Education.

CT—Miron, G. (2005). *Evaluating the performance of charter schools in Connecticut: A report commissioned by ConnCAN.* New Haven, CT: Connecticut Coalition for Achievement Now.

DC1—Henig, J. R., Holyoke, T. T., Lacireno-Paquet, N., & Moser, M. (2001, February). *Growing pains: An evaluation of charter schools in the District of Columbia; 1999-2000.* Washington, DC: The Center for Washington Area Studies, The George Washington University.

DC2—Nichols, A., & Ozek, U. (2010). *Public school choice and student achievement in the District of Columbia* (Working paper 53). Washington, DC: National Center for Analysis of Longitudinal Data in Education Research.

DE—Miron, G., Cullen, A., Applegate, E. B., & Farrell, P. (2007). *Evaluation of the Delaware charter school reform: Final report.* Dover, DE: Delaware State Board of Education.

FL1—Crew, R. E., Jr., & Anderson, M. R. (2003). Accountability and performance in charter schools in Florida: A theory-based evaluation. *American Journal of Evaluation, 24,* 189-213.

FL2—Office of Program Policy Analysis & Government Accountability. (2005). *Charter school performance comparable to other public schools; stronger accountability needed.* Tallahassee, FL: Florida Legislature.

FL3– Florida Department of Education. (2006). *Florida's charter schools: A decade of progress.* Tallahassee, FL: Author.

FL4—Sass, T. R. (2006). *Charter schools and student achievement in Florida.* Gainesville, FL: American Education Finance Association.

GA—Plucker, J., Eckes, S., Rapp, K., Ravert, R., Hansen, J., & Trotter, A. (2006, April). *Baseline evaluation of Georgia's charter schools program.* Atlanta, GA: Georgia Department of Education.

HI—Kana'iaupuni, S. M., & Ishibashi, K. (2005). *Hawai'I charter schools: Initial trends and select outcomes for native Hawaiian students.* Honolulu, HI: Kamehameha Schools-PASE.

ID– Ballou, D., Teasley, B., & Zeidner, T. (2008). Charter schools in Idaho. In M. Berends, M. G. Springer, & H. J. Walberg (Eds.), *Charter school outcomes* (pp. 221-241). New York, NY: Erlbaum.

IL1—Nelson, C., & Miron, G. (2002). *The evaluation of the Illinois charter school reform: Final report.* Springfield, IL: Illinois State Board of Education.

IL2—Hoxby, C. M., & Rockoff, J. E. (2004). *The impact of charter schools on student achievement.* Nashville, TN: Working Paper Series, National Center on School Choice.

IL3—Brown, L. & Gutstein, E. (2009). *The charter difference: A comparison of Chicago charter and neighborhood high schools.* Retrieved May 5, 2011, from http://www.uic.edu/educ/ceje

IL4—Chicago Public Schools. (2009). *2007-2008 Charter schools performance report.* Chicago, IL: Author.

IN1—Akey, T., Plucker, J. A., Hansen, J. A., Michael, R., Branon, S., Fagen, R., & Zhou, G. (2008). *Study of the effectiveness and efficiency of charter schools in Indiana.* Bloomington, IN: Center for Evaluation & Education Policy. Prepared for the Indiana General Assembly.

IN2—Nicotera, A., Mendiburo, M., & Berends, M. (2009). *Charter school effects in an urban school district: An analysis of student achievement gains in Indianapolis.* Nashville, TN: National Center on School Choice, Vanderbilt University.

LA—Scott S. Cowen Institute. (2009). *Public school performance in New Orleans: A supplement to the 2008 state of public education in New Orleans report.* New Orleans, LA: Author.

MA1—Massachusetts Department of Education. (2006). *Massachusetts charter school achievement comparison study: An analysis of 2001-2005 MCAS performance.* Boston, MA: Author.

MA2—Abdulkadiroglu, A., Angrist, J., Dynarski, S., Kane, T. J., & Pathak, P. (2009, November). *Accountability and flexibility in public schools: Evidence from Boston's charters and pilots.* National Bureau of Economic Research (Working paper 15549). Retrieved May 3, 2011, from http://www.nber.org/papers/w15549

MI1—Khouri, N., Kleine, R., & Cummings, L. (1999). *Michigan's charter school initiative: From theory to practice.* Lansing, MI: Public Sector Consultants, Inc.

MI2– Eberts, R. W., & Hollenbeck, K. M. (2002). *Impact of charter school attendance on student achievement in Michigan.* Kalamazoo, MI: Upjohn Institute Staff Working Paper. No. 02-080.

MI3—Miron, G. & Nelson, C. (2002). *What's public about charter schools?: Lessons learned about accountability and choice.* Thousand Oaks, CA: Corwin Press.

MI4—Bettinger, E. P. (2005). The effect of charter schools on charter students and public schools. *Economics of Education Review, 24*(3), 133-147.

MI5—Michigan Department of Education. (2007). *Public school academies: Michigan Department of Education report to the legislature.* East Lansing, MI: Author.

MN1—Office of the Legislative Auditor. (2008). *Evaluation report: Charter schools.* Minneapolis, MN: Author.

MN2—Institute on Race & Poverty. (2008). *Failed promises: Assessing charter schools in the twin cities.* Minneapolis, MN: Author.

MO—Metis Associates. (2004). *A study of the Kansas City, Missouri, charter public schools 2000-2003.* New York, NY: Author.

NC1—Noblit, G. W., & Corbett, D. (2001). *North Carolina charter school evaluation report.* Raleigh, NC: North Carolina State Board of Education.

NC2—Bilfulco, R., & Ladd, H. F. (2006, January). *School choice, racial segregation and test-score gaps: Evidence from North Carolina's charter school program.* Paper presented at the annual meeting of Allied Social Science Associations, Boston.

NJ1—Barr, J. M., Sadovnik, A. R., & Visonti, L. (2006). Charter schools and urban education improvement: A comparison of Newark's district and charter schools. *The Urban Review, 38*(4), 291-311.

NJ2—Barr, J. (2007).*Charter school performance in New Jersey* (Working paper #2007-006). Newark, NJ: Rutgers University.

NM—Andreson, K., Casey, J., Yelverton, B., & Rose, S. (2005). *2004-2005 evaluation of New Mexico charter schools.* Albuquerque, NM: New Mexico Public Education Department.

NY1—New York Board of Regents. (2003). *Report to the governor, the temporary president of the senate, and the speaker of the assembly on the educational effectiveness of the charter school approach in New York State.* Albany, NY: New York Board of Regents.

NY2—Dobbie, W., & Fryer, R. G. (2009). *Are high-quality schools enough to close the achievement gap? Evidence from a bold social experiment in Harlem* (Working Paper 15473). Cambridge, MA: National Bureau of Economic Research .

NY3—Hoxby, C. M., & Murarka, S. (2009). *How New York City's charter schools affect achievement, August 2009 report. Second report in series.* Cambridge, MA: New York City Charter Schools Evaluation Project.

OH1—Legislative Office of Education Oversight. (2003). *Community schools in Ohio: Final report on student performance, parent satisfaction, and accountability.* Columbus, OH: Author.

OH2—Carr, M., & Staley, S. (2005). *Using the Ohio proficiency test to analyze the academic achievement of charter school students: 2002-2004.* Columbus, OH: The Buckeye Institute.

OH3—Jenkins, P. (2005). *Effective or not: The plight of Ohio's charter schools* (Unpublished thesis). Miami University.

OH4—Thomas B. Fordham Institute. (2010). *Ohio urban school performance report for 2009-10.* Washington, DC: Public Impact.

OR—Oregon Department of Education. (2011). *Oregon charter schools 2009-2010 evaluation report.* Salem, OR: Author.

PA1—Enkishev, I. (2002). *Charter schools: A Philadelphia study* (Unpublished doctoral dissertation). Haverford College.

PA2—Miron, G., Nelson, C., & Risley, J. (2002). *Strengthening Pennsylvania's charter school reform: Findings from the statewide evaluation and discussion of relevant policy issues.* Harrisburg, PA: Pennsylvania Department of Education.

PA3—Zimmer, R., Blanc, S., Gill, B., & Christman, J. (2008). *Evaluating the performance of Philadelphia's charter schools.* Santa Monica, CA: RAND.

SW [unnamed Southwest district]—Imberman, S. A. (2007). *Achievement and behavior in charter schools: Drawing a more complete picture.* Unpublished manuscript. Retrieved May 5, 2011, from http://ssrn.com/abstract=975487

TN—Zoblotsky, T. A., Ross, S. M., Qian, H., & McDonald, A. J. (2008). *Student-level analysis of year 4 (2006-07) achievement outcomes for Tennessee secondary charter schools.* Memphis, TN: Center for Research in Educational Policy.

TX1—Gronberg, T., & Jansen, D. W. (2001). *Navigating newly chartered waters: An analysis of Texas charter school performance.* Austin, TX: Texas Public Policy Foundation.

TX2—Hanushek, E. A., Kain, S. G., & Rivkin, S. (2002). *The impact of charter schools on academic achievement.* Unpublished manuscript.

TX3—Gronberg, T., & Jansen, D. W. (2005). *Texas charter schools: An assessment in 2005.* Austin, TX: Texas Public Policy Foundation.

TX4—Booker, K., Gilpatric, S. M., Gronberg, T., & Jansen, D. (2007). The impact of charter school attendance on student performance. *Journal of Public Economics, 91,* 849-876.

TX5—Maloney, C., Sheehan, D., Huntsberger, B., Caranikas-Walker, F., & Caldera, S. (2007). *Texas open-enrollment charter schools: 2005-06 evaluation.* Austin, TX: Texas Center for Educational Research.

UT—Was, C., & Kristjansson, S. (2006). *An analysis of charter vs. traditional public schools in Utah.* Salt Lake City, UT: Utah State Charter School Board.

WI1—Molnar, A., Zahorik, J., Hoffman, L. M., Gobel, C., Walker, C. M., & Gosz, J. (2001). *Evaluation of the Wisconsin charter school program.* Milwaukee, WI: Center for Educational Research, Analysis, and Innovation, School of Education.

WI2—Witte, J., Weimer, D., Shober, A., & Schlomer, P. (2007). The performance of charter schools in Wisconsin. *Journal of Policy Analysis and Management, 26*(3), 573.

US1—Greene, J. P., Forster, G., & Winters, M. A. (2003). *Apples to apples: An evaluation of charter schools serving general student populations* (Education Working Paper No. 1). New York, NY: Center for Civic Innovation at the Manhattan Institute.

US2—Loveless, T. (2003). *The 2003 Brown Center report on American education: Charter schools: Achievement, accountability, and the role of expertise.* Washington, DC: The Brookings Institution.

US3—Finnigan, K., Adelman, N., Anderson, L., Cotton, L., Donnelly, M. B., & Price, T. (2004). *Evaluation of the public charter schools program: Final report.* Washington, DC: U.S. Department of Education, SRI International.

US4—Hoxby, C. M. (2004). *Achievement in charter schools and regular public schools in the US: Understanding the differences.* Cambridge, MA: Harvard University and National Bureau of Economic Research.

US5—Nelson, H. F., Rosenberg, B., & Van Meter, N. (2004). *Charter school achievement on the 2003 National Assessment of Educational Progress.* Washington, DC: American Federation of Teachers.

US6—U.S. Department of Education, Institute for Education Sciences, National Center for Education Statistics. (2004). *The nation's report card: America's charter school report* (NCES 2005-456). Washington, DC: Author.

US7—Mishel, L., & Roy, J. (2005, April). *Advantage none: Re-examining Hoxby's findings of charter school benefits* (EPI Briefing Paper #158). Washington DC: Economic Policy Institute.

US8—Braun, H., Jenkins, F., & Grigg, W. (2006). *A closer look at charter schools using hierarchical linear modeling* (No. NCES 2006–460). Washington, DC: National Center for Education Statistics, U.S. Department of Education.

US9—Lubienski, S. T., & Lubienski, C. (2006). School sector and academic achievement: A multilevel analysis of NAEP mathematics data. *American Educational Research Journal, 43*(4), 651-698.

US10—Miron, G., Coryn, C., & Mackety, D. (2007). *Evaluating the impact of charter schools on student achievement: A longitudinal look at the Great Lakes states.* East Lansing, MI: Great Lakes Center for Education Research and Practice.

US11—Center for Research on Education Outcomes. (2009). *Multiple choice: Charter school performance in 16 states.* Palo Alto, CA: Author.

US12—Zimmer, R., Gill, B., Booker, K., Lavertu, S., Sass, T. R., & Witte, J. (2009). *Charter schools in eight states.* Santa Monica, CA: RAND.

US13—Berends, M., Goldring, E., Stein, M., & Cravens, X. (2010). Instructional conditions in charter schools and students' mathematics achievement gains. *American Journal of Education, 116,* 303-335.

US14—Gleason, P., Clark, M., Tuttle, C. C., & Dwoyer, E. (2010). *The evaluation of charter school impacts: Final report* (NCEE 2010-4029). Washington, DC: National Center for Education Evaluation and Regional Assistance, Institute of Education Sciences, U.S. Department of Education.

US15—Tuttle, C. C., Teh, B., Nichols-Barrer, I., Gill, B. P., & Gleason, P. (2010). *Student characteristics and achievement in 22 KIPP middle schools.* Washington, DC: Mathematica Policy Research.

52. Determined using National Center for Education Statistics "Build A Table" feature for the 2009-2010 school year. Retrieved June 15, 2011, from http://nces.ed.gov/ccd/bat/

53. Zimmer, R., Buddin, R, Chau, D., Gill, B., Guarino, C., Hamilton, L., ... Brewer, D. (2003). *Charter school operation and performance: Evidence from California.* Santa Monica, CA: RAND.

54. Miron, G., Nelson, C., & Risley, J. (2002). *Strengthening Pennsylvania's charter school reform: Findings from the statewide evaluation and discussion of relevant policy issues.* Harrisonburg, PA: Pennsylvania Department of Education.

55. CREDO. (2011). *Charter school performance in Pennsylvania.* Palo Alto, CA: Center for Research on Education Outcomes (CREDO), Stanford University. Retrieved June 14, 2011 from http://credo.stanford.edu/reports/PA%20State%20Report_20110404_FINAL.pdf

CHAPTER 12: CONCLUSION

1. Levin, H. M. (2002). A comprehensive framework for evaluating educational vouchers. *Education Evaluation and Policy Analysis, 24*(3), 159-174.

2. Arsen, D., Plank, D., & Sykes, G. (1999). *School choice policies in Michigan: The rules matter.* East Lansing, MI: Michigan State University.

3. See for example, National Committee for Responsive Philanthropy. (2007). *Foundation giving leaves mark in the school choice movement.* Retrieved December 22, 2011 from http://ncrp.org/news-room/press-releases/101-11272007-foundation-giving-leaves-mark-in-the-school-choice-movement

4. OECD. (2008). *Growing unequal? Income distribution and poverty in OECD countries. Country note: United States.* Retrieved January 16, 2012 from http://www.oecd.org/dataoecd/47/2/41528678.pdf

5. See for example, Dansinger, S. H., Sandefur, G. D., & Wineburg, D. H. (1996). *Confronting poverty: Prescriptions for change.* New York, NY: Russell Sage Foundation.

ABOUT THE AUTHORS

David Arsen
Michigan State University
arsen@msu.edu
(517) 432-2276

David Arsen is a professor of educational administration and education policy in the College of Education at Michigan State University. He received his PhD in economics at the University of California, Berkeley. Dr. Arsen's research focuses on school finance and school choice policies.

Clive R. Belfield
Queens College, City University of New York
clive.belfield@qc.cuny.edu
(718) 997 5448

Clive Belfield is an associate professor of economics, Queens College, City University of New York. He is also a research fellow at the Center for Analysis of Postsecondary Education and Employment, Teachers College, Columbia University, and an associate editor, *Economics of Education Review*. He has published widely in the economics of education and is the author of *The Price We Pay: The Economic and Social Costs of Inadequate Education* (Brookings Press).

Martha Cecilia Bottia
University of North Carolina at Charlotte
(704) 687-2515
mbottia@uncc.edu

Martha Cecilia Bottia is assistant research professor of sociology at the University of North Carolina at Charlotte. Since 2005 she has surveyed

and synthesized the educational, social, and behavioral science literatures on the effects of school, racial and socioeconomic effects on educational outcomes. Her other research interests include illicit drugs,
terrorist organizations, and the education of immigrant students. Currently, she is working on a series of articles related to the unequal
impact of the implemented curriculum on socioeconomic and racially
diverse students, and on the role of structural characteristics of K-12
schools on student decisions to major in STEM.

Charleen Brantley
University of Massachusetts Boston
charlebrnt@aol.com
(617) 363-9514

Charleen Brantley, an adjunct professor, teaches undergraduate and
graduate students at the University of Massachusetts Boston. She
recently completed research on the State of Black Boston K-12. Her
research focus is twofold: literacy instruction in urban schools and literacy achievement of Black and Latino students in urban school districts.
Dr. Brantley received her EdD in leadership in urban schools from the
University of Massachusetts Boston.

Marisa Cannata
Vanderbilt University
marisa.cannata@vanderbilt.edu
(615) 322-1746

Marisa Cannata, PhD, is a senior research associate at Vanderbilt University, associate director of the National Center on School Choice and
the National Center on Scaling Up Effective Schools. Her research
interests focus on school choice and teacher quality, including teacher
career decisions, hiring, induction, work experiences, and professional
community. Dr. Cannata is the coeditor of *School Choice and School
Improvement* by Harvard Education Press. She has also been published
in the *Educational Administration Quarterly, Journal of School Choice, Elementary School Journal, Educational Policy Analysis Archives, Economics of
Education Review, American Journal of Education,* and *Teachers College
Record.*

Casey D. Cobb
University of Connecticut
casey.cobb@uconn.edu
(860) 486-0253

Casey D. Cobb is department head and professor of educational leadership and director of the Center for Education Policy Analysis at the Neag School of Education at the University of Connecticut. His research interests include policies on school choice, accountability, and school reform, where he examines the implications for equity and educational opportunity. Dr. Cobb is a member of the Research Advisory Panel for the National Coalition on School Diversity, a member of the NEA Foundation's Closing the Achievement Gaps Initiative Knowledge Group, and past president of the New England Educational Research Organization. He holds an AB from Harvard University and a PhD from Arizona State University.

Gregg Garn
University of Oklahoma
garn@ou.edu
(405) 325-1082

Gregg Garn is dean of the Jeannine Rainbolt College of Education at the University of Oklahoma where he also serves as the Linda Clark Anderson Presidential Professor and Professor of educational leadership and policy studies. Dr. Garn is also the director of the K20 Center for Educational and Community Renewal, a university wide research and development center focused on teaching and learning innovations. His research agenda is focused on school choice, policy development and implementation, and the politics of education.

Patricia H. Hinchey
Pennsylvania State University
pxh12@psu.edu
(570) 333-5285

Pat Hinchey is a professor of education at Penn State and a Research Fellow at the National Education Policy Center at the University of Colorado, Boulder. As a career-long supporter of social justice, she has taught graduate and undergraduate courses in education theory and policy, race and gender, action research, and media literacy. She is author of several journal articles and books on topics related to educational equity and engaged citizenship. Her review of research on teacher assessment was published by NEPC in 2010, and she has lectured extensively on this issue.

Natalie Lacireno-Paquet
WestEd
npaquet@wested.org
(781) 481-1100

Natalie Lacireno-Paquet, a senior research associate at Learning Innovations at WestEd, conducts research and evaluation to provide actionable data and analysis for program improvement at the federal, state, and local levels. She is currently leading a statewide evaluation of the Kansas Multi-Tier System of Supports initiative. She frequently combines quantitative and qualitative methods in her work. Her research interests are in education policy and school reform. She received her PhD in public policy from The George Washington University.

Christopher Lubienski
University of Illinois
club@illinois.edu
(217) 333-4382

Christopher Lubienski is associate professor of education policy at the University of Illinois. His research focuses on education policy, reform, and the political economy of education, with a particular concern for issues of equity and access. Dr. Lubienski held postdoctoral fellowships with the National Academy of Education and with the Advanced Studies Program at Brown University, and was named a Fulbright Senior Scholar for New Zealand. He has authored both theoretical and empirical papers on innovation and achievement in school choice systems, and has edited *School Choice Policies and Outcomes: Empirical and Philosophical Perspectives* (with Walter Feinberg, SUNY Press, 2008), and *The Charter School Experiment: Expectations, Evidence, and Implications* (with Peter Weitzel, Harvard Education Press, 2010).

William J. Mathis
University of Colorado Boulder
wmathis@sover.net
(802) 383-0058

Bill Mathis is the managing director of the National Education Policy Center, University of Colorado Boulder. He was superintendent of schools for the Rutland Northeast Supervisory Union, Brandon, Vermont and was a national superintendent of the year finalist and Vermont superintendent of the year. Earlier, Dr. Mathis was Deputy Assistant Commissioner in New Jersey and taught at a number of colleges and universities. He is a member of the Vermont state board of education and on the national board of directors of the Rural School and Community Trust. He previously served on the board for the Association for Education Finance and Policy. His research interests are in accountability, assessment, and finance.

Julie Fisher Mead
University of Wisconsin at Madison
jmead@education.wisc.edu

Julie F. Mead is a professor and chair of the Department of Educational Leadership and Policy Analysis at the University of Wisconsin-Madison. Dr. Mead researches, teaches, and writes about topics related to the legal aspects of education. Her research centers on special education law and legal issues raised by various forms of school choice. She is a member of the Education Law Association and the American Educational Research Association. She publishes regularly in education and law journals. Her most recent book is *Charter Schools and the Law: Establishing New Legal Relationships*, with Preston Green.

Roslyn Arlin Mickelson
University of North Carolina at Charlotte
RoslynMickelson@uncc.edu
(704) 687-4075 office

Roslyn Arlin Mickelson is professor of sociology, public policy, women and gender studies, and information technology at the University of North Carolina at Charlotte. Since 2005 Dr. Mickelson has been surveying and synthesizing the educational, social, and behavioral science literatures on the effects of school racial and socioeconomic demographic composition on various educational outcomes. The results of this ongoing synthesis have been published widely in sociology, law, public policy, and educational journals. Currently, she is writing a book synthesizing social science research on the effects of school and classroom diversity on outcomes across the life course including educational and occupational attainment, intergroup relations, and social cohesion in multiethnic democratic societies.

Gary Miron
Western Michigan University
garmiron@gmail.com
269-599-7965

Gary Miron is a professor of evaluation, measurement, and research at Western Michigan University. He has studied and evaluated school choice reforms in the United States and Europe. In the United States, he has conducted nine comprehensive evaluations of charter school reforms commissioned by state agencies and has undertaken dozens of other studies related to charter schools and private education management organizations that have been funded by the U.S. Department of Education, state agencies, private foundations, as well as advocates and critics of charter schools. In Europe, Dr. Miron has studied the national voucher reform in Sweden and conducted research on school restructuring in four countries. He has served as an external expert for the OECD and worked with a network of countries to develop international indicators related to school choice, parent voice, and school accountability.

Stephanie Southworth
Clemson University
southwo@clemson.edu
(704) 576-7759

Stephanie Southworth's research focuses on educational stratification. Specifically, she examines the effects of school racial and socioeconomic composition on students' opportunities to learn. In her coauthored 2007 *Social Forces* article she found that the racial composition of a school affected the track placement of students differently depending on their race and gender. In a 2010 article published in *Educational Policy Analysis Archives*, she examined school racial and poverty composition and teacher quality on elementary and middle school students' math and reading achievement. She found that all students performed higher in low poverty, racially balanced schools. She also found that the effects of teacher characteristics on achievement differed by grade.

Yongmei Ni
University of Utah
Yongmei.ni@utah.edu
(801) 664-4735

Yongmei Ni is an assistant professor in the Department of Educational Leadership and Policy at the University of Utah. Her research interests focus on school choice, economics of education, and quantitative research methods. Her current work examines how school choice affects student achievement through influencing teacher working conditions, teacher commitment, and principal turnover. She has published articles in journals such as *Economics of Education Review, Teachers College Record, Educational Administration Quarterly,* and *Educational Policy.* Dr. Ni was an associate editor of *Educational Administration Quarterly* and currently serves on its editorial board. She holds a PhD in education policy and a master's degree in economics from Michigan State University.

Jessica L. Urschel
Western Michigan University
j7urschel@wmich.edu

Jessica Urschel holds a master of arts in industrial/organizational psychology and is completing a PhD in behavior analysis at Western Michigan University. Ms. Urschel has been working on numerous grants regarding school choice, education management organizations, and other education policy issues since 2007. She also has process management consulting experience in health care, higher education, and local government.

Kevin G. Welner
University of Colorado Boulder
welner@colorado.edu
(303) 492-8370

Kevin Welner is professor of education and director of the National Education Policy Center (http://nepc.colorado.edu), housed at the University of Colorado Boulder School of Education. His work examines the use of research in policymaking, the intersection between education rights litigation and educational opportunity scholarship, and the school change process associated with equity-focused reform efforts. He has authored or edited more than eight books and 80 articles and book chapters, and he has received the American Educational

Research Association's Early Career Award, Palmer O. Johnson Award and Fellow status. His BA in biological sciences is from UCSB and his JD and PhD are from UCLA.

Terri S. Wilson
Southern Illinois University, Carbondale
wilson@siu.edu
(618) 453-7309

Terri S. Wilson is an assistant professor in the Department of Educational Administration and Higher Education at Southern Illinois University, Carbondale. She received her PhD from Teachers College, Columbia University in 2010. Dr. Wilson's work focuses on the philosophical foundations of education policy and politics. Her research interests include school choice, charter school reform and parent involvement. In particular, her research has explored the moral complexity and political significance of parents' school choices. A 2012 National Academy of Education/Spencer Foundation Postdoctoral Fellow, she is currently working on a book manuscript that explores how charter schools—particularly ones organized around linguistic and cultural communities—are reshaping how we understand schools as public spaces.

CPSIA information can be obtained at www.ICGtesting.com
Printed in the USA
BVOW011656151212

308271BV00002B/17/P